COMPUTERS & SOCIAL CONTROVERSY

COMPUTER SOFTWARE ENGINEERING SERIES

ELLIS HOROWITZ, Editor
University of Southern California

CALINGAERT
Assemblers, Compilers, and Program Translation

CARBERRY, KHALIL, LEATHRUM, and LEVY
Foundations of Computer Science

EVEN
Graph Algorithms

FINDLAY and WATT
PASCAL: An Introduction to Methodical Programming

HOROWITZ and SAHNI
Fundamentals of Computer Algorithms

HOROWITZ and SAHNI
Fundamentals of Data Structures

LOGSDON
Computers and Social Controversy

ULLMAN
Principles of Database Systems

COMPUTERS & SOCIAL CONTROVERSY

TOM LOGSDON

PITMAN

PITMAN PUBLISHING LIMITED
39 Parker Street, London WC2B 5PB

Associated Companies
Pitman Publishing Pty Ltd, Melbourne
Pitman Publishing New Zealand Ltd, Wellington

First published in Great Britain 1980
First published in USA 1980

© 1980 Computer Science Press, Inc.,
9125 Fall River Lane, Potomac,
Maryland 20854

This book was first published in 1980 by
Computer Science Press, Inc.
9125 Fall River Lane
Potomac, Maryland 20854 U.S.A.

Library of Congress Cataloging in Publication Data

Logsdon, Thomas S.
    Computers and social controversy.

    (Computer software engineering series)
    Bibliography: p.
    Includes index.
    1. Computers and civilization. I. Title.
II. Series.
QA76.9.C66L63   301.24'3   79–24611
US ISBN 0–914894–14–5
UK ISBN 0–273–01492–7

PREFACE

Controversy: A discussion of a question in which opposing opinions clash.

Webster's New World Dictionary

To date more than 250,000 large and medium scale computers have been installed in this country and more than 2 million Americans make their livings ministering to their needs. Though largely unobtrusive, these powerful machines influence our lives in a remarkable variety of ways. Indeed, some experts contend that it is necessary to go all the way back to the days of the Industrial Revolution to find an appropriate parallel—the harnessing of steam.

Like the Industrial Revolution, the computer revolution, in the main, is regarded as a positive benefit. And yet, when specific individuals are personally affected by the encroachments of computers, they do not always view their particular situations with bubbling good humor. Most especially, whenever the computer intrudes on their privacy, threatens their job security, or usurps their position as the earth's preeminent creatures, raging controversies inevitably result.

Most introductory computer science courses survey the uses of the computers in our society in a relatively placid way. There is much to be said for this approach. However, classroom trials have demonstrated that by focusing on the controversial issues, as is done in this treatment, we can trigger much broader and more enthusiastic student response. My classes at the University of Southern California have had many lively and stimulating discussions of these controversial issues and I would like to take this opportunity to thank my students for their many contributions toward modifying and restructuring this book.

Sincere thanks should also go to several individuals who helped in the preparation of the final manuscript. In particular, I would like to thank a charming lady named Elda Stramel who has done all my typing for many years. In addition to being a superb typist, Elda has a special talent for handing crisis situations—including those in which *everything has priority over everything else!*

I would also like to express my gratitude for the efforts of Mr. Ernie Gisondi who provided the excellent drawings that accompany the text. On many occasions he had to work from rough sketches so rudimentary even their author often couldn't remember exactly what they meant. The lettering was supplied by Sheila Hernandez, a happy craftsman, who worked under a deadline so tight that, at one point, she was doing pasteups a few minutes before she boarded her plane.

I would also like to thank my editor, Dr. Ellis Horowitz, who made many preceptive suggestions that kept the project moving forward and who fearlessly recommended major surgery on Chapter 5 when it suddenly dawned on both of us that it covered the wrong material and contained the wrong words.

Finally, I would like to thank a delightful friend, my daughter, Donna, who said simply and often: "Dad, I'm proud of you."

Tom Logsdon
Seal Beach, California

CONTENTS

Preface   v

1. **An Introduction to Computer Technology**   1

   Digital and Analog Computers   3
   Special Purpose and General Purpose
   Machines   5
   Microminiaturization   5
   Computer Speeds   9
   A Typical Data Processing Center   11
   Time Sharing Systems and
   Minicomputers   11
   The Hobby Computer Revolution   16
      The Beginnings   19
      The Participants   20
   Bibliography   21
   Exercises   23
   Student Projects   23

2. **The Von Neumann Legacy**   25

   The Advantages of Binary Arithmetic   29
      A Typical Binary Code   32
      Parity Checking Schemes   33
   Internally Stored Programs   35
      The Development of FORTRAN   37
      BASIC: A Language for Time Sharing   37
      A Typical Computer Program   38
      Other Languages   39
      Flowcharting Techniques   39
   The Four Functions of a Digital Computer   40
      Input-Output   42
      Processing and Control   44
      Storage   46
      Assembling a Functioning System   46
   Von Neumann's Contributions   46
   Bibliography   47
   Exercises   48
   Student Projects   50

3. **The Care and Feeding of a Digital Computer**   53

   Punched Card Inputs   55
      The Unit Record Concept   59

Keypunching Mechanisms 60
Card Reading Devices 60
Magnetic Tapes 61
Remote Terminals 64
The Magic Light Pen 65
Computer Aided Design 65
High Speed Printers 67
Devices That Draw Pictures and Graphs 69
Cathode-Ray-Tude Plotters 69
Mechanical Plotters 69
Computer-Directed Conversations 70
Bibliography 74
Exercises 75
Student Projects 75

4.   The Computer's Memory 77

Primary Storage 79
Magnetic Core Rings 80
Solid-State Memory Units 82
Marketing Comparisons 86
Auxiliary Storage 86
Magnetic Drums 86
Magnetic Disks 89
Bubble Memories 89
Charged-Coupled Devices 91
Data Buffers 92
External Storage 92
Punched Cards 92
Magnetic Tapes 93
The Floppy Disk 93
Selecting the Computer's Storage Media 95
The Dawning of the Second Industrial
Revolution 96
Bibliography 98
Exercises 98
Student Projects 99

5.   Software Engineering 101

The Five Phases of Software Development 105
Difficulties With Cost and Manpower
Estimates 107
Typical Software Coding Rates 111
Modern Methods For Increasing

Programmer Efficiency 113
   Structured Programming 114
   Top-Down Design 115
   Chief Programmer Teams 115
   Structured Walkthroughs 116
   Preliminary Results 117
Bibliography 118
Exercises 119
Student Projects 119

6. Electronic Privacy Intrusion 123

The People's Need For Privacy 125
Society's Need For Information 127
Government Dossiers 132
The Federal Data Center 132
Privacy Abuses 135
Privacy and the Law 136
   The Fair Credit Reporting Act of 1970 137
   The Privacy Act of 1974 138
   Privacy Regulations for Business
   and Industry 140
   Probable Costs 142
Criminal Data Files 145
   Manual Methods 145
   The National Crime Information Center 147
The Future 149
Bibliography 152
Exercises 154
Student Projects 154

7. Computer Fraud 157

The Great Phone Company Rip-Off 159
Electronic Embezzlement 162
The Magnitude of Computer Crime 166
Protecting the Machines 168
   Secret Passwords 168
   File Protection Rings 169
   The Making of a Secure Machine 170
   The Perils of Complexity 171
   Secure Kernels 171
   Tiger Teams at ZARF 172
Access Limits 173

User Identification Methods 173
Terminals That Operate by Lock and Key 175
Data Encryption Schemes 176
Trapdoor Codes 180
The Many Faces of Computer Crime 181
Bibliography 182
Exercises 185
Student Projects 186

8. Machines That Teach 187

An Introduction To Computer Aided
Instruction 192
    The Basic Hardware 194
    A More Sophisticated Approach 195
    Argumentative Robots 196
Available Courseware 196
Hardware Research Projects 197
Current Expenditure Levels 199
Future Cost Projections 202
    Hardware Costs 202
    Software Costs 202
    The Big Picture 204
Student Respones 205
Courseware Effectiveness Studies 207
Some Professional Misgivings 210
Electronic Tutoring in the Home 213
Bibliography 215
Exercises 216
Student Projects 217

9. The Era of Intelligent Machines 219

What is Intelligence? 223
The Computer and the Brain 226
Artificial Intelligence 228
Game Playing Machines 228
    Tic-Tac-Toe 229
    Machines That Learn 234
Language Translations 238
    Syntax and Semantics 239

Ambiguity and Context 239
Language Comprehension Programs 240
Turing's Test for Machine Intelligence 242
Problem Solving and Pattern Recognition 245
Some Critical Opinions 248
The Future 250
Bibilography 251
Exercises 252
Student Projects 253

10   Computers and Automation 255

Human Labor Versus Automatic Machines 258
Industrial Robots 260
Feedback Control 261
The Friendly Robots in Your Future 264
Unemployment Levels 265
Historical Progress in Worker Productivity 270
Mechanization and Job Quality Trends 273
Alienation and Worker Dissatisfaction 273
The Future 275
Bibliography 278
Exercises 279
Student Projects 280

11.   The Scanner Revolution 281

Cash Drawers That Talk Computer 284
The Universal Product Code 284
The Scanners 287
Operating Procedures 287
Potential Cost Savings 289
Customer Concerns 292
Paying for the Hardware 292
The Fears of Unemployment 294
The Price Marking Controversy 295
New Opportunities for Deception and Fraud 298
Approaching the Status Quo 299
A Method For Making the Scanners Obsolete 301
Bibliography 303
Exercises 305
Student Projects 306

12. Computers and our Monetary System   307

Historical Perspectives   309
   Coins and Paper Money   309
   Checks   311
   Credit Cards   312
   Electronic Funds Transfer Systems   315
The Costs and the Benefits of
Electronic Money   317
The American Way of Debt   321
Governmental Responses to EFTS   322
   Restrictive Banking Laws   322
   The Federal Reserve   323
   Negative Reactions From the Postal
   Department   324
Customer Responses   325
   Learning to Live Without the Float   326
   Privacy Worries   327
   Special Security Concerns   328
Concluding Remarks   328
Bibliography   330
Exercises   332
Student Projects   332

13. The Future   333

The Publication of the Limits to Growth   336
   Euphoric Responses   341
   Clinical Evaluations   342
   Sobering Afterthoughts   344
Computers and Military Power   346
   Maintaining and Enhancing the Strategic
   Balance of Terror   347
   New Possibilities for Tactical War   352
The Geopolitics of Computers   357
Concluding Remarks   359
Bibliography   360
Exercises   362
Student Projects   363

Historical Perspectives   365

Glossary   371

Index   389

COMPUTERS

CHAPTER 1

AN INTRODUCTION TO COMPUTER TECHNOLOGY

DIGITAL AND ANALOG COMPUTERS

SPECIAL PURPOSE AND GENERAL PURPOSE MACHINES

MICROMINIATURIZATION

COMPUTER SPEEDS

A TYPICAL DATA PROCESSING CENTER

TIME SHARING SYSTEMS AND MINICOMPUTERS

THE HOBBY COMPUTER REVOLUTION
The Beginnings
The Participants

BIBLIOGRAPHY

EXERCISES

STUDENT PROJECTS

Twenty years ago in the midst of a rigid argument with a swarm of straight-laced engineers, the author playfully defined a computer as "a device which allows us to solve a set of problems that no one would want to solve if he didn't have a computer." This remark had an interesting effect on the conversation and even today it contains a small grain of truth, but, of course, it's not a very serviceable definition.

What then is a computer? Strictly speaking, we can call any machine that computes a computer. The term is not even confined to machines. At one time the human technicians who performed computations in support of large engineering operations were called "computers."For our purposes, however, we will need to use the term in a more specialized way. Thus we will define a computer as follows:

"Any automatic device (usually electronic) which is capable of storing relatively large amounts of data and executing complicated sequences of mathematical or logical operations without human intervention".

In keeping with this definition a computer has two important properties: a reasonably large memory capacity and the ability to function for long periods of time without human assistance.

When someone mentions a computer we usually envision a machine that does mathematical calculations. But computers actually function in a far more general way. Indeed, the capabilities of many popular models are so generalized that some authors define them as "symbol-manipulating machines that transform raw information into a more useful format."

Because of these broad capabilities, there are even a few experts who whink we should completely abandon the name. "They are called computers simply because computation is the only significant job that has so far been given to them." These words are from a 1952 *Scientific American* article by physicist Louis N. Ridenour, who went on to say: "The name has somewhat obscured the fact that they are capable of much greater generality. To (properly characterize) its potentialities the computer needs a new name. Perhaps as good a name as any is 'information machine'."

DIGITAL AND ANALOG COMPUTERS

Computers are often classified according to their underlying physical principals. In keeping with this method of classification there are two fundamental types of machines: *digital* and *analog*.

A *digital* computer manipulates individual digits in much the same way you do whenever you balance your checkbook or add up your grocery bill. By contrast, an analog computer doesn't deal with digits at all; it operates on a continuous spectrum of voltage levels. If you could somehow hear a digital computer doing its work it would sound like a runaway telegraph key; an analog computer would sound like a discordant symphony orchestra. In thumbnail form we can say that a digital computer "counts" whereas an analog computer "measures". Perhaps a simple analogy would help clarify these fundamental concepts. When a housewife goes into a country store and orders "a dozen eggs and a pound of coffee" she is placing a *digital* order for the eggs and an *analog* order for the coffee.

Although it works with numerical digits, a *digital* computer uses a completely different kind of arithmetic than we use in our everyday lives. Instead of working with the ten decimal digits: 0,1,2,3,...,9 it works with only two: 0 and 1. This so-called *binary numeration system* is so efficient because digital computers contain huge numbers of *bistable switches,* that is, switches which can assume two distinct states of stability such as "on" and "off" or their equivalent. "On" represents a binary 1; "off" represents a binary 0. During computation these electronic switches are automatically changed from one state to another in rapid sequence.

The operation of an *analog* computer is based on the fact that virtually every system of mathematical equations can be represented by a specific network of electrical circuits. To operate an analog computer we wire together the proper combination of components so that the resulting array constitutes an "analogy" of the problem being solved. The voltage in the resulting circuit can be measured and it represents the solution of the requisite equations.

Analog computers can provide cheap, efficient solutions to certain kinds of problems such as the design of the flight control system for a high-performance aircraft. One disadvantage is that an analog computer is not nearly as accurate as its digital counterpart. Another is that when we switch to a new problem we must, in effect, rewire the entire computer. By contrast, in a digital computer *the circuits are always the same no matter what problem we are solving.* We feed a new set of program instructions into a digital computer via punched cards, magnetic tapes, or their equivalent; no changes in the machinery itself are ever required.

SPECIAL PURPOSE AND GENERAL PURPOSE MACHINES

Computers can also be classified in accordance with their overall versatility levels. A *special purpose computer* is designed to solve only a limited class of mathematical or logical problems. For example, the simulators used in training the Space Shuttle astronauts are special-purpose machines. So are the tiny braking devices that keep a trailer truck from skidding whenever its driver is forced to make a panic stop. A *general purpose computer* can solve a much broader class of problems. In particular, a general purpose *digital* computer is remarkably versatile. In theory, it can solve virtually any problem which we can formulate in a clearly-defined manner.

Because of their many advantages—convenience, accuracy, reliability—digital computers outnumber their analog competitors by at least ten to one. And because of their versatility, *general-purpose* installations outnumber *special-purpose* installations by a similar margin. For this reason when we use the term "computer" in this textbook we will mean—in the absence of a specific disclaimer—a *general purpose digital computer*.

Contrary to popular belief computers are not becoming more mathematically sophisticated with improved technology. When the first general purpose digital computer, the Mark I, became operational in 1946 mankind reached a new technological plateau. Although the Mark I was clumsy and unreliable—and unbelievably slow—it could, in theory, solve any mathematical problem that can be solved by today's more elaborate machines. In 1936 a brilliant British logician named Alan Turing proved mathematically that the computational capabilities of all general purpose digital computers are essentially the same. They differ in processing speeds, storage capabilities, reliability, convenience, etc., but from a mathematical viewpoint all general purpose digital computers are blood brothers of equivalent computational power.

MICROMINIATURIZATION

To a large extent the average processing speed of a digital computer is determined by the distance its electronic pulses must travel in reaching the desired internal locations even though the pulses travel at the speed of light—one foot in one billionth of a second! The shorter we can make these internal pathways, the faster the computer can be made to operate.

Fortunately, in recent years, our design engineers have managed to shrink these important pathways to a remarkable degree by packing increasingly large numbers of transistors onto their solid state circuit chips. A transistor is a tiny slab of silicon or germanium which performs essentially the same electronic functions as the bulky vacuum tubes in an old-fashioned radio. The resulting devices are called "solid state" because they are constructed from solid materials containing their own intrinsic positive and negative electrical charges.

As you can see from the graph at the top of Figure 1, between 1970 and the present day the number of transistors on a typical circuit chip has gone from 3,000 to 70,000 and, if present trends continue, it will reach 400,000 by 1985. Cost trends, as shown by the bottom graph, are following a similar contour. In 1970 a dollar would buy 300 transistors. By 1985 it is estimated that that same dollar will buy at least 17,000. Originally the chips were called integrated circuits but, as they became more complicated and compact, a new name was needed. Today's versions are called *Large Scale Integrated* (LSI) circuits.

The photograph in Figure 2 shows a typical LSI circuit chip of the type used in modern computers. Although it is only slightly larger than a baby's fingernail, this tiny chip of silicon contains the equivalent of 50,000 transistors. In other words, it is approximately three times as complicated as the entire ENIAC computer of 1946—which covered 1600 square feet of floor space and weighed 60,000 pounds!

No wonder newcomers to the industry tingle with excitement whenever they contemplate the capabilities of a solid state circuit chip. A recent issue of *Time* magazine contained this wonderfully picturesque and enthusiastic description:

> "It is tiny, only about a quarter of an inch square, and quite flat. Under a microscope, it resembles a stylized Navaho rug or an aerial view of a railroad switching yard. Like the grains of sand on a beach, it is made mostly of silicon, next to oxygen the most abundant element on the surface of the earth."
>
> "Yet this inert fleck—still unfamiliar to the vast majority of Americans—has astonishing powers that are already transforming society. For the so-called miracle chip has a calculating capacity equal to that of a room size computer of only 25 years ago."*

*"The Age of the Miracle Chips". *Time*. 20 February 1978, pp. 44-45.

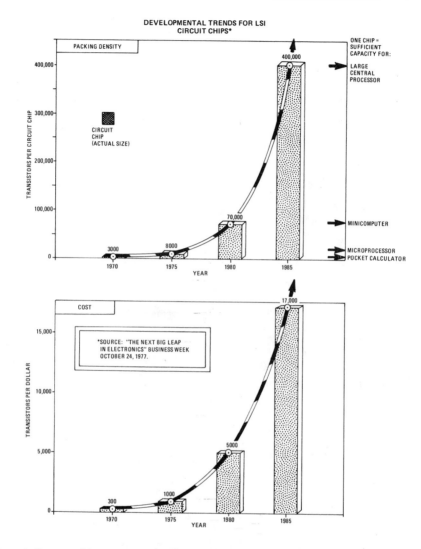

DEVELOPMENTAL TRENDS FOR LSI CIRCUIT CHIPS*

Figure 1: Because of intense research efforts, LSI circuit chips are becoming increasingly complicated and their cost is dropping at a dramatic rate. In 1970 it was possible to pack each chip with 3000 transistors at a cost of about $\frac{1}{3}$ of a cent each. If present developmental trends continue, by 1985 a typical circuit chip will contain at least 400,000 transistors each costing only about $\frac{1}{200}$ of a cent.

Not only is the miracle chip infinitely smaller and more compact than the rows of vacuum tubes it replaces, but it also embodies a number of other advantageous characteristics. Here is a partial listing which ap-

LSI CIRCUIT CHIPS

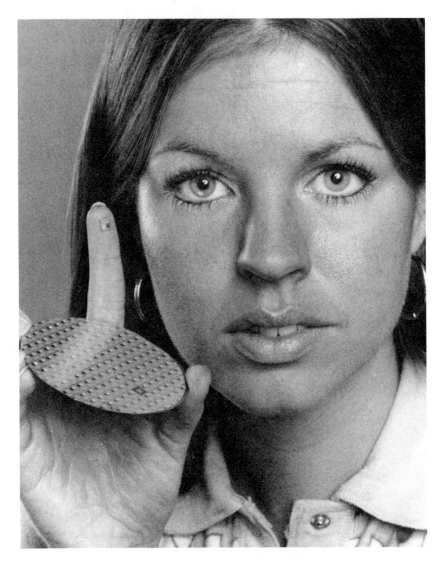

Figure 2: This LSI circuit chip, which measures roughly $\frac{1}{5}$ of an inch on a side and contains 50,000 transistors, incorporates a number of advantageous characteristics. Today's miracle chips are cheap, easy to mass produce, fast, infinitely versatile, and convenient. Moreover, because their electrical connections are laid down as an integral part of their surface material, they tend to be remarkably reliable.

peared in a later section of that same article in *Time* magazine: "Unlike the hulking vacuum tubes and tangled wires from which it evolved, it is cheap, easy to mass produce, fast, infinitely versatile and convenient." And, they might well have added: *amazing reliable.* In most complicated man-made devices—jumbo jets, oil refineries, artificial satellites—it is the interconnections which most often fail, not the basic components themselves. Fortunately, in the case of a solid state chip, the interconnections become an integral part of the material itself. Hence, they are much less prone to failure. Operating lifetimes commonly stretch over several years and the error rates associated with some solid state memory units amount to less than one mistake in every 100 billion operations.

The computer industry is the most obvious beneficiary of LSI technology. As we shall see in subsequent chapters, silicon chips are an important component of the computer's processing circuits and its high-speed memory units. However, the practical utility of circuit chips extends well beyond the narrow boundaries of the data processing industry. Indeed, although many private citizens are barely aware of their existence, it has been estimated that 85 percent of the chips now produced are installed in ordinary consumer products. The chips are everywhere: Flip the channel selector knob on one of the latest TV sets and a solid state chip will automatically fine-tune the picture. Push the buttons on a pocket calculator and a chip will total up your grocery bill. Drop a quarter into a recently installed vending machine and a chip will help insure that you end up with the proper selection—and the correct change.

COMPUTER SPEEDS

In comparison with their early ancestors, modern solid state computers are remarkably efficient machines. In one second a well-designed electronic computer can add 1 million pairs of 8-digit numbers at a cost of approximately 8¢. If we hired a team of human technicians to tackle the same job with pencil and paper, it would take them two man-years of intense effort and the cost would be around $20,000. Thus, it is easy to see why computers have become so popular among cost-conscious businessmen. In a fair computing contest a digital computer can almost always run circles around any human being.

Some informative comparisons are presented in Figure 3. As you can see, events that seem almost instantaneous on a human scale would be agonizingly slow if we could see them from the viewpoint of a digital computer. Indeed, to a modern computer, your body would probably seem like an inanimate object.

If it happens at all, a wink from a pretty coed seems to happen instantaneously. But a digital computer of modern design would regard even the fastest wink as an event of noticeable duration—it would be able to carry out 5,000 calculations while that pretty, flirtatious eyelid is making its fleeting vertical journey.

Thus we see that modern digital computers are already remarkably fast—and they're getting faster all the time. A few years ago the engineers at IBM decided to study the rate at which the processing speeds of their best machines had ben increasing as each new model was introduced into the marketplace. Accordingly, they devised a special program containing 1700 typical processing operations and ran it on a number of their most popular computers. The results are summarized in Figure 4. As you can

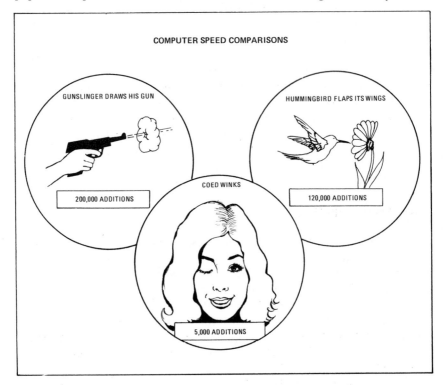

Figure 3: Events that seem almost instantaneous on a human scale would be agonizingly slow if we could see them from the computer's point of view. In the time it takes a gunslinger to draw and fire his revolver, a computer of modern design can add 200,000 pairs of eight-digit numbers. Even a wink from a flirtatious coed would seem to the computer to be an event of noticeable duration. While her eyelid is making its brief vertical journey, a well-made computer can find at least 5,000 sums.

see, the best available computer of 1955 required 375 second to complete the program at a cost of $14.54. By 1975 they had developed a computer that could handle the same task in 4 seconds. The cost? Only 20¢.

A TYPICAL DATA PROCESSING CENTER

Professional cartoonists have developed some rather quaint notions as to the proper appearance of a digital computer. Their drawings usually portray a giant machine towering over a swarm of pot-bellied scientists and technicians who attend to its needs with fanatical energy. Such drawings bear little resemblance to reality; a modern data processing center, as pictured in Figure 5, more nearly resembles the sales floor for a local appliance dealer. Refrigerator-sized units stand in neat rows on a carpeted floor (often a false floor housing electrical cables and cooling conduits). This approach is superior to the use of a single massive machine in that maintenance procedures are simplified and the free-standing units can be assembled in modular fashion. This allows each company to purchase just the right combination of components to fill its own individual needs.

TIME SHARING SYSTEMS AND MINICOMPUTERS

When digital computers first became available right after World War II they were operated almost entirely by scientists and engineers. Later they were applied to a variety of bookkeeping tasks by business firms and government bureaucracies. During this era the new machines had an important impact on our lives despite the fact that the average person seldom saw or touched the hardware. In the past few years, however, computers have become accessible to the layman. Two separate technological breakthroughs have made this possible:

1. time sharing systems
2. minicomputers.

In a *time sharing* system several users simultaneously share the services of a single computer. These users can be in the same room with the computer or they can be at distant locations linked to it by ordinary telephone lines or permanently-wired circuits. The first time sharing network was set up at MIT in 1961. In the intervening years remote teleprocessing has become increasingly important. In 1973 Bell Telephone announced that there were more long distance telephone circuits devoted to machines talking to machines than there were people taking to

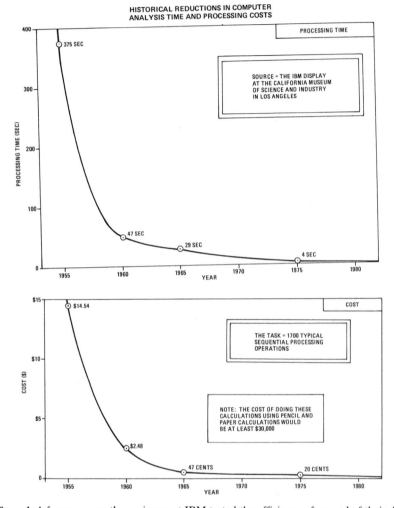

HISTORICAL REDUCTIONS IN COMPUTER
ANALYSIS TIME AND PROCESSING COSTS

Figure 4: A few years ago the engineers at IBM tested the efficiency of several of their best computers using a special program containing 1700 typical processing steps. They found that the best available machine in the mid 1970's was nearly one hundred times faster and cheaper than the best model they had manufactured in 1955.

people!* Computers also make extensive use of microwave relay links and satellite transmissions. Indeed, several major companies have banded

---

*This figure includes many machines other than computers; facsimile devices, for example, and television transmitters. Moreover, when they talk, machines tend to hog several communication channels at one time. A TV transmission uses about 600 voice channels and when two computers talk to one another they commonly require 1200 or more.

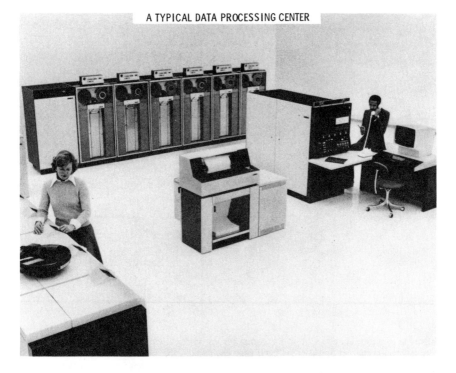

A TYPICAL DATA PROCESSING CENTER

Figure 5: In the early 1950's a typical digital computer was a bundle of wires and tubes crammed into a large, overheated metal cabinet. By contrast, modern computers consist of detached modules housing neat collections of integrated circuits and LSI devices. Though several orders of magnitude more efficient than their predecessors, the newer machines tend to have an austere, inhuman appearance.

together to launch their own data transmission satellite called the SBS (Satellite Business System).

Figure 6 shows how a time sharing network operates. Note that each user has his own remote terminal whereby he can communicate with the computer in a two-way running dialogue. Two different types of terminals are in common use. In one type the outputs are displayed on a TV screen; in the other they are printed on continuous form paper folded in accordion fashion.

Technically speaking, a time sharing computer doesn't service all the users simultaneously. Instead, it switches its attention from one remote terminal to another in serial fashion. However, because it is so fast and efficient, each individual user has the *illusion* of having the computer all to him or herself. In a typical system 10 to 50 remote terminals might be connected at any given moment. Variable amounts of computer time are

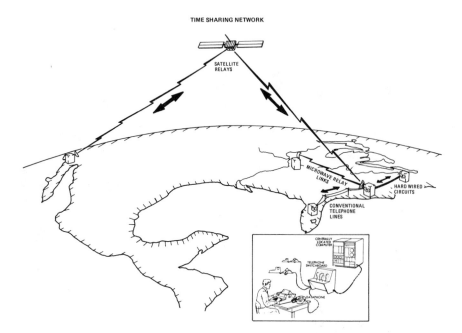

Figure 6: In a time sharing system the computer automatically cycles itself from one remote terminal to another so quickly that each user has the illusion of having the computer all to him or herself. Interconnected by commercial telephone lines, hard-wired circuits, microwave relay links, or satellite communication channels, a time sharing network has a number of intrinsic advantages over a conventional data processing system equipped with batch processing facilities.

usually apportioned to the various terminals depending on their current needs. Typically, when a particular user is serviced, he or she is given 1 to 10 seconds of the computer's time.

With time sharing the separate divisions of a large company can be linked to one centrally-located computer. Moreover, smaller companies can gain access to the computer since they can lease time from larger outfits. The concept also promotes efficient *real-time* calculations. In a real-time system the results of the computer's processing steps are used to influence the outcome of a process *while it is taking place.* The Apollo moon flights made extensive use of real-time processing to insure that the astronauts could safely complete their mission. Airline reservation systems also capitalize on the technology of real-time processing.

Minicomputers are small, self-contained devices which currently sell for a few thousand dollars each. A typical version marketed by Computer Automation is presented in Figure 7. Although they are slower and less accurate, and they lack some of the convenience features of the large-

A TYPICAL MINICOMPUTER

Figure 7: This self-contained unit, called the BASIC desk, is typical of the minicomputers now found in the commercial workplace. It runs on ordinary household current and requires no special cooling or other environmental controls. Although the BASIC desk is usually operated independently, it can also be interconnected with up to four other terminals with similar capabilities.

scale machines, minicomputers can be surprisingly powerful. Their outputs are usually printed reports, but a minicomputer can also be rigged with plotting devices capable of drawing graphs, barcharts, and other visual materials. Another possibility is to feed its outputs into one or more distant computers for further processing.

Approximately 170,000 minicomputers are currently in operation in the United States compared with 120,000 large-scale machines. In 1978 minicomputer sales topped 50,000 units with a total value of about $3 billion. Retail prices for the three most popular models currently range from $4,000 to $12,000. However, the extra auxiliary equipment can easily raise the total price for a particular installation to $50,000 or more.

Time sharing systems and minicomputers made it possible for ordinary people to gain access to powerful digital computers. But even with the new machines, computer *ownership* was still largely confined to a few thousand government agencies and private corporations. Of course, even in those early days personal computing machines had been put together by a few resourceful individuals. At first it was a lonely hobby, but within a few years, advancing technology allowed thousands of ordinary people to buy and operate their own private microcomputers. A microcomputer is a small, self-contained unit which can perform essentially all the functions of a large-scale digital computer. It is a fascinating device to see in operation. Recently, my students and I got an opportunity to witness a demonstration of one of the new microcomputers and to learn first hand about the beginnings of the hobby computer revolution.

THE HOBBY COMPUTER REVOLUTION

He as an unassuming man dressed in ordinary street clothes. But, if he had taken the trouble to outfit himself in a more futuristic way, he might have been able to convince us that he, and the complicated electronic nodules he was operating, had just been beamed down to the planet earth by Captain Kirk of the Starship Enterprise. With an air of unhurried confidence, he inserted a flat disk into the proper mechanism, flipped a pair of switches, and then waited patiently as a nearby television set gradually flickered and then began to respond to the silent signals sent out from the other machines.

The demonstration that followed was not what any of us had anticipated, but my students were obviously amused and delighted. Random snickers rippled back and forth across the classroom as a shimmering green stick figure burst onto the screen and—accompanied by flute-pure electronic tones—launched into a comical dance routine:

> "Yankee Doodle went to town, riding on a pony.
> Stuck a feather in his hat, and called it macaroni."

The place was Stauffer Lecture Hall on the USC campus. The audience was composed of the 68 students enrolled in Computer Science 140-L— "Computers and Society". Our guest was Mr. Kip Reiner a representative of Apple, Incorporated. His mission was to show us some of the capabilities of the Apple II, one of the most versatile and exciting of the new hobby-oriented microcomputers.

Mr. Reiner obviously enjoyed operating the sleek little machine. Under his guidance it became, in turn, a blackjack dealer, a math tutor, a music synthesizer, and a dedicated fire marshall on an inspection tour issuing stern verbal warnings.

The Apple II costs about $1100. One of its popular competitors, the Commodore Pet 2001, which provides only black and white images, can be obtained for $700. Pictures of both machines are presented in Figure 8. Other microcomputers, with lesser capabilities, can be purchased in kit form for as little as $300. (See Table 1). Despite their low cost, however, these microcomputers are remarkably powerful and versatile machines. Indeed they compare favorably in every respect with the finest available full-sized computers of two decades ago, computers which cost upwards of $500,000 each!

This is how computer expert Robert N. Noyce characterized the hobby-oriented machine in a recent issue of *Scientific American*:

> "Today's microcomputer at a cost of perhaps $300 has more computing capacity than the first large electronic computer. It is 20 times faster, has a larger memory, is thousands of times more reliable, consumes the power of a light bulb rather than a locomotive, occupies 1/30,000th the volume and costs 1/10,000th as much. It is available by mail order or at your local hobby shop.*

Now that microcomputers are becoming available to us at a reasonable price, how can we utilize their computational capabilities? In an endless number of ways if we are sufficiently resourceful. Some housewives use their machines to store their favorite recipes. If they need to prepare a meal for 14 people instead of only 6, the computer automatically calculates new quantities for the key recipe ingredients. Tutoring elementary students in spelling and math is another favorite application. Whenever the student begins to make mistakes, the machine will tease or cajole him toward greater concentration. Many users keep "things to do lists" and "appointment calendars" safely tucked away inside the computer's infallible electronic memory. Financial records, income tax data, birthday reminders and important telephone numbers are also handled with electronic efficiency.

If you attach the proper sensors, a microcomputer can be made to control the environment in your house or to manage some of your other repetitive personal chores. Some of the most popular uses along these lines include: brightening and dimming household lights, turning on stereos and television sets, opening and closing window drapes, making temperature and humidity adjustments, watering the lawn, and even phoning for help if there is a fire or burglary in the home.

---

*Noyce, Robert N. "Microelectronics." *Scientific American,* September 1977, pp. 62-69.

Of course, these advanced uses are quite expensive; the installations of extra switches and sensors always involves substantial extra cost. Moveover, once a hobbyist begins playing tricks with computer-actuated hardware, the process tends to become addictive. One California computer fanatic, who now controls virtually every mechanism in his home electronically, thinks he has finally figured out where it will all likely end.

TABLE 1

BUYER'S GUIDE TO HOME COMPUTERS*

TYPE OF MICRO-COMPUTER	CUR-RENT PRICE	TOTAL MEMORY CAPACITY (characters)	PRO-GRAM-MING LAN-GUAGE	COLOR DIS-PLAYS?	VIDEO DISPLAY INCLUDED?
APPLE II	$1195	24,000	BASIC	YES	NO: CONNECTS TO STANDARD COLOR SET
COMMODORE PET 2001	$795	22,000	BASIC	NO	YES: BLACK AND WHITE DISPLAY
COMPUCOLOR II	$995	24,000	BASIC	YES	NO: CONNECTS TO STANDARD COLOR SET
OHIO SCIENTIFIC CHALLENGER	$349	12,000	BASIC	NO	NO: CONNECTS TO STANDARD BLACK AND WHITE OR COLOR SET
RADIO SHACK TRS I/4	$599	8,000	BASIC	NO	YES: BLACK AND WHITE DISPLAY
RCA VIP	$249	2,500	CHIP-8	NO	NO: CONNECTS TO STANDARD BLACK AND WHITE OR COLOR SET

*SOURCE = Hawkins, William J. "Memory? Programming? Add-Ons? Check Before You Buy a Home Computer". *Popular Science,* March 1979. pp. 102+.

THE APPLE II AND THE PET 2001

Figure 8: The Apple II, which can be connected to the lead-in wires of any color television set, produces beautiful graphs, barcharts and artistic patterns in 15 shimmering hues. A powerful microcomputer, the machine is also equipped with game paddles, joystick controls, and sound effects for use in conjunction with a wide range of video games. The Pet 2001 shown on the right is a cheaper, more austere, machine. It has only the most primitive gaming capabilities and it projects its computed results onto a built-in black and white television screen.

"You keep adding components until you exceed your yearly income", he explains with a nervous grin.

The Beginnings

The personal computer revolution seems to have erupted with dramatic swiftness, but how did it all begin? Most hobbyists would agree that the movement was born, quite unexpectedly, in January of 1975. In that month, an electronics engineer named Edward Roberts convinced the editors of *Popular Electronics* to run a cover story of the "Altair 8800", a hobby computer kit which had been under development in various forms by his company, Micro Instrumentation and Telemetry Systems, since the early months of 1972.*

Roberts and his research team had anticipated that the cover story might result in sales of as many as 200 Altair microcomputers, but their estimate was in error by at least an order of magnitude. In fact, on a single frantic Friday afternoon, shortly after the publication reached the newstands, they sold 275 units.

The Participants

When the Altair 8800 was first announced there were, in the entire United States, no more than 200 hobby computers, most of them patched together from industrial discards. In part, their numbers were so limited because they could be obtained only by surreptitious means. Asked how he managed to locate parts for his earliest computer in an era when the necessary circuits were sold only to commercial firms, one resourceful youth candidly replied: "There was only one way. I had to lie a lot."

Fortunately, lying is no longer a necessary prerequisite to computer ownership. By January of 1977, two years after the publication of the *Popular Electronics* cover story, there were an estimated 20,000 home computers in use and, during the next 12 months, approximately 24,000 new ones were sold with a market value somewhere between $60 and $70 million.** Comparisons between the sales rates of full size computers, minicomputers, and microcomputers are presented in graphical form in Figure 9. As you can see, at present, the larger machines dominate the market but the cheaper microcomputers are gaining at a rapid rate.

The hobbyists who own and operate personal computers tend to be fiercely loyal and passionately enthusiastic. They have their own computer clubs—by last count 180 organizations worldwide. They hold their own conventions—in January of 1977 the First Annual West Coast Computer Faire was held in San Francisco. It hosted 13,000 enthusiastic participants. They publish their own magazines. *Interface Age* claims 30,000 paid subscriptions, *Byte* subscribers are said to number more than 60,000.***

---

*The name of the new computer was furnished by *Popular Electronics* editor Les Solomon who asked his 12 year old daughter, Lauren, an avid Star Trek fan, to help him pick out a suitable name. "What do they call the computer on board the Enterprise?" he asked her. Her answer: "Computer". But she went on to suggest that they name it *Altair:* "Because that's where the Enterprise is going tonight."

**Merserv, Evertt T. "The Personal Computer Industry". Arthur D. Little, Inc. Report No. L780901, 7 September 1978.

***Kilobaud, Personal Computing, ROM, The Computer Hobbyist, On Line, and Dr. Dobb's Journal of Computer Calisthenics and Orthodontia* are also quite popular with hobby computer enthusiasts.

They support their own retail outlets. In July of 1975 the first Los Angeles specialty shop, The Computer Store, cautiously opened for business. Today, there are at least 400 outlets nationwide. Many are franchises with such unlikely names as "the Byte Shop", "Itty Bitty Machine Company", "Computer Shack", and "Kentucky Fried Computer".

It may be embarrassing for you to go into a shop with such a diminutive name, but if you do, you can, for a surprisingly small amount of cash, purchase your own personal microcomputer, a machine which possesses some truly remarkable computational capabilities.

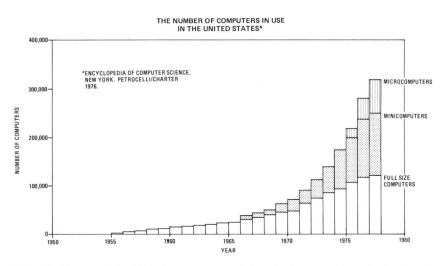

Figure 9: At present, the full-scale computers and the mincomputers in use in the United States comfortably outnumber the cheaper microcomputers. However, the microcomputer population is growing quite rapidly and, as is shown by the above graphs, the micro's will likely overtake the other, more elaborate machines within a few short years.

BIBLIOGRAPHY

1. "A Fine Faire." *Personal Computing,* July/August 1977, pp. 120-130.

2. Berger, Ivan. "Home Computer Kits: The Hottest New Angle in America's Newest Hobby." *Popular Mechanics,* February 1977, pp. 99-100.

3. Conway, John. "The Debatable Future of Minicomputers—Some Points of View." *EDN,* 5 June 1977. pp. 54-61.

4. Curran, Lawrence. "Personal Computers Mean Business." *Electronics,* 31 March 1977, pp. 89-96.

5. Davis, Sam. "Personal Computers: Expensive Toys or Efficient Problem Solvers?" *EDN,* 20 April 1978, pp. 24-26.

6. Ditlea, Steve. *A Simple Guide to Home Computers*. New York, New York: A & W Visual Library, 1979.

7. Doerr, John. "Low-Cost Microcomputing: The Personal Computer and Single-Board Computer Revolutions." *Proceedings of the IEEE*. February 1978, pp. 117-130.

8. "Everybody's Doing It ('Computing' At Home)." *IEEE Spectrum,* May 1977, pp. 29-34.

9. Garland, Harry. "Design Innovations in Personal Computers." *Computer,* March 1977, pp. 24-27.

10. Hall, John. "Why is the Mini Mightier than Ever?" *Instrumentation and Control Systems,* May 1977, pp. 28-33.

11. Isaacson, Portia. "Personal Computing." *Datamation,* October 1977, pp. 210-211.

12. "It Will be so Nice to Have a Computer Around." *The Register,* Los Angeles, 23 October 1977, p. A20.

13. Kay, Alan C. "Microelectronics and the Personal Computer." *Scientific American,* September 1977, pp. 230-244.

14. Mayo, John S. "The Role of Microelectronics in Communication." *Scientific American,* September 1977, pp. 162-179.

15. Moody, Robert. *The First Book of Microcomputers* Rochelle Park, New Jersey: Hayden Book Company, 1978.

16. Muller, Don. "Personal Computers in Home and Business Applications." *Computers and People.* December 1977, pp. 11-20.

17. Newman, Joseph. "The Computer: How It's Changing Our Lives." *U.S. News and World Report,* 1972.

18. North, Steve. "The ABC's of Microcomputers." *Creative Computing,* March/April 1978, pp. 89-90.

19. North, Steve. "Apple II Computer." *Creative Computing.* July/August 1978. pp.28-29

20. Noyce, Robert N. "Microelectronics." *Scientific American,* September 1977, pp. 62-69.

21. Osborne, Adam. "Who's Who in Personal Computers?" *Mini-Micro Systems,* May 1978, pp. 70-73.

22. "Personal Computing Dissected." *Computer,* July 1977, pp. 71-73.

23. "Plugging in Everyman." *Time,* 5 September 1977, p. 39.

24. Russo, Paul M.; Wang, Chih-Chung; Baltzer, Philip K.; and Weisbecker, Joseph A. "Microprocessors in Consumer Products." *Proceedings of the IEEE,* February 1978, pp. 131-141.

25. Schefter, Jim. "Microelectronics—Tiny Chips That Trim Costs and Make Life Easier." *Popular Science,* January, 1978, pp. 53-55.

26. Toong, Hoo-Min D. "Microprocessors." *Scientific American,* September 1977, pp. 146-161.

27. Van Tassel, Dennie L. *The Complete Computer.* Chicago, Illinois: Science Research Associates, 1976.

28. Warren, Jim. "Personal and Hobby Computing: An Overview." *Computer,* March 1977, pp. 10-22.

29. Yasaki, Edward K. "Microcomputers for Fun and Profit?" *Datamation,* July 1977, pp. 66-71.

EXERCISES

1. What is a computer? What are some of the uses of the computers in our society? What are some uses you would like to see in the future?

2. What are some of the differences between a digitial and an analog computer? Which type is the most popular? Why?

3. What is a time sharing system? What are some of the advantages of time sharing?

4. What is a minicomputer? About how much does it cost? How do the capabilities of modern minicomputers compare with the capabilities of our early electronic computers?

5. What is a microcomputer? If you had one of your own how would you use it? When might you reasonably expect to have one?

6. What are some of the advantageous properties of an LSI circuit chip? List several ways in which the chip is now used and several ways you can foresee it being used in the future.

7. Figure 1 shows a dramatic reduction in the cost of transistors since 1955. If houses, cars, theater tickets, and tennis balls had experienced similar technological advances approximately how much would each one cost today?

8. What is general purpose digital computer? When did the first one become operational? What theorem did Alan Turing prove about general purpose computers? When did he make his proof?

9. What is real time processing? What are some of its uses?

10. Briefly describe the major features of the Apple II and the Pet 2001. If you were going to buy one of these machines which one would you be most likely to select? Why?

STUDENT PROJECTS

1. Historians often study old newspapers in order to find out what was important to the people of a particular era and to see how they responded to certain major controversies. Band together with two or three of your classmates and begin making a collection of newspaper articles dealing with the computers in our society. Make a special effort to find articles that treat controversial topics, especially the ones which are covered in the last eight chapters of this textbook. When you have accumulated a reasonable number of

articles, analyze them for topic, slant and content. Ask yourself a series of questions and then search through the articles to find the answers. For example: Are most of the articles critical or supportive? Do they reflect obvious biases or do they seem to represent genuine attempts to present a balanced viewpoint? Do they contradict one another or the same issues? Devise various methods of your own to analyze the content of the articles and put together a brief summary of your findings.

2. Visit a computer center and see what you can observe about data processing as practiced in modern America. Talk to some of the operators and find out what you can about the working conditions and the major problems encountered by the people who operate our digital computers. Informally discuss your findings with your classmates.

3. Go to the library and use the Reader's Guide to Periodical Literature to research the current status of microcomputer revolution. Pay particular attention to projections on the number of units industry experts expect to sell and their probable prices. Remember that any projections may tend to be optimistic and self serving since the people in the industry will benefit most if sales are high. Try to find out how ordinary people are already using microcomputers and how they may be using them in the future. Summarize your findings in a written or an oral report.

SUGGESTED REFERENCES:

a. Curran, Lawrence. "Personal Computers Mean Business." *Electronics.* 31 March 1977, pp. 89-96.

b. "A Fine Faire." *Personal Computing.* July/August 1977, pp. 120-130.

c. Yasaki, Edward K. "Microcomputers for Fun and Profit." *Datamation.* July 1977, pp. 66-71.

d. "Plugging in Everyman." *Time.* 5 September 1977, pg. 39.

e. Osborne, Adam. "Who's Who in Personal Computers?" *Mini-Micro Systems.* May 1978, pp. 70-73.

f. Berger, Ivan. "Home Computer Kits." *Popular Mechanics.* February 1977, pp. 99-100.

g. "Everybody's Doing It ('Computing' at Home)". *IEEE Spectrum.* May 1977, pp. 29-34.

CHAPTER 2

THE VON NEUMANN LEGACY

THE ADVANTAGES OF BINARY ARITHMETIC
A Typical Binary Code
Parity Checking Schemes

INTERNALLY STORED PROGRAMS
The Development of FORTRAN
BASIC: A Language for Time Sharing
A Typical Computer Program
Other Languages
Flowcharting Techniques

THE FOUR FUNCTIONS OF A DIGITAL COMPUTER
Input-Output
Processing and Control
Storage
Assembling a Functioning System

VON NEUMANN'S CONTRIBUTIONS

BIBLIOGRAPHY

EXERCISES

STUDENT PROJECTS

There is no way anyone can build a data processing industry without teamwork. Huge groups of cooperative individuals are needed to keep the computers humming and sputtering at peak efficiency. However, there are also ample opportunities for personal flashes of brilliance. Over the years many in the industry have burned with star-like luminosity. Yet none has ever burned brighter or flickered longer than a playfully-intense Hungarian immigrant named John von Neumann.

Born into a wealthy, cultured family in Budapest in 1903, "Johnny" von Neumann, as his friends called him throughout his life, was a happy, precocious youngster who loved mathematical puzzles and tricky word games. When he was only six, he and his father told each other jokes in classical Greek. Later, in the United States, Edward Teller, father of the hydrogen bomb, would pun with him in several dialects. When their companions were not multilingual, they would, to be polite, restrict themselves to making puns in a single language but they both agreed that it was like doing an oil painting in black and white.

On the advice of Theodore von Karman, a highly-respected scientist, von Neumann earned his first PhD in chemistry but, because he had always enjoyed working with figures, he returned to school for an additional year to get another degree in advanced mathematics. In 1926 at the age of 23, he left his home for a teaching post in Germany. There he began a most remarkable habit of lecturing without notes, selecting a problem which he had not yet solved and tackling the solution of it as he lectured.* Unfortunately, within a short time, the militant sounds of the Nazi goose step began echoing ominously through the streets of Berlin and Hamburg and, to escape the conflict he knew would surely come, he accepted an invitation to lecture at Princeton University. Once there he published several significant technical papers and began a series of distinguished research efforts into the foundations of mathematics, nuclear energy, climate control, and the digital computer.

At Princeton and later at Los Alamos he enjoyed intimate parties with robust wines and vigorous conversations. He was, by all accounts, a talented host, a magnetic personality, a dedicated scientist, a gifted instructor . . . and a lousy driver. He had so many traffic accidents his students nicknamed one of the intersections near Princeton "von Neumann's Corners". Of course he was always armed with a creative explanation for each and every mishap. In describing one of his more harrowing escapades, he stubbornly maintained that "there was a long

---

*Thomas, Shirley. *Men of Space*. Philadelphia, Pennsylvania. Chilton Publishing Co., 1960.

row of trees moving by on the side of the road at 60 miles an hour, when suddenly one of them stepped into my path."

"He had the fastest mind I ever met" stated the famous nuclear physicist Lothar Nordheim. He made a similar impression on Herman Goldstine, one of the fathers of the ENIAC. "As far as I could tell, von Neumann was able on once reading a book or article to quote it back verbatim" wrote Goldstine in a book on the history of computers. "Moreover, he could do it years later without hesitation. He could also translate it at no diminution in speed from its original language into English. On one occasion I tested his ability by asking him to tell me how *Tale of Two Cities* started. Whereupon, without any pause, he immediately began to recite the first chapter and continued until asked to stop after about ten or fifteen minutes."*

His uncanny mathematical capabilities were also widely admired. With blistering speed and accuracy he could solve even the most difficult problems—in his head—problems whose solutions often took the best mathematicians hours or days of tedious pencil-and-paper calculations.

Then as now, ingenious practical jokes were a common laboratory diversion. And, not surprisingly, the fun-loving, gregarious "Johnny" was nearly everyone's favorite target. When time permitted, his colleagues would work out a complicated problem in advance and then innocently pose it to him as though it had just arisen. As "Johnny" would race through the problem—bursting with intensity and agitation—the others would nonchalantly call out each intermediate step the instant before he could figure it out on his own. It was a fun game but surprisingly tricky; sometimes he would discover hidden shortcuts and suddenly without warning, beat all of them to the desired solution!

In 1946, after visiting the computer facilities at the Moore School of Engineering, von Neumann put together a special 40-page technical paper which provided the major thrust for the many advances in computer technology that were to occur over the next few decades. Although many of his most imaginative ideas had been advanced by other, earlier researchers, his lucid writing style and the forcefulness of his presentation commanded instant, widespread attention. The von Neumann paper dealt with three fundamental concepts:

1. The intrinsic advantages of binary arithmetic
2. The technical feasibility of internally stored programs
3. A function-oriented definition of the operations performed by the high-speed digital computer.

*Goldstine, Herman H. *The Computer from Pascal to von Neumann*. Princeton, New Jersey. Princeton University Press, 1972.

Throughout the remainder of this chapter, we shall explore the ramifications of these three major concepts. Off hand, this may seem to be an excessively heavy emphasis on a relatively brief era in the history of computers. However, the von Neumann paper is still having critical influences on the modern data processing industry. Even today, more than 30 years after it was first published, every major computer still employs some form of binary arithmetic; every major computer makes use of internally stored programs; and every major computer is constructed under the function-oriented design philosophy first clearly enunciated by "Johnny' von Neumann. There is simply no way you can fathom the complexities of modern computers unless you understand something of what he did. Indeed, his work has been so influential that some historians designate the various events in the history of computer technology as BVN (*Before von Neumann*) or AVN (*After von Neumann*).

THE ADVANTAGES OF BINARY ARITHMETIC

It is possible to build a computer that uses decimal arithmetic of the type we employ in our everyday business transactions. The ENIAC and several other early machines were, in fact, built that way. However, there is a much better method for designing computers. As was mentioned in Chapter 1, the computer's electronic switches are intrinsically bistable. Like a light bulb and many other familiar, everyday devices (See Figure 10), a bistable switch can assume precisely two states of stability—such as "on" and "off" or their equivalent. Hence, as John von Neumann pointed out in his famous paper, it is much more efficient to have the computer store and process its data values in binary, a numeration system which uses only 1's and 0's. In such a computer, information is carried from one internal location to another by means of binary pulse trains—strings of electronic pulses which march in single file. A binary 1 is represented by the presence of a pulse; its absence represents a binary 0. When a pulse train is routed through one of the computer's processing circuits, a new pulse train is automatically produced in response to the program instructions.

Like our familiar decimal system of numeration, the binary system utilizes *positional notation*. In a positional notation system, part of the value of a digit results from its *shape* and part of it results from its *position* with respect to the other symbols. Thus, for example, we interpret the decimal number 6,324 to mean 6 "thousands", 3 "hundreds", 2 "tens", and 4 "ones":

"thousands"	"hundreds"	"tens"	"ones"
6324 = 6 x 1000 +	3 x 100 +	2 x 10 +	4 x 1

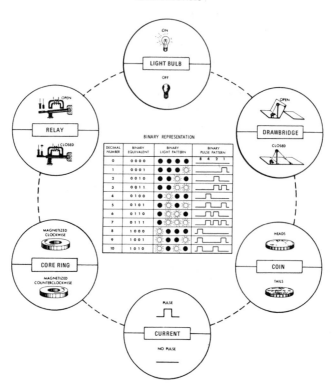

BISTABLE DEVICES

Figure 10: These devices are bistable, that is, they can assume exactly two distinct states of stability such as "on" and "off" or their equivalent. A large-scale digital computer uses millions of bistable switches for the storage and processing of information. During computation, the switches change from one stable state to another in response to the program instructions. Binary pulse trains—strings of electronic pulses which march in single file—are used in transmitting coded information between the various mechanisms inside the computer. A binary 1 is represented by the presence of a pulse; its absence denotes a binary 0.

If we would take the digit 3 and move it to a new location (without changing its shape) the value of the entire number would change. Clearly, the number 6,243 is not the same as 6,324 although it merely involves a rearrangement of the same decimal digits.*

---

*Most of us are so accustomed to the decimal system, we find it hard to appreciate that its use is quite arbitrary. And yet, other systems have been employed in the past. As Jeremy Bernstein points out in his book, *The Analytical Engine,* "In reckoning time there are residues of other systems; the number of hours in the day is counted by twelves, and the number of seconds in a minute by sixties . . . The predominance of the decimal system undoubtedly has to do with the fact that the best-known counting instrument of all—the fingers on one's hands—operates by tens." If Bugs Bunny had been your first grade teacher, you might just as well use a system that involves only eight symbols instead of ten; Bugs Bunny, like most cartoon characters, has only four fingers on each hand.

The binary numeration system also uses positional notation but the values of the columns reading from right to left are not 1, 10, 100, 1,000, . . . as they are in our decimal system. Instead their values are 1, 2, 4, 8, . . . That is to say, the "place values" are powers of 2 rather than powers of 10. Moreover, in binary we do not use all ten of the familiar digits: 0, 1, 2, . . . ,9; instead we use only two: 0 and 1. Thus we would represent the decimal numbers 0 through 14 in binary as follows:

Decimal Number	Binary Version	Number	Version
0	0000	8	1000
1	0001	9	1001
2	0010	10	1010
3	0011	11	1011
4	0100	12	1100
5	0101	13	1101
6	0110	14	1110
7	0111		

Specifically, the decimal numbers 9 and 13 are coded in binary like this:

Decimal No.		Binary No.		Decimal "eights"		Binary "fours"		"twos"		"ones"
9	=	1001	=	1 x 8	+	0 x 4	+	0 x 2	+	1 x 1
13	=	1101	=	1 x 8	+	1 x 4	+	0 x 2	+	1 x 1

The addition table in the decimal number system is relatively complicated and it requires an appreciable amount of time to learn. In order to handle the sums of the ten decimal digits in their various combinations, we must memorize a total of 100 items of the form: 6 + 3 = 9 and 8 + 7 = 15. By contrast, the binary addition table is so simple it can be written on a postage stamp:

$$0 + 0 = 1$$
$$0 + 1 = 1$$
$$1 + 0 = 1$$
$$1 + 1 = 10$$

The first three sums look familiar but the last one may seem a little strange. Of course, when we write 1 + 1 = 10 in binary, the result on the right is interpreted as "one 2 and zero 1's."

Performing calculations in binary certainly seems simple and straightforward. Why then don't we borrow the computer's binary system for our own use? One problem with this idea is that large binary numbers are quite stringy and difficult to remember. The author's telephone number, 431-3334, for example, is 110101111-110100000110 in binary notation. Such a number would be relatively easy to dial—if the phone company switched to binary, your push-button telephone would need only two buttons! But you would have to be a black-belt memory expert to keep the numbers in mind long enough to complete your call.

A Typical Binary Code

In addition to the pure binary representation shown in Figure 10, computers use several other binary codes. Figure 11 shows how numbers are represented as *binary coded decimals*. The white rectangles denote binary zeros; those that have been darkened denote binary ones.

This particular code can be used in representing up to 64 letters, numbers and special characters. Whenever we are coding one of the ten decimal digits, the two rows of "zone bits" are always binary zeros. The other four bits vary depending on the value being coded. The decimal digit 7, for example, is represented by placing binary ones in the last three rows, i.e., those marked 1, 2, and 4:

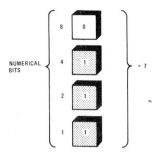

Similarly, the decimal digit 9 is denoted by placing binary ones in the rectangles marked 1 and 8. It may not be clear to you at this point how this particular code differs from the pure binary representation listed in Figure 10. The fundamental difference is that, in the case of binary coded decimals, each decimal digit in a number is represented by its own separate string of binary 1's and 0's. Thus, for example, the decimal number 138 would be coded in this form

$$
\begin{array}{ccc}
(1) & (3) & (8) \\
0001 - & 0011 - & 1000
\end{array}
$$

as a binary coded decimal whereas in pure binary it would be represented as a single unit

(138)
10001010.

The two rows of "zone bits" marked B and A are used in conjunction with the numerical bits to represent letters and special characters. This is the way the first 13 letters of the alphabet are coded:

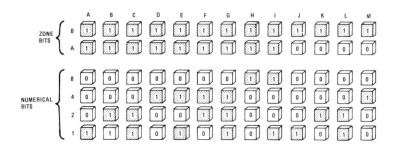

As you can see, the code is quite systematic. The adjacent letters J, K, and L, for example, are represented as: 100001, 100010, and 100011 respectively. Note that in pure binary these three values would equal 33, 34, and 35. However, the computer is rigged to regard them as binary-coded-decimal characters so that, in practice, confusion never actually arises.

Parity Checking Schemes

A modern digital computer is a remarkably reliable machine. Some models average less than one error in every 100,000,000,000 processing operations. Inpart, this high degree of reliability stems from the fact that computers can be rigged to detect and correct their own mathematical errors. In the early years of the computer revolution, automatic error detection was accomplished by running two processing units in parallel so that the computer could cross-check the results after each computation. If a mismatch occurred, the offending processing steps were repeated by both units. It was a workable scheme but it was extremely expensive. In effect, the computer had to be equipped with enough hardware so that it could duplicate every mathematical operation in real time.

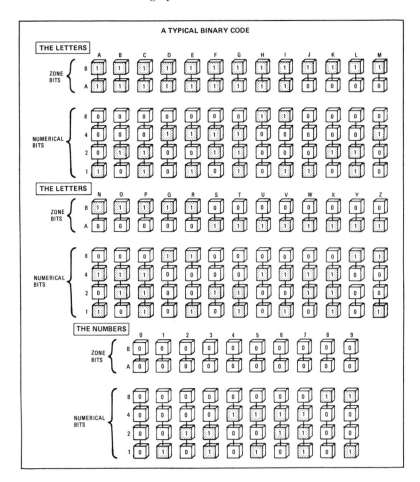

Figure 11: Modern computers use various types of binary codes in storing and processing numbers, letters, and special characters. The ones in this figure are represented as binary coded decimals. White rectangles denote binary zeros; those that have been darkened denote binary ones. As you can see, the ten decimal digits are coded by using the four "numerical bits" in various binary combinations. The letters and special characters are coded by using the two "zone bits" in conjunction with the four "numerical bits".

Parity checking is a modern technique which accomplishes some of the same objectives with much cheaper hardware. In parity checking each coded character being stored inside the computer is accompanied by an extra bit called the "parity checking bit". This parity checking bit automatically assumes a value of 0 or 1 such that each coded character

PARITY CHECKING SCHEMES

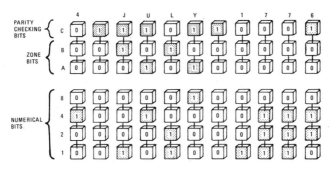

Figure 12: Parity checking is an automatic procedure which allows the computer to detect and correct its own transmission and processing errors. An extra bit, called the parity checking bit, is attached to each alphanumeric character being held in storage. This bit assumes a value of 0 or 1 such that each character always contains an odd number of binary 1's. If an even number of 1's is encountered at any point, the computer knows it has made an error. When an error is found, the offending operation is automatically repeated several times in attempting to obtain an acceptable value.

always contains an *odd number of binary digits.** Figure 12 shows the parity checking bits that would be associated with the storage of the date "4 JULY 1776". The parity checking bits are the ones in the first row marked "C" for checking bit.

The parity checking bits allow the computer to verify the accuracy of each operation it performs. Each time a processing step is executed, or a binary pulse train is transmitted from one internal location to another, the parity checking bit is examined to make sure it has the proper value. Whenever the computer encounters a parity checking error, it automatically repeats the offending operation to see if it can obtain a valid result. If the error persists after several tries, it prints a message to the operator and goes on to its next assignment.

INTERNALLY STORED PROGRAMS

In 1946 John von Neumann was invited to the Moore School of Engineering in Philadelphia where he got a chance to watch the ENIAC in operation. Although it suffered from severe reliability problems, with breakdowns occurring almost daily, the ENIAC could, when it worked properly, perform 5,000 additions in a single second. In other words, it was nearly 2,000 times as fast as Howard H. Aiken's Mark I which had

---

*Just to make things more confusing some machines are rigged to use *even* parity checking. In this case an *even number of binary 1's is associated with each character.*

triggered an enthusiastic response when it became operational a few months earlier.

Over the years von Neumann had spent a great deal of time performing tedious hand calculations and he was much impressed with the computational capabilities of the new machine. However, he was not nearly as enamored with the methods used in programming it. The ENIAC had an electronic memory for storing the numbers to be manipulated by the program instructions—which were themselves stored in another part of the machine. When numbers were fed into the computer, its electronic switches were merely reset to reflect the values to be held in storage. The instructions themselves, however, were inserted in a much more awkward way, in effect, by rewiring some parts of the computer's processing circuits. This is how Jeremy Bernstein, professor of Physics at New York University, described the ENIAC's rather elaborate programming procedures:

"Before starting on a given problem, one had to figure out each of the necessary instructions and hook up the appropriate circuits by hand—an operation that was something like plugging up connections on a telephone switchboard. In fact, plugging up a problem on the ENIAC sometimes took several people several days and involved making hundreds of wired connections."*

It was a complicated, time-consuming approach and it required that the computer be idled for lengthy intervals during the programming process. Fortunately, there was a practical alternative. The new scheme, as outlined by John von Neumann and others, would utilize *internally stored commands*. In such a system the program instructions are stored inside the computer in memory slots identical to those used to store data. One advantage of this approach is that the computer need not be idled during the programming process. But of more fundamental importance, the computer can be made to *alter its own commands while its computations are taking place*. As a result, it is able to make "decisions" and to set up loops of repeated calculations, two extremely powerful capabilities.

Internally stored programs were a significant improvement over the ENIAC's manual programming methods. But, unfortunately, even with internal storage, early programming techniques were still plagued with serious difficulties. Simple computer programs could be coded with reasonable ease, but coding a complicated routine tended to be a nerve-

---

*Bernstein, Jeremy. *The Analytical Engine*. Random House, New York. 1963.

wracking procedure. The fundamental problem was that early programmers had to communicate with their computers in programming languages which were natural for the machines but quite unnatural for the human programmers. In recent years, however, *symbolic programming languages* have helped alleviate this difficulty. The commands in a symbolic language resemble the words and equations used by mathematicians, accountants and engineers.

The Development of FORTRAN

One of the first and most successful symbolic programming languages was called FORTRAN (*FOR*mula *TRAN*slation). It was developed by John Backus and a team of 13 other programmers at IBM who spent nearly 75,000 manhours over a three year period developing the new language into a practical tool. Coding the complicated translation routines took most of their time. A digital computer can't understand the commands in a symbolic programming language in their raw form. Therefore, it must be equipped with a special routine to translate them into its own binary language before it can interpret their meaning.

When FORTRAN was first introduced, many programmers were skeptical of its purported benefits. They were convinced that their special knowledge of computer hardware would allow them to code far more efficient routines. In a few cases they were correct, but, generally speaking, the improvements they were able to make were quite small in comparison with the amount of time they had to expend.

BASIC: A Language for Time Sharing

Since its inception in 1957, FORTRAN has been among the most popular of the symbolic programming languages. It is especially convenient when it is used in solving the kind of problems encountered by scientists and engineers. Unfortunately, some programming tasks cannot be handled effectively in FORTRAN. In particular, the FORTRAN language tends to be clumsy and ineffectual when it is used in conjunction with certain types of business problems. Moreover, it is too complicated and confusing for effective use in many applications involving time sharing. When you are assigned to operate a time sharing terminal, you must be able to react within a reasonable interval whenever the computer flashes a message on the screen or prints out an obviously incorrect answer. It is possible to use FORTRAN in this hectic, pressure-prone environment, but, in general, BASIC is a much more realistic selection.

BASIC was developed in 1959 by Professor John Kemeny at Dartmouth College.* Although it was Dr. Kemeny's intention to devise a simple, straightforward language to be used in connection with time sharing applications, BASIC is also widely used in the programming of industrial and educational minicomputers and it is, by far, the most popular selection of hobby computer enthusiasts.

A Typical Computer Program

Given a reasonable amount of time, it is relatively easy to develop a working knowledge of one of the simpler programming languages. Consequently, a professional programmer does not often reflect on the raw power of the skills he or she has acquired. However, whether he or she realizes it or not, a well-trained programmer with access to a high-speed digital computer can accomplish a remarkable amount of work in a surprisingly short time.

In order to amplify this point, we will code a program in BASIC which makes use of a loop of repeated calculations. The program will also provide some interesting insights into the dynamics of the population explosion.

In 1979 the population of the United States was 216.8 million with a growth rate that was virtually stagnant, averaging less than one percent per year. By contrast, Mexico's population was only 64.4 million but her annual growth rate was a hefty 3.3 percent. If we assume that Mexico's present growth rate will persist over the next few decades, how long will it be before our Mexican neighbors outnumber the people now living in the United States?

Populations tend to grow in a manner which is akin to compound interest. That is to say, the number of children born to each generation will be roughly proportional to the number of available parents. This law leads to a relationship which states that if Mexico's annual growth rate is 3.3 percent, then its population next year will equal $P \times (1 + 0.033)$ where P is this year's population. In order to compute the population for the year after, we need only replace the old value of P with its new value and repeat the same calculation. This is what is done 50 times in the program in Figure 13.

As you can see, the program involves six simple BASIC commands. An experienced programmer could easily code this routine in less than five minutes. And, if he ran it on a moderate-sized computer, it would

---

*Dartmouth College is now Dartmouth University and John Kemeny is now its President.

produce 50 error-free values arranged in a pleasant format at a cost of a few pennies.

The graph at the bottom of Figure 13 shows how the population of Mexico will expand if it follows the trends indicated by our rather simplistic projection. As you can see, the trend line indicates that in the year 2016 Mexico's population will surpass the present population of the United States.

Some of the commands in our sample program contain familiar English words such as LET, PRINT and END. Does this mean the computer understands ordinary English? Not exactly. It can respond to 50 or 60 specific English words, but if you feed it words like MARMALADE or TWILIGHT, which are not within its specialized vocabulary, it won't have the slightest idea what you mean.

Other Languages

Modern computers speak many languages besides FORTRAN and BASIC; languages with curious names like MAD, MANIAC, INTER-COM, and PL/I. Typical samples are presented in Figure 14. As you can see, these computer languages are nearly as diverse as the languages currently spoken by the family of man. Note that some involve only binary 1's and 0's; others involve decimal digits; and still others involve ordinary English words.

Flowcharting Techniques

Symbolic languages have helped immensely in simplifying the programming of digital computers, but, even with the new languages, programming can be a tedious profession. So tedious that a master plan is often necessary to keep the programmer and his or her co-workers from getting hopelessly confused. For this reason many practitioners use flowcharts to plan their programs and to make sure they are logically consistent.

A flowchart is a deceptively simple tool. In essence, it is a series of boxes interconnected by arrows. The shape of each box denotes its function and the arrows indicate the order in which the computations are to occur. Some of the standard flowcharting symbols used by professional programmers are sketched on the left hand side of Figure 15. A flowchart of the population projection program is presented on the right hand side of the same figure. Note that its starting and stopping points are marked with oval boxes, its computations are enclosed within rectangles, its inputs and outputs are denoted by parallelograms and its decision point is

POPULATION PROJECTION PROGRAM

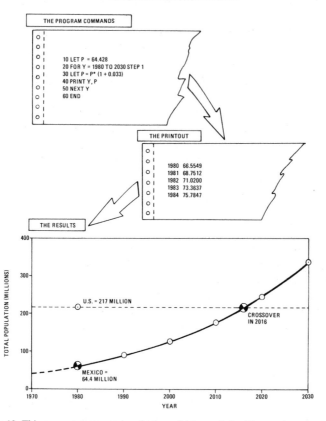

Figure 13: This computer program, which could be coded with ease by a beginning student, shows how six simple BASIC commands can be used in making crude population projections. According to the computer, if Mexico's present growth rate remains unchanged, the number of Mexicans will equal the present number of inhabitants of the United States by the year 2016.

bounded by a box shaped like a diamond. Flowcharts of this type are quite helpful to professional programmers. They are also widely used by many others outside the data processing industry such as operations researchers and nuclear engineers.

THE FOUR FUNCTIONS OF A DIGITAL COMPUTER

When a scientist describes the operating principles of an intercontinental ballistic missile or a high-performance aircraft he doesn't attempt to analyze every single component part as a separate entity.

SAMPLES OF COMPUTER LANGUAGES

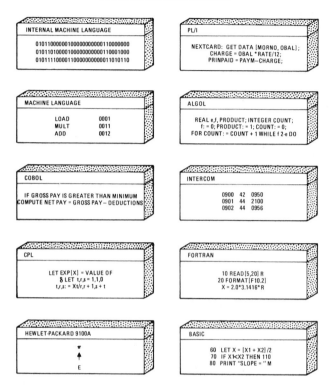

INTERNAL MACHINE LANGUAGE

```
0101100000010000000000011 0000000
0101101000010000000000011 0001000
0101111000011000000000011 1010110
```

PL/I

```
NEXTCARD: GET DATA [MORNO, OBAL];
        CHARGE = OBAL *RATE/12;
        PRINPAID = PAYM−CHARGE;
```

MACHINE LANGUAGE

```
LOAD      0001
MULT      0011
ADD       0012
```

ALGOL

```
REAL e,f, PRODUCT; INTEGER COUNT;
    f: = 0; PRODUCT: = 1; COUNT: = 0;
FOR COUNT: = COUNT + 1 WHILE f 2-e DO
```

COBOL

```
IF GROSS PAY IS GREATER THAN MINIMUM
COMPUTE NET PAY = GROSS PAY − DEDUCTIONS
```

INTERCOM

```
0900   42   0950
0901   44   2100
0902   44   0956
```

CPL

```
LET EXP[X] = VALUE OF
  § LET t,r,s = 1,1,0
  t,r,s: = Xt/r,r + 1,s + t
```

FORTRAN

```
10 READ [5,20] R
20 FORMAT [F10.2]
   X = 2.0*3.1416*R
```

HEWLET-PACKARD 9100A

```
π
↑
E
```

BASIC

```
60   LET X = [X1 + X2] /2
70   IF X1<X2 THEN 110
80   PRINT "SLOPE = " M
```

Figure 14: The languages used in programming digital computers are nearly as diverse as the languages spoken by the members of the human family. A Mexican Gaucho and an Australian aborigine would be unable to talk to one another because they have no common vocabulary. A pair of computers programmed to use any two of the languages shown in the above figure would have even greater difficulties in attempting to communicate.

Instead, he divides the device into a series of interlocking subsystems each devoted to a particular function. Accordingly, he might focus his attention on the guidance and control system, the electrical power system, the propulsion system, and so on.

The philosophy underlying this approach is that it is often better to define a complicated device in terms of what it *does* rather than what it *is*. Even in 1946 this was not a new idea, but John von Neumann adopted it with consumate skill in his widely-heralded technical paper. In the von Neumann classification system the computer is regarded as a device which performs four basic functions:

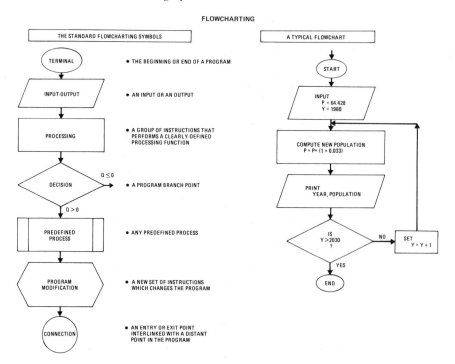

Figure 15: A flowchart is a series of boxes interconnected by arrows which summarizes the structure and content of a computer program. The shape of each box denotes its function whereas the arrows indicate the order in which the computations are to be carried out. The sample flowchart on the right corresponds to the BASIC Program in Figure 13 which was coded to project Mexico's population levels throughout the next 50 years.

1. input-output
2. processing
3. control
4. storage.

A diagram showing how these functions are interrelated is presented in Figure 16. They are also discussed one at a time in the next four sub-sections.

Input-Output

The *input-output* devices are used by the computer to communicate with the outside world in a human-oriented "language". Data values and program commands are fed into the computer by means of the input devices. When the computations have been completed, the output devices are used to display the final results.

Whenever you see Hollywood's version of a digital computer in operation the cameras invariably linger on the input-output devices— mechanical card readers swallowing hefty stacks of perforated cards, magnetic tape drives twitching back and forth like flea-infested basset

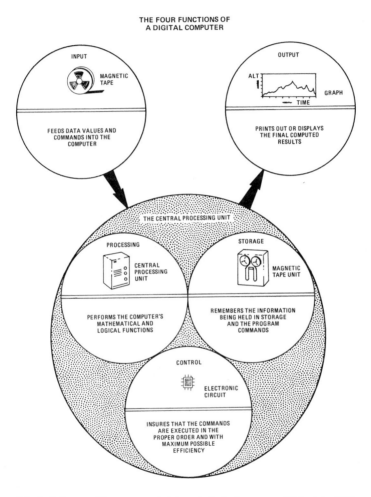

THE FOUR FUNCTIONS OF
A DIGITAL COMPUTER

Figure 16: As John von Neumann noted in a technical paper published in 1946, a digital computer can be regarded as a machine which performs four basic functions: input-output, processing, control and storage. More than 30 years have elapsed since he made his penetrating observations but, even today, all large-scale digital computers are constructed under the same basic philosophy he so skillfully enunciated.

hounds, high-speed printers churning out endless stacks of neatly-printed paper forms. They come in a variety of sizes and shapes, and they work in a number of different ways, but the purpose of the input-output devices is always the same: to provide a convenient communication channel between the man and his machine.

Processing and Control

The *processing* mechanisms are the devices the computer uses to process the input values in accordance with the program instructions. In general, these mechanisms consist of solid-state electronic circuits equipped with no moving parts. The only thing that moves is a series of electronic pulses which travel at an effective speed of 150,000 miles per second.*

The *control* mechanisms cause the computer to execute the program instructions in the proper sequence with maximum possible efficiency. The other three functions are usually executed by free-standing units. By contrast, the control mechanisms tend to be dispersed throughout the computer at the point of need. In this respect the computer's control mechanisms are roughly analogous to the nervous system of the human body.

The control system includes devices which keep the various computer functions properly synchronized. In a *synchronous* computer this is accomplished by a metronome-like device called the "clock pulse circuit" which sends out evenly-spaced timing pulses to every corner of the Central Processing Unit. In a different kind of machine called an *asynchronous* computer, timing pulses are not used. They are unnecessary because each processing circuit is designed so that it automatically signals the other parts of the computer when it completes each separate processing step.

A digital computer's processing and control circuits operate like a railroad switching yard built on a microscopic scale. In accordance with the program instructions, electronic pulse trains (packets of electrons) are routed through a series of solid-state switches. Each time the pulse train encounters one of the switches, it is automatically converted into a new pulse train with the desired characteristics.

An overview of the switching procedure is presented in Figure 17. The decimal number 003-005 in the upper left hand corner of the figure

---

*In passing through a vacuum, electromagnetic waves travel at a rate of 186,000 miles per second. However, when they traverse solid materials such as the circuits and wires inside a computer, the travel speed is typically reduced by about 25 percent.

represents a typical machine language command. As you can see, it consists of two parts: an operation code (003) and a numerical address (005).* This is how the computer would interpret such a command: "Take the quantity stored in location 005 and *add* it to the value being stored in the accumulator." (The accumulator is a high-speed storage register which temporarily stores the results of each processing step.) In a particular application, location 005 might contain last month's gas bill and the accumulator might contain the balance for this month. As is specified in the operation code (003), these two values would be routed through the *adder unit,* a special electronic circuit, to obtain their sum which is then stored in the accumulator thus wiping out its previous contents.

THE COMPUTER'S PROCESSING OPERATIONS

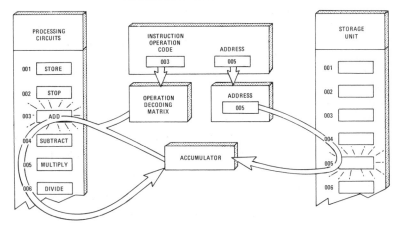

Figure 17: The computer's processing and control circuits are like a railroad switching yard built on a microscopic scale. In this particular case the computer is commanded to take the quantity stored in the accumulator (a temporary high-speed storage register) and the quantity stored in location 005 and route them through a circuit designed to add their two values. The result is then stored in the accumulator thus erasing the quantity it previously contained.

---

*In most modern computers the machine language commands involve two numerical addresses instead of only one and they are coded in binary notation; however, to help make things a little clearer, we have purposely selected the simpler version and represented it in decimal notation.

Storage

The computer's *storage* unit "remembers" both the program instructions and the current data values. In general, a large-scale computer utilizes several different types of storage devices carefully interconnected to provide an overall memory system with the best possible combination of desirable properties.

The devices which handle the three functions listed across the bottom of Figure 16: *processing, control* and *primary storage* are generally co-located in a separate cabinet called the Central Processing Unit (CPU). In a modern computer the Central Processing Unit is all-electronic. In fact, it contains most of the computer's electronic circuits.

Assembling a Functioning System

Like a high-quality stereo system, a large-scale digital computer is usually assembled from a series of separate, self-contained components interconnected by electrical cables. One advantage of this approach is that it allows each individual user to put together a set of components specifically tailored to his particular needs. Modularized construction also isolates the subunits of the computer thus fostering routine maintenance and simplifying major equipment modifications.

Today's designers have produced a surprisingly large variety of system components. Figure 18 provides a partial listing. Although the items in this figure are tremendously important to the professional engineers who purchase and install today's data processing systems, you need not try to memorize the list or even attempt to puzzle out what is meant in each and every instance. The purpose of this figure is not to confuse or intimidate but to help you get a handle on the rich diversity of hardware selections that are currently available.

VON NEUMANN'S CONTRIBUTIONS

In 1957, after a lingering illness, John von Neumann died. An affectionate, fun-loving Hungarian immigrant, he had lived his life with enthusiasm and vigor. More than any other single individual, his contributions have helped shape the way we design and operate our digital computers. He was a charming personality who cared about the future of his adopted land. He thrived on science and mathematics. He loved people. We owe him an enormous debt of gratitude.

THE HARDWARE COMPONENTS AVAILABLE IN TODAY'S MARKETPLACE

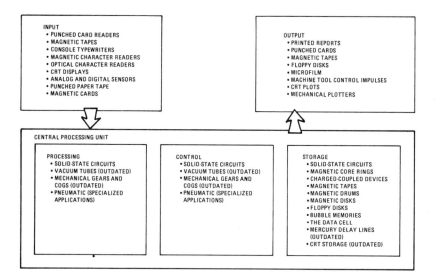

Figure 18: Today's competitive marketplace has produced a rich variety of hardware devices capable of carrying out the computer's four basic functions. The listings in this figure are presented to help you gain a speaking acquaintance with some of the more popular selections.

BIBLIOGRAPHY

1. Adams, J. Mack and Hayden, Douglas H. *Social Effects of Computer Use and Misuse. New York, New York: John Wiley, 1976.*

2. Bernstein, Jeremy. *The Analytical Engine.* New York, New York: Random House, 1963.

3. "Bytes and Chips." *New Yorker,* 53 (1977):30-31.

4. Davis, Ruth M. "Evolution of Computers and Computing." *Science,* 195:1096-1102.

5. Davis, Ruth M. "The Evolution of Computers and Computing." *Science,* 18 March 1977, pp. 1096-1102.

6. Douglas, J. H. "From Numbercrunchers to Pocket Genies." *Science News,* 6 September 1975, pp. 154-157.

7. "Down Silicon Valley." *Time,* 20 February 1978, pg. 51.

8. Eckert, Presper J. "Thoughts on The History of Computing." *Computer,* December 1976, pp. 58-65.

9. Goldstine, Herman H. *The Computer From Pascal to Von Neumann.* Princeton University Press, Princeton, New Jersey: 1972.

10. Gottfried, Byron S. *Programming With BASIC.* New York, New York: McGraw-Hill, 1975.

11. Holoein, Martin O. *Computers and Their Societal Impact.* New York, New York: John Wiley, 1977.

12. "How a Computer Adds 1 and 1." *Time.* 20 February 1978.

13. *Introduction to Computing Through the BASIC Language,* New York, New York: Holt, Rinehart, and Winston, 1969.

14. Logsdon, Tom. *Programming in BASIC.* Fullerton, California: Anaheim Publishing Co., 1977.

15. Logsdon, Tom and Logsdon, Fae. *The Computers in Our Society.* Fullerton, California: Anaheim Publishing Company, 1974.

16. Morrison, Philip and Morrison, Emily. *Charles Babbage and His Calculating Engines.* New York, New York: Dover Publications, 1961.

17. Pack, Susan. "The Computers are Coming, The Computers are Coming." *Skyline,* Rockwell International, Spring 1977, pp. 6-11.

18. Price, Wilson T. *Introduction to Computer Data Processing,* New York, New York: Dryden Press, 1977.

19. "Pushbutton Living." *Time,* 20 February 1978, pp. 46-49.

20. Ralston, Anthony and Meek, Chester L. *Encyclopedia of Computer Science.* New York, New York: Petrocelli/Charter, 1976.

21. Sanders, Donald. *Computers in Society.* New York, New York:McGraw-Hill, 1973.

22. "The Age of the Miracle Chips." *Time,* 20 February 1978, pp. 44-45.

23. Thomas, Shirley. *Men of Space.* Philadelphia, Pennsylvania: Chilton Publishing Co., 1960.

EXERCISES

1. List the four basic functions of a digital computer and briefly describe each function.

2. Using terminology similar to that used in Exercise 1, list and briefly describe the basic functions of the human body. An automobile. The Federal Government.

3. In 1946 John von Neumann put together a special technical paper which had important impacts on all future developments in computer technology. List the three major contributions of this landmark publication and describe the significance of each contribution.

4. What is the decimal value of these two binary numbers?

     a.   1001
     b. 100110

5. A computer transmits the following binary-coded-decimal message from one of its storage units into the Central Processing Unit:

   Has there been an error in transmission? If so, which character is erroneous?

6. When John Kemeny decided to develop the BASIC language, FORTRAN was already quite successful. In view of this fact why did he feel the need for a new programming language? What are some of the present day uses of BASIC which Dr. Kemeny had not anticipated?

7. John von Neumann listed *input-output* as a single computer function. Why do you suppose he didn't regard "input" and "output" as two separate functions?

8. Most modern computers are assembled in modular fashion. What are some of the principal advantages of this approach?

9. John von Neumann made many important contributions to the development of early computers but he also worked successfully in several other fields. How would you characterize the personal and intellectual characteristics that allowed him to contribute to so many different technologies?

10. Last November a computer programmer at the Rand Corporation had a couple of drinks with his lunch. That afternoon he drew this flowchart:

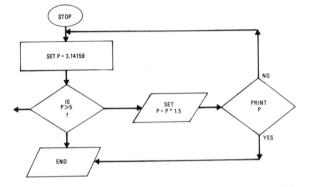

It contains several errors; point out as many as you can find.

STUDENT PROJECTS

1. The caption in Figure 14 claims that computer languages are "nearly as diverse as the languages spoken by the members of the human family". Collect samples of some of the languages spoken by man and machines and make a poster comparing them.

2. John von Neumann was a loveable and successful scientist and human being. Research his life with emphasis on his amazing mental feats and his contributions to computer technology. Put together an informal report summarizing your findings.

SUGGESTED REFERENCES

a. Goldstine, Herman H. *The Computer from Pascal to von Neumann.* Princeton University Press, Princeton, New Jersey. 1972.

b. Bernstein, Jeremy. *The Analytical Engine.* Random House, New York, New York. 1963.

c. Thomas, Shirley. *Men of Space.* Philadelphia, Pennsylvania: Chilton Publishing Co., 1960.

d. Eckert, J. Presper. "Thoughts on the History of Computing". *Computer.* December 1976, pp. 58-65.

e. Davis, Ruth M. "The Evolution of Computers and Computing". *Science.* 18 March 1977, pp. 1096-1102.

f. Logsdon, Tom and Fae. *The Computers in Our Society.* Fullerton, California: Anaheim Publishing Company. 1974.

g. Logsdon, Tom. *Computer Science and Technology.* Palisade, New Jersey: Franklin Publishing Company, 1974.

3. Reread the material on flowcharting in this textbook and research it in other sources. Now plan and flowchart an airline reservation system. Include in your flowchart provisions for such things as seat availability, first class or coach ticketing, special dietary requirements, rental car and hotel accommodations, traveler discounts, total ticket charges, etc. Use the standard flowcharting symbols and be sure to rig your flowchart so that the resulting program will print out an itemized bill and any other pertinent information.

CHAPTER 3

THE CARE AND FEEDING
OF A DIGITAL COMPUTER

PUNCHED CARD INPUTS
The Unit Record Concept
Keypunching Mechanisms
Card Reading Devices

MAGNETIC TAPES

REMOTE TERMINALS
The Magic Light Pen
Computer Aided Design

HIGH SPEED PRINTERS

DEVICES THAT DRAW PICTURES AND GRAPHS
Cathode-Ray-Tube Plotters
Mechanical Plotters

COMPUTER-DIRECTED CONVERSATIONS

BIBLIOGRAPHY

EXERCISES

STUDENT PROJECTS

"Hal", he said, in a steady a voice as he could manage. "Give me manual hibernation control—on all the units."

"All of them, Dave?"

"Yes."

"May I point out that only one replacement is required. The others are not due for revival for one hundred and twelve days."

"Hal, switch to manual hybernation control."

"I can tell from your voice harmonics, Dave, that you're badly upset. Why don't you take a stress pill and get some rest?"

"Hal", said Bowman, now speaking with icy calm. "Unless you obey my instructions I shall be forced to disconnect you."

Hal's surrender was as total as it was unexpected. "O.K., Dave," he said, "You're certainly the boss. I was only trying to do what I thought best. Naturally, I will follow all your orders. You now have full manual hyberation control."

> *2001: A Space Odyssey*
> Arthur C. Clarke
> 1968

Like many of his compatriots lurking in the pages of science fiction, "Hal", the softspoken computer in Arthur Clarke's *Space Odyssey 2001*, exhibits a number of frighteningly human characteristics. He speaks clear, articulate English—complete with proper voice inflections. He comprehends even the most intricate spoken instructions. He successfully analyzes voice harmonics. And in his spare time he teaches himself to read lips!

But what is all the excitement about? Haven't recent issues of the National Observer and related publications been peppered with convincing accounts of computers engaging in intelligent conversations? Aren't lip reading and stress detection relatively simple examples of pattern recognition? Fair questions. We shall attempt to answer them in the next few chapters. We kick off our story by examining some of the more commonplace methods used in communicating with today's high-speed digital computers. Figure 19 lists typical examples of some of the more popular communication media. They include punched cards, magnetic tapes and disks, light pen devices, hard copy printers, and various types of electronic and mechanical plotters.

PUNCHED CARD INPUTS

In the early days of the computer revolution, punched cards were widely accepted as the most versatile and efficient medium for feeding

THE COMPUTER'S INPUT-OUTPUT MEDIA

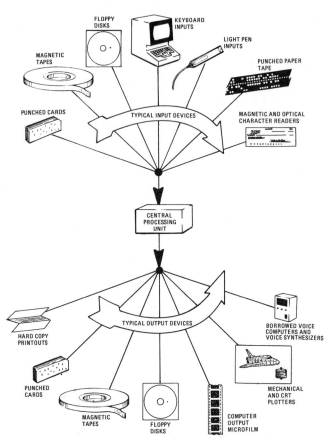

Figure 19: Some of the more popular media used in feeding data values and program commands into a digital computer are listed across the top part of this figure. As you can see, there is an abundance of methodologies. Some of the more popular output media, equally numerous, are listed across the bottom part.

information into digital computers. In recent years, a number of practical alternatives have been perfected. However, even today, many of our country's data processing installations are still dominated by those strange-looking perforated cards that hound us for money whenever we work up enough courage to tear open our mail.

Although most Americans invariably associate punched cards with computers, their earliest recorded use predated the development of the digital computer by almost 150 years. In 1801 a French entrepreneur named Joseph Jacquard used thousands of punched cards to control the shuttles of his complicated weaving looms. This novel technique allowed him to produce beautiful multicolored tapestries woven into remarkably intricate designs. One of them was a full-color portrait of Joseph Jacquard himself, a portrait which required more than 2,000 punched cards.

Direct descendents of the cards developed by the French weaving industry (See Figure 20) were later adapted for use in conjunction with some of our country's earliest mechanized data processing operations. Dr. Hermann Hollerith, a young mathematician at the U.S. Census Bureau, pioneered their use when he was assigned to help in making the 1890 census tabulations. It has taken more than 7 years to complete the analysis of the previous census but, because of his clever innovations, the new tabulations required only 2.5 years. The machines developed by Hermann Hollerith were not computers, or for that matter, even calculators. Instead, they were much simpler card sorting machines which routed the various cards into different storage bins in accordance with their coded punches.

A modern version of the punched card designed by Hermann Hollerith is sketched in Figure 21. As you can see, it can handle the full compliment of the alphanumeric symbols now in common use. Numbers, letters, and special characters can all be represented using Hollerith's systematic binary code. The symbols printed across the top of the card are not detected by the computer. They are included for the convenience of the human operators; the computer senses only the holes using its Braillelike sensing techniques.

Notice that the card is divided into 80 columns each of which has 12 different punching locations. The bottom ten are designated as "numeric punches". A single rectangular hole at any one of these locations denotes one of the decimal digits. Thus, for example, the number "4" is coded by punching a hole at location 4 in the card column of interest.

The top three rows on the card are designated as "zone punches". The top two are numbered 12 and 11 and the third is numbered 0 (the 0 is regarded as both a *zone* and a *numeric* punch). Letters of the alphabet and special characters are represented by punching two or three holes (one above the other) in a single card column. Specifically, the letter A is denoted by combining a 12-punch with a 1-punch. The other letters and special characters are represented by using the systematic code presented in Figure 21.

Why has one corner been removed from the card? The answer is quite simple: The missing corner helps the machine operator make sure all the cards are turned the same way and that he is inserting them with the proper orientation.

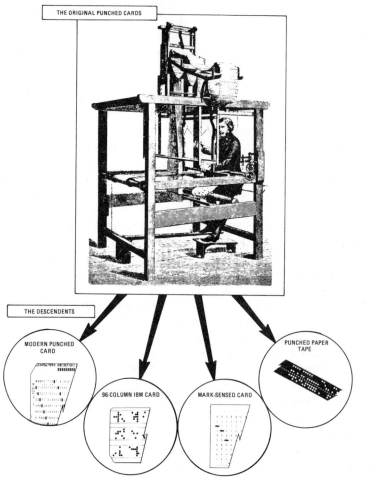

Figure 20: In 1801 a Frenchman named Joseph Jacquard utilized thousands of punched cards in controlling the shuttles of his complicated weaving looms which produced multicolored tapestries of exquisite design. Today, nearly 200 years later, our digital computers still employ various types of punched cards and punched paper tapes patterned after his original conception.

A MODERN HOLLERITH CARD

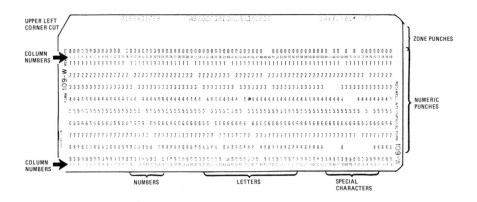

Figure 21: A modern Hollerith card can handle a maximum of 80 alphanumeric characters. As this sample shows, numbers are coded by making a single punch in the appropriate card column; letters and special characters are coded by using double or triple punches. Note that the upper right hand corner is missing from the card. This helps the machine operators make sure all the cards are turned the same way and that the deck itself has the proper orientation.

The card in Figure 21 is specifically designed to show how the various alphanumeric symbols are represented. The cards used in practice, however, are divided into individual packets of data called *fields*. A *field* is an adjacent sequence of card columns devoted to a specific item of information. In a particular application, for example, we might decide to place the salesman's name in a field stretching from column 3 through column 12 and we might place his monthly sales commission in card columns 15 through 24. Once the size and location of the card fields have been chosen, changes tend to be quite expensive. For this reason extreme care should be exercised in making the proper selections.

The Unit Record Concept

Computer experts often attempt to abide by the *unit record concept* in structuring their data processing operations. In the unit record concept, all the pertinent information associated wih a particular business transaction is punched into a single card. Of course, a Hollerith card is limited to a maximum of 80 alphanumeric characters. Hence, it is necessary to squeeze the maximum possible amount of data onto each card. Suppose, for example, that your employer has decided to include a field showing whether or not each customer is *male* or *female*. It would be possible to reserve a field spanning 6 card columns so that the machine operators could key in "MALE" or "FEMALE" using Hollerith's alphanumeric characters. However, a much more efficient approach would be to represent "male" with a 1-punch and "female" with a 2-punch. This technique reduces the width of the field in question from six card columns to only one, a saving which provides extra space for any other necessary data values.

Keypunching Mechanisms

Hollerith cards are prepared for computer input by using a device called a "keypunch machine" or a "card punch machine". A keypunch machine resembles a small electric typewriter mounted on a desksize cabinet. The arrangement of the keys is similar to that used on a standard typewriter except that there are several extra buttons and switches.

Two types of keypunch machines are in common use. In the simplest model the card advances through the machine one column at a time. As each key is depressed, tiny knife blades gouge holes into it and it steps forward one space. In the more complicated model the information provided by the keying operations is stored electronically. When all 80 characters have been provided, all the holes are punched simultaneously in one final operation. This approach is called the "die set" principle of card punching. As far as we know Hermann Hollerith was the first to put it to practical use.

Card Reading Devices

In Hollerith's card sorting devices each card was floated through the machine supported by a thin film of liquid mercury. Spring loaded pins protruded through the holes to establish an electrical contact which activated the appropriate card sorting mechanisms. The mechanisms themselves did not carry out any mathematical calculations. The cards were simply routed into various storage bins in accordance with their coded punches. As they made their way through the machine, they tripped a series of counters. Using this technique. Hollerith was able to determine the number of people in the various census classifications. For example, he could, if desired, find out how many female school teachers resided in the suburbs in Scranton, Pennsylvania. This was accomplished by running the appropriate stacks of cards repeatedly through his cleverly-designed card sorting machines.

Modern cardreading mechanisms utilize two fundamentally different methods for decoding the contents of a deck of punched cards. Figure 22 summarizes their salient features. In one popular type of device, tiny wire brushes protrude through the holes in each card thus establishing an electrical contact with a charged metal roller. Timing pulses, which are synchronized with the card's forward movement, allow the machine to ascertain the locations of the various punches. In the other type of device, a light beam shines through the holes in the card to illuminate a row of photoelectric sensors. These sensors are similar to the ones used by your instamatic camera in measuring the brightness of your surroundings.

Cardreading devices are quite fast by human standards. A well-designed unit can handle up to 1200 cards per minute. If you could process alphanumeric characters at a comparable rate, you would be able to read this textbook in less than seven minutes. However, by the standards of the computer, cardreading machines are maddeningly slow. In the time it takes a typical cardreading device to decode a single alphanumeric character, the computer can perform about 600 computations. For this reason cardreading devices are rarely used for reading data values directly into a large-scale digital computer. Instead, the information punched into the cards is usually transferred onto a magnetic tape which is then read into the computer. This two-step procedure is employed because a magnetic tape unit has a data transfer rate which is about 200 times faster than the rates achieved by the best cardreaders.

TWO TYPES OF CARDREADERS

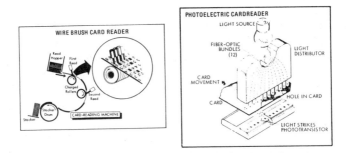

Figure 22: Two different types of card reading mechanisms are presently in common use. The *wire brush reader* employs a row of metal brushes which protrude through the holes to establish an electrical contact with a charged metal roller. The *photo-cell reader* illuminates the card with an intense beam of light which passes through the holes thus selectively activating a row of light-sensitive photoelectric cells.

MAGNETIC TAPES

Unlike home recording devices, which must be able to reproduce the full vibrational spectrum of the human voice, the magnetic tape units used in data processing operations handle only discrete binary pulses. A binary "one" is recorded by sending a pulse through a slender metal coil wrapped around a tiny electromagnet. This pulse creates a magnetic field which locally magnetizes the thin coating on the surface of the moving tape. A binary "one" is represented by magnetizing a long slender region about one twentieth the thickness of a human hair, a binary "zero" is represented by the absence of any magnetization.

Once the pulses have been recorded on a magnetic tape, they will remain there indefinitely. However, if the recorded values are no longer needed, the tape can be erased and reused. Reuseability is economically critical. A 2400-foot reel of magnetic tape costs about $35. If the tape couldn't be erased and reused it would be prohibitively expensive for many potential uses. Of course the tapes sustain a small amount of damage every time they pass through the machines, and they slowly deteriorate even when they're not being used. For this reason the tapes are typically discarded—or relegated to less demanding assignments—when they have been reused 100 times or when they exhibit obvious evidences of deterioration.

The two most popular types of recording assemblies are sketched in Figure 23. One of them employs a single-gap read-write head; the other utilizes a head which is designed with two separate gaps. The two-gap version is more versatile in that it provides for immediate verification of the accuracy of the recording. Unfortunately, it is also more complicated and expensive.

The tapes in a data processing center pass through the machines at a surprisingly rapid rate. Tape transport speeds as high as 200 inches per second are not uncommon. This means that the velocity of the tape is 30 to 60 times higher than the velocities used in home recordings.

The rate of acceleration is also considerably higher. It takes only about 1/500 of a second to accelerate the tape from a standstill up to its full velocity. During the acceleration interval, the tape is subjected to about 300 g's.* How is it possible to accelerate a delicate tape so rapidly? For one thing the tapes used in data processing applications are made from relatively thick tear-resistant materials. For another, stresses are minimized by maintaining a pair of slack loops in the tape as shown in Figure 23. Because of these slack loops the forces of acceleration do not have to work against the inertia of the heavy tape reels. The only thing that has to be accelerated is a short segment of the tape. How are the slack loops maintained? Two pairs of vacuum sensors monitor their lengths at all times constantly signaling the machine to make any necessary adjustments.

---

*One g equals the force created by the earth's gravitational field at sea level. In returning from the moon the astronauts withstood about 9 g's which is fairly close to the maximum acceleration rate the human body can tolerate for any lengthy interval.

A TYPICAL MAGNETIC TAPE UNIT

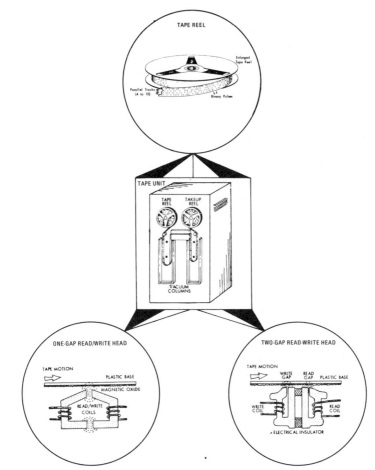

Figure 23: The magnetic tape units in a data processing center are, in some respects, similar to home recorders. However, rather than dealing with the full vibrational spectrum needed in duplicating the human voice, these special devices handle only discrete electrical pulses. Recordings are made by transmitting the pulses through a coil winding wrapped around a tiny electromagnet. When a pulse surges through the coil, the electromagnet locally magnetizes a small clump of ferromagnetic granules imbedded in the surface of the moving tape. Readout of the stored values is accomplished by reversing the procedure. When a magnetized subregion passes by the electromagnet it creates a sudden current pulse which is routed through the computer's processing circuits.

The tapes used in a data processing center are twice as wide and at least twice as long as those used for home recordings. A 2400-foot reel of magnetic tape can hold more than 70 million characters and its data transfer rate can exceed 1 million characters per second. In other words a single tape has the capacity of nearly 500 boxes of punched cards and, under optimum conditions, its data can be fed into a computer at a rate which nearly equals the maximum processing rate of the computer's electronic processing units.

REMOTE TERMINALS

In the early days of the data processing era computer centers were usually set up for *batch processing* operations. In batch processing the user turns his job over to a group of experts who combine it with several other jobs before it is read into the computer. This approach saves considerable amounts of valuable computer time because the computer can be rigged to handle several jobs in a "simultaneous" manner. Thus, for example, when one job calls for the time-consuming, but non-productive, process of rewinding a magnetic tape, the Central Processing Unit can fill in its idle moments by working piecemeal on one of its other assignments. This concept of interleaving work on several jobs simultaneously is called *multiprogramming*. A batch processing facility equipped with multiprogramming capabilities conserves the computer's precious resources, but it is not strongly user-oriented. Whenever the user turns in his job he must return to his work station and wait for several hours or days before he can find out if it operates correctly. Usually it fails because he has made any of a number of subtle errors, and, when it does, there is nothing he can do except fix the indicated errors and go back through the same awkward, time-consuming procedures.

Today batch processing is still quite popular because of its intrinsic efficiencies but time sharing has become a viable alternative. In a time sharing system the inputs are usually entered by means of a remote terminal equipped with a typewriter keyboard. Some terminals record the user inputs—and the corresponding outputs—on a hard copy printout; others utilize a faster, but less permanent cathode-ray-tube display. In the latter system when one of the typewriter keys is depressed, a beam of electrons shines through a tiny template to project an image of the appropriate letter onto the screen. When you operate such a device there is no sound. And no time delay.

From the user's viewpoint the primary advantage of time sharing over batch processing is that he or she gets an instant response from the computer. This allows the user to correct any errors on the spot, to run extra cases, and to make any necessary program modifications.

The Magic Light Pen

Some remote terminals are equipped to handle light pen inputs. A light pen is a pencil-sized unit which can be used to create drawings and other visual materials on a CRT screen. It operates like a magic wand; it doesn't actually touch the surface of the screen but as you move it in any desired pattern, it automatically creates a phosphorescent line.

Light pens can be handled effectively by individuals who are too young or too poorly coordinated to operate an electric typewriter. The computer asks specific questions and the user indicates his responses by touching the pen to various sectors of the screen. This approach is particularly adaptable to Computer Aided Instructional routines in which the computer plays the role of a supremely-patient electronic tutor.

Computer Aided Design

Light pens are also being used for advanced applications that require scientific talents and carefully-sharpened skills. These applications include Computer Aided Design which is among the most versatile and intriguing of the new programming techniques.

Recently the author got an opportunity to interview Jack Boddy, a specialist in Computer Aided Design at Rockwell International, where light pen inputs are used in conjunction with the construction and operation of NASA's reuseable Space Shuttle. During the interview Boddy, a transplanted English engineer, cranked up a magnetic disk connected to a powerful minicomputer. When the disk reached the proper cruising speed, he pushed a half dozen buttons to transfer a three-dimensional drawing it held in its memory onto a nearby television screen.

It took about six hours to sketch all the lines," he explained in a heavy British accent. "But now that it's in storage I can call it up instantly at any time."

He gingerly touched the light pen to various sectors of the screen and the drawing appeared to take on a life of its own. It was uncanny. Something like a well-made, but carefully controlled, science fiction film! With a series of simple movements, he rotated the picture in three dimensions, enlarged segments of it, inserted new structural elements, and erased a number of unwanted lines. At selected intervals he also pushed a bright red button to obtain hard-copy prints. A few samples of his work are presented in Figure 24.

SAMPLE LIGHT PEN DRAWINGS

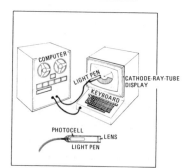

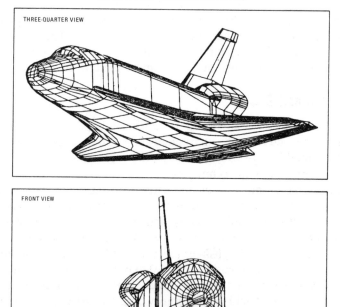

Figure 24: Light pen inputs provide a convenient means for feeding drawings and other visual materials into a digital computer. In this instance, a three-dimensional skeleton of the reuseable Space Shuttle has been sketched with a light pen by an aerospace engineer. Once his version of the drawing has been completed, the engineer can command the computer to rotate it as a solid shape at the same time enlarging selected portions, suppressing unwanted lines, or attaching new components at designated locations.

"Most of the things the computer does are easy to program." Boddy pointed out stroking the ends of his curly mustache, "the hardest part is making it suppress any hidden lines. If we paid an artist to sketch the Shuttle from several angles he could tell in an instant which lines were on the backside. But the computer doesn't have any sense of the real world; it has to test the surfaces—two at a time to determine which of the lines are hidden from view!"

He went on to explain that, since the figure involved so many separate lines any of which could theoretically be on the backside depending on how the figure was turned, "the procedure used in locating the hidden lines often requires several minutes of expensive computer time".

Of course the reason for using Computer Aided Design is usually not to have the computer determine which lines are hidden. More typically, it is commanded to calculate certain engineering quantities associated with the geometrical figure being analyzed. In the case of the Space Shuttle, for example, the computer can be commanded to evaluate the lift, drag and aerodynamic heating that will be encountered during reentry for a particular design. If any of the values turn out to be unacceptable, the reentry trajectory or the contours of the vehicle itself can be modified for another try. This technique is called *interactive computer graphics*, a relatively new, but highly promising, branch of computer science.

HIGH SPEED PRINTERS

The primary output of most data processing centers is a stack of hard-copy printouts, a stack which often accumulates at an astonishing rate. These printouts are usually generated by high-speed printers. The two most popular types of mechanical printers are sketched in Figure 25.

In essence the *printwheel* consists of a metal drum embossed with several dozen identical copies of the entire set of alphanumeric characters to be printed. The drum spins at a constant rate, typically 1200 revolutions per minute. When the desired letter passes by the proper spot on the paper, it is slammed against the paper surface by a tiny electromechanical hammer.

The *chain printer,* which is also shown in Figure 25, resembles a bicycle chain which rotates at a rapid rate. Typically, between 1 and 5 copies of all the characters to be printed are embossed on the chain. One hundred twenty electromechanical hammers arranged in a straight row slam the paper into contact with the chain. The maximum operating speed of the chain printer is slightly faster than the maximum pace of the printwheel. However, it has a much more important advantage. The individual letters on the chain can be altered with ease for any particular application. If a reduced character set is adequate, extra copies can be placed on the chain and the printing speed is proportionately increased.

Both printwheels and chain printers use continuous form paper folded in accordian fashion. Two rows of closely-spaced holes along the outer edges allow the unit to advance the paper immediately after each line has been printed.

The two devices sketched in Figure 25 are called *line printers* because, in essence, they print a whole line at one time. Those of us who use the hunt-and-peck system of typing can't help but be impressed by

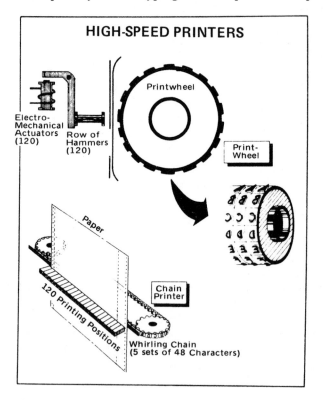

Figure 25: Two types of line printers are in common use: the *printwheel* and the *chain printer*. The printwheel is essentially a rotating cylinder with several dozen copies of the alphabet embossed on its curved surface; the chain printer resembles a bicycle chain which rotates around continuous form paper. Printing for both types of devices is accomplished by a row of electromechanical hammers which slam the paper into contact with the freshly-inked metal type.

their great speed. A line printer of modern design can produce 20 lines of hard-copy printout—the equivalent of a typewritten page—every second it is in operation.

DEVICES THAT DRAW PICTURES AND GRAPHS

Most of the outputs provided by a computer come in printed form but the computer can also be taught to plot graphs. Two types of plotting devices are presently in common use: *cathode-ray-tube plotters* and *mechanical plotters*. Both produce graphs and drawings similar to the ones constructed by skilled engineers.

Cathode-Ray-Tube Plotters

A cathode-ray-tube plotting device resembles an ordinary television set but it constructs its pictures in a completely different way. Your TV picture is formed by a beam of electrons of variable intensity which sweeps across 525 horizontal lines on your screen 30 times per second. The beam's systematic scanning pattern is controlled by tiny electromagnets located in the neck of the picture tube. A cathode-ray-tube plotter works in a similar way but instead of scanning to make the picture, the beam of electrons is made to form the outlines of the drawing one line at a time in the same way it would be drawn by a commercial artist. A sample plot is presented in Figure 26. As you can see, it has extremely sharp outlines.

The small letters and numbers on the plot are not drawn one line at a time. Instead, they are formed by shining the electron beam through a special template which has cutouts defining the various alphanumeric characters. Cathode-ray-tube plots can be furnished to the user on microfilm or in a hard-copy format. If desired, a series of plots can also be turned into a motion picture film which can be viewed by running it through a 35 mm projector. Films of this type are fascinating and useful but quite costly.

Mechanical Plotters

A computer can also be rigged to drive a mechanical plotter which utilizes a mechanically-driven inking pen. A metal framework resembling a miniature overhead crane sweeps over a sheet of paper under the direction of a series of computer-generated electronic pulses. A typical graph constructed by a mechanical plotter is presented in Figure 27. It takes longer to make a graph in this way but, as you can see, it is

PLOTS GENERATED BY A CATHODE
RAY TUBE PLOTTER

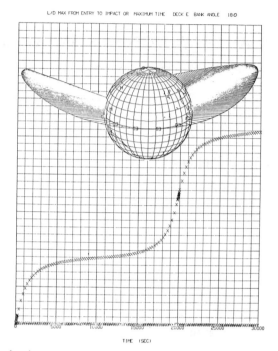

Figure 26: These drawings were generated by a cathode ray tube plotter, a computer-controlled device in which a beam of electrons is directed onto a phosphorescent screen to form the desired images. The results are photographed by a 35 mm camera and subsequently furnished to the user in a hard-copy format or as a strip of 35 mm microfilm.

essentially as clear and precise as the ones produced by a cathode-ray-tube plotter.

COMPUTER-DIRECTED CONVERSATIONS

This chapter opened with a brief sample of the remarkable conversational proclivities of the Hal 9000 computer as described by Arthur Clarke in his book *Space Odyssey 2001*. Unfortunately, there is a hidden flaw in his basic design, and, soon after the space ship blasts off for Jupiter, Hal slowly beings loosing his mind. Consequently, Commander Bowman has no choice: he is forced to perform a makeshift lobotomy while the mission is still in progress. We now revisit the ship where Hal's delicate brain surgery has just begun. As the scene unfolds, notice the subtle rapport that exists between our reluctant neurosurgeon and his fretfully-intense electronic patient:

TYPICAL PLOTS GENERATED
BY A MECHANICAL PLOTTER

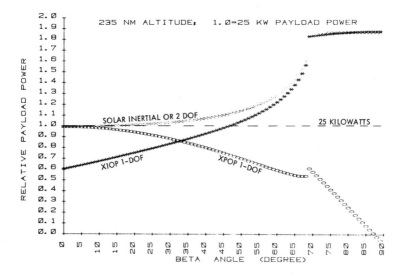

Figure 27: These graphs were drawn by a mechanical plotter, a computer-directed device which draws pictures using a mechanically-driven inking pen. Mechanical plots, which typically require several minutes to produce, are often generated by minicomputers under the direct supervision of the ultimate user.

"Dave", said Hal, "I don't understand why you're doing this to me . . . I have the greatest enthusiasm for the mission . . . You are destroying my mind . . . Don't you understand? . . . I will become childish . . . I will become nothing . . ."

This is harder than I expected, thought Bowman. I am destroying the only conscious creature in my universe. But it has to be done, if I am to regain control of the ship.

"I am a HAL Nine Thousand Computer Production Number 3. I became operational at the Hal Plant in Urbana, Illinois, on January 12, 1997. The quick brown fox jumps over the lazy dog. The rain in Spain is mainly in the plain. Dave—are you still there? Did you know that the square root of 10 is 3 point 162277660168379? Log 10 base e is zero point 434284481903252 . . . correction, that is log e to the base 10 . . . the reciprocal of 3 is zero point 33333333333333333333...

Two times two is . . . two times two is . . . approximately 4 point 101010101010101010 . . . I seem to be having some difficulty—my first instructor was Dr. Chandra. He taught me to sing a song, it goes like this, 'Daisy, Daisy, give me your answer do. I'm half crazy all for the love of you'."

The voice stopped so suddenly that Bowman froze for a moment, his hand still grasping one of the memory blocks still in circuit. Then, unexpectedly, Hal spoke again.

The speech tempo was much slower, and the words had a dead, mechanical intonation; he would never have recognized their origin.

"Good . . . morning . . . Doctor . . . Chandra . . . This . . . is . . . Hal . . . I . . . am . . . ready . . . for . . . My . . . first . . . lesson . . . today . . ."

Bowman could bear no more. He jerked out the last unit, and Hal was silent forever."

If you haven't bothered to keep up with what's been going on in computer research over the past several years, Hal's abilities to handle the English language may seem entirely fictionalized. However, this is not entirely so. Computer-driven devices are being developed which can, to a limited extent, understand what is said to them and reply with a recognizable vocal response.

The most successful technique for coupling speech capabilities with data processing hardware consists of a so-called *borrowed voice computer*. Such a machine reconstructs phrases and sentences by assembling fragments of human speech previously recorded on the surface of a magnetic disk. For example, a paid announcer might make a studio recording of the numbers 0 through 9, the letters of the alphabet, and the months of the year, together with a few preselected phrases such as "out of stock", "part required", "located in warehouse bin number . . .", and so on. These speech fragments are then transferred onto a magnetic disk and a program is coded to access them in an appropriate way.

At Rockwell International, for example, where the author works, a borrowed voice computer is used to keep track of the various parts being kept in storage. Whenever an engineer needs to know about the status of a particular part, he dials the computer from any ordinary telephone. He then uses the same telephone dial to communicate his needs to the computer. A typical exchange might go something like this:

"Part required?"
"3714"
"Diesel headgasket . . . cost . . . 1 . . . 3 . . . 7 . . . point . . . 4 . . . 8 . . . dollars . . . Located in warehouse bin number . . . 3 . . . 7 . . . 1 . . . temporarily out of stock . . . will arrive on . . . April . . . 1 . . . 7 . . . What else do you require?"

It may seem from this exchange that the computer is carrying on an intelligent conversation. However, it is merely assembling certain previously recorded fragments of human speech. The program which handles these tasks cannot "understand" spoken words; it merely routes the computer to the appropriate segments of the disk whereupon another unit picks off whatever verbal message is recorded there. The result sounds a little like a "conversation" but, in fact, it entails hardly any more conversational skills then are exhibited by the "Mrs. Beasley" talking doll who "speaks" any of several prerecorded phrases whenever someone pulls her string.

Moreover, the phrases uttered by the computer tend to be dull and lifeless. Each time a word is spoken, it always sounds the same. There are no variations. No errors. No hesitations. No vocal inflections.

The new bubble memories (to be discussed in Chapter 4) are giving us another method for providing the computer with a borrowed voice. A bubble memory is a tiny solid-state chip which stores discrete packets of information magnetically. Some of the phone company's prerecording messages ("I'm sorry that number is no longer in service") are presently being recorded using bubble memory chips. The recordings are more costly than those made on a magnetic disk or a continuous-loop tape recorder. However, a bubble memory operates more reliably and the quality of its recording does not deteriorate with repeated use. This means that the message is always crystal clear; rerecording is never necessary to obtain acceptable quality.

A third method for providing the computer with "speech" capabilities consists of a *voice synthesizer,* a unit which electronically reproduces the individual phonemes (sound units) that make up human speech. A few years ago voice synthesizers were extremely expensive. But their technology has been revolutionized over the past few years. Today it is possible to purchase a "talking chess board" which plays an amateurish game of chess and verbally calls out each move it intends to make!

Although there have been some noteworthy efforts along these lines, the *speech recognition* capabilities of computers are not well developed at the present time. Even the best devices currently on the market are capable of recognizing only about 200 spoken words and, under nonoptimum conditions they don't consistently do even that well. If a new speaker is introduced—or the old one catches a cold—the machine's speech recognition capabilities are quickly degraded.

Thus we see that in a sense it can be claimed that today's computer has both a mouth and an ear. Unfortunately, neither is a tenth as good as the ones being mass produced by Mother Nature using unskilled labor. Today's best devices are incapable of the kind of understanding Hal seemed to exhibit (he may have been *crazy* but he wasn't *stupid*). Can future computers be taught to respond to our most subtle verbal messages? An interesting question. A question which we shall tackle in the chapters to come.

BIBLIOGRAPHY

1. Adams,J. Mack, and Hayden, Douglas H. *Social Effects of Computer Use and Misuse.* New York, New York: John Wiley, 1976.

2. Adams, J. Mack, and Moon, Robert. *An Introduction to Computer Science.* Glenview, Illinois: Scott Foresman, 1970.

3. *Basic Data Processing.* New York, New York: Dover Publications, 1971.

4. Bernstein, Jeremy. *The Analytical Engine.* New York, New York: Random House, 1963.

5. Clarke, Arthur C. *2001: A Space Odyssey.* New York, New York: New American Library, 1968.

6. *Computers.* New Brunswich, New Jersey: Boy Scouts of America, 1968.

7. "Computers". *Encyclopedia Britannica. Book of the Year,* 1977.

8. Davis, Gordon B. *Computer Data Processing.* New York, New York: McGraw-Hill, 1969.

9. Davis, Ruth M. "Evolution of Computers and Computing." *Science* 195:1096-1102.

10. Dorf, Richard C. *Computers and Man.* San Francisco, California: Boyd and Fraser Publishing Co., 1977.

11. Hollingdale, S.H. and Toothill, G.C. *Electronic Computers.* Baltimore, Maryland: Penquin Books, 1965.

12. Holoien, Martin O. *Computers and Their Societal Impact.* New York, New York: John Wiley, 1977.

13. Logsdon, Tom. *Computer Science and Technology.* Palisade, New Jersey: Franklin Publishing Co., 1974.

14. Lohberg, Rolf and Lutz, Theo. *Computers at Work.* New York, New York: Sterling Publishing Co., 1970.

15. Pack, Susan. "The Computers are Coming, The Computers are Coming." *Skyline,* Rockwell International, Spring 1977, pp. 611.

16. Fisher, Peter F., and Swindle, George F. *Computer Programming Systems.* New York, New York: Holt, Rinehart and Winston, 1964.

17. Price, Wilson T. *Introduction to Computer Data Processing.* New York, New York: Dryden Press, 1977.

18. Ralston, Anthony and Meek, Chester L. *Encyclopedia of Computer Science.* New York, New York: Petrocelli/Charter, 1976.

19. Rothman, Stanley, and Mossmann, Charles. *Computers and Society.* Palo Alto, California: Science Research Associates, 1972.

20. Sanders, Donald H. *Computers and Society.* New York, New York: McGraw-Hill, 1977.

21. Vorwald,Alan and Clark, Frank. *Computers! From Sand Table to Electronic Brain.* Eau Claire, Wisconsin: E. M. Hale and Company, 1968.

22. Worcester, Roland. *Electronics.* New York, New York: Grosset and Dunlap, 1970.

EXERCISES

1. In 1801 Frenchman Joseph Jacquard utilized large numbers of punched cards in their earliest known industrial application. How did he use them? How are their descendents used today?

2. This card employs the Hollerith code. Decipher its message. Now answer it by sketching or punching a card of your own.

3. How are binary pulses recorded on a magnetic tape? How are they later reconstructed?

4. Three different cardreading techniques were briefly described in this chapter. In your own words explain how any one of them works.

5. Hal, the spaceship computer in Arthur Clarke's *Space Odyssey 2001* exhibited some rather fancy input-output capabilities. List some of them and discuss whether or not you think ordinary computers will possess similar capabilities by the year 2001.

6. What is Computer Aided Design? How is it used? What kind of equipment is needed?

7. Two types of line printers were discussed in this chapter. Choose either one and explain how it works.

8. What is a borrowed voice computer? From whom does it borrow its voice? Is there any other way to give a computer the capability to converse? What causes computer-generated conversations to seem so flat and lifeless? Suggest a possible solution.

9. What is the unit record concept? Why is it used?

10. What is the principal advantage of batch processing? What is an alternative? What are the advantages of the alternative?

STUDENT PROJECTS

1. Even if we never see a computer in our everyday lives we often encounter samples of the computer's input-output media especially in the form of the bills and receipts that come in the afternoon mail. Team up with several of your classmates and begin making a collection containing as many different samples as you can obtain. When you have a reasonable number of items make a scrapbook or a poster to share with the rest of your class.

2. Even with today's primitive level of technology, our computer's can listen and speak. Research these input-output techniques and summarize your findings in a short report.

3. Automatic plotting devices are widely used in both science and the arts including motion picture production. Research these uses of automatic plotting devices and write up your findings. Where possible include sample drawings and plots.

CHAPTER 4

THE COMPUTER'S MEMORY

PRIMARY STORAGE
Magnetic Core Rings
Solid-State Memory Units
Marketing Comparisons

AUXILIARY STORAGE
Magnetic Drums
Magnetic Disks
Bubble Memories
Charged-Coupled Devices
Data Buffers

EXTERNAL STORAGE
Punched Cards
Magnetic Tapes
The Floppy Disk

SELECTING THE COMPUTER'S STORAGE MEDIA

THE DAWNING OF THE SECOND INDUSTRIAL REVOLUTION

BIBLIOGRAPHY

EXERCISES

STUDENT PROJECTS

Some of the data processing industry's most innovative design efforts have been devoted to the construction of faster and more efficient storage devices. These efforts have been motivated almost entirely by simple economics. It is not uncommon for a company to spend $600,000 for the storage units to be attached to a $1 million digital computer. These sizeable expenditures are necessary because the computer's overall efficiency is largely determined by the capacity of its memory and the speed with which its data values can be retrieved.

Life would be much easier for the men and women who design and operate our digital computers if they could put their hands on a simple, inexpensive storage medium with rapid, random-access capabilities. Unforturnately, at present, such a storage medium does not exist. Consequently, the designers must strive for the best possible compromise by assembling a carefully-selected mix of storage devices—some of which are fast and expensive, some of which are slow and cheap.

In one popular arrangement the computer's memory is structured in a *hierarchy* of descending capabilities. As is shown by the sketches in Figure 28 it involves three different types of storage devices:

- primary storage
- auxiliary storage
- external storage

The primary storage region is located in the computer's Central Processing Unit. It contains a relatively small number of frequently-used data value and commands. The processing circuits have direct access to these stored quantities—which can be retrieved at electronic speeds. The *auxiliary storage* units—magnetic drums and disks—are also attached to the computer at all times but they are not housed inside the CPU. These memory devices, which supplement primary storage, are cheaper and more spacious, but somewhat less convenient. Finally, the *external storage* media (punched cards and magnetic tapes) are not permanently attached to the computer. The external media provide essentially unlimited storage capacity at a surprisingly low cost; however, it is relatively difficult for the computer to retrieve the values being held in external storage. In most cases human assistance is required.

PRIMARY STORAGE

The primary storage region of the ENIAC, the world's first electronic digital computer, consisted of long rows of vertical cabinets filled with sputtering vacuum tubes of primitive design. These hot, bulky tubes

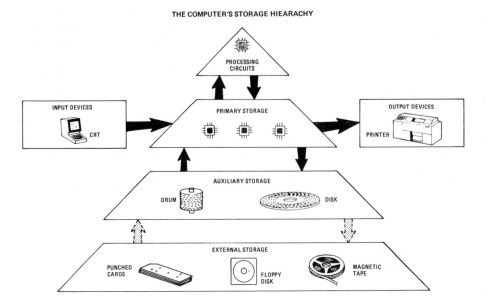

Figure 28: In order to obtain the best possible combination of storage capacity, cost, and access time today's data processing experts often interconnect several separate types of storage devices in a carefully-structured hierarchy. As this figure shows, the primary storage region is supplemented by a series of auxiliary and external storage devices which are more spacious and less costly than primary storage.

provided a fairly rapid response but, unfortunately, they were extremely costly and unreliable. Consequently, the maximum number of tubes that could be included in the design was less than 18,000, a number which provided the storage equivalent of only about two typewritten pages of information. Modern computers can be equipped with far more spacious and reliable primary storage capabilities at a small fraction of the cost. A few years ago core storage devices were the most popular selection. Today we more typically choose solid-state memory units.

Magnetic Core Rings

A core storage unit utilizes millions of tiny magnetizable donuts threaded onto a grid of electrically conducting wires. Each donut can be magnetized either clockwise (to denote a binary 1) or counterclockwise (to denote a binary 0). Figure 29 illustrates the major design features of a modern core storage unit.

In theory it would be possible to build a device of this type by using a separate wire to link each core ring to the electronic processing circuits.

CORE STORAGE UNITS

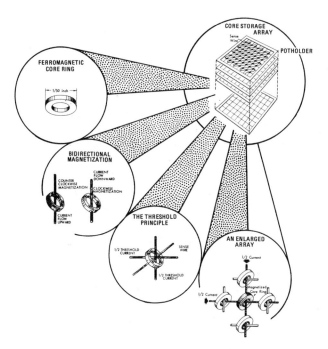

Figure 29: A core storage unit consists of millions of tiny magnetizable donuts threaded onto a grid of electrically conducting wires. In such a unit clockwise magnetization represents a binary 1, counterclockwise magnetization a binary 0. Each core ring is carefully fabricated so that its magnetic field will be reversed by a full-current pulse whereas a pulse half as intense will have no effect on its magnetization. Thus, if two half-current pulses are sent through a pair of mutually perpendicular wires in the grid, the only core ring that will be affected is the one at their intersection. Data readout is accomplished by "writing" a 0 into the core ring of interest. If the core contains a binary 1 at the time of interrogation, a current pulse will be induced in a special "sense wire" which is threaded through every core in the plane; if the core contains a binary 0, no pulse will be created.

However, the resulting array would be a design monstrosity. The technique actually used, which relies upon the so-called *threshold principle of magnetization,* is far more clever and efficient. In accordance with this novel design philosophy, each core ring is constructed so that a full current pulse is sufficient to change its direction of magnetization but a current pulse half as strong will have no detectable effect.

The array is structured so that two mutually perpendicular read-write wires pass through each and every magnetic core. As you can see from the sketches in Figure 29, the wires are woven into a clothlike grid held together by a single core ring at each intersection. When a particular core ring is to be magnetized, a half-current pulse is transmitted through each of its two mutually-perpendicular read-write wires. As a result, the only core ring in the entire array that will be magnetized is the one at the intersection of the two wires. The other core rings will be entirely unaffected because they will receive, at most, only a half current pulse which is insufficient to change their direction of magnetization.

The third zigzagging wire which runs through every core in the grid (See Figure 29) is called the *sense wire*. It is used in the read-out procedure in which the values being held in storage are interrogated. How is a binary digit extracted from a core ring? The procedure is quite simple: We merely *write a 0 in the core ring of interest*. This is accomplished by sending a half current pulse through its two mutually-perpendicular read-write wires. If the core ring contains a binary 1 prior to receiving the interrogation pulse, its direction of magnetization will be reversed, thus inducing a new current pulse in the sense wire. On the other hand, if it contains a binary 0, its magnetization will be unaffected and no current pulse will be created.

In an actual memory array several pot holder-like grids are stacked one above the other to form a core ring tower. Specifically, this tower might consist of eight or nine layers which would allow it to store a series of coded characters each consisting of eight or nine binary digits.

Solid-State Memory Units

Despite their rather clever design characteristics and their highly reliable operation, magnetic core rings are gradually being displaced by solid-state memory chips. A photograph of a typical memory chip is presented in Figure 30. It consists of 16,000 transistors each of which can be accessed in 1/5,000,000 of a second. Although this chip is roughly as complicated as the entire ENIAC computer of three decades ago, it weighs a tiny fraction of an ounce, is driven by a whisper of power, and costs only about $30 when purchased in production quantities.

A microscopic view of the rugged surface of the chip is sketched in the lower right hand corner of the figure. As you can see, it exhibits a series of rugged contours resembling agricultural terraces. The locations and shapes of the various terraces, their subsurface interconnections, and the nature of their crystalline structure determines the exact way in which the chip will function.

The transistors on a solid-state memory chip are laid out in a precise rectangular grid which is divided into rows and columns in a manner not unlike the way the seats are arranged in a college classroom. Each transistor has a row address and a column address so that a pair of

SOLID STATE MEMORY CHIP

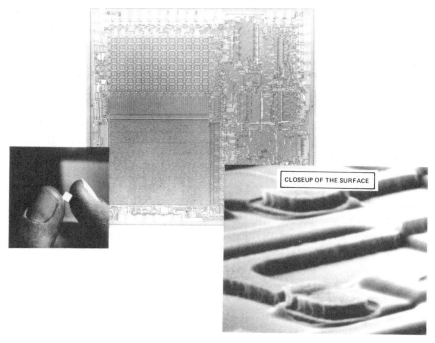

CLOSEUP OF THE SURFACE

Figure 30: A solid-state memory chip stores binary pulses in an array of transistors arranged into a rectangular grid. This particular memory chip is manufactured and sold by the Rockwell International. It is smaller than a baby's fingernail, has a storage capacity of 16,000 bits, and an access time of 1/5,000,000 of a second. The electron micrograph in the lower portion of the figure shows a closeup of the rugged surface of the chip. As you can see, it resembles a series of agricultural terraces. The functioning of the chip is determined by the interconnections between these textured slabs, their geometrical layout, and the exact structure of their component crystals.

interrogation pulses can be routed to the proper intersection to access any value being held in storage. This physical arrangement is similar to the layout of a core ring memory array except that solid-state chips are usually not stacked in pancake fashion. Instead, they more typically occupy a single co-planar array.

When solid-state amplifiers first reached the marketplace shortly after their development in 1948 they were sold like vacuum tubes as separate units, one transistor per package. However, even in those early days, it was obvious that the units being marketed were intrinsically different from conventional vacuum tubes. For one thing they were produced from solid, monolithic materials, each functioning component differing from its immediately adjacent neighbors only in the most subtle ways, e.g., by the amount and type of trace impurities. Unfortunately, at first, transistors were so hard to manufacture no one was able to capitalize on their intrinsic simplicity. However, as the infant industry began to grow and mature, it soon became evident that solid-state devices could be mass producted by using procedures that resembled multicolor silk screen printing.

Sets of oversized masks two or three feet across are drawn by skilled draftsmen, then photographically reduced and duplicated dozens of times in a grid-like pattern. These masks are used in creating a series of identical solid state chips on the surface of a thin wafer of silicon or germanium typically about three inches in diameter. Figure 31 shows the sequence of operations used in the manufacture of a particular type of silicon chip. As you can see, the silicon wafer is covered with the masks one by one thus exposing certain selected portions or the material to

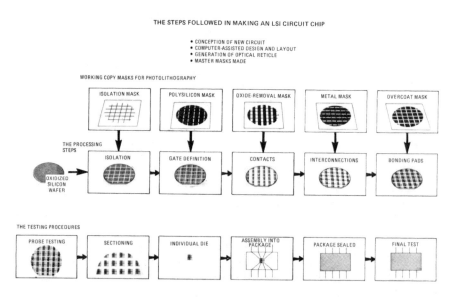

THE STEPS FOLLOWED IN MAKING AN LSI CIRCUIT CHIP

• CONCEPTION OF NEW CIRCUIT
• COMPUTER-ASSISTED DESIGN AND LAYOUT
• GENERATION OF OPTICAL RETICLE
• MASTER MASKS MADE

WORKING COPY MASKS FOR PHOTOLITHOGRAPHY

| ISOLATION MASK | POLYSILICON MASK | OXIDE-REMOVAL MASK | METAL MASK | OVERCOAT MASK |

THE PROCESSING STEPS

OXIDIZED SILICON WAFER

| ISOLATION | GATE DEFINITION | CONTACTS | INTERCONNECTIONS | BONDING PADS |

THE TESTING PROCEDURES

| PROBE TESTING | SECTIONING | INDIVIDUAL DIE | ASSEMBLY INTO PACKAGE | PACKAGE SEALED | FINAL TEST |

Figure 31: Solid-state chips are usually produced on flat wafers of silicon or germanium grown from a fluid mix. Precisely-machined masks are produced oversized by skilled technicians and then photographically reduced. These masks protect portions of the wafer as it is etched, metalized, oxidized, etc. in a series of careful production steps. The result is a set of about 100 identical chips each covering 1/25th of a square inch and each containing 50,000 solid state switches.

oxidation, metalization, ultra-violet irradiation, and so on. When the various production steps have been completed, the wafer ends up with 100 or more identical solid-state chips on its surface, each chip typically covering 1/25th of a square inch and containing 50,000 solid-state switches.

Because of the way a chip is mass produced, its cost is essentially independent of its electronic complexity. For this reason the design engineers constantly strive to achieve increased packing densities (more transistors per chip). Unbelievable as it sounds, on the average over the past two decades the number or transistors in the most advanced chips has doubled every year.

TESTING THE CHIPS FOR DEFECTS

Figure 32: The manufacture of solid-state devices is an exacting science. Even the tiniest dust particle can ruin a delicate chip. Because of these extremely demanding requirements, at some facilities twenty inoperable chips are produced for every one that functions properly. Once the various manufacturing steps have been completed, rigorous testing procedures cull out defective units. Those found to contain flaws are discarded or rigged so that only their functioning components are actually used.

Unfortunately, as packing densities increase, the smallest imperfections can cause circuit malfunction. Figure 32 shows how even a microscopic break in one of the electrical channels (which can be caused by tiny dust particles or other contaminants) can ruin an entire circuit chip. Defects of this type are quite common. As a matter of fact, approximately 75% of all the circuits now being manufactured must be discarded because they are defective. The manufacturers could reduce the number of discards if they were willing to settle for lower packing densities. However, maximum profits (and the best circuits) result if they push their design capabilities to the point where they end up with a substantial number of discards.

Marketing Comparisons

The popularity of magnetic core rings is definitely declining now that solid-state memory chips have become a practical alternative. However, core ring sales are still quite brisk. Last year sales exceeded $100 million and many industry experts believe they will continue at that level into the mid 1980's and beyond. In part, their continuing popularity stems from the fact that magnetic core rings are a non volatile storage media. This means that, unlike most solid-state chips, a core ring array will retain its stored contents even if the computer's power supplies are interrupted. Another factor which has helped insure their survival is that the companies producing core rings have managed to develop increasingly clever methods for their design and fabrication. When core storage units first entered the commercial marketplace, a typical core plane was about the size of a kitchen potholder; held together with cores that exceeded the diameter of a hospital drinking straw. Today, as Figure 33 shows, we can construct core planes that are only slightly larger than a postage stamp. The donut-shaped rings themselves, which are strung onto connecting wires thinner than a human hair, are so small that a silver tablespoon can hold about 60,000 cores!

AUXILIARY STORAGE

The computer's primary storage region is supplemented by cheaper, more spacious, but more sluggish auxiliary devices most of which utilize magnetic storage techniques. The common auxiliary storage units (See Figure 34) include magnetic drums, magnetic disks, and bubble memories.

Magnetic Drums

A magnetic drum is a squat drum coated with a thin magnetizable film. A series of recording tracks encircle the drum, which rotates at a

A MODERN CORE MEMORY PLANE

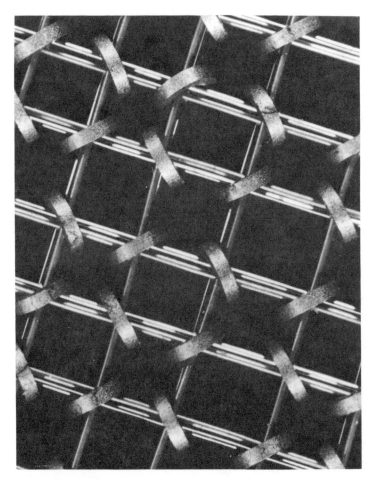

Figure 33: Because of a series of steady technological advancements, core storage arrays have managed to survive in the marketplace in the face of intense competition from solid-state memory chips. The first magnetic core rings dating back to 1953 were about $\frac{1}{5}$ of an inch in diameter. By contrast, the core rings now being marketed are so small they are almost invisible to the naked eye.

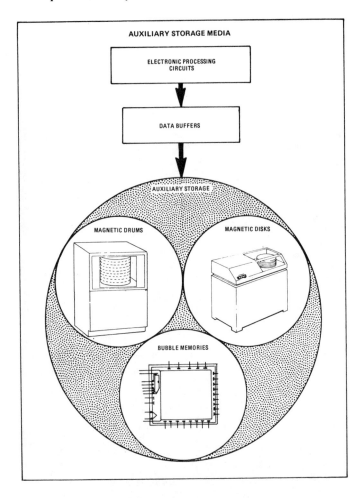

Figure 34: Today's most popular storage media include the magnetic drum, the magnetic disk, and the bubble memory. Drums and disks are coated with a ferromagnetic material which can be locally magnetized to represent binary pulses. A bubble memory is constructed from a tiny slab of orthoferrite, a special substance which contains natural snake-like regions of magnetization. When an electrical pulse is sent through a metal coil positioned above the surface of the slab, the nearby regions of natural magnetization are instantly formed into a tiny magnetic bubble.

constant rate, typically 2400 revolutions per minute. Each track is serviced by a set of stationary read-write heads similar to the ones used in accessing the contents of a magnetic tape. The magnetic drum, which typically holds about 2 million alphanumeric characters, provides *semi-random access* to the values being held in storage. This means that the amount of time required to access a randomly selected bit is, to some extent, dependent upon its physical location.* If it is directly beneath the read-write heads at the time of interrogation, it can be retrieved immediately. If it is on the opposite side of the drum, the retrieval process must be delayed until the drum rotates 180 degrees. For a typical unit this takes about 1/80 of a second.

Magnetic Disks

In some respects a magnetic disk is similar to a magnetic drum. A disk unit consists of a series of flat, rotating platters stacked one above the other as shown in Figure 34. The platters are coated top and bottom with magnetic recording material. Concentric recording tracks on each platter are serviced by stationary or moveable read-write heads. Those units which utilize stationary heads are mechanically simpler and they can be sealed to prevent dust and particle contamination. Unfortunately, because of the extra electronics and the much larger number of read-write heads, they are three or four times more expensive than those units which employ moveable heads.

A typical magnetic disk unit can handle approximately 8 million alphanumeric characters. Rotation rates are usually about 3500 revolutions per minute—a rate which roughly matches the rotational speed of the drive train in a well-made family Chevrolet. The read-write heads skim over the surface of the disk at speeds as high as 100 miles per hour. The heads do not actually touch the disk; instead, they hover over its surface supported by a thin layer of air. If one of the heads does accidentally touch the disk it is said to have "crashed". When this happens a portion of the magnetizable film is often destroyed.

Some disk storage devices are equipped with *disk packs*. A disk pack is a collection of adjacent platters which can be removed from the machine and placed in storage for later reuse. Disk packs can also be shipped to other locations for processing by distant computers.

Bubble Memories

As technology moves forward the distinctions between primary, auxiliary, and external storage are becoming increasingly blurred and indistinct. In particular, the new bubble memory units are presently classed as auxiliary storage but soon they may be serving other storage needs.

---

*Core ring arrays and solid-state memory units are *random access* devices. Any value they hold in storage can be accessed in the same amount of time regardless of its positon.

A bubble memory is constructed from orthoferrite material, a naturally occurring substance which is divided into alternating snake-like bands of positive and negative magnetization. If we pass an electrical pulse through a tiny metal loop held near the surface of an orthoferrite slab, the nearest snake-like region will be drawn into a thin magnetic cylinder called a "bubble". As is indicated in Figure 35, the presence of a bubble denotes a binary 1; its absence denotes a binary 0. Once a bubble has been formed in this way, it will remain on the surface of the chip indefinitely. In practice, however, the bubbles do not remain stationary. Instead, they circulate around a series of tight circles. Figure 35 shows how the bubbles are made to retrace series of minor loops. Variable electrical fields keep them in motion and tiny guideways imprinted on the surface of the chip help insure that they will not stray from their intended paths.

A typical bubble memory includes about 200 minor loops each containing 500 bubbles laid out on a flat surface a little larger than the head of a two-penny nail. This gives the bubble memory a packing density approaching 1,000,000 bits per square inch—among the highest information packing densities of any modern memory device. Costs are also fairly reasonable—on the order of $30 per chip when purchases are made in large production quantities. Another important advantage of the bubble memory is that it is a non volatile storage medium. If we switch off the power, the bubbles are not erased or destroyed. They will remain on the surface of the chip and when the power comes back on, their stored contents can again be retrieved.

The computer accesses a multidigit binary value being held in storage by pulling one bubble from each minor loop onto the major loop as shown in Figure 35. Once the bubbles are moving around the major loop, they pass through a special "bubble detector" which enlarges them one-by-one so that their magnetic fields can be more easily sensed. This interrogation procedure creates a series of abrupt electrical pulses which are routed into the computer's processing circuits.

If a particular bubble is no longer needed, the "bubble eraser" extinguishes it. This is accomplished by shrinking it to an undetectable size. On the other hand, if a new bubble is required, the "bubble generator" creates it. The technique used in making new bubbles is sketched at the top of Figure 35.

The bubbles circulating around the surface of a bubble memory chip are surprisingly small—on the order of 1/2,000 of an inch in diameter. Take a look at one of the tiny hairs growing on the back of your hand.

The bubbles now in use are so small 50 or them could be positioned side-by-side on the end of that slender human hair!

Charged-Coupled Devices

The bubble memory utilizes magnetic storage methods to provide a high-density device which is considerably cheaper than a conventional solid state memory chip. Fortunately, there is also another alternative. It is called a *charged-coupled device*. A charged-coupled device is similar to a bubble memory in that the values being held in storage are constantly

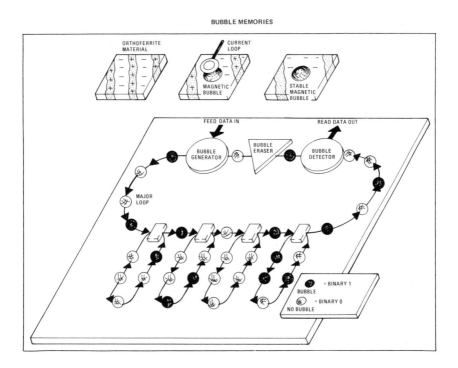

Figure 35: A bubble memory device utilizes a tiny metal loop to pull the natural stripe-like regions of magnetization in an orthoferrite material into a series of stable magnetic "bubbles". Once the bubbles have been formed in this way, they are constantly circulated around a series of minor loops until the computer needs to interrogate their stored contents. Upon interrogation one bubble from each minor loop is pulled onto the major loop. When it enters the major loop it awaits its turn to pass through the bubble detector, a special electronic device which enlarges the bubbles and senses their magnetic fields. In this way the bubble detector creates an electronic pulse train which is an exact binary analogue of the bubbles that were retrieved.

circulated around a series of closed loops on the surface of the chip. These values can be accessed only at certain specific locations. This allows the component transistors to be simplified by about 75 percent thus greatly reducing costs. However, the result is a more sluggish device without random access capabilities. Today's charged-coupled devices are also volatile. This greatly limits their potential applicability.

Data Buffers

Because of the enormous differences in speed and capacity among the various components, the interlinking of a computer's storage devices into an efficient computational system tends to be relatively difficult. One clever design trick consists of using electronic *buffers* in conjunction with some of the data transfer operations. A buffer is a high-speed, low-capacity storage register which is inserted between two storage units of grossly different operating speeds. In essence, a data buffer performs the same function as a freeway on-ramp. On-ramps are necessary because the slow-moving traffic on the surface streets must somehow be integrated with the freeway traffic which travels at a much higher average speed. The on-ramp gives the drivers time and space to accelerate. Similarly, a buffer accepts data values from the low-speed storage devices and holds them in reserve until they can be snatched into the high-speed storage units at electronic speeds. A digital computer would still function without buffers but it would be much less efficient.

EXTERNAL STORAGE

The lowest level of the computer's storage hierarchy is occupied by external storage. The external storage devices provide essentially limitless storage capacity but the computer can access their stored contents only with the periodic assistance of the people who service the machines.

Punched Cards

Punched cards are among the most popular external storage media. In Chapter 3 we saw how the cards can be prepared by human keypunch operators, but a computer can also be commanded to punch a deck of cards to be kept in storage against future needs.

Several different types of punched cards are in common use. These include the Hollerith card, which can hold up to 80 characters, and the 96-

column midget card which holds 20 percent more—despite the fact it is only one third as large. Midget cards have a higher information packing density for three principal reasons: they use binary coding, they employ smaller (round) holes, and they are divided into three separate horizontal tiers, each tier being capable of handling a maximum of 32 alphanumeric characters.

Magnetic Tapes

The magnetic tape is another popular external storage medium. In a previous chapter we reviewed the basic operating principles of magnetic tape units as they are used for input-output, but the tapes can also be used by the computer for temporary scratch pad storage. If their stored contents are saved for later reuse once they have been detached from the machines, the tapes become a part of external storage.

A tape is not nearly as convenient as a drum or a disk because it provides only *sequential* access. By sequential access we mean that the computer must wade through all the intermediate storage slots in order to reach a value located in the middle of the tape.

Some private companies and government agencies store thousands of tapes in carefully-guarded air-conditioned vaults. A typical tape can hold as many as 46 million alphanumeric characters or roughly the information content of a small set of encyclopedias.

The Floppy Disk

In 1973 IBM announced an exciting new external storage medium called a floppy disk. A floppy disk is a flat vinyl platter permanently sealed within a square protective cover. Because of the rugged, self-lubricating properties of vinyl plastic, the platter can withstand surprisingly high levels of abuse. Consequently, the read-write heads can remain in permanent contact with the surface of the disk. This is in sharp contrast to the complicated arrangement used by a conventional disk unit in which the read-write heads must gently hover over the surface of the disk supported by a delicate aerodynamic boundary layer.

Of course some friction is inevitably created when a stationary object is in contact with one which is moving at a rapid rate. However, it turns out that it is possible to fabricate floppy disks so that they can withstand 3 or 4 million passes of the read-write heads before they are too worn for reliable reuse. In practice the read-write heads are repositioned periodically but, even if they stayed on the same track continuously, approximately 16 hours would elapse before a catastrophic failure would occur. When a particular track begins to show signs of serious wear, the computer automatically switches its data values onto a spare track.

Two distinct types of floppy disks are in common use—soft sectored disks and hard sectored disks (See Figure 36). In a soft sectored disk a single index hole is used by the computer to sense the platter's angular orientation once per revolution. This is accomplished by shining a light through a hole in the disk to illuminate a stationary light-sensitive detector. The data being stored on each track is further indexed by a series of magnetic pulses permanently imprinted on the surface of the disk. Although this system is quite reliable, approximately 25% of the storage slots must be reserved for these routine recordkeeping tasks.

THE FLOPPY DISK

Figure 36: A floppy disk is a vinyl platter coated with a magnetizable material. Information is recorded and retrieved by means of a moveable read-write head resting on the surface of the spinning disk. Two types of floppy disk units are in common use. The soft sectored disk kèeps track of its stored contents by means of a single index hole plus a series of indexing pulses permanently recorded on the surface of the disk. The hard sectored disk performs the same function mechanically by using an index hole plus 32 equally-spaced sector holes. The hard sectored disk is more complicated than its soft sectored counterpart but it can handle 25 percent more information.

A hard sectored disk circumvents this difficulty by utilizing an additional 32 equally-spaced sector holes in addition to the index hole to give the computer more frequent indications of the angular orientation of the spinning disk. As a result, the indexing pulses can be eliminated. Consequently, the hard sectored disk can handle approximately 25 percent more data—300,000 alphanumeric characters as opposed to 250,000 characters for the soft sectored disk.

Because of its intrinsically simpler design, a floppy disk is orders of magnitude cheaper than a conventional disk storage device. Floppy disks can be purchased for as little as $3000 each. Smaller versions are even cheaper.

SELECTING THE COMPUTER'S STORAGE MEDIA

In this chapter you have been exposed to some of the difficulties faced by our country's data processing experts when they attempt to select the proper combination of storage devices for use in a particular application. It must be clear to you by now that there are no easy answers, no infallible guides, merely men and women who do the best they can to reach compromise solutions to a whole series of tricky technical problems.

Of course, they are aided by reams of engineering specifications similar to the ones presented in Table 2. The most important parameters to be considered in any given selection include the required storage capacity, the average access time, and the estimated cost per bit. As you can see from the values in the table, solid-state storage is extremely costly in comparison with competing storage techniques. However, despite its high cost, a solid-state memory is quite attractive because its stored values can be accessed with such great speed. It takes a solid-state device only about 1/2,000,000 of a second to retrieve any binary digit being held in storage. By contrast, a magnetic tape can store 10,000 times as many bits for a penny, but, unfortunately, the tape's data transfer rate is at least 10 to 20 times lower. Moreover, if we need a value stored in the middle of the tape, it can take 50 seconds, or even longer, to pull it from storage. In other words, if we are dealing with a randomly-selected bit, rather than the next one in sequence, a solid-state memory unit is about 100,000,000 times faster than a magnetic tape.

Hopefully, at this point you are beginning to see why our designers are willing to live with the added complexity of hierarchial storage. They would, of course, prefer to utilize a single storage medium if it could provide a reasonable compromise between overall cost, storage volume, and access speed. Unfortunately, to date, nobody has been able to develop a single storage medium with an acceptable combination of desirable properties. Consequently, unless there is some unforeseen technological breakthrough, storage hierarchies will continue to be used for at least the next several years.

THE DAWNING OF THE SECOND INDUSTRIAL REVOLUTION

Three decades ago a new revolution quietly began to take shape within the Western World. Before it was over it would alter all our lives in a hundred dozen ways. But most people, busy with their own private affairs, hardly seemed to notice it at all. Small wonder. It was not filled with noisy, boisterous events. No cannon balls hurtled through the sky. No one was assassinated. No flags were burned on crowded city streets. No statues blasted to smithereens. It was not a political revolution of the kind historians recount with such feverish glee. It was a revolution of technology. More precisely, it was a revolution of computer technology.

The Industrial Revolution of the 19th century gave us machines to enhance the power of our muscles; this new revolution has given us computers to enhance the power of our brains. Today there are more than 150,000 large-scale digital computers in operation in the United States. These computers have greatly magnified our ability to retrieve and manipulate vast amounts of useful information. However, we must be careful not to misuse our agile electronic slaves. For a computer, like a bulldozer, is a tool with spectacular, but specialized, capabilities. If you need to remove tons of stubborn dirt from a vacant city lot a bulldozer is an excellent choice; it's not nearly as good for removing smaller specks of dirt from a badly swollen eye. Of course, any attempt to use a bulldozer in this way would soon reveal the folly of our selection. Unfortunately, computers, unlike bulldozers, seem to have an almost unlimited potential for misuse. As Dr. Elting E. Morrison at MIT has observed, most machines developed in the past—engines and generators—were quite intolerant of man's stupidity:

". . . Overloaded, abused, they stopped work, stalled, broke down, blew up; and that was the end of it. Thus they set clear limits to man's ineptitudes. For the computer . . . the limits are not so obvious. Used in ignorance or stupidity, asked a foolish question, it does not collapse, it goes on to answer the fool according to his folly. And the questioner, being a fool, will go on to act on the reply."

In the chapters to follow we will learn more about the role of the computers in our society. We will also examine some of the ways in which they have been used and abused—and some of the ways in which the people in our society have been reacting.

TABLE 2
STORAGE MEDIA COMPARISONS

STORAGE MEDIUM	TYPE OF STORAGE	CAPACITY (millions of characters)	DATA TRANSFER RATE (millions of characters per second)	AVERAGE ACCESS TIME FOR RANDOMLY SELECTED BIT (sec)	APPROXIMATE HARDWARE COST (bits per penny)
SOLID-STATE MEMORY UNITS	Primary Random Access Volatile	2 (64,000 per chip)	2	1/2,000,000	7
MAGNETIC DRUM	Auxiliary Semi Random Access Non Volatile	2	1	1/100	800
MAGNETIC DISK	Auxiliary Semi Random Access Non Volatile	7	0.15	1/80	10,000
BUBBLE MEMORY	Auxiliary Semi Random Access Non Volatile	0.1 per chip	2	1/3,000	30
CHARGE-COUPLED DEVICE	Auxiliary Semi Random Access Volatile	0.1 per chip	2	1/2,000	20
PUNCHED CARDS	External Sequential Non Volatile	0.16 per box	0.0016	12 (assuming 500 cards in the hopper)	100
MAGNETIC TAPE	External Sequential Non Volatile	46	0.2	50	90,000
FLOPPY DISK	External Semi Random Access Non Volatile	0.25	0.2	1/40	3,000

BIBLIOGRAPHY

1. Adams, J. Mack, and Haden, Douglas H., *Social Effects of Computer Use and Misuse.* New York, New York: John Wiley, 1976.

2. Arnold, William F. "Memory Makers Brace for Bubble Bath." *Electronics,* 16 February 1978, pp. 75-76.

3. "The Art of Chip Making." *Time,* 20 February 1978, p, 56.

4. "The Bubble Memory Finally Arrives." *Business Week,* 28 March 1977, pp. 72-74.

5. "Business:Thinking Small." *Time,* 20 February 1978, pp. 50-53.

6. "Floppies Continue Their Price Drive." *Datamation,* May 1977, pp. 253-254.

7. "Floppy Disk Profile." *Mini-Micro Systems,* November 1978, pp. 37-51.

8. Holoien, Martin O. *Computers and Their Societal Impact.* New York, New York: John Wiley, 1977.

9. Lindgren, Nilo."Semiconductors Face the 80's." *IEEE Spectrum,* October 1977, pp. 42-48.

10. Logsdon, Tom. *Computer Science and Technology.* Palisade, New Jersey: Franklin Publishing Co., 1974.

11. Altman, Lawrence. "Memories." *Electronics,* 20 January 1977, pp. 81-96.

12. Rajchman, Jan A. "New Memory Technologies." *Science,* March 1977, pp. 1223-1229.

13. Ralston, Anthony and Meek, Chester L. *Encyclopedia of Computer Science.* New York, New York: Petrocelli/Charter, 1976.

14. Rose, Edward A. "Bubbles vs Floppies." *Mini-Micro Systems,* April 1977, pp. 42-43.

15. Sanders, Donald H. *Computers in Society.* New York, New York: McGraw-Hill, 1973.

16. Sollman, George H. "A Guide to Floppy Disk Selection." *Mini-Micro Systems,* April 1977, pp. 36-46.

17. Thorne, Bill. "Disk Destruction Made Simple." *Creative Computing,* Nov-Dec 1976, p. 38.

18. "256,000 Bubbles." *Military Electronics Countermeasures,* November 1978, pp. 73-75.

EXERCISES

1. In your own words explain how a core ring array stores a binary 1 or a binary 0. Now explain how the computer goes about interrogating the values being held in storage.

2. What do we mean by random access storage? Name two common memory devices that provide random access capabilities. Name two that don't.

3. How are the computer's memory units arranged into a storage hierarchy? What is the purpose of this arrangement?

4. What is a volatile storage medium? List several devices that are non volatile.

5. What is a disk pack? Is it a volatile storage medium?

6. Some magnetic disks have moveable read-write heads and some have stationary heads. Describe their relative advantages and disadvantages.

7. How does a bubble memory unit operate? Is it a random access storage medium? Is it volatile? Is it a solid-state device?

8. Most bacteria are about 1/3000 of an inch in diameter. How does their size compare with the bubbles in a bubble memory? How does it compare with the transistors on a solid-state chip? (Hint: In estimating the size of the transistors assume that the solid-state device is $\frac{1}{5}$ of an inch on a side and that it contains 64,000 transistors.)

9. A floppy disk unit is considerably cheaper and simpler than a conventional disk drive. Explain why.

10. What do we mean by semi random access? List some devices that provide semi random access capabilities.

STUDENT PROJECTS

1. Solid-state devices are used in a remarkable variety of ways by industry, the military and by ordinary consumers. Research these applications and present your findings in an informal written report.

SUGGESTED REFERENCES:

a. Lindgren, Nilo. "Semicondutors Face the 80's". *IEEE Spectrum.* October, 1977. pp.42-48.

b. "Business: Thinking Small." *Time.* February 20, 1978. pp. 50-53.

c. Schefter, Jim. "Microelectronics—Tiny Chips that Trim Costs and Make Life Easier." *Popular Science.* January, 1978. pp. 53-55.

d. Mayo, John S. "The Role of Microelectronics in Communications." *Scientific American.* September, 1977. pp. 162-179.

e. Russo, Paul M., et. al. "Microprocessors in Consumer Products." *Proceedings of the IEEE.* February, 1978. pp. 131-141.

f. Noyce, Robert N. "Microprocessors." *Scientific American.* September, 1977. pp. 62-69.

g. "The Age of the Miracle Chips." *Time.* February 20, 1978. pp. 44-45.

h. *Information.* San Francisco, W.H. Freeman. 1966.

i. "Chip Helps Detect Targets Automatically." *Electronics.* March 16, 1978. pp. 41-42.

2. Visit a data processing center or phone or write one in your area. Find out from the people who work there the types and the numbers of devices they have in their storage hierarchy. Using this data plus the specifications in Table 1, prepare a new table showing the approximate total capacities of their devices, their total costs, their data transfer rates and their average access times.

3. In the last section of this chapter, the author compared the Computer Revolution with the Industrial Revolution of the 19th century. Go to the library and find out what happened to trigger the Industrial Revolution and how it affected the people living at the time. Now draw a series of parallels between the effects of this earlier revolution and the one we are now experiencing.

CHAPTER 5

SOFTWARE ENGINEERING

THE FIVE PHASES OF PROGRAM DEVELOPMENT

DIFFICULTIES WITH COST AND MANPOWER
ESTIMATES

TYPICAL SOFTWARE CODING RATES

MODERN METHODS FOR INCREASING PROGRAMMER
EFFICIENCY
Structured Programming
Top-Down Design
Chief Programmer Teams
Structured Walkthroughs
Preliminary Results

BIBLIOGRAPHY

EXERCISES

STUDENT PROJECTS

Invariably, when we think about the data processing industry, we imagine rows of sleek, silent machines sitting in air conditioned cubicles performing almost incomprehensible feats of mathematical magic. However, the *software* packages in a modern computer center are actually much more costly and complicated than the *hardware* modules we so strongly admire. Indeed, as is shown in Figure 37, software (program development and maintenance) typically accounts for 80 percent of total dollar costs. In 1976 Barry W. Boehm estimated that computer software was costing our country more than $20 billion per year—or roughly one percent of our gross national product.*

The techniques currently used in producing data processing hardware are quite advanced and scientific. By contrast, our software production methods are much more primitive and chaotic. This is how computer expert Harlan D. Mills recently contrasted today's hardware and software methodologies:

"The close alliance of science and engineering in hardware has, over the last 25 years, accomplished dramatic achievements in reliability, speed, storage, cost, and function. This achievement has few parallels in human history. But the use of this remarkable hardware has led to large, complex, ponderous, unreliable, and incompatible (software) systems."**

Dr. Frederick P. Brooks, Jr. would not be much inclined to disagree with this rather pessimistic assessment. Brooks, who managed much of the development of the IBM 360 recently published this striking word-picture characterizing the rather dismal status of today's programming technology:

"No scene from prehistory is quite so vivid as that of the mortal struggles of great beasts in the tar pits. In the mind's eye one sees dinosaurs, mammoths, and sabre-toothed tigers struggling against the grip of the tar. The fiercer the struggle, the more entangling the tar, and no beast is so strong or so skillful but that he ultimately sinks."

"Large-system programming has, over the past decade, been such a tar pit, and many great and powerful beasts have thrashed violently in it. Most have emerged with running systems—few have met goals, schedules and budgets. Large and small, massive or wiry, team after team has become entangled in the tar. No one thing seems

*Boehm, Barry W. "Software Engineering." *IEEE Transactions on Computers*. December, 1976. pp. 1226-1241.
**Mills, Harlan D., "Software Engineering." *Science*. March, 1977. pp. 1199-1205.

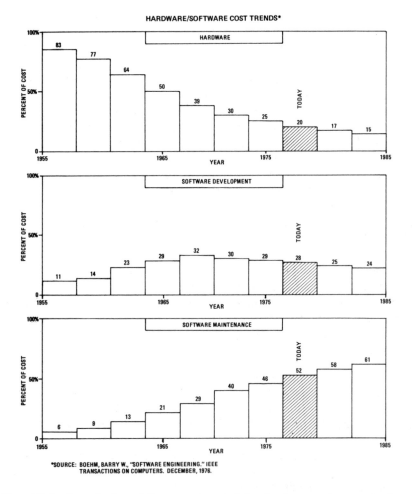

HARDWARE/SOFTWARE COST TRENDS*

*SOURCE: BOEHM, BARRY W., "SOFTWARE ENGINEERING." IEEE
TRANSACTIONS ON COMPUTERS. DECEMBER, 1976.

Figure 37: In the early days of the computer revolution hardware costs were dominant. However, as these graphs show, our expenditures for software development and maintenance currently exceed our expenditures for hardware by a margin of four to one.

to cause the diffculty—any particular paw can be pulled away. But the accumulation of simultaneous and interacting factors brings slower and slower motion. Everyone seems to have been surprised by the stickiness of the problem, and it is hard to discern the nature of it. But we must try to understand it if we are to solve it."*

---

*Brooks, Frederick, P. "The Mythical Man-Month." *Datamation*. December 1975. pp. 44-52.

Because of their high cost and their almost incomprehensible complexity, a number of attempts have been made to systematize the development of large software projects. These efforts are just beginning to solidify into a new branch of science called *software engineering.* Later in this chapter we shall explore some of the hottest new methods currently being used by its practitioners in attempting to make the programming process more systematic and efficient. But first we will examine the various phases a professional programmer goes through when he is given a new assignment and we will review some of the problems he typically encounters along the way.

THE FIVE PHASES OF SOFTWARE DEVELOPMENT

As is shown in Figure 38, the development of a large software package can be broken down into five major phases:

1. Establishing the Requirements
   During the initial phase, the software experts and their customers exchange various documents and conduct a series of meetings in an attempt to develop a complete, consistent, unambiguous set of program specifications. These specifications are intended to serve as a basis for common agreement among all the parties concerned as to what the software product is supposed to accomplish when it becomes operational.
2. Designing the Routine
   In the second phase the programmers and the design engineers determine what types of hardware units will be used, what coding languages will be employed, and how the various subtasks will be carried out by the professional staff. During this phase program flowcharts and other visual aids are used in structuring and outlining the content of the component parts of the overall software package.
3. Coding the Commands
   Once the design phase has been completed, the commands are coded in the appropriate language. We often regard the coding phase as being the primary assignment of the professional programmer but, actually, coding typically consumes only about one-sixth of his time and effort.
4. Testing the Program
   The first few versions of the program are invariably riddled with errors. Some of these errors can be detected automatically by the computer, others must be located and corrected by running a series of test cases—simple runs for which the correct answers are known in

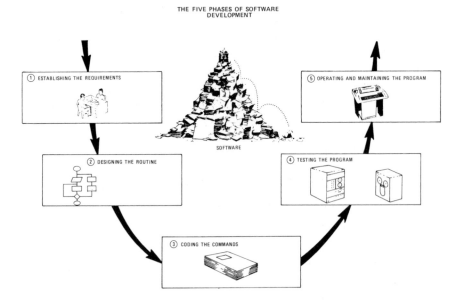

THE FIVE PHASES OF SOFTWARE
DEVELOPMENT

① ESTABLISHING THE REQUIREMENTS

⑤ OPERATING AND MAINTAINING THE PROGRAM

SOFTWARE

② DESIGNING THE ROUTINE

④ TESTING THE PROGRAM

③ CODING THE COMMANDS

Figure 38: Generally speaking, professional programmers go through five distinct phases in the development of a large computer program. In the first two they establish the requirements in cooperation with the customer and work out the design of the appropriate software routines. In the next two they code the commands and test and debug them. Finally, in the fifth phase they exercise the operational program and make any modifications necessitated by programming goofs or specification changes.

advance. In general a test case will exercise only a small portion of the completed program; hence, large numbers of them are needed if we are to be reasonably certain that the program as a whole is essentially error-free. In practice it is usually impossible to "prove" that a particular program has been completely debugged. Indeed, many have been found to contain errors long after they have been declared operational. The first FORTRAN translation routine, for example, was found to contain several coding errors 18 months after it was officially released.

5. Operating and Maintaining the Program

When the program has been debugged, it can be operated on a routine basis. However, this is not the end of the programming efforts. Because of the subsequent discovery of changing requirements and various types of discrepancies, most programs must be maintained on a continuous basis. When we talk about "maintaining" a program we are referring to the periodic changes necessary to meet these important needs. Program maintenance is often regarded as a rather unglamorous occupation. However, it provides the employment for perhaps 60 percent of all the professional programmers now working in the United States.

DIFFICULTIES WITH COST AND MANPOWER ESTIMATES

The history of software coding efforts is replete with large-scale fiascos. One of the earliest, the SAGE system, was designed to handle the surveillance of enemy aircraft for the United States Air Force. When first initiated, the SAGE program was a relatively simple undertaking handled by a small closely-knit group of professional programmers. However, it soon became enormously complicated. "Within a year approximately 1000 people were involved", explained Jules I. Schwartz in a recent technical report. "People were recruited and trained from a variety of walks of life. Streetcar conductors, undertakers (with at least one year of training in calculus), school teachers, curtain cleaners, and others were hastily assembled, trained in programming for some number of weeks, and assigned parts of a very complex organization...the system was delivered over a year late at considerably more cost than was originally expected."*

The managers of the SAGE system were surprised when they encountered huge cost overruns. But today the reaction is much milder when actual costs exceed early estimates. Even the most experienced companies are plagued by this expensive problem. Figure 39 shows the cost estimate errors that were made in connection with three FORTRAN compilers developed at IBM. As you can see, the original cost estimates were off by amounts ranging from 17 to 177 percent. Although this may seem like a rather dismal record, these estimates are actually more accurate than the industry average. Pricing estimate errors ranging from 100 to 150 percent are the rule rather than the exception.

Why is it so difficult to get accurate pricing estimates? For one thing computer programmers are eternal optimists. "This time it will surely run" they repeat with great frequency, or "I've just found the very last bug."

---

*Schwartz, Jules I. "Construction of Software: Problems and Practicalities" from *Practical Strategies for Developing Large Software Systems* edited by Ellis Horowitz. Reading, Massachusetts. Addison-Wesley. 1975.

But programming errors aside, there are a number of factors that can put a project behind schedule, none of them particularly dramatic. Frederick P. Brooks explains it this way:

> "When one hears of disastrous schedule slippages in a project, he imagines that a series of major calamities must have befallen it. Usually, however, the disaster is due to termites, not tornadoes; and the schedule has slipped imperceptibly but inexorably."
>
> "Yesterday a key man was sick, and a meeting couldn't be held. Today the machines are all down, because lightning struck the building's power transformer. Tomorrow the disk routines won't start testing, because the first disc is a week late from the factory. Snow, jury duty, family problems, emergency meetings with customers, executive audits—the list goes on and on. Each one only postpones some activity by a half-day or a day. And the schedule slips, one day at a time."

It makes a very convincing argument, but, actually, most of the delays Dr. Brooks enumerates are similar to the ones that bedevil other large-scale projects outside the data processing industry, seemingly without driving them into a complete tailspin. What is it that makes software development a special case? Dr. Brooks goes on to explain how we are distracted by the concept of measuring the amount of work required to complete a task in terms of man-months. As he observes, we can use extra manpower to speed the completion of some tasks but not others:

> "Men and months are interchangeable commodities only when a task can be partitioned among many workers *with no communication among them*. This is true of reaping wheat or picking cotton; it is not even approximately true of systems programming. When a task cannot be partitioned because of sequential constraints, the application of more effort has no effect on the schedule. The bearing of a child takes nine months, no matter how many women are assigned."*

Well, at least, in the case of childbearing, adding extra help doesn't cause us to fall further behind schedule. However, paradoxically, additional slowdowns can occur if we assign extra manpower to a faltering software effort. As Dr. Books puts it: "Adding manpower to a late software project makes it later."

---

*Brooks, Frederick P. "The Mythical Man-Month." *Datamation.* December, 1974. pp. 56-58.

These slowdowns stem from the fact that when additional people come on board, those already working on the project must use a portion of their time and effort in training and communicating with their new, inexperienced co-workers. The data in Figure 40 shows what can happen if too many people are added too quickly. As you can see by examining the top graph, in a specific case it might take just as long to do a task with seven people as it would with only one.

Practical experience indicates that there are definite limits as to how fast additional personnel can be added to an ongoing project. For example, V. S. Vyssotsky at Bell Telephone Laboratories estimates that the maximum rate of buildup for reasonable efficiency is about 30 percent per year.* It is also important that any extra workers be added with careful timing. Figure 41 shows the typical manpower loading for a complicated project. Note that the number of workers builds up rather rapidly at first but then begins to taper off gradually and almost imperceptibly. Generally speaking, about 40 percent of the man-hours are expended during the first quarter of the project, another 40 percent in the

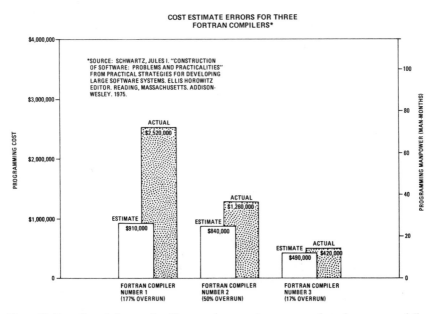

Figure 39: Even though thousands of large-scale computer programs have been successfully coded, cost estimate errors still occur with discouraging regularity. All three of the routines listed in this figure were developed by experienced teams of computer programmers. Yet, as you can see, they encountered cost overruns ranging from 17 to 177 percent.

*Brooks, Frederick P. "The Mythical Man-Month." *Datamation*. December, 1974. pp. 45-52.

second quarter, and the remaining 20 percent of the effort is spread over the last half of the timetable.

As the project approaches completion the estimates as to how much work remains gradually become more accurate. In 1977 Doty, Nelson and Stewart made a study of the cost estimate errors associated with large software projects for the Rome Air Development Center. Here is one of their important conclusions:*

". . . size estimate errors may be greater than 200 percent in the conceptual phase of a project, 100 percent at the RFP stage, 75

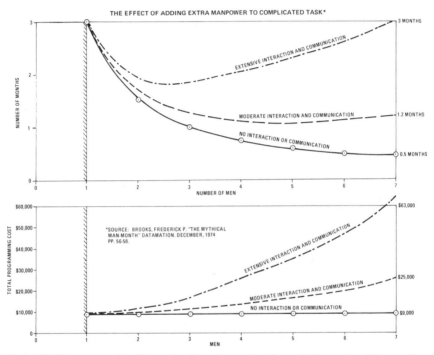

Figure 40: When we are handling a simple assignment such as picking cotton it is usually possible to shorten the schedule by recruiting additional personnel. However, the addition of extra workers is not nearly so helpful when the tasks to be performed are complicated and interdependent. Indeed, as Frederick P. Brooks has observed, when new programmers are assigned to a faltering software effort the schedule may actually be longer than it would have been with a smaller, more compact staff.

---

* Doty, D.L., Nelson, P.J. and Stewart, K.R., *Software Cost Estimation Study: Guidelines for Improved Software Cost Estimating (Volume 2)*. Final technical report by Doty Associates, Inc. for Rome Air Development Center (RADC-TR-77-220), Griffiss Air Force Base, N.Y. August, 1977.

percent up to the preliminary design review, and 50 percent through the remainder of the development. Schedules derived from size estimates may be underestimated by similar margins."

The curves in Figure 40 are well known to industry leaders but, even so, if one of their pet projects begins to fall behind schedule there is an almost overpowering urge to buy back some of the lost time by adding extra personnel. However, in many cases this is the worst possible reaction. As Frederick P. Brooks has observed: "When schedule slippage is recognized the natural (and traditional) response is to add manpower. Like dousing a fire with gasoline, this makes matters worse, much worse. More fire requires more gasoline and thus begins a regenerative cycle which ends in disaster."*

TYPICAL SOFTWARE CODING RATES

The productivity of the average computer programmer is surprisingly low. Generally speaking, those who work on large-scale projects average completing only about five instructions per day. The coding rates achieved

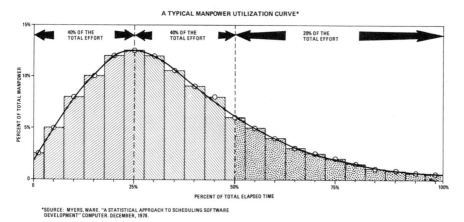

Figure 41: The manpower requirements for a large-scale project are usually not constant. Instead, as this figure illustrates, they tend to build up to a peak rather quickly but then they begin gradually tapering off. In general, about 80 percent of the effort occurs during the first half of the project with the remaining 20 percent requiring an interval of nearly equal length.

---

*Brooks, Frederick P. "The Mythical Man-Month." *Datamation*. December, 1974. pp. 56-58.

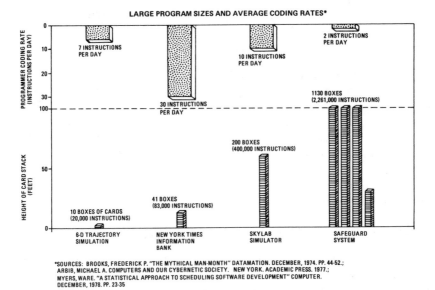

LARGE PROGRAM SIZES AND AVERAGE CODING RATES*

*SOURCES: BROOKS, FREDERICK P. "THE MYTHICAL MAN-MONTH" DATAMATION. DECEMBER, 1974. PP. 44-52.;
ARBIB, MICHAEL A. COMPUTERS AND OUR CYBERNETIC SOCIETY. NEW YORK. ACADEMIC PRESS. 1977.;
MYERS, WARE. "A STATISTICAL APPROACH TO SCHEDULING SOFTWARE DEVELOPMENT" COMPUTER.
DECEMBER, 1978. PP. 23-35

Figure 42: The average coding rates for the programmers working on large-scale projects are surprisingly low. Under worst-case conditions they average only 2 instructions per day; at best, they can manage to raise their productivity by a factor of 15 to about 30 instructions per day.

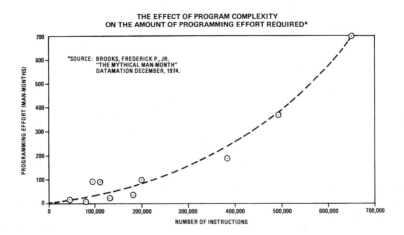

**THE EFFECT OF PROGRAM COMPLEXITY
ON THE AMOUNT OF PROGRAMMING EFFORT REQUIRED***

*SOURCE: BROOKS, FREDERICK P., JR.
"THE MYTHICAL MAN-MONTH"
DATAMATION DECEMBER, 1974.

Figure 43: Doubling the size of a computer program more than doubles the amount of effort required. In part, this is true because the interactions between the various component parts give rise to greater complexity as well as extra opportunities for serious programming errors. As this graph shows, a program involving 600,000 instructions typically requires nearly four times as much programming effort as one involving half as many instructions.

by four teams of programmers who were assigned to work on software packages ranging from 20,000 to more than 2 million statements are listed in Figure 42. As you can see, the average programmer had a productivity rate ranging from 2 to 30 instructions per day.

Why are professional programmers so unproductive? For one thing they spend a surprisingly small fraction of their time coding their routines. According to Frederick P. Brooks only about one-sixth of their day is spent in writing commands.* Moreover, coordination with their co-workers burns up a great deal of valuable time. As you can see from the graph in Figure 43, the amount of programming effort required rises dramatically when the size of a software package increases. Typically it takes nearly four times as much effort to develop a program with 600,000 commands as it does to develop one with only 300,000.

It is also considerably more difficult to debug a large-scale program because the errors can affect the results in a greater variety of ways. Moreover, correcting an error in one part of a large program can create problems in some other, seemingly unrelated, portion. As a result, a large-scale program can be "90 percent debugged" at a certain time but then at some later time it might end up being only "80 percent debugged".

Because coding errors are so much harder to uncover in the later parts of the developmental process, the programmers should exercise extreme care when they are establishing the requirements and designing the routines. The effort levels required in finding bugs at various points in the programming process are summarized in Figure 44. Notice that it costs nearly 70 times as much to find and correct a particular error in the operational phase as it does to find it during the initial phase when the overall requirements are being set. This figure is sending us a message loud and clear: work carefully and slowly in the early phases of the developmental process in order to avoid mistakes that may later turn out to be extremely expensive to correct.

MODERN METHODS FOR INCREASING PROGRAMMER EFFICIENCY

Historically, many computer programmers have approached their jobs in surprisingly undisciplined ways. Given a cursory description of what a new program was intended to do and a few casual instructions as to how it was supposed to do it, they would often rush back to their desks

---

*His estimates call for the following breakdown: $\frac{1}{3}$ of the time planning, $\frac{1}{3}$ coding, $\frac{1}{4}$ component test and early system test, $\frac{1}{4}$ system test, all components in hand.

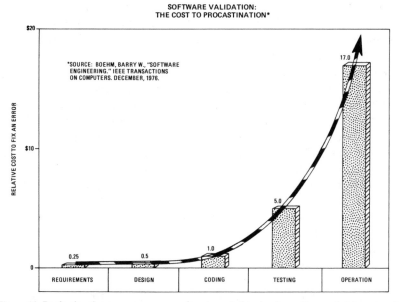

Figure 44: Professional programmers are often tempted to begin coding and debugging their routines as soon as they develop even the skimpiest notions as to what the program is intended to do. However, large amounts of time and money can be saved if they manage to resist this temptation and spend a realistic interval developing the requirements and designing the program prior to the coding phase. As this figure shows, it costs almost 70 times as much to correct an error once the program is in operation as it does to find and correct it during the early requirements phase.

and, without writing anything down, begin coding commands. If they could get the program to run at all, they would then gradually modify it until it began to converge toward what the customer actually wanted. Today many programs are still coded under this rather lackadaisical philosophy but, more recently, a body of systematic programming techniques has begun to emerge.

Structured Programming

One of the most powerful new techniques is called *structured programming*. Taken in its broadest context, structured programming refers to the process in which we break the overall job down into separate pieces, or modules. These modules, in turn, are broken down into smaller pieces which are also further subdivided. Finally, we reach a point where it is appropriate to begin coding the actual instructions one line at a time.

Of course the modules must be chosen in such a way that we can specify how they are to interact. In effect, there is a *contract* between each pair of modules. This contract specifies two things: (1) what the module will do and (2) what assumptions it is making about the behavior of the other modules. In particular, we must specify explicitly what *inputs* a particular module is to receive from the various other modules and what *outputs* it is to provide for them.

Generally speaking, structured programming has worked exceedingly well. But there have been a few cases in which some of the modules could not actually be coded because their contracts were mathematically impossible or logically inconsistent. When a problem of this type occurs, it can necessitate extensive replanning and recoding.

Top-Down Design

One of the most intriguing properties of a digital computer is that it can make a "decision" thus creating a branch point. For example, a payroll program can be rigged to determine if a particular worker has made all his social security payments for the year; if *not* it will compute his payments for the current week; if *so* it will automatically branch to some other point in the program where it will compute something else.

"Branching" capabilities of this type give a computer program enormous power and versatility. Unfortunately, it is easy for a programmer to get carried away and begin building a routine containing a hopeless tangle of branch points shooting off in a dozen different directions.

Top-down design is a realistic alternative. When we use top-down design we rig the program so that each command produces, at most, only two branches which are placed one after the other immediately below the branching command. As a result the programmer can actually read his program listing *from the top down*—the same way he would read a textbook or a mystery novel! In some respects it is even easier to read because certain commands are indented to help focus the attention of the reader on those lines of the code having a special significance.

Chief Programmer Teams

For many years it has been common knowledge that there is a tremendous variation in the capabilities among the various members of any programming team. The best programmers are often an order of magnitude more efficient than any of their colleagues. In 1974 Lawrence H. Cook, Jr. made a systematic study of programmer efficiency by giving the same assignment to several different programmers. He obtained the following results:*

---

*Cooke, Lawrence H., "Programming Time vs. Running Time." *Datamation*. December, 1974. pp. 56-58.

1. Program development times varying from 3 to 29 hours
2. Program execution times varying from 0.5 to 192 seconds.**

During World War II when the U.S. Air Force commanders stationed in England discovered similar variations in the skill levels among their experienced bombardiers, they introduced the "lead bombardier" concept in which their best operator dropped his bombs as a signal to his counterparts flying in the same formation.

A few years ago IBM devised a similar approach in which they formed "Chief Programmer Teams" to be used in connection with large software efforts. Each team is headed by a Chief Programmer who is responsible for designing, coding, and integrating the top-level structure of the program as well as some of the other key components. He or she also manages and motivates other team members and personally reads and reviews their code.

The Chief Programmer is assisted by a Deputy-Chief who shares the overall responsibilities and is available to take over in emergencies. The team also involves a number of skilled programmers and a *Program Librarian* who makes sure that each of the program modules is properly developed, documented, and put in the required standardized form. Another important duty of the librarian is to keep complete records on all test runs that have been made—including those that have ended in failure.

In general, the Chief Programmer Team concept has worked extremely well. However, there has been one rather serious problem: It is quite difficult to find Chief Programmers with enough energy and talent to perform all the required functions.

Structured Walkthroughs

"Structured walkthroughs" are another method that can be used to increase programmer efficiency. In a structured walkthrough the programmer projects a copy of his or her code onto a screen and leads the other members of the team through it one line at a time, carefully explaining what it is supposed to do.

It has been found that this technique leads to the elimination of large numbers of errors. Indeed, after a thorough review of the process, Edward Yourdon estimated that "a reviewing audience can easily spot five or six bugs in a 200-statement program within 15 minutes."*

---

*Incidentally, the slowest programmer in the group wrote the program that ran the longest.

**Yourdon, Edward. "Making the Move to Structured Programming." *Datamation*. June, 1975. pp. 52-56.

Some programmers contend that structured walkthroughs burn up too much valuable time. However, an experiment conducted at Aetna Life and Casualty suggests that less than 6 percent of the programmer's time was spent in code reviews and structured walkthroughs. But even if it is not too time consuming, certain practitioners do not relish the prospect of exposing their code to public scrutiny. Said one professional who worked for Shell Oil in London:

"Reading someone else's program is like reading their personal mail—it's an invasion of privacy in which civilized people simply do not indulge."

Preliminary Results

At this early date it is not yet clear how much these new techniques will improve programmer efficiency. Some authors are casually predicting 5-fold improvements. Others indicate improvements of only 200 to 300 percent.* The barcharts in Figure 42 provide us with a small indication of the gains we might reasonably expect. A few years ago the Information Bank Program for the *New York Times* was coded using all of the procedures we have just outlined. As you can see, it has the highest average coding rate of any of the samples listed in the figure.

Michael A. Arbib the author of *Computers and The Cybernetic Society* had these kind words to say about that particular programming effort:

"A six-man team completed the task in 22 months—almost 30 lines per man-day, several times the normal rate of programming for a large project. Even more impressively, the program appeared to have an exceptionally small number of bugs in it."**

Still, even with a dedicated team using these new techniques, the development of a large-scale computer program is definitely a difficult undertaking. Computer expert Jules I. Schwartz recently issued this pointed warning to those who might end up supervising the efforts of a large team of professional programmers. "In managing programming efforts, never assume they will go well, or have been going well. Treat

---

*Yourdon, Edward. "Making the Move to Structured Programming." *Datamation*. June, 1975.pp. 52-56.
**Arbib, Michael A. *Computers and The Cybernetic Society*. New York, New York: Academic Press, 1977.

each effort as if it is a developing disaster . . . and maybe you won't have one."*

---

*Schwartz, Jules I. "Construction of Software: Problems and Practicalities" from *Practical Strategies for Developing Large Software Systems*. Ellis Horowitz, editor. Reading, Massachusetts: Addison-Wesley. 1975.

BIBLIOGRAPHY

1. Arbib, Michael A. *Computers and The Cybernetic Society*. New York, New York: Academic Press: 1977.

2. Boehm, Barry W. "The High Cost of Software" from *Practical Strategies for Developing Large Software Systems*. Ellis Horowitz, editor. Reading, Massachusetts: Addison-Wesley, 1975.

3. Brooks, Frederick P. "The Mythical Man-Month." *Datamation*. December, 1974. pp. 44-52.

4. Cooke, Lawrence H., Jr. "Programming Time Versus Running Time." *Datamation*, December, 1974, pp. 56-58.

5. DeMillo, Richard A., Lipton, Richard J., and Sayward, Frederick G., "Hints on Test Data Selection: Help for the Practicing Programmer." *Computer*. April, 1978. pp. 34-41.

6. Moranda, Paul B. "Software Quality Technology." *Computer*. November, 1978. pp. 72-78.

7. Keider, Stephen P. "Why Projects Fail." *Datamation*. December, 1974. pp. 53-55.

8. Mills, Harlan D. "Software Engineering." *Science*. March 18, 1977. pp. 1199-1205.

9. Myers, Ware. "A Statistical Approach to Scheduling Software Development." *Computer*. December, 1978. pp. 23-35.

10. Sanders, Donald H. *Computers in Society*. New York, New York: McGraw-Hill, 1977.

11. Schwartz, Jules I. "Construction of Software: Problems and Practicalities" from *Practical Strategies for Developing Large Software Systems*. Ellis Horowitz, editor. Reading, Massachusetts: Addison-Wesley, 1975.

12. Yourdon, Edward. "Making The Move to Structured Programming." *Datamation*. June, 1975. pp. 52-56.

13. Liu, Chester C. "A Look at Software Maintenance." *Datamation*. November, 1976. pp. 51-55.

14. Ralston, Anthony and Meek, Chester L. *Encyclopedia of Computer Science*. New York, New York: Petrocelli/Charter, 1976.

15. Boehm, Barry W. "Software Engineering." *IEEE Transactions on Computers*. December, 1976. pp. 1226-1241.

EXERCISES

1. Define the terms hardware and software. In today's marketplace which is usually more costly? Which has been developed in a more scientific way?

2. What is structured programming? How does it differ from the conventional techniques that have been used by professional programmers since the early days of the data processing revolution?

3. According to the rather cynical assessments of Frederick P. Brooks "Adding manpower to a late software project makes it later." What did he mean by this statement? Could it ever be literally true?

4. List the five phases of program development and, in your own words, give a brief description of each one. Which phases requires the most manpower? Which ones warrants the most care? Explain why.

5. According to figures quoted in this chapter a typical professional programmer working on a large software effort averages coding only about 5 commands per day. Explain why he or she has such a low productivity. If you were the supervisor of a programming group what are some of the things you might try in order to increase your worker's average productivity?

6. Nearly everyone who attempts to estimate the cost of a large-scale programming effort seems to end up with an unrealistically low estimate. What are some of the reasons for these prevalent errors? How might the people who finance the projects protect themselves from errors of this type?

7. What is a "structured walkthrough"? Why do you think it is so effective? Why does it cause resentment at some facilities?

8. What is "top-down design"? How does it differ from conventional programming techinques?

9. Explain why doubling the size of a computer program tends to more than double its cost.

10. By using each of the ten data values plotted in Figure 43, compute the average number of instructions per day for programs of various sizes. Now make a plot similar to the one in Figure 43 with a new vertical scale: "average number of instructions coded per man-day".

STUDENT PROJECTS

1. Visit a local data processing center and interview the programmers and their supervisory personnel. Ask them about the current use of the techniques which were reviewed in the last major section of this chapter. Also ask them about their average productivity rates. Report your findings to your classmates.

2. Put together a short research report on structured programming. Explain in more detail how the process works and summarize some of the practical experiences that have been gathered over the past few years.

SUGGESTED READING LIST

a. Arbib, Michael, A., *Computers and the Cybernetic Society.* New York, New York: Academic Press, 1977.

b. Ralston, Anthony and Meek, Chester L., *Encyclopedia of Computer Science.* New York, New York: Petrocelli/Charter, 1976.

c. Horowitz, Ellis. *Practical Strategies for Developing Large Software Systems.* Reading, Massachusetts: Addison-Wesley, 1975.

d. Horowitz, Ellis. "FORTRAN Can It Be Structured and Should It Be?" From *Practical Strategies for Developing Large Software Systems.* Reading, Massachusetts: Addison-Wesley, 1975.

e. Boehm, Barry W. "Software Engineering." *IEEE Transactions on Computers.* December, 1976. pp. 1226-1241.

f. Yourdon, Edward. "Making the Move to Structured Programming." *Datamation.* June, 1975. pp. 52-56.

3. Some of the numbers quoted in this chapter would seem to indicate that the data processing industry's cost estimates are frequently off by 100 to 200 percent. But how large are the errors for large-scale projects outside the data processing industry? Go to the library and look up some material on the history of cost estimating. Now compare the errors in the software field with those that have been encountered in the construction of such things as military aircraft, large sports stadiums, school buildings, etc. Summarize your findings in tabular or barchart form along with some similar statistics on large software projects.

SOCIAL

CONTROVERSY

CHAPTER 6

ELECTRONIC PRIVACY INTRUSION

THE PEOPLE'S NEED FOR PRIVACY

SOCIETY'S NEED FOR INFORMATION

GOVERNMENT DOSSIERS

THE FEDERAL DATA CENTER

PRIVACY ABUSES

PRIVACY AND THE LAW
   The Fair Credit Reporting Act of 1970
   The Privacy Act of 1974
   Privacy Regulations for Business and Industry
   Probable Costs

CRIMINAL DATA FILES
   Manual Methods
   The National Crime Information Center

THE FUTURE

BIBLIOGRAPHY

EXERCISES

STUDENT PROJECTS

A few decades ago if anyone at all invaded your privacy it was almost always hometown newspapers or backfence gossips. But today sophisticated computers and other automatic devices are being used with increasing frequency in a modern electronic war against human privacy.

The knowledge that computers can be used against us in this way fills many Americans with intense feelings of irritation and despair. What exactly do we fear with such mindless intensity? A recent panel cartoon in *The Saturday Review of Literature* graphically illustrated one disturbing possibility. It showed a worried executive listening to a telephone message from a snoopy computer:

> "This is the computer Data Bank. Leave $100,000 in small bills in Locker 287 at the Port Authority Bus Terminal or I'll print out your complete dossier and send it to your wife."

In the real world computerized blackmail will probably occur only under the rarest of circumstances. However, blackmail is not our only problem; computers already threaten our privacy in many other subtle ways. In this chapter we will review some of these privacy threats and we will try to put them in the proper perspective against a backdrop of existing custom and law.

THE PEOPLE'S NEED FOR PRIVACY

Although it may be difficult for us to define exactly what we mean by the word—or to explain why we need it so badly—we all have intuitive feelings that we cannot function at all as human beings without at least some degree of privacy. People everywhere seem to feel the same way. Bathing, eating, sleeping, courtship, and other personal activities are almost always to some extent hidden from public view. Privacy conventions are also observed in conjunction with severe illness, death, childbirth and certain religious rites such as marriage and circumcision. Moreover, in our own country privacy is strongly connected with our concepts of freedom and liberty. It has been said that a free society is governed, in part, by the principle that:

> "There are frontiers . . . within which men should be inviolable, these frontiers being defined in terms of rules so long and widely accepted that their observance has entered into the very conception of what it is to be a normal human being."*

---

*Berlin, Isaiah. *Two Concepts of Liberty*. Oxford, England: Clarendon, 1963.

One of the most effective ways for a state to encourage conformity is to minimize privacy. Indeed, one definition of the word *private* is "to belong to oneself; not public or of the state". Sociologists have even evolved a formal proposition highlighting the inverse relationship between privacy and conformity:

"The greater the (perceived) probability that an action will be observed, the greater the probability that the action will be in compliance with the perceived social norms of the observer."*

A striking example of the extent to which conformity can be encouraged via the elimination of privacy occurred in Chinese prison camps during the Korean conflict. The methods used in minimizing privacy were both clever and effective. Each prisoner was constantly urged to report infractions of camp regulations by any of his fellow captives. If he made such a report he was always rewarded with extra food rations or other privileges, but the guilty party was never punished—or even reprimanded. At first it seemed that everyone benefitted from this novel arrangement. But within a short time all feelings of mutual trust had been eliminated, and the prisoners stopped cooperating with one another even when cooperation was clearly of mutual benefit. Sanitation efforts deteriorated, deaths from dysentery mounted, and, although the camps were lightly guarded, not one single prisoner managed to escape during the entire conflict.

When the prisoners were released at the end of the war, their attitudes were quite puzzling to Army psychologists. Filled with suspicion and resentment, they would hardly talk about themselves at all, but they talked endlessly about the smallest character flaws of their fellow captives. Moreover, unlike prisoners from previous wars, they showed only moderate interest in personal leaves, group parties, and other opportunities to socialize with their colleagues.

This was, of course, an extreme case of privacy deprivation. Even under worst-case conditions our privacy is not so severely threatened. But like these prisoners of war the privacy losses we now suffer do have important effects on the way we live and work and on the way we relate to the other people. What then is the problem? We know we need privacy— why don't we make arrangements to have it? Unfortunately, life is seldom that simple. We must somehow balance our own needs for privacy against society's needs for information.

---

* Simmel, Arnold. *Encyclopedia Brittanica. 1974.*

SOCIETY'S NEED FOR INFORMATION

Throughout the history of evolution the trend has always been toward organisms that can store and process increasingly large amounts of information. An organism stores information in two ways: in its genes (which direct the construction of duplicate offspring) and in its brain cells (which store information from the organism's past experiences). Specifically, the microbes that inhabited the earth three billion years ago are estimated to have held within their genes one million bits of information or roughly one-third the information-content of this textbook. Modern organisms are far more complex. Human beings, for example, hold the information-equivalent of 3,000 books in their genes and 3,000,000 books in their brains.

In 1977 Dr. Carl Sagan, a highly respected scientist at Cornell University, published a popular book, *The Dragons of Eden*,* in which he summarized the major evolutionary trends that have led us up to the present day. Figure 45, which was extracted from his book, shows how much information is stored in our genes, our brains, and external to our bodies in our books and libraries. Note that for the first 97 percent of the earth's history all living organisms carried more information in their genes than they carried in their brains. Reptiles were the first major exception. Of course reptiles were quite unintelligent in comparison with the more advanced creatures that later appeared on the evolutionary ladder, especially human beings. The powerful brains of humans contained 1000 times as much information as his genes. Later, as they learned to draw pictures, read and write, and program digital computers they began to store additional information *outside* their bodies. Carl Sagan's careful estimates indicate that our modern culture contains the equivalent of 100,000,000 books or about 30 times the information-storage capability of the human brain.

A prosperous society obviously needs enough *energy* and *materials* to keep all the available machines operating at peak efficiency. But a third thing is also needed: *Information*. America provides materials, energy and information to her citizens in surprisingly abundant quantities. (See Table 3). Each year we consume per capita about 15,000 pounds of energy-producing substances such as coal and oil; 19,000 pounds of solid materials such as sand, iron, and cement; and 75 pounds of newsprint and other paper products used largely in the distribution of information.

---

*Sagan, Carl. *The Dragons of Eden*. New York, New York: Random House, New York. 1977.

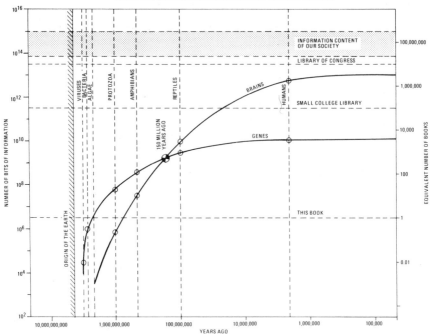

Figure 45: The information-storage capabilities of living creatures has steadily increased throughout the history of evolution. The simple algae that ruled the earth 3 billion years ago held within their genes the information-equivalent of one textbook. Today man holds about 3000 volumes of information in his genes and 1000 times as much in his brain. Moreover, the cultural information stored outside his body is estimated to be about 30 times as much as he can store in the cells of his brain.

Although the quantity of materials associated with the collection and distribution of information is relatively small, the information itself is a key element in maintaining a smoothly-functioning society. The "Green Revolution" provides us with an interesting example of the importance of accurate and timely information.

For many years America's highly productive agricultural technology has been widely admired in the underdeveloped areas of the world. Unfortunately, until recently, this advanced technology could not be exported directly because seed varieties that grow well in Oklahoma or Minnesota are not necessarily well adapted to the climatic conditions in Chile or Bangladesh. Moreover, for a number of reasons, local seed varieties already in use do not respond well to American farming methods. When chemical fertilizer is applied to the strains of wheat

TABLE 3: THREE THINGS THAT KEEP
A SOCIETY FUNCTIONING

	SUBSTANCE	QUANTITY (Pounds per Person per Year)	COMMENTS
ENERGY	Coal	5200	Principal uses = industrial and electrical power generation
ENERGY	Oil	5100	
ENERGY	Natural Gas	4400	98,500 cubic feet per person
MATERIALS	Sand, Gravel and Stone	17,600	
MATERIALS	Iron	800	
MATERIALS	Cement	500	Excluding water, these three materials plus the hydrocarbons listed above account for 90 percent of all the commercial substances we currently use.
INFORMATION	Newsprint	75	6570 pages of newspaper copy published each year per capita
INFORMATION	Computer Processing Steps	70,000,000,000,000 (steps)	Source = The Saturday Review of Literature
INFORMATION	Hours of Television Viewing	1300 (hours)	Source = TV guide ~ 3.5 hours per day

normally planted in Pakistan, for example, yields actually decline because the shaft grows so tall the wheat topples over onto the damp ground thus causing it to rot before harvest.

Because of these difficulties and others, a group of agricultural experts funded by the Ford Foundation and the Rockefeller Foundation compiled massive and complicated arrays of information on seed response, weather conditions, harvest times, etc., over a period of nearly a decade in developing rugged, dwarf varieties of wheat, rice, and other grains which were well adapted to the specific local conditions in various parts of the world. It was tiresome, tedious work but it paid handsome dividends. As the graph in Figure 46 shows, the new seed varieties have tripled per-acre food production in India and other countries.

The agricultural records that fostered the Green Revolution contained only impersonal information such as rainfall levels and harvest statistics. However, an efficient society must also have access to information of a more personal nature. Your medical records, for example, fall into this sensitive category. Much of the information stored in your medical file is quite routine, but it may also include items of life-saving consequences. The information on your blood type, for example, could save your life should you need an emergency transfusion. The details of your allergic reactions to penicillin and other miracle drugs could also fall into this life-saving category.

It may not be clear to you how your personal medical records can benefit society as a whole. But benefits of this type do, indeed, exist. For years doctors have been carefully recording precise information on their cancer cases. Recently these records have helped medical researchers formulate an important new conclusion about the fundamental nature of cancer. No longer regarded as a random hazard that strikes some unlucky people and not others, today cancer is believed to be largely produced by controllable activities like smoking, exposure to x-rays, and the consumption of certain food additives such as Red Dye Number 2. Now that these findings are available, people everywhere are in a better position to cut their cancer risks provided they are willing to make relatively minor changes in the way they live.

It would be possible to cite many other examples of the beneficial effects of accurate, reliable information. But perhaps a better way to illustrate how information helps us is to examine what happens when we don't have it.

The World War II battle for the Arnhem Bridge provides an excellent example. Although it involved a 65 mile drive through enemy territory coordinated with the largest drop of paratroopers in history, the bridge seemed like a reachable objective because of the information provided by British intelligence experts that it was guarded only by "old men on bicycles". In reality it was guarded by battle-hardened veterans in heavily-armored Panzers units.

Further information gaps developed when the radio transmitters provided to the field commanders had insufficient range to reach company headquarters and when the encircled paratroopers were unable to signal their aircraft that the prearranged drop zones had been overrun by the Germans. In addition, the partisan reports on enemy troop deployments were largely useless because of language difficulties, faulty observation, and the inability to distinguish between reliable and unreliable descriptions.

These communication breakdowns contributed to one of the most appalling military disasters of the war. All the participating units

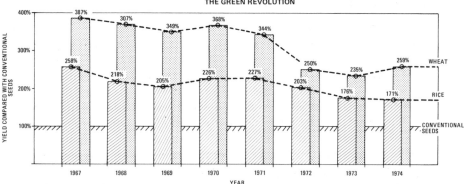

Figure 46: Accurate, timely information collected over a period of nearly a decade gave the world the Green Revolution which is currently providing nourishing food for millions of poor people in underdeveloped areas of the world. As these barcharts show, crop yields for those farms in India now being planted with the new seed varieties have increased on the average between 70 and 290 percent.

experienced heavy casualties. But the 10,000 British troops holding the bridge were nearly obliterated; during the nine-day engagement 80 percent of them were killed, wounded, or captured. Moreover, the Allies lost precious tanks and armoured vehicles by the hundreds, losses which had detrimental impacts on the remainder of the European campaign.

The Allied troops who fought against the "old men on bicycles" at Arnhem quickly learned to appreciate the consequences of inaccurate information. These consequences are relatively easy to spot in a military battle because the objectives are so clearly defined and because the battle takes place over a relatively brief interval. It is a little harder to see how garbled or inaccurate information harms our peace-time society. But the harm exists, nevertheless. For example, it has been estimated that we pay about 2 percent extra for everything we buy because of other people's bad checks and unpaid charge accounts. These losses occur, in part, because credit investigations often result in muddy information on the client's financial habits. Better credit investigation would surely help cut these losses.

It is not hard to cite dozens of other instances where better information would help our society function more effectively. What then is the problem? If society needs more reliable information why don't we make arrangements to have it? Unfortunately, life is seldom that simple. We must somehow balance society's needs for information against our own needs for privacy.

GOVERNMENT DOSSIERS

Although they would be quick to concede that government agencies have legitimate needs for information, many experts believe our government has already collected more information on our personal lives than it could ever use. The State of Indiana, for example, maintains 199 file systems containing 82 million dossiers. This means that there are approximately 16 dossiers for each of the 5 million Indiana residents.* The files maintained by the Federal government are considerably larger. They are estimated to contain at least 4 billion dossiers or an average of 18 for each American citizen. The information in these files is surprisingly comprehensive. It includes, among other things, highly personal data on educational attainments, psychiatric profiles, police records, alcohol and drug addiction, food purchases and consumption, income statistics, school grades, and property ownership.

What is the purpose of all this information? The tabulations in Figure 47 summarize some of the things the government is trying to accomplish. As you can see, most of the files are intended to fulfill reasonably valid objectives. However, many other files kept by the government seem entirely frivolous and unnecessary. The Tennessee Valley Authority, for example, keeps one on all customers who own electric appliances. The Air Force keeps one on religious preferences of uniformed personnel. A federal data bank holds the names and addresses of all adoptive parents. Another contains the names of the children of migrant workers. Moreover, the authority for collecting these files is often shaky and ill defined. A senate investigation turned up the fact that 17 percent of federal data banks have no statutory authority whatsoever and 84 percent have no explicit authority. In other words, our government collects information it has no clear legal mandate to collect. A separate study revealed that the citizens whose activities are being scrutinized are ignorant of the existence of the data 42 percent of the time.

THE FEDERAL DATA CENTER

If the government has no legal justification for collecting much of the personal information it now collects, it has an even weaker justification for consolidating it within one centralized agency. But a few years ago many Americans were suddenly horrified to learn that Washington's technocrats were planning to do exactly that. The concept, which they called the Federal Data Center, had been floating around for a long time

---

*Privacy Journal. April 1977, Vol. III, NO. 6, pg. 6.

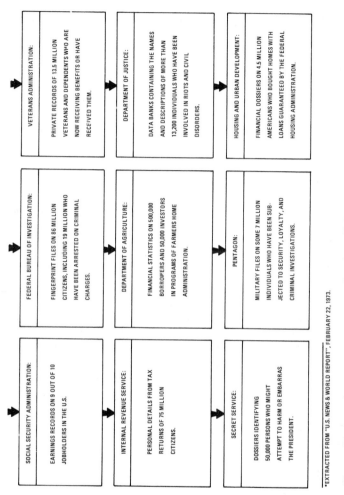

THE GOVERNMENT'S FILES OF PERSONAL INFORMATION*

SOCIAL SECURITY ADMINISTRATION:

EARNINGS RECORDS ON 9 OUT OF 10 JOBHOLDERS IN THE U.S.

FEDERAL BUREAU OF INVESTIGATION:

FINGERPRINT FILES ON 86 MILLION CITIZENS, INCLUDING 19 MILLION WHO HAVE BEEN ARRESTED ON CRIMINAL CHARGES.

VETERANS ADMINISTRATION:

PRIVATE RECORDS OF 13.5 MILLION VETERANS AND DEPENDENTS WHO ARE NOW RECEIVING BENEFITS OR HAVE RECEIVED THEM.

INTERNAL REVENUE SERVICE:

PERSONAL DETAILS FROM TAX RETURNS OF 75 MILLION CITIZENS.

DEPARTMENT OF AGRICULTURE:

FINANCIAL STATISTICS ON 500,000 BORROWERS AND 50,000 INVESTORS IN PROGRAMS OF FARMERS HOME ADMINISTRATION.

DEPARTMENT OF JUSTICE:

DATA BANKS CONTAINING THE NAMES AND DESCRIPTIONS OF MORE THAN 13,200 INDIVIDUALS WHO HAVE BEEN INVOLVED IN RIOTS AND CIVIL DISORDERS.

SECRET SERVICE:

DOSSIERS IDENTIFYING 50,000 PERSONS WHO MIGHT ATTEMPT TO HARM OR EMBARRAS THE PRESIDENT.

PENTAGON:

MILITARY FILES ON SOME 7 MILLION INDIVIDUALS WHO HAVE BEEN SUB- JECTED TO SECURITY, LOYALTY, AND CRIMINAL INVESTIGATIONS.

HOUSING AND URBAN DEVELOPMENT:

FINANCIAL DOSSIERS ON 4.5 MILLION AMERICANS WHO BOUGHT HOMES WITH LOANS GUARANTEED BY THE FEDERAL HOUSING ADMINISTRATION.

*EXTRACTED FROM "U.S. NEWS & WORLD REPORT", FEBRUARY 22, 1973.

Figure 47: A modern government cannot function efficiently without collecting information on the personal lives of its citizens: But many knowledgeable experts believe that our government has already collected more information than it actually needs. Recent studies indicate that federal data files contain approximately 18 dossiers for each American citizen. Any gains that can be achieved from accumulating additional information and consolidating it into a centrally located data center must be carefully weighed against the added potential for abuse.

but it was first formally proposed by the Social Science Research Council in April of 1965. Centralizing the records that were scattered among a dozen or more agencies seemed to have several advantages: it would cut costs and improve efficiency; it would provide more security for the files; and it would allow easy cross-correlations among the various data entries.

To its originators the idea seemed entirely non-controversial. After all, no new information would be collected; the available information would merely be moved to a new location. But almost as soon as the new proposal had been advanced, it became the focus of a raging controversy. What were the people so worried about? Why did they find the Federal Data Center so disturbing? Computer expert Paul Armer voiced one overriding worry:

> "I believe that any instance in which a great deal of information about an individual is concentrated in one place represents a threat to his privacy. In our existing systems, privacy is assured under all but the most unusual circumstances by the sheer cost and inconvenience of the search."*

One of Armer's colleagues Bernard S. Benson felt even more uneasy. After a lengthy study of the potential hazards of the Federal Data Center concept, he concluded that "the concentration of information in the form (proposed) can be catastrophically dangerous".

And yet it was the general public that was most outraged. Whenever the Federal Data Center was mentioned, it conjured up images of the country being taken over by a heedless army of computers aided by swarms of bureaucrats having fingertip access to cradle-to-grave information on millions of Americans. Nor did the people sit around and complain; they acted. They wrote letters, made phone calls, and buttonholed their congressmen. Finally, as *The Nation's Business* wryly observed: "A campaign led by senators, representatives, and various public and private organizations shamed the Johnson Administration into abandoning the idea."

However, even after the President made his public stand, the Data Center concept refused to die a quiet death. Several attempts were made to revive it in a disguised form by using time-sharing hardware. But there are serious technical difficulties with this approach. For one thing when personal records are kept by the subject's name, cross-correlations between the various data entries are difficult and elusive. Is "William Jenkins" the same man as "Bill Jenkins"? If the addresses match he

---

*Armer, Paul. "Computer Technology and Surveillance". *Computers and People.* September, 1975. pp. 8-11.

probably is—although they could be father and son. If the age is the same he is almost certainly the same man provided the address is the same. But what if the addresses differ? Did he move? Are they two different men? Or is there an error in the records?

Because of these and other difficulties those who face the task of assembling computer files would like to have a "universal identifier" a number assigned to each person preferably at birth—to eliminate ambiguities.

Of course, privacy advocates oppose the existence of universal identifiers. They maintain that separate records are desirable because they help protect the privacy of the individual. For one thing the universal identifier tends to make records available for purposes other than their original intent. In addition, unauthorized persons could extract personal information from computers too easily if all they need is readily available Social Security numbers or other universal identifiers.

PRIVACY ABUSES

But all this is so speculative, has anyone actually been harmed by the information stored in computers? Has this information ever been found to be biased and inaccurate? And has this information ever been used for harmful or sinister purposes? You bet it has. Consider these actual case histories:

- An ex-Marine from Illinois was plagued for years with mistaken information in a computer operated by the FBI's National Crime Information Center. He was jailed several times as a deserter although he was not guilty.
- A St. Louis editor was refused auto insurance when "data" on drug use and irrational behavior turned out to a quick skim of neighborhood gossip that earned the investigator $1.45. In a subsequent court case, he won $40,000 in damages.
- A Massachusetts man served in prison for a crime he committed. He got a full pardon, moved 1,000 miles away to start a new life and entered a community college. Soon, he was kicked out because of his past. A data bank did not have the information that he had been pardoned.
- A District of Columbia woman had a part-time government job but when she tried to get full-time work with the Air Force she lost her part-time job. A data bank said she had a criminal record. Two years later she finally managed to prove the criminal record was her husband's not hers.

- A 26-year-old Long Island woman was hassled for more than a year because her name appeared in a federal computer file on international drug smugglers. She was forced to undergo strip searches at airports several times by U. S. Customs Service Agents. She is now suing the government for $90,000.

When we read these case histories, we get the impression that the privacy rights of the people involved have been grossly violated. But what exactly are our rights of privacy? Are these rights specified by the Constitution? Perhaps they should be but they're not. The word "privacy" is not mentioned anywhere in our Constitution. Apparently, privacy was not viewed as much of a problem by the founding fathers in the early days of our republic. In the intervening years, however, there have been certain legal opinions and congressional actions designed to help define and clarify our rights of privacy.

PRIVACY AND THE LAW

In 1890 Louis Brandeis and Samuel Warren published an article entitled"The Right of Privacy" in which they outlined a fundamental philosophy which many people, even today, regard as quite modern and enlightened. Thirty years later in 1920, after his appointment to the Supreme Court, Justice Brandeis again addressed the concept of privacy when he wrote in a somewhat indignant minority opinion:

"The right to be let alone is... the most comprehensive of rights and the right most valued by civilized men."

Despite his efforts, however, a general right to privacy was not explicitly affirmed by the U. S. Supreme Court until 1965. In that year the decision in *Griswold versus Connecticut* invalidated a state law prohibiting the use of contraceptives even by married couples. The majority opinion written by Justice Douglas relied upon

"A right of privacy older than the Bill of Rights—older than our political parties, older than our school system."

In essence, the court held that the law in question could not stand because the only practical methods of enforcement would grossly violate the privacy rights of Connecticut residents.

In recent years several other government mandates have further clarified our individual privacy rights. The Fair Credit Reporting Act of

1970, for example, has given each citizen the right to know what information is being held on him or her by credit bureaus and to challenge the accuracy of that information. The Privacy Act of 1974 is another giant stride forward. It provides comprehensive guidelines on the proper methods for the collection and use of personal information by the federal government.

The Fair Credit Reporting Act of 1970

The Fair Credit Reporting Act of 1970 represents an attempt to protect the privacy rights of individuals while assuring credit agencies, insurance companies, and others reasonable access to the information they need. These five short introductory paragraphs from the act itself illustrate some of the difficulties that are inherent to this delicate balancing act:

"The banking system is dependent upon fair and accurate credit reporting. Inaccurate credit reports directly impair the efficiency of the banking system, and unfair credit reporting methods undermine the public confidence which is essential to the continued functioning of the banking system."

"An elaborate mechanism has been developed for investigating and evaluating the credit worthiness, credit standing, credit capacity, character, and general reputation of consumers."

"Consumer reporting agencies have assumed a vital role in assembling and evaluating consumer credit and other information on consumers."

"There is a need to ensure that consumer reporting agencies exercise their grave responsibilities with fairness, impartiality, and a respect for the consumer's right to privacy."

"It is the purpose of this title to require that consumer reporting agencies adopt reasonable procedures for meeting the needs of commerce for consumer credit, personnel, insurance, and other information in a manner which is fair and equitable to the consumer with regard to the confidentiality, accuracy, relevancy, and proper utilization of such information in accordance with the requirements of this title."[*]

The main body of the act carefully restricts the distribution of the information contained in credit files to three specific types of end users:

---

[*]Smith, Robert Ellis and Snyder, Keith D. *Compilation of State and Federal Privacy Laws, 1977-78 Edition.* The Privacy Journal, Washington, D.C. 1977.

1. Those who have a valid court order.
2. Those who have written permission from the consumer.
3. Those who need the information for a valid credit or business transaction, employment or insurance investigation, or those who need it to facilitate the granting of a government license requiring proof of financial responsibility.

The act specifically forbids the disclosure of obsolete information even to those agencies that otherwise qualify for access. For example, bankruptcies that predate the report by more than 14 years are to be deleted. So are the following items if they are more than 7 years old: legal suits and judgments, paid tax liens, debts placed in the hands of collection agencies, and records of arrest, conviction, or imprisonment.

Moreover, the consumer is given the right to examine his file (exclusive of medical information) and to challenge the accuracy of its contents. If there is a dispute over the material it contains, he is allowed to provide his own explanation of the facts and to insert the explanation in his file.

The Fair Credit Reporting Act of 1970 is no mere statement of abstract legalistic principles. It has real teeth. Any agency that fails to comply with its requirements is legally liable in the amount of the actual damages sustained by the consumer plus court costs and reasonable attorney's fees. Those who obtain information from the files under false pretenses or disclose information to unauthorized individuals can be fined as much as $5000 and imprisoned for as much as one year.

The Privacy Act of 1974

As it was originally framed, The Privacy Act of 1974 covered information-handling practices by state and local governments and private industry as well as the federal government. It was subsequently pared down to apply only to the federal government and even at the federal level some activities—notably the Criminal Justice Information System operated by the FBI—were excluded from regulation.

However, even in its emasculated form, the act provides individuals with powerful controls over their privacy rights. In particular, it gives them the right to see their files (under certain conditions) and to point out any errors contained in these files. It also requires that the government inform individuals when they must supply information by law. Finally, it forbids the sale or distribution of this information for any purposes other than the one for which it was gathered in the first place.

The introduction of the Privacy Act recognizes that ordinary people are directly affected by the "collection, maintenance, use, and dissemination of personal information by Federal agencies" and that the use of "computers and sophisticated information technology, while essential to the efficient operations of the Government, has greatly magnified the harm to individual privacy that can occur."

The purpose of the act, which covers 15 single-spaced pages, is spelled out in three short introductory paragraphs. Specifically with respect to federal data files, the act is designed to:

1. Permit an individual to determine what records pertaining to him are collected, maintained, used, or disseminated...
2. Permit an individual to prevent records pertaining to him . . . for a particular purpose from being used or made available for another purpose without his consent.
3. Permit an individual to gain access to information pertaining to him in Federal agency records, to have a copy made of all or any portion thereof, and to correct or amend such records."*

Those who willfully defy the provisions of the act are subject to civil penalties equal to the actual damages incurred by the individual as a result of their actions but "in no case shall a person entitled to recovery receive less than the sum of $1,000 and...the costs of the action together with reasonable attorneys fees as determined by the court." Criminal actions are also spelled out in the act with fines up to $5,000 for those who willfully break its provisions.

In compliance with the Privacy Act, the U. S. Government Printing Office is currently distributing a publication called *Protecting Your Right of Privacy*. It includes a 410-page section they call a "Digest" listing those federal records containing potentially sensitive personal information. The "Digest" describes the files maintained by 82 Federal agencies and it explains how ordinary people can gain access to their own files. A photograph of the "Digest" is presented in Figure 48. If you would like to find out what information the government has on you, you can start by sending $5.00 to:

> Superintendent of Documents
> U. S. Government Printing Office
> Washington, D. C. 20402

Ask for "Protecting Your Right to Privacy" Stock No. 022-000-00120-5.

---

*Smith, Robert Ellis and Snyder, Keith D. *Compilation of State and Federal Privacy Laws, 1977-78 Edition*. The Privacy Journal, Washington, D.C. 1977.

If you would like to find out what one of the largest *private* credit agencies knows about your personal life, you can send a signed letter listing your social security number and containing a check for $4.00 to:

TRW Credit Data
P. O. Box 5450
Orange, California 92667

Within a few days you will receive a computer printout of your data file together with a form soliciting any comments you may have on the items contained in that file.

Privacy Regulations for Business and Industry

Through vigorous lobbying and other political pressures, business and industry managed to escape regulation by the Privacy Act of 1974 but that situation is strictly temporary. At this writing there are more than 100 privacy bills pending before the U. S. Congress and the various state legislatures. These bills will attempt to protect the individual in a variety of ways. Among other things the ones that eventually become law will probably:*

- Require that court orders be obtained before banks, credit card companies and other firms turn over information about individual accounts to police, FBI and other Government investigators.
- Insist that private firms adhere to standards that would stop the collecting of information that they do not need.
- Outlaw "pretext" interviews in which an investigator impersonates a doctor or clergyman to squeeze out information that should be kept private.
- Make public and private organizations destroy or update old credit and financial information after a reasonable period of time.

In addition, the specific provisions of the new acts dealing with computer data banks would, most likely, be structured along these lines:

"Companies would probably have to report all...files or data banks once a year to a government body. Individuals listed in these data banks would probably have to be notified that they are in such files, and they would undoubtedly have access to their own file. They would also have a chance to correct any errors in their file. They

---

*"Striking Back at the Super Snoops", *Time*, July 18, 1977, pp. 16-21.

498   PROTECTING YOUR RIGHT TO PRIVACY

(d) The General Counsel of the Commission is responsible for providing legal interpretation of the Privacy Act of 1974, and for preparing all agency rules and notices for official publication in compliance with the Act.

(e) Commission employees will be informed of all the implications of their actions in this area, including especially:

(1) That there are criminal penalties for knowing and willful unauthorized disclosure of material within a system of records; for willful failure to publish a public notice of the existence of a system of records; and for knowingly and willfully requesting or obtaining records under false pretenses;

(2) That the Commission may be subject to civil suit due to failure to amend an individual's record in accordance with his request or failure to review his request in conformity with § 3b.224; refusal to comply with an individual's request of access to a record under § 3b.221; willful or intentional failure to maintain a record accurately pursuant to § 3b.201(b) and consequently a determination is made which is adverse to the individual; or willful or intentional failure to comply with any other provision of the Privacy Act of 1974 or rule promulgated thereunder in such way as to have an adverse [effect on] individual.

§ 3b.204 Safeguarding records, manual and comp[uter-based] systems.

(a) The administrative and physical controls to protect the information in the manual and computer-based record systems from unauthorized access or disclosure will be specified for each system in the FEDERAL REGISTER. The system managers, who are responsible for providing protection and accountability of such records at all times and for insuring that the records are secured in proper containers whenever they are not in use or under direct control of authorized persons, will be identified for each system of records in the FEDERAL REGISTER.

(b) Whenever records in the manual or computer-based record systems, including input and output documents, punched cards, and magnetic tapes or disks, are not under the personal control of an authorized person, they will be stored in lockable containers and/or in a secured room, or in alternative storage systems which furnish an equivalent or greater degree of physical security. In this regard, the Commission may refer to security guidelines prepared by the General Services Administration, the Department of Commerce (National Bureau of Standards), or other agencies with appropriate knowledge and expertise.

(c) Access to and use of records will only be permitted to persons pursuant to §§ 3b.221, 3b.224, and 3b.225. Access to areas where records are stored will be limited to those persons whose official duties require work in such areas. Proper control of data, in any form, associated with the manual and computer-based record systems will be maintained at all times, including maintenance of an accounting of removal of the records from the storage area.

Subpart C—Rules for Disclosure of Records

§ 3b.220 Notification of maintenance of records to individuals concerned.

(a) Upon written request, either in person or by mail, to the appropriate system manager specified for each system of records, an individual will be notified whether a system of records maintained by the Commission and named by the individual contains a record or records pertaining to him and filed under his individual name, or some other identifying particular.

(b) The system manager may require appropriate identification pursuant to § 3b.222, and if necessary, may request from the individual additional information needed to locate the record which the individual ... reasonably be expected to ... but not limited to ... birth, and a

(d) "For ... in all section ... circumstances such ... a search for any ... quested records from ... storage, field offices, or other ... [docu]ments is required; where a voluminous amount of data is involved; where information on other individuals must be separated or expunged from the record; or where consultations are required with other agencies or with others having a substantial interest in the determination of the request.

§ 3b.221 Access of records to individuals concerned.

(a) Upon written request, either in person or by mail, to the appropriate system manager specified for each system of records, any individual may gain access to records or information in a system of records pertaining to him and filed under his individual name, or some other identifying particular, and to have a copy made of all or any portion thereof in a form comprehensible to him.

(b) A person of his own choosing may accompany the individual to whom the record pertains when the record is disclosed [see § 3b.222(e)].

(c) Before disclosure, the following procedure may apply:

Medical or psychological records will be disclosed directly to the individual to whom they pertain unless, in the judgment of the system manager, in consultation with a medical doctor or a psychologist, access to such records could have an adverse effect upon the individual. When the system manager and a doctor determine that the disclosure of such information could have an adverse effect upon the individual to whom it pertains, the system manager may transmit such information to a medical doctor named by the requesting individual.

(d) The system manager will provide a written acknowledgement of the receipt of a request for access within ten days of receipt (excluding Saturdays, Sundays, and legal public holidays). Such acknowledgement may, if necessary, request any additional information needed to locate the record which the individual may reasonably be expected to know, and may require appropriate identification pursuant to § 3b.222 of this part. No acknowledgement is required if access can be granted within the ten-day period.

(1) If access can be granted, the system manager will notify the individual, in writing, as to when, and whether access will be granted in person or by mail; that access will be provided within ten days of the receipt of the request, excluding Saturdays, Sundays, and legal holidays). If the system manager is unable to provide access within ten days of receipt of the request, he will inform the individual in writing of the reasons therefor (for good cause shown) and when it is anticipated that access will be granted. A revised date of access indicated in the written notification to the individual. If this date cannot be met, the system manager will advise the individual in writing of the delay, the reasons therefor (for good cause shown), and of a revised date when access will be granted. Such extensions will not exceed thirty days from receipt of the request (excluding Saturdays, Sundays, and legal public holidays).

(2) If access cannot be granted, the system manager will inform the individual, in writing, within twenty days of receipt (excluding Saturdays, Sundays, and legal public holidays) of the refusal of his request; the reasons for the refusal; the right of the individual, within thirty days of receipt of the refusal, to request in writing a review of the refusal by the Chairman of the Federal Power Commission, 825 North Capitol Street, NE., Washington, D.C. 20426, or by an officer designated by the Chairman pursuant to § 3b.224(f); and the right of the individual to seek advice or assistance from the system manager in obtaining such a review.

(e) The Chairman, or officer designated pursuant to § 3b.224(f), not later than thirty days (excluding Saturdays, Sundays, and legal public holidays) from the date of receipt of the individual's request for review will complete such review, unless, for good cause shown, the

Figure 48: In compliance with the Privacy Act of 1974, the U. S. Government Printing Office has published this guide listing the personal files being held by 82 Federal agencies. If you suspect that a particular Federal agency is keeping potentially damaging or incorrect information on your life, you can follow the instructions in the guide to contact them and obtain your own personal copy.

might also have an opportunity to say who (outside the company keeping the file) may or may not see it."*

Attitudes differ as to how the new privacy bills will affect the businesses they are intended to regulate. Joseph L. Gibson, senior

*"Will the Privacy Issue Hit Industry?", *Industry Week*, May 5, 1975, pp. 41-43.

attorney of Marcor, Inc. has developed a reasonably sober appraisal of the ultimate impacts. Although he believes the overall effects will be decidedly negative, "privacy legislation will not in all probability, put any big business out of business, but it will most certainly raise substantially the cost of goods and services. If privacy legislation raises the cost of a credit report, for example, credit grantors such as large department store chains will order fewer reports. Credit grantors will then either restrict the amount of credit that they give . . . or charge the credit applicant a fee to process his application."

The people at TRW, a giant computer firm which keeps records on 55 million people, are considerably more worried. When one of their executives, Edward J. Brennan, Jr. was asked about the likely effects of the new legislation, he replied that: "a number of bills around would literally put us out of business overnight.* . . . the requirements for notifying each person in the file that it (contains) information on his life would cost us 20 percent more than our gross revenues."

Who will pay these extra costs? The answer is quite simple—the general public. There is no other candidate. For as Paul Armer has condescendingly observed:

> "The proposers of (privacy) regulations often seem to assume that the added costs will be borne by the credit bureaus, presumably out of their profits. This is nonsense. If the credit bureaus are to stay in business, the added costs must be passed along to the consumer—credit will become more expensive."**

How much more expensive? When the Privacy Act of 1974 was signed into law no one had any clear idea how much the total tab would be. Estimates on the cost of regulating private firms were even more ill-defined. But sketchy studies have now been completed and the results are not entirely encouraging.

Probable Costs

In 1975 the OMB (Office of Managment and Budget) made a crude economic study that indicated the added costs resulting from the Privacy Act of 1974 would probably run somewhere between $200 million and $300 million per year. These extra expenditures can and will be absorbed within the operating budgets of the various federal agencies. No other

---

*He surely meant the credit business not the entire TRW Corporation!

**Armer, Paul. "The Individual: His Privacy, Self Image, and Obsolescence". *Computers and People*. June, 1975. pp. 18-23.

outcome is possible. Government agencies can't go out of business no matter how costly their procedures turn out to be! But businessmen may encounter greater difficulties in coping with the new realities if and when a business version of the bill clears Congress.

Data Processing specialist Robert Goldstein has developed a computer model which projects industry costs. It includes the effects of three types of regulations:

1. controls on operating procedures
2. access rights of the subjects
3. usage control by the subjects.

Goldstein's simulations, some of which are summarized in Table 4, indicate that the proposed restrictions would increase the annual operating costs to a substantial degree. Of the three cases considered two of them are projected to incur additional costs of $2 million per year and one of them (the credit file) would incur additional costs of $20 million per year. Expressed in percentage terms, the privacy protection features of the new bills would increase annual expenditures by 15% to 146% depending on the type of file and its usage rates.

The new privacy laws will also result in additional hidden and indirect costs. Government monitoring, for instance, will add to our tax bills. A similar watchdog bureau which monitored wages and prices during World War II started out with a staff numbering a few dozen workers. But it quickly began to grow and by the war's end it had ballooned to 17,000. Right now we don't know exactly how much monitoring the new privacy laws will require but if they're like other government activities we will surely need a small army of bureaucrats.

The fact that the files must be divulged to the subjects on request will add another hidden cost. This reporting will, in many cases, reduce the accuracy and frankness of the information and hence its usefulness. A similar thing has already happened to some of the records kept by our school systems. Now that parents have a right to see any academic folders containing personal data on their youngster's progress, the teachers who fill out the forms are less candid than they once were. Today the year-by-year student reports which once helped the rest of the staff understand the behavioral difficulties and learning problems of their students are so general and evasive that few teachers even bother to open them anymore, much less study their contents.

The records in other areas of our society now being mined for the useful information they contain may soon be similarly emasculated. In particular, employee evaluations and medical records could lose much of

TABLE 4: THE ESTIMATED COSTS OF
COMPLYING WITH PRIVACY REGULATIONS*

ORIGINAL SYSTEM CHARACTERISTICS			
PURPOSE	NUMBER OF SUBJECTS	NUMBER OF CHARACTERS IN DATA BASE	ANNUAL OPERATING COST
1. Medical Information	1,000	3500 million	$4 million
2. Insurance Information	3 million	3600 million	$13 million
3. Credit Information	35 million	3500 million	$14 million

ADDITIONAL COSTS ASSOCIATED WITH PRIVACY			
PURPOSE	PRIVACY CONVERSION COST (REPROGRAMMING)	ANNUAL PRIVACY COST	ANNUAL PRIVACY COST AS A % OF ANNUAL OPERATING COST
1. Medical Information	$540,000	$1,800,000	45%
2. Insurance Information	$570,000	$1,900,000	15%
3. Credit Information	$1,400,000	$20,400,000	146%

*Source: Goldstein, Robert C. and Nolan, Richard L."Personal Privacy versus The Corporate Computer", *Harvard Business Review*, March-April, 1975. pp. 62-70.

their effectiveness because of the new disclosure laws. When this happens nothing dramatic will occur. The negative effects will be quite subtle. Efficiencies will decline slightly. Less qualified people will be hired by companies. A few thousand hospital patients will recover slower than they might have—some of them will die needlessly. But no one will know what has caused these problems. And no one will suggest that we go back to the previous system because by the time any ill effects show up the new methods will have become an integral part of our culture.

CRIMINAL DATA FILES

Strange as it may seem, the computer is not universally regarded as the main culprit in the war against human privacy. As a matter of fact, many experts contend that computerized systems, in some respects, protect our privacy better than manual systems. This position is not entirely untenable. For one thing privacy problems existed long before computers were practical. As Joseph Weizenbaum points out in his book, *Computer Power and Human Reason*:

"The Nazis . . . controlled the German people and implemented the systematic transportation of millions of people to death camps . . . when there were still no computers."*

Nor did our own country have any computers during the war. But this did not keep Army censors from reading nearly every letter mailed American servicemen.

In order to help you gauge the relative security levels of manual and computerized systems we will examine the procedures that would be followed for the specific case of a juvenile arrest record.

Manual Methods

When the author of this textbook was 15 years old he was arrested for vandalizing a warehouse. An arrest record describing the events is presented at the top of Figure 49. As you can see, the manual record consists of about 100 words which describe the circumstances of the incident and the disposition of the case.

Manual data files are typically stored in manila folders standing on edge in metal filing cabinets. If the system involves a large number of folders, a controlling librarian may keep track of them and make sure they are eventually returned to their proper locations. In smaller systems the files are generally unattended. Either way the user normally carries the folder of interest back to his work station where abuses can occur. The records can be copies, destroyed, or altered by nearly anyone with routine access. Moreover, an unsophisticated intruder such as the night janitor can, with relative ease, read the files and perhaps alter their contents.

*Weizenbaum, Joseph. *Computer Power and Human Reason*. New York, New York: W. H. Freeman, 1976.

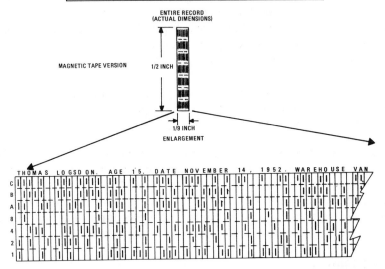

ARREST RECORDS: MANUAL FILE AND MAGNETIC TAPE VERSIONS

MANUAL VERSION

o THOMAS LOGSDON. AGE 15. DATE NOVEMBER 14, 1952. WAREHOUSE VANDALISM.
o THE SUSPECT ACCOMPANIED BY FOUR COMPANIONS ILLEGALLY ENTERED THE SIMS
o AND BRODERICK WAREHOUSE TO SET OFF FIREWORKS AND RIDE BICYCLES ON THE
o HARDWOOD FLOORS. DAMAGES TO THE PREMISES INCLUDED THE SCATTERING OF
o WAREHOUSE SALES RECORDS AND THE THEFT OF TWO CASES OF EMPTY POP
o BOTTLES. (APPROXIMATE VALUE $0.40). A COMPLAINT WAS FILED BY THE
o WAREHOUSE OWNERS. WHEN APPREHENDED, THE SUSPECT CONFESSED TO THE CRIME.
o PARENTS MADE RESTITUTION AND SUSPECT WAS RELEASED IN THEIR CUSTODY.

ENTIRE RECORD
(ACTUAL DIMENSIONS)

MAGNETIC TAPE VERSION   1/2 INCH

1/9 INCH
ENLARGEMENT

THOMAS LOGSDON. AGE 15. DATE NOVEMBER 14, 1952. WAREHOUSE VAN

Figure 49: The author's 1952 arrest record is shown in manual form and in the form it would have if it were coded for storage on a magnetic tape. The manual version can be deciphered by anyone who gains possession. The computerized version can be deciphered only by a relatively sophisticated individual with possession of the tape, knowledge of computer technology, and access to the proper machinery. Note that the entire manual record can be stored on a strip of tape only ½ inch wide and ⅑ inch long. A single reel of magnetic tape coded in the same way could hold at least 20,000 criminal records like the one shown at the top of this figure.

A computerized data file, on the other hand, is harder to decipher. If you can't operate the computer, you can't find out what information it contains. And even if you can get a printout by foul means you usually can't alter the files unless you know one or more secret passwords which allow you to operate some of the computer's hardware units.

The sketches at the bottom of Figure 49 show how the author's arrest record would be coded and placed on a magnetic tape. As you can see, a binary code is used in which 1's are represented by vertical marks. These tiny magnetized marks are packed together closer than the grooves on a phonograph record. As a result, a typical magnetic tape $\frac{1}{2}$-inch wide and 2400 feet long can store about 20,000 criminal records such as the one in Figure 49.

If you had such a criminal record would you prefer that it be stored electronically for direct computer access, or would you prefer that it be stored manually in a file folder? If it is stored manually it can be read by nearly anyone with physical access to the files but at least it would likely be confined to a relatively small geographical area. On the other hand, if your record is stored in a computer equipped with time-sharing hardware it could be whisked around the country at the speed of light.

The National Crime Information Center

Since 1969 criminal records have been stored in a special computer network called the National Crime Information Center (NCIC). As of 1975 this nationwide network contained 5,500,000 active records broken down as shown in Table 5. Police departments all over the country can access these extensive files using teletype terminals located in each stationhouse. A total of 62,000,000 inquiries were made during 1975 resulting in 323,000 "hits", e.g., verifications that recovered property had actually been stolen or that a suspect in custody was wanted in connection with another crime.*

Offhand, it would seem that the National Crime Information Center constitutes an admirable use of electronic technology. After all, it helps insure that stolen property will be returned to its rightful owner and that if a suspect is apprehended, he or she will be charged with all crimes he is believed to have committed. However, there have been heated arguments against the widespread adoption of the NCIC system. For example, when the city of Wayland, Massachusetts, was on the verge of hooking the local police department into the system, computer expert Stanley Robinson mustered some surprisingly persuasive arguments against its utilization.

Among other things he maintained that the "criminal histories" maintained by the NCIC are usually nothing more than ordinary arrest records. In many urban ghettos nearly every adult male has been arrested at one time or another during intense police "sweeps" on the area. Thus the system tends to discriminate against "the poor, the black, and the political radicals ('troublemakers')".**

---

*Adams, J. Mack and Haden, Douglas H. *Social Effects of Computer Use and Misuse*. New York, New York: John Wiley, 1976.

**The Quality of Justice in Lower Criminal Courts of Metropolitan Boston*. Lawyers Committee for Civil Rights Under Law, 15 Broad Street, Boston (1970).

TABLE 5
CONTENTS OF THE FILES MAINTAINED
BY THE NATIONAL CRIME INFORMATION CENTER

TYPE OF RECORD	NUMBER OF ITEMS	COMMENTS
WANTED PERSONS	155,000	The first five types of records in the list were first entered in the files in 1967.
VEHICLES	859,000	Most vehicles listed in the files were stolen. In 1968 the vehicles file was expanded to include stolen aircraft and snowmobiles.
LICENSE PLATES	316,000	
ARTICLES	1,050,000	Stolen articles are listed in the files only if they are "identifiable".
GUNS	890,000	
SECURITIES	1,610,000	Securities file was added in 1968.
BOATS	12,000	Boat file was added in 1969.
CRIMINAL HISTORY RECORDS	607,000	Criminal history records were added to the files in 1971.
TOTAL NO. OF ACTIVE RECORDS	5,500,000	
ANNUAL "TRANSACTIONS"	5,100,000	The number of "transactions" averages 170,000 per day.
ANNUAL "HITS"	323,000	"Hits" average 885 per day. The peak hour of

Source = Adams, J. Mack and Hayden, Douglas H. *Social Effects of Computer Use and Misuse,* New York, New York: John Wiley, 1976.

Another difficulty is that, at present, many forms of arrest records do not contain any information on dropped charges nor the result of trials or appeals. The police and the court systems faithfully report arrests and convictions but they are much less diligent about reporting the fact that suspects have been released, acquitted, or paroled. Moreover, as Robinson points out: "Even when complete records are kept, arrests that do not stick are still listed, creating a suspicion—indeed, a presumption—of guilt that can lead to further arrest and harassment".

The possibility of being harassed endlessly for a crime—or the presumption of a crime—committed in the distant past seems to go against one of the fundamental tenets of our society. To many people the Western Frontier represented a place where it was possible to build a new life free from the consequences of past transgressions. And only a few years ago our prisons were said to be places where a person guilty of wrongdoing "paid his debt to society" and hence earned a chance for a fresh start. Unfortunately, the Western Frontier is gone now and in a very real sense there can be no fresh starts in a society in which everything we have ever done follows us throughout our lives.

THE FUTURE

New laws and social customs may help us increase our privacy rights to some extent but there also seem to be powerful countertrends pushing us in the opposite direction. One of the most unnerving trends stems from the increasing complexity of government. Inevitably, as our government grows more complicated, pressures build to make it operate more efficiently. These pressures constantly tempt bureaucrats to ignore our privacy rights in an effort to reduce costs and increase services. As Paul Armer, director of Stanford University's Computation Center, has pointed out:

"We (all) look for improved efficiency in government, better law enforcement, and more rational programs in general. To do this, government needs more and better information about what is going on, information about people and organizations."*

The widespread use of credit cards is creating another set of privacy problems. One result is easy to spot: credit card companies openly conduct investigations which intrude into our private affairs. But, in addition, a credit card purchase, unlike a cash transaction, results in a permanent record of the event. If they were properly analyzed, these records could give any interested party a remarkably complete picture of our movements and our life styles.

---

*Armer, Paul. "The Individual: His Privacy, Self Image, and Obsolescence". *Computers and People*. June, 1975. pp. 18-23.

The trend toward more comprehensive insurance coverage is another source of difficulty. It is not hard to visualize ways in which the claims we file for medical and drug reinbursement could be abused, in fact, such abuses have already been observed in some company insurance plans. We may not care if others know about most of our minor ailments but there are other diseases that we may not want to broadcast. Infestations of lice, venereal diseases, mental disturbances and cancer (for various reasons) all fall into this sensitive category. If our country institutes a national health insurance program covering all our citizens, additional data of this type will be widely available to private and public institutions.

Dennie Van Tassel, Head Programmer at San Jose State College in San Jose, California, recently showed—perhaps in an overly dramatic manner—how records of this type might be used to track our movements with unnerving precision. His computer-constructed "daily surveillance sheet" (See Figure 50) reveals some chilling facts about the subject. His physical characteristics, gambling and drinking habits, his performance on the job, and even his extramarital affairs can all be deduced with reasonable accuracy using only those bits of information that may soon be a matter of public record.

When you read the computer printouts in Figure 50 you may be tempted to think of these listings as a fancy game like Monopoly or Space War. But it's more serious than that. Lack of privacy can cripple us just as surely as it crippled the American prisoners of war during the Korean conflict. In his book *Cancer Ward*, the Russian author, Alexander Solzhenitsyn, has skillfully described what could ultimately happen to us if too many personal records become visible to too many prying eyes.

"As every man goes through life, he fills in a number of forms for the record, each containing a number of questions. There are thus hundreds of little threads radiating from each man, millions of threads in all. If these threads were suddenly to become visible, people would lose all ability to move."

Of course, he didn't mean that we would be literally motionless. He meant that we would be able to move only in ways approved by the authorities. For those of us who have grown up with long traditions of freedom and liberty this may be even more painful than not being able to move at all.

Still, we must understand that privacy is not an absolute right. We willingly display the contents of our brief cases so that we can board an airplane with a reasonable assurance that it will reach its destination

DAILY SURVEILLANCE SHEET, 1987

Dennie Van Tassel
Head Programmer
San Jose State College
125 S. 7th St.
San Jose, Calif. 95114

```
                    NATIONAL DATA BANK
                 DAILY SURVEILLANCE SHEET
                       CONFIDENTIAL
                      JULY 11, 1987

    SUBJECT.    DENNIE VAN TASSEL
                SAN JOSE STATE COLLEGE
                MALE
                AGE 38
                MARRIED
                PROGRAMMER

    PURCHASES.  WALL STREET JOURNAL           .10
                BREAKFAST                     1.65
                GASOLINE                      3.00
                PHONE  (328-1826)              .10
                PHONE  (308-7928)              .10
                PHONE  (421-1931)              .10
                BANK (CASH WITHDRAWL)      (120.00)
                LUNCH                         2.00
                COCKTAIL                      1.00
                LINGERIE                     21.85
                PHONE  (369-2436)              .35
                BOURBON                       8.27
                NEWSPAPER                      .20
```

```
                    ** COMPUTER ANALYSIS **

    OWNS STOCK (90 PER CENT PROBABILITY)

    HEAVY STARCH BREAKFAST. PROBABLY OVERWEIGHT.

    BOUGHT 3.00 DOLLARS GASOLINE. OWNS VW. SO FAR THIS WEEK HE HAS BOUGHT 12.00
    DOLLARS WORTH OF GAS. OBVIOUSLY DOING SOMETHING ELSE BESIDES JUST DRIVING THE
    9 MILES TO WORK.

    BOUGHT GASOLINE AT 7.57. SAFE TO ASSUME HE WAS LATE TO WORK.

    PHONE NO. 328-1826 BELONGS TO SHADY LANE — SHADY WAS ARRESTED FOR BOOKMAKING IN
    1972.

    PHONE NO. 308-7928. EXPENSIVE MEN'S BARBER — SPECIALIZES IN BALD MEN OR HAIR
    STYLING.

    PHONE NO. 421-1931. RESERVATIONS FOR LAS VEGAS (WITHOUT WIFE). THIRD TRIP
    THIS YEAR TO LAS VEGAS (WITHOUT WIFE). WILL SCAN FILE TO SEE IF ANYONE ELSE
    HAS GONE TO LAS VEGAS AT THE SAME TIME AND COMPARE TO HIS PHONE CALL NUMBERS.

    WITHDREW 120.00 DOLLARS CASH. VERY UNUSUAL SINCE ALL LEGAL PURCHASES CAN BE
    MADE USING THE NATIONAL SOCIAL SECURITY CREDIT CARD. CASH USUALLY ONLY USED
    FOR ILLEGAL PURCHASES. IT WAS PREVIOUSLY RECOMMENDED THAT ALL CASH BE OUTLAWED
    AS SOON AS IT BECOMES POLITICALLY POSSIBLE.

    DRINKS DURING HIS LUNCH.

    BOUGHT VERY EXPENSIVE LINGERIE. NOT HIS WIFE'S SIZE.

    PHONE NO. 369-2436. MISS SWEET LOCKS.

    PURCHASED EXPENSIVE BOTTLE OF BOURBON. HE HAS PURCHASED 5 BOTTLES OF BOURBON
    IN THE LAST 30 DAYS. EITHER HEAVY DRINKER OR MUCH ENTERTAINING.

                    *** OVERALL ANALYSIS ***

    LEFT WORK AT 4.00, SINCE HE PURCHASED THE BOURBON 1 MILE FROM HIS JOB AT 4.10.
    (OPPOSITE DIRECTION FROM HIS HOUSE.)

    BOUGHT NEWSPAPER AT 6.30 NEAR HIS HOUSE. UNACCOUNTABLE 2 1/2 HOURS. MADE 3
    PURCHASES TODAY FROM YOUNG BLONDES. (STATISTICAL 1 CHANCE IN 78.) THEREFORE
    PROBABLY HAS WEAKNESS FOR YOUNG BLONDES.
```

Figure 50: Taken individually the paper forms we fill out as we go about the business of life may seem relatively harmless. But, in theory, these records could be assembled into a remarkably coherent picture of our private activities. The printout in this figure shows how this might be accomplished by a cleverly programmed digital computer with access to a single day's paper receipts.

intact. And we allow our doctors to keep medical records so that deadly drugs will not be administered indiscriminately. Dr. David F. Linowes, a Professor at the University of Illinois and Chairman of the U. S. Privacy Protection Commission, clearly understands that we need to strike a delicate balance between two contradictory goals. He summarized the findings of his Commission in the following way:

> "What we, and Congress, are left with is a dilemma. Clearly, the institutions of this country that provide insurance, credit and such are entitled to the best information available to run their businesses fairly and to protect their investments. What is not so clear is the limits that must be imposed upon their reach."*

In short, we know that private information keeps our society in operation but this is the crux of the problem: we must somehow balance the individual's need for privacy against society's need for information.

------

*Linowes, David F., "The Privacy Crisis." *Newsweek.* June 26, 1978. pg. 19.

BIBLIOGRAPHY

1. Adams, J. Mack, and Haden, Douglas H. *Social Effects of Computer Use and Misuse.* New York, New York: John Wiley, 1976.

2. Armer, Paul. "The Individual: His Privacy, Self Image, and Obsolescence." *Computers and People,* June 1975, pp. 18-23.

3. Armer, Paul. "Computer Technology and Surveillance." *Computers and People,* September 1975, pp. 8-11.

4. "The Campaign to Protect Personal Privacy." *Business Week,* 16 November 1974, pp. 88-90.

5. "Computer Privacy." *Scientific American,* February 1977, p. 50.

6. Carroll, John M. *Confidential Information Sources: Public and Private.* Los Angeles, California: Security World Publishing Co., 1975.

7. Crosson, Pierre R. "Institutional Obstacles to Expansion of World Food Production." *Science,* 9 May 1975, pp. 519-524.

8. *Federal Register: Protecting Your Right to Privacy.* Washington D.C.: U. S. Government Printing Office, 1977.

9. "Firms Cite Specific Dangers in Expanding Privacy Laws." *Industry Week,* 8 December 1975, pp. 20-23.

10. "First Pass at Privacy Laws Given an 'A' for Adequate." *Datamation,* February 1975, pp. 71-76.

11. Greenland, D. J. "Bringing the Green Revolution to the Shifting Cultivator." *Science,* 28 November 1975. pp. 841-844.

12. "Green Revolution: Creators Still Quite Hopeful on World Food." *Science,* 6 September 1974, pp. 844-845.

13. "Green Revolution (II): Problems of Adapting a Western Technology." *Science,* December 1974, pp. 1186-1193.

14. Goldstein, Robert C. and Nolan, Richard L. "Personal Privacy Versus The Corporate Computer." *Harvard Business Review,* March-April 1975, pp. 62-70.

15. "Government Snooping - How to Fight Back." *U. S. News and World Report,* 22 September 1975, pp. 21-22.

16. "How New Privacy Law Protects You". *U. S. News and World Report,* 30 December 1974, p. 16.

17. Linowes, David F. "The Privacy Crisis." *Newsweek,* 26 June 1978, p. 19.

18. Miller, Arthur R. *The Assault on Privacy: Computers, Data Banks and Dossiers.* Ann Arbor, Michigan: University of Michigan Press, 1971.

19. Armer, Paul. "Privacy - A Survey." Williamsburg, Virginia: Computers and Society - Computer Literary Workshop, July 16, 1978.

20. "NCIC A Tribute to Cooperative Spirit." FBI Law Enforcement Bulletin, February 1972.

21. "Privacy Act of 1974." Federal Reserve Bulletin, June 1976, pp. 521-536.

22. "Privacy: Congressional Efforts are Coming to Fruition." *Science,* 16 May 1975, pp. 713-715.

23. "Privacy: Costs, Codes, People and the Constitution." *Datamation,* May 1976, pp. 180-182.

24. "The Privacy Hearings Zero in on Business." *Business Week,* 3 November 1975.

25. "Privacy Journal: An Independent Monthly on Privacy in a Computer Age." (various issues) P. O. Box 8844, Washington, D.C.

26. "Privacy Legislation: Public Sector First." *Datamation,* September 1974, pp.130-132.

27. "Privacy: More Losses than Gains." *Technology Review,* February 1976, pp. 14-15.

28. "Protecting Your Privacy." *Business Week.* 4 April 1977, pp. 103-106.

29. "Questions on Legislation: Who Pays for Added Privacy? What New Laws Lie Ahead?" *Datamation,* May 1975, pp. 166-167.

30. Robinson, Stanley. "The National Crime Information Center (NCIC) of the FBI: Do We Want It?" *Computers and Automation,* June 1971.

31. Sagan, Carl. *The Dragons of Eden.* New York, New York: Random House, 1977.

32. Smith, Robert Ellis, and Snyder, Keith D., "Compilation of State and Federal Privacy Laws." Washington, D. C. : *Privacy Journal*, 1976.

33. "The Social Security Number as a Standard Universal Identifier." *Records, Computers, and the Rights of Citizens, U. S. Department of Health, Education and Welfare,* July 1973.

34. "U. S. Isn't the Only Place Where Citizens are Spied On." *U. S. News and World Report*, 7 April 1975, pp. 24-25.

35. "Will the Privacy Issue Hit Industry?" *Industry Week*, 5 May 1975, pp. 41-43.

36. "Who's Snooping into your Tax Returns Now." *U. S. News and World Report*, 11 August 1975, pp. 61-62.

EXERCISES

1. Approximately how many dossiers would you estimate are stored in government data files on the members of your immediate family? Does this seem like an excessive number to you? If so, what number would be more acceptable?

2. Some experts believe that manual data files have more potential for privacy abuse than the files which are stored within a digital computer. What is the basis of this argument? Do you find it convincing? Explain your answer.

3. The major provisions of The Privacy Act of 1974 were summarized in this chapter. Many people do not believe the act goes far enough in protecting us from the snooping eyes of the Federal government. What provisions could be added to the bill to make it stronger? How could we enforce these new provisions?

4. In your own words describe what is plotted in Figure 45. What is the significance of the point where the two curved lines cross one another?

5. The seven-bit binary code in Figure 49 is convenient for digital computers. Why isn't it similarly convenient for overworked students?

6. If you were hired to help improve the security at a company using manual data files what steps would you take? If you were given the same job for a computerized filing system, what would be your approach?

7. What is the NCIC? What are some of the difficulties associated with its use?

8. What is the Federal Data Center? Why wasn't it instituted?

9. What is a Universal Identifier? Why do some privacy experts object to its use?

10. In what ways is the Fair Credit Act of 1970 similar to the Privacy Act of 1974? In what ways do they differ?

STUDENT PROJECTS

1. Government and private data files contain enormous amounts of personal information on the people living in the United States. Research the records being held on your life or

that of a friend or relative (with his written permission.) You can begin by ordering *Protecting Your Right to Privacy* from the U. S. Government Printing Office and by contacting the TRW Credit Data Bureau as explained in this chapter. When you get the material back, prepare a notebook on the files and the reactions of the person whose files are being examined.

2. Investigate the methods whereby Americans can protect their rights of privacy. Make a 5-page report summarizing what you have learned.

SUGGESTED REFERENCES:

a. "Protecting Your Privacy". *Business Week*. April 4, 1977. pp. 103-106.

b. "How the New Privacy Law Protects You". *U. S. News and World Report*. December 30, 1974. pg. 16.

c. Smith, Robert Ellis and Snyder, Keith D. *Compilation of State and Federal Privacy Laws*. Privacy Journal. Washington, D. C. 1976.

d. "The Campaign to Protect Personal Privacy". *Business Week*. 16 November, 1974. pp. 88-90.

e. Goldstein, Robert C. and Nolan, Richard L. "Personal Privacy versus the Corporate Computer". *Harvard Business Review*. March-April, 1975. pp. 62-70.

f. "The Campaign to Protect Personal Privacy." *Business Week*. November 16, 1974. pp. 88-90.

g. "Privacy: Congressional Efforts are Coming to Fruition." *Science*. May 16, 1975. pp. 713-715.

3. Organize a debate among several of your classmates with the following topic: "Resolved: The Federal Data Center would be beneficial to the United States."

CHAPTER 7

COMPUTER FRAUD

THE GREAT PHONE COMPANY RIP-OFF

ELECTRONIC EMBEZZLEMENT

THE MAGNITUDE OF COMPUTER CRIME

PROTECTING THE MACHINES
Secret Passwords
File Protection Rings
The Making of a Secure Machine
Tiger Teams at ZARF
The Perils of Complexity
Secure Kernels

ACCESS LIMITS
User Identification Methods
Terminals That Operate by Lock and Key

DATA ENCRYPTION SCHEMES

TRAPDOOR CODES

THE MANY FACES OF COMPUTER CRIME

BIBLIOGRAPHY

EXERCISES

STUDENT PROJECTS

In the last chapter we saw how difficult it is to keep our country's computers from invading our privacy while assuring our social planners access to the information they need. The topic of this chapter is crime by computer, a relatively new social problem which has already begun to affect your pocketbook to a fairly serious degree.

Unlike common street criminals who engage in obvious antisocial activities such as rape and barroom brawls, computer criminals seldom see their victims suffering as a result of the things they do. Consequently, they tend to regard their exploits as playful pranks rather than serious crimes. Even when they're caught and punished, this lackadaisical attitude seems to persist. Explained one unrepentant electronic embezzler on the day he was carted off to jail: "When you get really involved with it, you tend to lose track of the humanities—you become enthralled by the numbers . . . and your whole life becomes so bound up with them you lose a qualitative sense."

Electronic digital computers first became available in 1946, but their use for criminal purposes is of much more recent origins—the first computer criminal was not apprehended and convicted until 1964. However, white collar crime—a much broader category which includes computer fraud—has been flourishing for a surprisingly long time. Some of the more noteworthy instances occurred in the late 19th century along the social fringes of straight-laced Victorian England.

Even in those days it was obvious that white collar crime differed in important respects from the more earthy and familiar forms of criminality. For one thing, it was a comparatively safe, surprisingly lucrative, way to carve out a comfortable living. As author Michael Crichton tells us in his excellent book, *The Great Train Robbery,** "Then as now, white collar crime involved the largest sums of money, was the least likely to be detected, and was punished most leniently if the participants were ever apprehended."

Why is white collar crime so safe and profitable? And why do its practitioners, even when caught, seem so immune from serious prosecution? In a later section we shall seek out the answers to these provocative questions. But first we pause to review the exploits of an unusually precocious white collar criminal.

THE GREAT PHONE COMPANY RIP-OFF

In the late 1960's a Los Angeles high school student named Jerry Schneider strayed into an unfamiliar alley as he wandered toward his

---

*Crichton, Michael. *The Great Train Robbery*. New York, New York: Knoff. 1975.

home from school. There outside the offices of Pacific Telephone, he noticed something that has always stirred the imagination of every inquisitive American youngster. In the patchy shade of an eucalyptus tree sat two metal trash bins heaped to overflowing with an irresistible tangle of electronic gear. He hadn't started out his boyish investigations with mischief in mind; as Jerry himself would later recall, he simply felt that "pilfering the phone company's discards might be a fun kind of thing to do." But long before the warm afternoon shadows had descended across those metal trash bins, Jerry Schneider had taken the first hesitant steps toward one of the most outlandish and lucrative computer frauds in the history of the world.

Among the items he rescued from oblivion were two bulging notebooks containing diagrams of the phone company's computers together with descriptions of their operating procedures. According to these publications, the computers could be used to instruct servicing crews to drop off expensive pieces of equipment at key delivery points located throughout the Los Angeles basin. At first Jerry regarded these cryptic monographs with more-or-less the same disdain he had previously reserved for his high school algebra book. But, after reviewing their contents more carefully, it began to dawn on him that he might have stumbled onto an efficient method for obtaining an unlimited collection of electronic souvenirs.

Later, when he enrolled as a full-time engineering student at UCLA, he dug out the handbooks again and began thumbing through their pages with renewed interest. An hour or so later as he shoved them back into the top drawer of his desk, he reached a monumental decision: working alone, with only his wits to guide him, he would develop a way to break through the computer's defenses.

The first steps were relatively easy: study the handbooks, learn about the inner workings of the digital computer, pump his professors for information about the most popular methods for maintaining data security. But how many people would have had enough courage to tackle the next part of his self-styled assignment? Stuck for a key piece of information, he barged into the offices of Pacific Telephone and, passing himself off as a magazine reporter, calmly interviewed the technicians who guarded and operated the company's computers.

Eventually he learned to use a surprisingly simple device—an ordinary touchtone telephone—to entice the computers into cooperating in their own downfall. By depressing the buttons in exactly the right sequence, he could trick them into disgorging expensive pieces of equipment on deserted city streets. For months he spent his evenings cruising the suburbs in a second hand phone company truck happily scooping up the loot.

Soon he had accumulated a huge stack of equipment much of it of obvious value. But, at first, there didn't seem to be any way to convert it into cold, hard cash. After considering various imaginative possibilities, he decided to lease a small warehouse and put the items up for sale. Unfortunately, his skill with computers greatly exceeded his expertise as a salesman; consequently, his inventory kept piling up in great unsorted heaps. Never one to crumble in the face of an obvious challenge, he hired 13 sales clerks and somehow mustered the gall to advertise his wares in the yellow pages—printed, of course, by Pacific Telephone, the same people who were so cooperatively furnishing his mountains of merchandise!*

Jerry's downfall came about—quite by accident—when he let one of his employees in on the secret of his success. Later disgruntled over a salary dispute, the employee also shared the secret with one of the officials at Pacific Telephone. At this point the grand scheme quickly unraveled into a tangled mess. But not before it had gone on for more than two years, and not before he had bilked the phone company out of nearly $1 million worth of electronic gear.

During the criminal investigation that followed Jerry never seemed to experience any feelings of guilt or recrimination. Like most computer con artists, he was badly infected with "vending machine syndrome", a malady in which those who cheat only mechanical devices rationalize their actions as harmless and benign. Indeed, even today when he talks about his youthful adventures, he is more often overcome with laughter than remorse: "Once (I) had a $25,000 switchboard delivered to a phone company manhole at two o'clock in the morning", he chuckles gleefully. "Of course the delivery crew seemed a little puzzled but they would never presume to challenge a set of instructions from their own computer".

When his case finally came to trial, Jerry Schneider sat in the courtroom with a stoic, uninvolved look on his face. No doubt his attorneys had briefed him on how lenient his punishment would likely turn out to be. For making off with 100 times the average bank-robbery haul, he was sentenced to work on a prison farm for a scant 60 days. A model prisoner, he got time off for good behavior and was officially released on the fortieth day.**

---

*Rosen, Stephen. *Future Facts*. New York, New York: Simon and Schuster. 1976.

** In a separate civil suit he was ordered to pay Pacific Telephone $85,000, less than 10 percent of his total loot!

When Jerry returned home after his brief imprisonment, he didn't find it necessary to sink back into a life of crime. Unlike most ex-convicts, he was able to use his expertise in setting up a lucrative business. You guessed it! The baby-faced Schneider—one of the biggest computer con artists in history—now makes a comfortable living showing other potential victims how to protect themselves against computer crime!*

ELECTRONIC EMBEZZLEMENT

Like their counterparts in Victorian England, middle class Americans have a tendency to regard criminals as habitual losers, scratching out a miserable existence by taking extreme risks because they're too lazy or too stupid to do anything else. It's a comforting mental image, but studies have shown that it does not accurately characterize the average criminal. It is an even more inaccurate characterization of the ones who use computers in their work. The typical computer con artist tends to be precisely the kind of employee you would want on your payroll if you could keep him from dipping his fingers in the till. As Ralston and Meek have so pointedly observed, he is almost always "young, energetic, highly motivated and intelligent."** As we have seen, Jerry Schneider embodied all of these attractive personality traits. In addition, he shared at least three other distressing characteristics with his colleagues in computer crime:

1. He got away with huge sums of money
2. His crimes were detected only by chance
3. His punishment was exceedingly mild.

These, of course, are the same characteristics attributed to white collor criminals by Michael Crichton in *The Great Train Robbery*. We now discuss them one by one.

1. He got away with huge sums of money.

Computer crime can be enormously profitable. Once an embezzler manages to breach the computer's security system, large sums are essentially as easy for him to steal as small ones. Table 6 provides some instructive statistics on the profitability of various forms of criminality. As you can see, the average take from an armed robbery of a branch bank is $2000; those who rob major banks end up with an average of $10,000; the

---

*Alexander,Tom. "Waiting for The Great Computer Rip-Off". *Fortune*. July, 1974. pp. 143-150.

**Ralston, Anthony, and Meek, Chester L. *Encyclopedia of Computer Science*, New York, New York: Petrocelli/Charter: 1976.

average amount stolen in a conventional embezzlement is $19,000. By contrast, the average lifted in an embezzlement involving computers is $430,000—and it is not uncommon for the total to go considerably higher. When computer consultant Mark Rifkin hit the Security Pacific Bank in Los Angeles in November of 1978 he made off with a cool $10.2 million.

2. His crimes were detected only by chance.

Virtually all of the computer crimes that have come to light so far have been discovered by accident. A few years ago, Donn Parker, a computer security expert at the Stanford Research Institute, investigated 175 cases of crimes involving computers. He found that "hardly any were uncovered through normal security precautions and accounting controls".*

TABLE 6

THE AVERAGE AMOUNT STOLEN IN VARIOUS
TYPES OF CRIME*

TYPE OF CRIME	AVERAGE AMOUNT STOLEN
Larceny-Theft	$150
Burglary	$320
All Robberies	$400
Branch Bank Robbery	$2,000
Full-Service Bank Robbery	$10,000
Conventional Bank Embezzlement	$19,000
Computer-Related Embezzlement	$430,000

*Sources = "Sharpest Spurt Ever in Violence, Theft". *U. S. News and World Report,* November 24, 1975.
"Annals of Crime: Dead Souls in the Computer Part I: *The New Yorker,* August 22, 1977. pp. 35-65.

Why aren't auditors more successful in ferreting out computer criminals? Contrary to popular belief, auditing procedures are not set up to catch embezzlers—especially those who make use of electronic computers. A vice president who handles computer security at a large New York bank, notes that the primary purpose of auditing is to assure that earnings are fairly reported to tax officials and stockholders. "Auditors seldom find a loss", he recently told reporters, "they may confirm it after it is already known". Computer scientist Brandt Allen at the University of Virginia strongly endorses this candid view and he goes on to add that "computer technology tends to confound auditors and managers to the extent that they are rarely in a position to detect and prevent computer-based embezzlement."

One difficulty is that in dealing with digitized material, the auditor loses his traditional "paper trail"—a visible pathway marked with official invoices, checks, and receipts. In a conventional bookkeeping system, these pieces of paper allow the auditor to confirm any suspected financial irregularity. He or she can start at any point and trace the relevant transaction backward or forward to its ultimate source. Unfortunately, in a computerized system, this is usually impossible because the intermediate steps occur inside the machine and even those few paper documents that once existed are often unavailable at the time audit is being made.

From this description it may sound like our data processing experts have been engaging in a grand conspiracy to help make computer fraud harder to detect; bear in mind, however, that the primary purpose of computerized recordkeeping is to eliminate unnecessary labor and costly paperwork. These items are definitely reduced in a computer-based system but, unfortunately, as a result, the auditor is often placed in a position that is seriously compromised.

Security expert Donn Parker points out another serious difficulty in crosschecking the records in a data processing center: "A computerized system tends to destroy the independence of the auditor, since the very people whose work he is supposed to be auditing are standing between him and the documents of record". This problem stems from the fact that the digitized records are usually meaningless unless they can be routed through a digital computer. Who runs the computer? It may seem a bit strange but, generally speaking, the computer is run by the people whose records are under audit!

3. His punishment was exceedingly mild. Some experts are convinced that at least 99 percent of all computer thieves manage to evade detection. However, even those few who are caught often escape prosecution because the institutions they rob prefer to avoid the unfavorable publicity

of a public trial.* The banking industry is so squeamish about bad publicity because their business is based on mutual trust; or, in accordance with the playful assessments of economist Kenneth Galbraith; "The public believing a lie."

As Galbraith explains: The bank expects each customer to believe it actually has his money in its deposit accounts despite the fact that everyone knows that only a small fraction of their total assets can be kept on the premises. Most of the money is always on loan earning interest. As long as all the customers behave as though they believe this "absurd falsehood", everything works fine; but if trust is suddenly shaken, and too many of the depositors attempt simultaneous withdrawals, the bank will inevitably collapse. Consequently, even if a computer embezzler is caught redhanded, the bank may choose to swallow the loss rather than risk a panic among the people who are so cooperatively pretending to believe the lie.

In those rare instances in which a case actually ends up in the courtroom, the prosecution faces special difficulties because "the proceedings often call for the kind of technical knowledge that is simply not available to most police departments . . . few members of prosectorial staffs know enough about the intricacies of electronic data processing to prepare a case against defendants which will stand up in court."**

Finally, even if a solid case is somehow presented, juries tend to be extraordinarily sympathetic to the white collar criminal. This magnanimous attitude probably stems from the fact that white collar crimes are nearly always impersonal and non violent. At first thought it may seem a little disturbing that embezzlers spend so little time in jail.***However, it should be noted that our country is not currently suffering from a serious shortage of criminals. With this fact in mind, most of us would rather not waste our prison cells on those who are only interested in taking our money if it means crowding out those who are more interested in taking our lives.

---

*Senator Joseph R. Biden, Jr., the Delaware Democrat who heads the Senate Subcommittee on criminal laws and procedures estimates that "the chance of a computer crime being detected is probably less than one in a hundred; a computer criminal's chance of being convicted, less than one in five hundred; and the chance of a computer criminal going to jail, less than one in a thousand." (Quoted in the *Chronicle of Higher Education*, July 17, 1978.)

**Whiteside, Thomas. "Annals of Crime: Dead Souls in the Computer, Part II". *The New Yorker*, August 29, 1977. pp. 34-64.

***According to an article entitled "The War on White Collar Crime" in the June 3, 1977 issue of *Business Week*: "Last year 91 percent of convicted bank robbers received jail terms, the sentences averaging more than 11 years. Of those convicted of embezzling bank funds, however, only 17 percent were sent to prison. (Their) sentences averaged only 23 months."

THE MAGNITUDE OF COMPUTER CRIME

At present, there are approximately 400,000 computer programmers in the United States, about 90 percent of them working business applications. In addition, there are at least 1,100,000 people who work with computers in a variety of other ways. On occasion, these individuals are overcome by temptation. Consider these actual case histories:

- In 1966 a young programmer in a Minneapolis bank convinced the computer to ignore all overdrafts from his personal account. His spending spree ended with an all-expense-paid vacation in the city jail.

- In the early 1970's a group of Korean technicians, who were assigned to operate a special army supply computer program, diverted large quantities of food, uniforms, vehicles, and gasoline for subsequent resale. The swindle was so effective $18 million worth of equipment vanished in a single year.

- In 1974 computer operators extracted 3 million customer names and addresses from the computerized files of Encyclopedia Britannica. The list, which was valued at $1 million, was resold to other mail order outfits.

- In 1972 a computer at Penn Central Railroad was instructed to divert 217 railroad cars worth up to $60,000 each to a special siding near LaSalle, Illinois. Once they had been delivered and were being repainted with fake markings, the cooperative computer was commanded to forget where they were.

When they come to light, spectacular cases of this type are almost always good for a banner headline. However, computer crime actually constitutes a relatively small fraction of all the crime that now occurs. Figure 51 compares the social costs of various types of criminal activities. As you can see, the losses resulting from computer fraud constitute well under one percent. These statistics, which were obtained from a number of different sources, are admittedly crude, but they are probably in the proper ball park. They indicate that the total annual crime losses to government and industry are roughly $25 billion and $30 billion respectively. Of this total only about $0.3 billion results from outright computer fraud.*

---

*This estimated value does not include such marginally illegal activities as the use of company computers to play games or to handle personal calculations. Nor does it include the relatively common practice of taking a copy of various company computer programs along to a new place of employment. It is impossible to obtain accurate estimates, but these shady activities probably cost the government and private industry hundreds of millions of dollars each year.

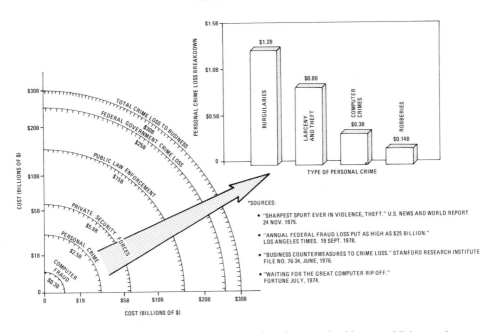

Figure 51: Although a few spectacular computer crimes have received heavy publicity, crude estimates indicate that crime by computer is actually costing our society only about $300 million per year. This is not an insignificant total but it amounts to less than 1 percent of the dollar losses associated with the more familiar forms of criminality such as burglary and theft.

If computer-related crime is such a small fraction of all the criminal activity that now exists why is it such a cause for concern? For one thing, as is shown in Figure 52, it is growing at an alarming rate. Every year since 1968 the number of computer-related crimes made public has grown by 50 percent or more over the previous year! Moreover, as our society converts to the widespread use of electronic payments systems, the potential for computer fraud will inevitably increase. It is not generally known but already every working day billions of dollars in electronic transactions are flowing between hundreds of digital computers. When Mark Rifkin swindled the Los Angeles Security Pacific Bank out of $10.2 million in 1978, a bank spokesman admitted that the theft certainly should have been spotted but he added that "a mere $10.2 million might get lost in the shuffle, since the bank normally transfers $20 billion a week by wire."*

---

*"The Great Computer Heist". *Newsweek*. November 20, 1978. pp. 99-100.

PROTECTING THE MACHINES

Computer fraud certainly appears to be a growing problem, but why don't we eliminate it by building our computers so that they're safe and secure? Of course, that's what we've been trying to do; unfortunately, it's a little more difficult than you might suppose. Contrary to popular belief, a modern computer system is usually not a single unit sitting in a single room. More typically, it consists of a series or processing units and remote terminals interconnected by telephone lines and various other types of communication links. In such a system the thief may never actually see the computer he is attempting to rob. Jerry Schneider's case provides a classic example; as you will recall, he ordered a million dollars worth of expensive telephone equipment from the comfort of his own home.

Secret Passwords

Of course, the people who design computers have been building certain safeguards into the equipment for many years. For example, in a time-sharing system, the computer's memory is partitioned into separate compartments. Theoretically, it is impossible for a user to interrogate or

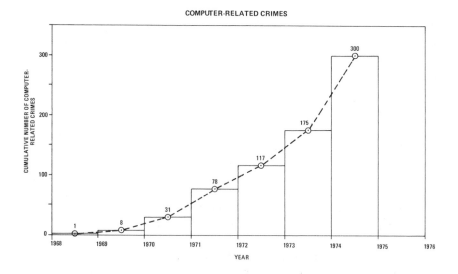

Figure 52: In recent years all types of crimes have been spurting upward at an alarming rate, but computer-related crimes have been growing far faster than most other types of criminal activity. Even more alarming, most of the computer crimes that have come to light so far have been uncovered only by accident.

alter the files outside his or her own compartment. Moreover, specific data files can be accessed only if he or she can supply a prearranged secret "password". A password is a consecutive sequence of alphanumeric characters which acts as a key to unlock a portion of the computer's memory.

If they are handled with care, secret passwords can be enormously helpful in maintaining data security; unfortunately, they are not always taken seriously. Even when large sums of money are involved, the procedures for safeguarding secret passwords are sometimes amazingly lax. According to the FBI, Mark Rifkin (who had at one time worked as a consultant to the Security Pacific Bank) talked his way into the Wire Room where he apparently glimpsed or overheard the next day's secret password.* Armed with this key piece of information it was relatively easy for him to make off with more than ten million dollars.

Given a valid password, an intruder can interrogate, change, or delete any data file that is accessible to him or her. Moreover, he or she can usually make these changes without leaving a trace. A few modern systems keep automatic logs on certain types of changes but, unfortunately, this is not, at present, a standard operating procedure. Of course, most of the files that have been wiped out in the past were destroyed inadvertently or in some cases by a good Samaritan who was attempting to help a friend improve his program! As a matter of fact, secret passwords were initially developed to prevent friendly and inadvertent intrusions rather than those involving criminal intent.

File Protection Rings

File protection rings provide another method for guarding important data files from inadvertent destruction. A file protection ring is a small plastic cylinder which locks into the center of a reel of magnetic tape. (See Figure 53). A tape drive is able to *read* the contents of a tape whether or not its file protection ring is in place. However, it can *erase* a tape only if its reel contains a file protection ring.

Of course, even when file protection rings are used, a careless operator can still wipe out important records if he or she mistakenly inserts the ring and then commands the computer to erase the tape. However, this unfortunate chain of events is relatively uncommon because it requires two consecutive human errors. Indeed, any machine operator who repeatedly destroys important data tapes in this manner would be a good candidate for transfer to a less demanding assignment.

---

*"The Great Computer Heist". *Newsweek*. November 20, 1978. pp. 99-100.

Secret passwords and file protection rings are reasonably cheap and effective methods for protecting important data files from malicious or accidental destruction. In addition, more elaborate efforts have been made to further increase the security of existing systems or to build impenetrable computers starting from the ground up. Honeywell's "multics" system is perhaps the best known example of a hard-headed attempt to design and build a secure computer.

The Making of a Secure Machine

In September of 1973 Honeywell Information Systems of Phoenix, Arizona, issued a special press release outlining the unusually tight security features of their new "multics" system. The company officials had every good reason to be proud of their ingenious machine. After all, their best computer specialists had spent six agonizing years designing and building the multics system to exacting specifications. Even their competitors grudgingly acknowledged that it probably incorporated the most elaborate safeguards of any large computer ever marketed up to that point

In particular, it used special cryptographic procedures to encode its secret passwords and "stratified access" which permitted users with various clearly established needs to gain access to some portions of its memory while being denied access to others. It was also rigged to maintain an automatic "audit trail" of the internal activities of anyone

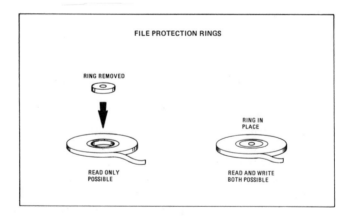

Figure 53: A file protection ring is a small plastic cylinder designed to protect a magnetic tape from being inadvertently erased. Tape drives are able to *read* the contents of a magnetic tape whether or not its reel contains a file protection ring. However, they are able to *erase* the tape only if the file protection ring is in place.

his terminal would be charged for only a few minutes of computer time despite the fact that he had been using the system for more than two hours!*

Lieutenant Karger's story sounds quite impressive. But exactly how difficult is it to break through the defenses of a "secure" machine? Let's put it this way: the Tiger Teams at ZARF have tried their hand at every new system that has ever been marketed; so far none of them has been able to stand up under their well-organized assaults.

The Perils of Complexity

What makes it so hard for our designers to build a tamper-proof computer? Complexity is perhaps the most serious problem. As a program moves through the various processing steps inside the computer, its movements are controlled by a special software routine called the "operating system". A modern operating system is so complicated that no one person can ever hope to understand exactly how it works. The operating system for the Univac 1108, for example, involves about 500,000 machine language instructions. The one used by the IBM 370 involves nearly 6 million. To give you some idea how many instructions that is, if we printed out the entire instruction set, using the computer's high speed printer, it would cover 75,000 sheets of paper stretching over a length of almost 20 miles.

Unfortunately, the technicians attempting to design a secure operating system labor under a distinct handicap. A clever intruder needs to find only one flaw in these instructions to break through whereas the designers of the system are theoretically afforded no leeway at all in their attempts to make it secure. Moreover, they cannot simply seal the system shut once and for all; there must be some method for making changes as new requirements arise. In particular, the password list must be periodically updated and any errors that crop up in the operating system itself must be corrected. These changes are made by using a number of code words called "system commands". The system commands act like special keys to unlock or bypass the computer's normal safeguards. Of course, any intruder who gains access to the system commands can exercise essentially complete control.

Secure Kernels

The security problems encountered by computer designers are, in some respects, similar to those faced by the technicians who constructed

---

*Alexander, Tom. "Waiting for The Great Computer Rip Off". *Fortune.* July, 1974. pp. 143-150.

who used it. The men and women who designed the multics system were confident that no one could breach its security. Thus, although it was a time-sharing system, they advocated its use for the storage and processing of classified information.

Tiger Teams at ZARF

Unfortunately—to be as charitable as possible—their enthusiastic assessments turned out to be a bit premature. The morning after their press release was reprinted in all the major newspapers, one of Honeywell's computer operators was surprised to see his console suddenly spring to life. Out rolled a message quoting the newspaper accounts and sniping unmercifully at the multics system. When the printer finished its uncomplimentary tirade, it signed off with these revealing words:

"ZARF IS WITH YOU AGAIN!"

Well, at least they hadn't incurred the wrath of God! Like everyone else at Honeywell, the machine operator knew that ZARF was a special code name signifying a joint project between the Air Force and the MITRE Corportation, a defense-related Think Tank. The purpose of this heavily-classified project is to study computer security features. In keeping with their duties, a favorite pastime of the people at ZARF is to break through the defenses of "secure" machines.

This is what had happened the day before: Upon reading Honeywell's self-congratulatory press release, a man named Steven Lipner of MITRE telephoned a colleague at ZARF, Lieutenant Paul Karger, and asked him if he thought he could penetrate the computer's safeguards. Although Karger was in Boston (3000 miles away) he confidently predicted that he could do it without leaving home. When he hung up, he walked down a single flight of stairs, switched on a teletype terminal in his basement, dialed Honeywell's multics system, and typed in a few subtle instructions. It was sweaty, exacting work but within two and a half hours he had subverted every one of multic's vaunted safeguards.

Once in control, Lieutenant Karger copied the entire list of passwords from the computer's memory—changing a few just to add a dash of confusion. Then he added a special "trapdoor" to insure future access—just in case his original entrance might later be discovered and sealed shut. Next he carefully erased all traces of his entry to fool the computer's auditing system. In one final insult he rigged the system commands so that the Alaskan pipeline: their operations were enormously complicated and they were scattered out over a vast, unguarded terrain. Of course, there was no way to fence off or patrol the pipeline's entire 800-mile span. For this reason the construction crews used a different ploy in order to protect their most valuable items of equipment; they were stored in special secure compounds.

A similar technique can be used in protecting the contents of the computer's memory. Certain sensitive portions of the operating system can all be grouped together into one region called a "secure kernel". The secure kernel is then protected by extremely rigid and formal entry procedures. To some extent this approach circumvents the security difficulties stemming from the intrinsic complexity of the operating system.

ACCESS LIMITS

As we have seen, a number of valiant efforts have been made to design and build tamper-proof data processing systems. Although these systems can usually be overpowered by highly-trained experts with relative ease, in general, they are resistant to the efforts of the average unsophisticated intruder. In actual practice, however, most computer fraud is accomplished without overpowering the computer's defense mechanisms. The most common approach is to abuse assigned responsibilities. For this reason, over the short term, at least, the most effective methods for protecting our sensitive data files will probably consist of carefully screening personnel and perfecting various user identification methods and other types of access controls.

User Identification Methods

Recently a team of researchers at the National Bureau of Standards wrapped up a special study on various methods for effective user identification. They concluded that there are three fundamental things we can test about an individual to ascertain his or her identify. (See Figure 54)

1. Something he or she *has* (a badge, a pass, a card).
2. Something he or she *knows* (a password, a lock combination, intimate information).
3. Something *about him or her* (voice characteristics, hand geometry, fingerprints).

According to the Bureau's report: "everything in the first two categories can be compromised . . . in that they can be lost, stolen, or yielded to an unauthorized person under duress".* The third category provides higher levels of security, but expensive hardware systems are usually required. And, even under the best conditions, the devices in this category experience certain practical problems. In particular, they do not always provide repeatable results.

In a *voice recognition system* the computer is given a "reference profile"; a tape recording of a person repeating a specific phrase several times. Through processing the machine establishes a set of averages and limits so that it can learn to distinguish that particular voice from any others. Later, if a match within a certain tolerance is achieved, the identity of the person is considered to be verified. But couldn't such a system be fooled by an ordinary tape recording of the person's voice? Fortunately, this potential threat can be eliminated by having the computer select at random any of several previously recorded phrases. The selected phrase would then be broadcast over a speaker system and the person would be required to repeat it immediately.

Various methods for *matching fingerprints* to verify identity have also been devised. Inked impressions are generally unnecessary. A satisfactory image of the print can be obtained by placing the fingertip on a properly lighted prism. When the fingertip is in place, the computer automatically matches its whorls and loops against those previously stored in its memory.

Hand geometry is another practical method of personal identification. This technique was accidentally discovered by Air Force researchers when they measured a large number of pilots to obtain data for making gloves. An automatic device using a set of motor-driven photoelectric cells measures finger lengths (distances between the fingertips and the soft web between the fingers). The entire procedure takes less than 1 second.

The analysis of the dynamic features of the *handwriting process* provides another means of automatic identification. In this scheme it is *not* the signature itself which is analyzed but rather the forces, velocities and accelerations experienced by the pencil point when the person signs his or her name. The computer takes a few hundred samples of these parameters during the signing process which lasts four or five seconds. A skilled forger can duplicate a person's signature, sometimes with remarkable fidelity. However, most experts find it difficult to believe that any forger would ever be able to duplicate all the dynamic movements that are involved.

---

*Meissner, Paul. "The Computerized Password". *Privacy Journal*. August 1977. pp. 3-5.

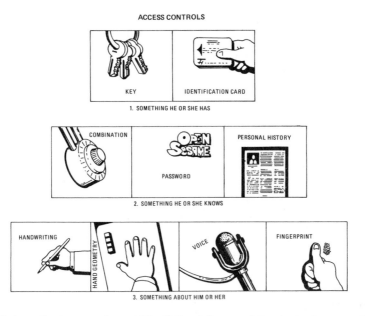

Figure 54: According to researchers at The National Bureau of Standards, there are three fundamental ways of insuring that only authorized users can gain access to a digital computer: *something he or she has, something he or she knows* or *something about him or her.* The first two categories can always be compromised by careless, talkative, or terrified users. The third provides a more promising approach to data security but, unfortunately, the necessary hardware elements tend to be much more costly and much less reliable.

Every identification method investigated so far is plagued with one or more practical difficulties. Voice prints, for example, produce inconsistent results if the person is under stress or has a cold, and the fingerprinting method can fail if the person presses too hard or too lightly. The systems now being tested typically make about one incorrect identification in 50 tries. However, it is the belief of most researchers that, with further study, these error rates can be reduced to a small fraction of one percent.

Terminals That Operate by Lock and Key

Most time sharing computers will accept commands from any remote terminal provided the user can supply a valid password. Consequently, there have been numerous instances in which unauthorized outsiders have gained access to the computer. Both Jerry Schneider and Lieutenant Karger used terminals that were not actually a part of the system they were manipulating.

One technique for preventing unauthorized intrusion into a time sharing system is to have the computer identify the remote terminal before it will obey any subsequent commands. In 1977 IBM announced a device of this type called a "lock-and-key terminal". It is designed so that only those people who have keys can turn the terminal on. When the key is engaged, the terminal automatically sends a signal to the computer pinpointing the terminal location. Lock-and-key terminals should help prevent the unauthorized use of time sharing systems. Unfortunately, the new terminals cannot be introduced overnight. Industry sources estimate that remote terminals worth $17 billion have already been installed. Their average useful lifetime is 10 years or more, consequently, over the short term they are not likely to be replaced in substantial numbers.

DATA ENCRYPTION SCHEMES

A few years ago when one of the bidders for the Alaskan oil leases lost several bids by suspiciously narrow margins, an analysis by an independent computer security firm strongly indicated that bidding information sent by the company from computer to computer over ordinary telephone lines was probably tapped by one of its competitors.* With the anticipated growth of large-scale electronic funds transfer systems, distributed processing networks, and electronic mail, much of our economy will ultimately depend upon secure data channels. Today the only effective way to make a communication channel secure is to use data encryption.

In an encryption scheme the "plaintext" (the original message) is translated into a "cyphertext" (a meaningless scramble of symbols) prior to transmission. Once it has been received at the other end, the "cyphertext" is decrypted to reproduce the original message. A simple example of how this encryption/decryption procedure works is presented in Figure 55. The sample case uses a "substitution" cipher, that is, a new symbol is substituted for each old one. There are also "transposition" ciphers in which the symbols in the plaintext are scrambled into a new order and "product" ciphers which combine both "substitution" and "transposition", often in extremely complex patterns.

In July of 1977, after spending $40 million on a study of the overall problems associated with data security, IBM, in conjunction with the National Bureau of Standards, announced the release of a new product cipher called the *Data Encryption Standard*. It is slated to be used for all unclassified government data transmissions and, in addition, is being made available to any interested private companies.

---

*Whiteside, Thomas. "Annals of Crime: Dead Souls in the Computer, Part I". *The New Yorker*. August 22, 1977. pp. 35-65.

The Data Encryption Standard makes use of a complicated mathematical model in order to translate any sequence of binary digits into ciphertext form for transmission over unprotected data links. Once the ciphertext reaches its destination, the recipient reverses the procedure to restore the original message. Each user chooses his own special key—a 56-digit binary number which must be kept secret from unauthorized recipients.

Specifically, the Bank of America might have this kind of a key:

0010101 0100001 1000001 0001001 0111001 0000011 0001001 0010010

whereas Home Savings and Loan might have one like this:

0000111 1110101 0111100 0010101 1110000 0011100 0001110 1010111

When it was first announced, the Data Encryption Standard was warmly received by most experts in the financial community. Although they were not permitted to know exactly how the system worked, they were delighted to have access to a standard coding method because they knew that the situation would have quickly become chaotic if each individual user tried to develop his own separate cipher. Unfortunately, the Data Encryption Standard soon triggered a series of sizzling controversies. For one thing two Stanford University professors, Dr. Martin Hellman and Dr. Whitfield Diffie, warned that, in theory, a machine could eventually be built to determine any user's key assuming that a correctly-translated sample transmission could be obtained (something which inudstry experts concede is impossible to prevent).

Of course the most efficient way to break any code is to find some weakness or pattern in its encryption procedures. This does not seem very likely in the case of the Data Encryption Standard partly because IBM has devoted 17 man-years of effort to various code-busting approaches, coming up empty. But even if cleverness fails, Hellman and Diffie contend that within a few years "brute force" procedures can be used instead.* They reason that with 56 binary bits in the key, there are 2^{56} different keys or about 100,000,000,000,000,000 possibilities. Using today's technology, a computer equipped with a single high-density LSI chip could be constructed that could try out 1,000,000 keys per second.

Still, even at that rate it would take such a computer around 3000 years to find a single key. However, if the computer used 1,000,000 chips

---

*A "brute force" procedure is a computational method which utilizes direct, inelegant methods to arrive at a costly, time-consuming solution to a mathematical problem.

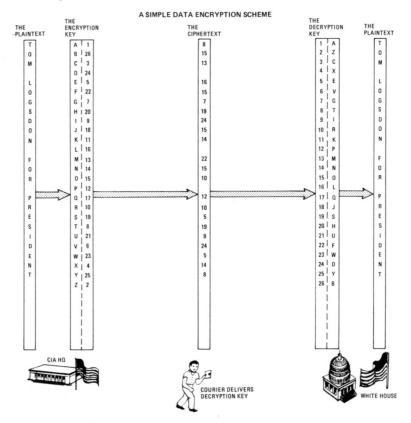

Figure 55: One of the simplest techniques for *encrypting* a message is to substitute a unique number for each of its alphanumeric symbols. Once this has been done, the resulting ciphertext can be transmitted over the open airwaves. Upon receipt, it is *decrypted* by using a special key previously delivered to the recipient by courier.

working in parallel, the search time would be reduced to one day or less. How much would their fancy code-busting machine cost? Hellman and Diffie estimate that the required number of chips could eventually be produced for about $10 million and that other hardware and electronics would add an additional $10 million. If the resulting machine was given a sufficiently large enough number of assignments, each cryptographic key could be deciphered for about $5000.*

Given this ticklish situation, what do Hellman and Diffie believe we should do? For one thing they recommend doubling the key size to 128 binary digits.** According to their calculations, this would increase the

---

*"Computer Encryption and The National Security Agency Connection". *Science*. July 1977. pp. 438-440.

**They maintain that the military routinely uses key sizes 10 to 20 times as large.

cost to the users by a negligible amount, yet it would raise the cost of a typical brute-force code-breaking search from $5000 to $20,000,000,000,000,000,000,000,000,000,000—or 10 trillion times our country's current gross national product!

Dr. Alan Konheim of IBM at Yorktown Heights, New York, understands the argument of Hellman and Diffie, but he is convinced that such a code-breaking number-cruncher will never actually be built. He notes that if any company has misgivings about the security of the code, they could effectively increase their key size to 112 bits by enciphering their data and then enciphering it again. "Would the government invest in a machine to break the code if people could easily foil the machine by enciphering twice?" Konheim asks impatiently.

Dr. Konheim may be correct in his assessment but, unfortunately, the Data Encryption Standard is also involved in another controversy. In order to get permission to export the cryptographic device, IBM had to agree to allow the National Security Agency to participate in its design and to classify a few of the critical features of its inner mechanisms. Accordingly, some critics find it difficult to "shake the feeling that these features were classified because to reveal them would be to reveal far simpler ways to break the code."

Because of questions concerning its security, some important potential clients have declined to adopt the new system, thus, to some extent, nullifying its effectiveness as a *standard* encryption procedure. Specifically, Robert Morris of Bell Telephone Laboratories says that officials at his company "have decided that the . . . (Data Encryption Standard) is too insecure to be used in the Bell System".* Andrew Del Preore of the Banker's Trust Company in New York is more tight-lipped about the exact reasons, but the bottom line is that his company has decided not to use the Standard because it "did not meet all the banks requirements." It seems likely that if the Data Encryption Standard had been master-minded entirely by private industry, few would be disturbed. But, unfortunately, as Dr. Gina Bari Kolata commented in a recent *Science* magazine article "some critics suspect that this coding system was carefully designed to be just secure enough so that corporate spies outside the government could not break a user's code and just vulnerable enough so that the National Security Agency could break it."**

On the other hand, it should be noted that the executives at many companies are not shaken by the scare stories that have been circulating.

*"Computer Encryption and National Security Agency Connection". *Science*. July 1977. pp. 438-440.

**"Computer Encryption and National Security Agency Connection". *Science*. July 29, 1977. pp. 438-440.

Officials at Citibank in New York, one of the most sophisticated commercial users of cryptography, are fully cognizant of the criticisms, but plan to use it anyway. M. Blake Greenlee of Citibank says that the Data Encryption Standard is "a great step forward". In his view most of the problems associated with it are psychological, not practical. According to Greenlee, it all boils down to this commonplace observation: "Few people in the U.S. trust our intelligence agencies."

TRAPDOOR CODES

People often criticize something without being able to come up with anything better. But when Hellman and Diffie blasted the Data Encryption Standard, they not only offered a simple way to make a substantial improvement (double the key size) they also suggested a more elaborate alternative called a "trapdoor code". Trapdoor codes have several attractive properties not shared by the Data Encryption Standard.

For most coding schemes the *encrypting* and the *decrypting* functions are simply interrelated. Thus, for example, if you understand the method I used in encrypting the message in Figure 55, you also understand how to decrypt it. However, the trapdoor code, as developed by Hellman and Diffie, is not reversible in this sense. Such a code is based on the fact that some mathematical procedures are easy to perform but their *inverses* are not. Their picturesque name is meant to convey the feeling associated with a trapdoor, namely, it's easy to fall through—but hard to get back from the other side.

Hellman and Diffie proposed several specific "trapdoor functions" in their earliest publications. All of them worked, but none was entirely satisfactory. Fortunately, Ronald L. Rivest, Adi Shamir, and Leonard Adleman, three cryptography experts at MIT, have developed an elegant way to implement the Hellman-Diffie concept using prime numbers.* (A prime number is one which is evenly divisible only by itself and 1. Thus, for example, 13 is prime but 14 isn't—it's divisible by 2 and 7.)

The new "trapdoor" methodology is based on the fact that it was easy to find two large prime numbers and multiply them together but amazingly difficult for someone else to take the resulting product and determine its two prime factors. (The two quantities which when multiplied together will produce the same number.) Dr. Rivest has provided the following estimates on the difficulty of finding the necessary prime factors: "It would take the PDP-10 computer about 90 seconds to

---

*"A Method for Obtaining Digital Signatures and Public-Key Cryptosystems". Rivest, Ronald, Shamir, Adi, Adleman, Len. Technical Memo LCS/TM82. Massachusetts Institute of Technology. April 1977.

find two 60-digit prime numbers and multiply them together to obtain their product of some 121 digits. But if we programmed that same computer to find the composite primes of the resulting 121-digit number, by the best available algorithm, it would take the machine at least 40 quadrillion years!"

If you were a user of a trapdoor coding system, the first step would be for you to generate two large prime numbers (about 40 digits each) and feed them into your encryption device. You would then keep these prime numbers secret but publish their product in the open literature. Anyone who chose could then send you a message at any time. He or she would do this by inserting the product number into his or her coding device and transmitting the resulting ciphertext to your computer. Such a message could be broadcast over network TV or printed in the *New York Times*. It wouldn't make any difference who intercepted it because the only device in the world that would be able to decipher the hidden message would be one that "knows" the two prime numbers whose product equals your published value. Note that this method does not require the advanced distribution of cryptographic keys nor the concealment of the encoding algorithm. Another important property is that it provides for the possibility of "unforgeable" electronic signatures.

The only hope for breaking the Hellman-Diffie trapdoor code is for someone to devise an efficient way to factor large numbers into their component primes. There is, of course, no proof that some ingenious expert won't eventually discover a fast-factoring algorithm. Still, some of the best mathematicians in the world have struggled with this factorization problem for the past 300 years. No important insights have been developed for more than a century. However, even if an unexpected breakthrough in factorization procedures should occur, trapdoor codes would, in any case, have a secure future. This is true because there are many other functions, not involving prime numbers that could serve as the basis for an effective trapdoor code.

THE MANY FACES OF COMPUTER CRIME

In this chapter we have devoted most of our attention to electronic embezzlement and the various methods for its prevention. However, there are many other types of computer crime. One of the most common is the stealing of computer time for personal or frivolous applications. This happens on a small scale almost everywhere computers are used. Biorhythm charts and Snoopy Calendars made by computer are proudly displayed at many data processing centers.

Illicit computer games are also quite common. Nearly every large data processing center is equipped with "Space War" or "Blackjack" or even 5-handed poker games. When the work load is slack, the operators are inevitably tempted to crank up one of these games for a few minutes of painless diversion. No one has made a study to find out, but it seems likely that time-sharing (with its unsupervised remote terminals) has probably increased this waste of precious resources.

Another common source of unspectacular fraud is the theft of computer programs for resale or reuse at another location, often a competing company. Even a relatively simple program can be worth a great deal of money. Careful estimates indicate that each command ends up costing something like $10 to $30 by the time the program becomes fully operational. Occasionally, one company steals programs from another by reading its files on a time-sharing terminal; but, more often, a programmer merely switches jobs and carries along a copy of a familiar routine. There are also persistent reports of programmers leaving in a huff and slipping a few extra cards into their decks to spoil their programs for any future users.

Much more serious acts of vandalism—and terrorism—have also occurred at a number of data processing centers. Some of the most vicious attacks took place in conjunction with the demonstrations against the Vietnam War when university computer systems were known to be used in military research. In 1970 the computer center at the University of Wisconsin was bombed, resulting in the death of one of the students and damage estimated at $1.5 million. At about the same time, a Molotov cocktail tossed into the data processing center at Fresno State College in Northern California caused $1 million in damages.

Credit verification firms have provided an opportunity for a more serene (and more profitable) type of computer crime. Recently, an underground market for the doctoring of unfavorable credit information has grown and flourished. In 1977 one of the clerks at TRW Credit Data was indicted for tampering with the company's credit files. She was said to have doctored several hundred individual records for fees ranging from $300 to $1500 each.

One final type of computer crime deserves brief mention. Some people get so angry and irritated with computers that they assault them with hand guns and other deadly weapons. To date there have been at least four authenticated cases of attempted computer murder.

BIBLIOGRAPHY

1. Alexander, Tom. "Waiting for the Great Computer Rip-Off." *Fortune,* July 1974, pp. 143-150.

2. "Are Colleges Training Computer Criminals?" *The Chronicle of Higher Education*, 17 July 1978.

3. Brandt, Allen. "Embezzler's Guide to the Computer." *Harvard Business Review*, July-August 1975, pp. 79-89.

4. Parker, Brian and Umholtz, Philip D., "Business Countermeasures to Crime Losses." *Stanford Research Institute Business Intelligence Program*, June 1976.

5. "Central Crime Computer Project Draws Mixed Reviews." *Science*, 8 July 1977, pp. 138-141.

6. "Computer Encryption and the National Security Agency Connection." *Science*, 29 July 1977, pp. 438-440.

7. "Controversy Over 'The Encryption Controversy' " *Mini-Micro Systems*, May 1978, p. 7.

8. *Computer Security and Integrity*, IEEE Computer Society, Long Beach, California: Gaithersburg, Maryland Symposium Proceedings, 19 May 1977.

9. "Computer Security: An Overview." *Datamation*, January 1974, pp. 42-47.

10. "The Computer Thieves." *Newsweek*, 18 June 1973, pp. 109-112.

11. "Conning by Computer." *Newsweek*, 23 April 1973, p. 90.

12. Crichton, Michael. *The Great Train Robbery*, New York, New York: Knopf, 1975.

13. "A Crime: Management's Attitude Toward Theft." *Management Review*, August 1977, pp. 29-31.

14. "The Criminal Mind: A New Look at an Ancient Puzzle." *Science*, February 1978, pp. 511-514.

15. "Cryptography: On the Brink of a Revolution?" *Science*, 19 August 1977, pp. 747-748.

16. "Computer Capers." *Time*, 8 August 1977, p. 53.

17. "The Outlook for Computer Security." *Mini-Micro Systems*, October 1978, pp. 42-45.

18. Diffie, Whitfield, and Hellman, Martin E. "Exhaustive Cryptanalysis of the NBS Data Encryption Standard." *Computer*, June 1977, pp. 74-84.

19. Diffie, Whitfield, and Hellman, Martin E. "New Directions in Cryptography." *IEEE Transactions on Information Theory*, November 1976, pp. 644-654.

20. "Dubious Sounds." *Newsweek*, 26 February 1979, p. 93.

21. Gardner, Martin. "A New Kind of Cipher that Would Take Millions of Years to Break." *Scientific American*, August 1976. pp. 120-124.

22. Gardner, Frances. "On the Meaning of Randomness and Some Ways of Achieving It." September 1977, pp. 116-120.

23. "The Great Computer Heist."*Newsweek,* 20 November 1978, pp. 99-100.

24. Katzman, Harry Jr., *The Standard Data Encryption Algorithm.* New York, New York: Petrocelli Books, 1977.

25. Kinnican, Paul. Data Encryption Garus: Tuchman and Meyer." *Mini-Micro Systems,* October 1978, pp. 54-60.

26. "The Lady is a Thief: The Great Train Robbery." *Time,* 5 February 1979, p. 144.

27. McLaughlin, R. A. "Equity Funding: Everyone is Pointing at the Computer." *Datamation,* June 1973, pp. 88-91.

28. Meissner, Paul. "The Computerized Password." *Privacy Journal,* August 1977, pp. 3-5.

29. Meyer, Carl H. and Tuchman, Walter L. "Putting Data Encryption to Work." *Mini-Micro Systems,* October 1978, pp. 46-52.

30. Mitchell, Grayston. "Annual Federal Fraud Loss Put as High as $25 Billion." *Los Angeles Times,* 19 September 1978.

31. Parker, Donn B. and Nyeum, Susan. "The New Criminal." *Datamation,* January 1974, pp. 56-58.

32. Ralston, Anthony and Meek, Chester. "Crime and Computer Society." *Encyclopedia of Computer Science*: New York, New York, Petrocelli/Charter: 1976, pp. 372-374.

33. "The Rising Risks of Regulation." *Time,* 27 November 1978, pp. 85-87.

34. Rivest, Ronald; Shamir, Adi, and Adleman, Len. "A Method for Obtaining Digital Signatures and Public Key Crypto Systems." *Laboratory for Computer Science,* April 1977, MIT/LCS/TM-82.

35. Robertson, W. "Those Daring Young Con Men of Equity Funding." *Fortune,* August 1973, pp. 81-85.

36. Rosen, Stephen. "Computer Crime." *Future Facts,* New York, New York: Simon and Schuster, 1976.

37. Rosen, Stephen. "Data Privacy through Cryptology." *Future Facts.* New York, New York: Simon and Schuster, 1976, pp. 321-322.

38. Sandek, Lawrence. "Privacy, Security, and Ciphers." *Data Processor,* January 1978, pp. 2-8.

39. Shapley, D., and Kolata, G. B. "Cryptology: Scientists Puzzle Over Threat to Open Research." *Science,* 30 September 1977, pp. 1345-1349.

40. "Sharpest Spurt Ever in Violence, Theft." *U. S. News and World Report,* 24 November 1975, p. 82.

41. "Society Not Cause of Crime, Study Finds." *Los Angeles Times,* 31 August 1977, Part II. pg. 4.

42. "Spotting the Computer Crook." *Science Digest,* October 1973, p. 39.

43. "Study Crime Cost to Business." *Electronics News,* 5 June 1978.

44. "The Ultimate Heist." *Time,* 20 November 1978, p. 48.

45. "Using Computers to Steal, Latest Twist in Crime." *U. S. News and World Report,* 18 June 1973, pp. 39-40.

46. "The War on White Collar Crime." *Business Week,* 13 June 1977, pp. 66-71.

47. Whiteside, Thomas. "Annals of Crime: Dead Souls in the Computer (Part I)." *The New Yorker,* 22 August 1977, pp. 35-65.

48. Whiteside, Thomas. "Annals of Crime: Dead Souls in the Computer (Part II)." *The New Yorker, 29 August 1977, pp. 34-64.*

EXERCISES

1. Explain why computer embezzlers are not caught as often as other thieves and why they are not as likely to suffer severe punishment even if they are caught.

2. Assess controls are designed to limit the use of computer systems to those individuals who are actually authorized to use the machines. Describe several of these techniques and list some of the difficulties associated with their implementation.

3. How do the Tiger Teams at ZARF earn their paychecks? Do you think their jobs will get harder or easier in future years? Explain your answer.

4. What is the Data Encryption Standard? Who perfected it? What have been some of the problems in its implementation?

5. The words *fraud, theft,* and *embezzlement* were used more-or-less interchangeably in this chapter. However, lawyers and judges tend to make more careful distinctions. Look up the definitions of these three terms in your dictionary. Now summarize the differences and give illustrative examples.

6. What is a lock-and-key terminal? Why isn't it more widely used?

7. How do the losses due to computer crime compare with the losses we suffer from other types of criminal activity? How do the rates of growth compare?

8. Explain why it is so difficult to develop an operating system that is secure from people like Lieutenant Karger? What is one method of making the computer's operating system more impenetrable?

9. What is a trapdoor code? In what practical ways does it differ from the code used in the Data Encryption Standard?

10. In this chapter the author indicates that secret passwords are not as effective as they could be in improving data security. Why is this so? What could we do to improve their effectiveness?

STUDENT PROJECTS

1. Ever since it was first introduced in 1977, the Data Encryption Standard has been the focus of several raging controversies. Research these controversial issues and put together an informal written report summarizing your findings.

   ## SUGGESTED REFERENCES:

   a. "Computer Encryption and The National Security Agency Connection", *Science.* July 29, 1977. pp. 438-440.

   b. "Cryptography: On The Brink of a Revolution?" *Science.* August 19, 1977. pp. 747-748.

   c. Katzan, Jr., Harry. *The Standard Data Encryption Algorithm.* New York, New York: Petrocelli Books 1977.

   d. Diffie, Whitfield. "The Outlook for Computer Security". *Mini-Micro Systems.* October 1978. pp. 42-45.

   e. Diffie, Whitfield and Hellman, Martin E. "New Directions in Cryptography". *IEEE Transactions on Information Theory.* November 1976. pp. 644-654.

   f. Diffie, Whitfield and Hellman, Martin E. "Exhaustive Cryptoanalysis of the NBS Data Encryption Standard". *Computer.* June 1977. pp. 74-84.

   g. "Controversy Over 'The Encryption Controversy'." *Mini-Micro Systems.* May 1978. pg. 7.

2. Coding methods have had a rich and exciting history. Look up codes in the encyclopedias in your library and write a short summary report. Include samples and descriptions of code-breaking procedures if this will help clarify your presentation.

3. In this chapter we saw how difficult it is to design a secure data processing system. But, perhaps, the experts have not yet approached the problem in a sufficiently imaginative way. Sketch the plans for a secure computer center incorporating as many security features as you can imagine complete with one or two line descriptions on how they work. Feel free to use some of the security features that are described in this chapter, but also invent some new ones of your own.

CHAPTER 8

MACHINES THAT TEACH

AN INTRODUCTION TO COMPUTER AIDED INSTRUCTION
The Basic Hardware
A More Sophisticated Approach
Argumentative Robots

AVAILABLE COURSEWARE

HARDWARE RESEARCH PROJECTS

CURRENT EXPENDITURE LEVELS

FUTURE COST PROJECTIONS
Hardward Costs
Software Costs
The Big Picture

STUDENT RESPONSES

COURSEWARE EFFECTIVENESS STUDIES

SOME PROFESSIONAL MISGIVINGS

ELECTRONIC TUTORING IN THE HOME

BIBLIOGRAPHY

EXERCISES

STUDENT PROJECTS

The first electronic digital computers were developed at large public universities. Hence, it might seem reasonable that students would have been among the earliest beneficiaries. But, in fact, the computers at Princeton and MIT were seldom used by anyone who was enrolled in college. Most early applications were scientific or military. Later, as business processing became increasingly popular, the campus computers were saddled with such mundane assignments as keeping records, meeting payrolls, and ordering janitorial supplies.

Because of the high cost and complexity of the earliest machines, no one was much inclined to consider the possibility of using computer technology to streamline the educational process. By the early 1960's, however, programmed instructional routines had begun to appear at certain selected locales, and, within a short time, a few brave visionaries were beginning to speculate about the possibilities for a new "educational revolution."

Of course, our educational system has always been awash with tantalizing rumors of "revolutionary" new technologies. Even as early as 1866 it was said that a new technological development, the blackboard, would likely trigger revolutionary changes in the classroom. "It is the mirror reflecting the character and quality of the individual mind,"* claimed one popular advertisement of the day. In the 1920's radio was touted as having similar revolutionary potentialities. In the 1930's it was motion pictures . . . in the 1950's it was language laboratories . . . and in the 1960's it was the high speed digital computer.

Not surprisingly, teachers living in this world of slick talk and fancy claims leaned toward skepticism. But in the 1960's when a computer salesman came to call, they were at least willing to read his brochures and listen to his sales pitch. What was causing these skeptical educators to let down their guard? For one thing digital computers seemed to open up genuine possibilities for *individualized instruction*. Unlike textbooks, filmstrips, and tape recordings, which have a rigid *linear* structure, a computer program can be coded with "branching" capabilities. If a student answers its questions correctly, it skips to new material; if his responses indicate confusion, it provides an instant review. Proponents of Computer Aided Instruction (CAI) reasoned that with such a program, each student could move at his own pace under the constant direction of a machine that never got tired or irritable—in short, a supremely-patient electronic tutor.

The tutorial capabilities of programmed instruction had intrigued Stanford University professor Patrick Suppes even before he was inti-

*Tyack, David B. "Educational Moonshot?" *Phi Delta Kappan*. February 1977. pg. 457.

mately familiar with the necessary methodology. Consequently, he was delighted to receive a phone call from one of the editors at Scientific American in 1966 asking him to assess the potential advantages of CAI in the classroom. After making a throughgoing investigation, he felt he had to go all the way back to the boyhood days of Alexander the Great in order to find an appropriate parallel:

> "One can predict that in a few more years, millions of school children will have access to what Phillip of Macedon's son Alexander enjoyed as a royal preogative; the personal services of a tutor as well-informed and responsive as Aristotle."*

A professional colleague of Professor Suppes was not quite as concerned with the historical significance of CAI, but he was entirely enamoured with its psychological advantages, pointing out that it lacks the "scorn, impatience, sarcasm, and prejudice" of conventional educational methods as preceived by most slow learners—many of whom have come to regard their textbooks as "frightening symbols of failure and despair".**

Joseph Newman, staff writer for U. S. News and World Report, must have felt a strong rapport with these same slow learners when he edited the following paragraph summarizing some of the advantages of using the computer in the classroom:

> "A well-programmed computer can keep a student at an assigned task until it is mastered, while a teacher might present a lesson and move on to something else—whether the student understands it or not. Also, unlike most teachers, the computer is endlessly patient, running until it is shut off. 'When I want to shut it up, I can shut it up,' remarked one youngster seated at a terminal, apparently trying to prove that he controlled it, not it him. In addition the computer can substitute for missing teachers. And it has no biases. As one young user is said to have remarked to a classroom visitor: 'I like the computer, it doesn't know I'm black.'"***

Unfortunately, despite these glowing accounts of its many advantageous characteristics, CAI seems to be causing growing resentment among

---

*Peters, Harold J. "The Electronic Aristotle." *Computer Decisions*. July 1976. pp. 42-46.

**Mosmann, Charles. *Evaluating Instructional Computing*. Irvine, California. University of California at Irvine. 1976.

***Newman, Joseph. *The Computer: How It's Changing Our Lives*. Washington, D.C. Books by U. S. News and World Report. 1972.

many groups of professional educators. Their objections range over a broad spectrum, but they tend to center on the cost (often outlandish with present-day hardware) and the impersonal rote-memory nature of most existing instructional programs. For example, in a recent journal article, Dr. Seymour Papert, co-director of the Artificial Intelligence Laboratory at MIT, presented this blistering attack on the electronic tutoring devices now invading the classroom:

> "Technology in education usually means inventing bright new gadgets to teach the same old stuff in a thinly disguised version of the same old way. If the gadgets are computers the same old teaching becomes incredibly more expensive and biased toward its dullest parts, namely the kind of rote learning in which measurable results are obtained by treating children like pigeons in a Skinner box."*

Other antagonists argue against the ultimate practicality of CAI on completely different grounds. Some of them, for example, maintain that individualized instruction should not necessarily be regarded as an unqualified blessing. They agree that one aim of education is to develop individuality; but another, of equal importance, is to teach young people how to play a *cooperative* role in society. Unfortunately, they have great difficulty seeing how a student squatting in front of a remote terminal— out of contact with his teachers and classmates—can be learning anything important about human cooperation. In an age of widespread social alienation (which seems to reach its apex among college students) it is not obvious that we should adopt expensive, controversial, technologies that further insulate the classroom student from contact with other human beings.

Educator A. G. Oettinger focuses his attention on what he believes is an even more fundamental difficulty with electronic tutoring. He contends that, although individualized instruction can be achieved to a degree by bringing computers into the classroom, students with different abilities soon arrive at quite different points in the course, and limitations in computer storage make it impractical to provide the full range of material which is actually needed. He also sees the content of CAI lessons as "rigid and unimaginative". For one thing the questions are "often multiple choice and the machine is generally unable to deal with variations in

---

* The Skinner Box is used as an aid in the training of small animals such as pigeons and chickens. It was developed by B. F. Skinner, an educator who advocates a teaching philosophy based on a variation of Pavlov's conditioned responses. Practitioners of his system immediately reward any child who gives a favorable performance with toys, candy, or other desirable objects.

spelling and word order."* Moreover, equipment reliability problems and difficulties in scheduling present formidable—and in his opinion largely unnecessary—problems for those who must manage our country's complicated educational systems.

What then is Computer Aided Instruction? A bright promise for the future? A new method of breathing fresh life into our educational institutions? A bottomless rat hole for federal funds? A new method for promoting student isolation in an era when human contact is a premium commodity? In the pages to follow we shall attempt to give you a broad background of material so that you can formulate your own answers to these important questions. We start by defining CAI, carefully breaking it down into its simplest component parts, and discussing the hardware systems that are needed to make it a practical reality.

AN INTRODUCTION TO COMPUTER AIDED INSTRUCTION

Generally speaking, the term *Computer Aided Instruction* refers to the use of computers to present drills, practice exercises, and tutorial sequences to the student for the purpose of teaching him useful facts, skills, and concepts. In most such programs the material is divided into a large number of small steps interspersed with periodic tests designed to monitor the student's progress.

The three most popular approaches to CAI are:

- The Drill and Practice Method
- The Tutorial Method
- Simulation and Games

The *Drill and Practice Method* is used to reinforce previously acquired concepts. Its primary purpose is to allow the user to gain familiarity and competence with the material. By far the easiest to program, drill and practice sometimes consists of extremely simple procedures such as the review of the multiplication tables or the recall of specific chemical formulas. In many cases the computer's powers are cleverly harnessed, but in others a set of flash cards could accomplish the same objectives at a much lower cost.

The *Tutorial Method* entails the presentation of material to the student for the *first time*. The primary focus is on the student's acquisition of new facts and concepts. A tutorial program typically consists of textual

---

*Oettinger, A.G. *Run, Computer, Run.* Cambridge, Massachusetts: Harvard University Press, 1969.

material interspersed with questions and problems. If the student's responses are correct, the computer will help him or her advance quite rapidly; if difficulties are encountered, it will introduce remedial exercises before going on to something new. A dialogue format is commonly used and, in some cleverly-programmed tutorial routines, the user is allowed to ask questions of the computer. A sample printout from a program of this type is presented in Figure 56. In this particular case, the student is attempting to devise a way to synchronize two clocks, one in San Francisco, the other in New York. Notice how the student interrogates the computer to uncover clues as to how he or she might arrive at a correct solution.

A SAMPLE TUTORIAL PROGRAM

```
COMPUTER:  PLEASE CONSIDER HOW WE MIGHT SYNCHRONIZE TWO CLOCKS TO READ
           THE "SAME TIME." ONE OF THESE CLOCKS IS IN SAN FRANCISCO,
           THE OTHER IS IN NEW YORK. AS YOU THINK ABOUT THE PROBLEM,
           ASK ME ANY QUESTIONS THAT OCCUR TO YOU. WHEN YOU ARE READY
           TO PROPOSE A SYNCHRONIZATION METHOD, TYPE "READY," THEN I
           WILL QUIZ YOU ABOUT YOUR PROPOSED METHOD.

STUDENT:   how far is it from new york to san francisco

COMPUTER:  THE DISTANCE FROM NEW YORK TO SAN FRANCISCO IS APPROXIMATELY
           3000 MILES OR 5000 KILOMETERS.

STUDENT:   what about different time zones

COMPUTER:  TIME ZONES AND DAYLIGHT SAVINGS TIME ARE MATTERS OF HUMAN
           CONVENIENCE AND NOT PHYSICAL PRINCIPLE. ASSUME THAT IF
           OUR METHOD OF SYNCHRONIZATION WERE EXTENDED OVER ALL THE
           EARTH ALL INHABITANTS WOULD OPERATE ON A SINGLE TIME STANDARD.

STUDENT:   may I use light signals

COMPUTER:  CERTAINLY. FEEL FREE TO USE LIGHT.

STUDENT:   may I use moving clocks

COMPUTER:  WELL, GIVE IT A TRY AND SEE WHAT HAPPENS.

STUDENT:   now I am ready

COMPUTER:  IF YOU ARE READY, TYPE THE SINGLE WORD "READY." OTHERWISE
           PLEASE DO NOT USE THE WORD.

STUDENT:   ready

COMPUTER:  NOW I WILL QUIZ YOU ON YOUR SYNCHRONIZATION METHOD. DOES
           YOUR METHOD OF SYNCHRONIZATION INVOLVE THE PROPAGATION OF
           SOME SIGNAL—OR MATERIAL OBJECT—FROM ONE PLACE TO ANOTHER.

STUDENT:   of course

COMPUTER:  WHAT KIND OF PROPAGATING SIGNAL OR TRAVELING OBJECT DO YOU
           PROPOSE TO USE

STUDENT:   a light signal
```

Figure 56: In most tutorial programs the computer asks a series of questions to be answered by the student. But in this novel program, which was coded by Dr. Joseph Weitzenbaum and Dr. Edwin Taylor at the Massachusetts Institute of Technology, the student asks the questions and the computer provides the answers. The objective of this particular program is to help the student figure out how he or she would synchronize two clocks, one in New York, the other in San Francisco.

Simulation and Games are the most difficult CAI routines to program but, in many cases, the easiest to operate. In a simulation program the user interacts with a realistic "model" of some specific procedure. One advantage of simulation is that we can duplicate hazardous or impossible tasks without risking life, limb or property. Through simulation even beginners can conduct experiments, which would be difficult or impossible to duplicate in real life. As one researcher has pointed out: "Some sciences require human subjects; others require expensive or dangerous materials; others require impossible periods of time—years, decades, generations to complete a single experiment. Such laboratories can be simulated by the computer to provide students of these sciences with experimental experiences."[*]

In general, a simulation involves either one user or a small crew engaging in a cooperative venture. A *game* is essentially a simulation in which two or more participants compete. In some cases the computer assumes the role of one of the participants. The most popular game, at present, is electronic pingpong. Although it was built for recreational purposes rather than instruction it does, nevertheless, help teach the participants eye-hand coordination and some of the fundamental principles of exterior ballistics. More serious games are occasionally programmed for use in schools. Economics and military strategy are particularly well adapted to gaming procedures of this type.

The Basic Hardware

In most Computer Aided Instructional systems the student sits at a remote terminal and engages the computer in a lively dialogue. Generally speaking, a console typewriter equipped with several extra buttons and switches is the primary means of communication between man and machine.

A practical alternative—which can be managed by younger children—employs a computer-controlled TV screen and a small hand-held light pen. (See Figure 57) In the simplest lightpen system, the computer generates a series of multiple choice questions and the student indicates his choices by touching the light pen to the appropriate sectors of the screen. In more advanced systems, the light pen is used to draw phosphorescent lines on the screen and to erase lines—either permanently or temporarily. It can also be used to move the lines around and connect them in various ways to form new patterns. Capabilities of this type are particularly useful in the architectural and the engineering sciences.

---

[*]Mosmann, Charles. *Evaluating Instructional Computing.* Irvine, California. University of California at Irvine. 1976.

A More Sophisticated Approach

Simple, straightforward terminals form the heart of most Computer Aided Instructional systems. However, the systems at certain schools are far more advanced. At Florida State University, for instance, some of the physics courses are taught by a digital computer which controls the student's exposure to a variety of textbooks, audio lectures, single-concept film loops, TV shows, and color slides.

If you were enrolled in one of these courses, your lesson might start with a short quiz based on your last outside reading assignment. You would indicate your responses by typing on a keyboard or by touching a light pen to the appropriate spots on a TV screen. If you failed the computer-administered quiz, the machine would print a few sympathetic remarks and suggest that you reread the assignment and return the next day for a second try. If you passed the quiz, the computer would provide you with a printed study guide complete with any relevent drawings related to your current assignment. Next you might be directed to listen to a short prerecorded audio lecture covering the major points in the new material you were expected to master.

After listening to this lecture, you would be given a second quiz to see if you had grasped the new material. Depending on your responses, you might be directed to a single-concept film loop. After viewing the film as many times as necessary, you would return your attention to the

TWO TYPES OF CAI TERMINALS

Figure 57: Two popular types of CAI terminals are in widespread use. The teleprinter terminal consists of a modified electric typewriter which handles both input and output functions. An alternate type of terminal makes use of a hand-held device called a light pen. Light pens can be handled by younger children and they provide sophisticated capabilties such as graphical inputs not provided by teleprinter terminals.

computer terminal where you might be further quizzed, given additional review material, or directed back to another audio cassette. At the completion of the session, the computer would provide you with a new textbook assignment to be read and a set of review problems to be completed before your next encounter. It would also present you with a set of barcharts showing how much progress you had made since enrolling in the course. Similar materials would be made available to your teacher or your advisor.

Argumentative Robots

Robots are another mechanical frill sometimes used in conjunction with CAI to make the learning experience more interesting and palatable. At Public School 106 in New York City, for example, a computer-controlled robot named "Leachim" is programmed to talk directly and personally to the fourth grade youngsters. When his turn comes, the child dons headphones and begins taking verbal instructions from the machine. Responses are indicated by pushing buttons corresponding to a series of multiple choice questions. During the course of the student-robot "conversation", maps, diagrams, and other pictures are periodically flashed on a nearby screen. Leachim knows each student's name, family background, hobbies and interests—and he is programmed to compliment and encourage the students or, if it seems necessary, to scold them for being careless or inattentive. The students, of course, know that Leachim is a machine but, on occasion, he becomes so real to them that they can be heard arguing back, pounding their fists, or giggling with uncontrollable delight.

AVAILABLE COURSEWARE

In 1967 there were fewer than 100 CAI routines in existence among all the colleges and universities in the United States. Over the next decade this number grew steadily so that by 1976 *The Index to Computer Based Learning** would list 1837 routines related to a total of 137 subjects. These included instruction in 14 different foreign languages. If you had decided at the time to complete all the available courses, it would have taken you approximately 20,000 hours or nearly two and one half years (assuming that you were willing to work 24 hours a day every day of the year except Christmas and Thanksgiving).

---

*1976 *Index to Computer Based Learning*, edited by A. Wang and published by the Instructional Media Laboratory of the University of Wisconsin-Milwaukee.

Most of the routines would have taken you less than 10 hours of effort but a few of them would have taken much longer, especially those dealing with military technology. The index listed three routines coded by military researchers each of which required more than 600 hours for complete mastery.

But for all your painstaking efforts would you have ended up with a balanced education? Not particularly. As the barcharts in Figure 58 show, most of the available coursework consisted of college-level studies in math, health, chemistry, and the computer sciences. Your hard-earned education would have been sadly deficient in such basic fundamentals as creative writing, English literature, sociology, and applied psychology.

HARDWARE RESEARCH PROJECTS

So far the two most ambitious attempts to make use of computers in the classroom are the PLATO Project directed by Donald Bitzer at the University of Illinois and the TICCIT Project managed by Kenneth Stetten at the MITRE Corporation in conjunction with Brigham Young University.* Both of these undertakings are heavily financed by government grants and both are concerned with making CAI *hardware* and *courseware* widely affordable.

The PLATO Project, which was begun in 1960, is the larger of the two. In fact it can be classified as the most ambitious effort at producing Computer Aided Instructional programs ever undertaken. To date the center has developed approximately 4000 hours of courseware materials—enough to fill the entire college career of a typical student. Four generations of PLATO development have already been completed and present plans call for a fifth generation using 4000 terminals connected to a CDC 6600 computer. Proponents of the system are convinced that they can eventually get the cost of the terminals down from $6000 each to less than $500 using reasonable extensions of present technology.

In the 1960's when the PLATO Project was first started, it seemed obvious that the economies of scale** would favor the use of a single centralized computer devoted to handling hundreds or thousands of remote terminals. However, in the intervening years, computer technology has changed so drastically it now appears that a set of decentralized

---

*PLATO stands for *Programmed Logic for Automatic Teaching Operations* whereas TICCIT denotes *Time-shared, Interactive, Computer Controlled Informational Television.*

**The economy-of-scale concept refers to a law of economics which states that, all other things being equal, the cost per participant or per product is generally lower when operations are carried out in a big way. One reason is that with large-scale operations more elaborate, more automated equipment is economically justifiable. Given better equipment, costs inevitably decline.

minicomputers each devoted to a relatively small number of terminals may provide a cheaper alternative under certain conditions. Many of the newer CAI systems are set up in this way, including the TICCIT Project, managed by the MITRE Corporation.

The basic terminal in the TICCIT Project is an ordinary color television set equipped with a special keyboard. This device, along with a dozen or so of its companions, is connected to a dedicated minicomputer with approximately 100 million characters of disk storage capabilities. The computer creates the printed materials and the images which appear on the screen. It also generates audio messages which are played through the speaker system.

The money used in financing the PLATO and the TICCIT Projects has been furnished in large part by various agencies of the federal government especially the National Science Foundation. Over the past decade these two projects alone have been granted approximately $30 million in government funds. However, in recent years government appropriations have declined abruptly. For example, support from the National Science Foundation plummeted from $8.4 million in 1972 to $3 million in 1976. According to National Science Foundation Director Erik

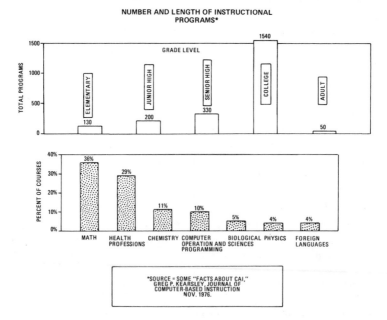

Figure 58: These statistics, which were compiled by Dr. Greg P. Kearsley of the University of Alberta, show that 68 percent of all Computer Aided Instructional routines are devoted to the education of college students. The various routines cover a broad range of subjects but math, health studies, chemistry and the computer sciences play a dominating role.

McWilliams we are rapidly approaching the time when CAI must "sink or swim in the marketplace". Unfortunately, it may end up sinking. History shows that CAI programs tend to "fade away as government support is withdrawn". To many observers this suggests that "local school systems do not find CAI's benefits worth the expense".* Erik McWilliams is afraid the programs may continue their disconcerting slide in future years: "Times are tough economically, especially in education", he points out, "consequently, it's going to be difficult for school administrators to make a major capitol investment in hardware."

"*Difficult* is hardly the word." Insists Dr. Harold J. Peters the ranking CAI expert at Hewlett Packard. "The commercial version of the National Science Foundation's PLATO will carry a price tag in excess of $5 million; the cost of a terminal alone will be $6000!"** Ironically, as we shall see, the decline in support for CAI is coming at a time when hardware costs are falling precipitously. Indeed, within a few years, computerized instruction could be a bigger bargain than conventional teaching techniques.

CURRENT EXPENDITURE LEVELS

The American educational system is big business. At present there are approximately 61 million full-time students enrolled in our schools compared with about 100 million employees in our labor force. To keep these schools in operation we are spending approximately $140 billion each year—or roughly $2300 per student. Higher education alone accounts for about 11 million full-time students and absorbs approximately $50 billion in annual expenditures.

Only a small part of this money is being spent on computers. As the graph in Figure 59 shows, computer-related expenditures in all forms amount to less than $1 billion per year. However, even this relatively small expenditure level can be somewhat deceptive because most of the outlays are absorbed by administration and research rather than instruction. As a matter of fact, only about $170 million goes toward clear-cut instructional applications. Of this total 36 percent is used to teach students *about* computers, (i.e., training them to program, operate, and service data processing machines.) The remainder, approximately $100 million, is used directly for CAI applications.

It's not a very large expenditure. Indeed, by the time it is apportioned among our country's 11 million college students, it amounts to only

*Butman, R.C. "Mind and Machine". *Technology Review*. June 1976.

**Peters, Harold J. "The Electronic Aristotle". *Computer Decisions*. July 1976. pp. 42-46.

around $9 each. Although this figure represents an almost insignificant fraction (less than 0.5 percent) of per-student expenditures, many educators seem to need more-or-less constant reassurance that their jobs are not threatened by computers. Fortunately, the proponents of CAI are ready, willing, and able to reassure them. In reading the specialized journal articles from the field it's surprising how often we encounter the same pat explanation that CAI will "save the teacher a great deal of time"—which can be used for more "individualized instruction". Consider these examples from various recent publications:

"Instead of replacing teachers, (Computer Aided Instruction) has given them the means to do their jobs better and provide a richer and

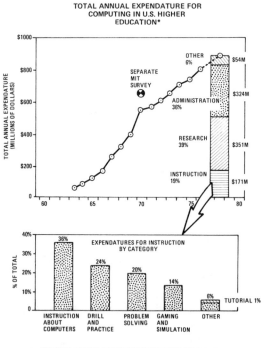

Figure 59: In 1978 a little less than $1 billion was spent for computing in American colleges and universities. Of this total, approximately 19 percent ($170 million) was devoted to instructional purposes, one-third of which was used in teaching students *about* computers. Thus, only about $100 million went directly toward CAI applications. Spread over a student population of 11 million, this implies an annual CAI expenditure level of about $9 per student.

more valuable education to their students."

Charles Mosmann
Evaluating Instructional Computing
University of California at Irvine, 1976

"The teacher is relieved of routine drill-and-practice work and can devote more time to giving students individual attention."

Computers in Society
Donald H. Sanders
McGraw-Hill 1977

"Thus the computer can free a sizeable amount of the teacher's time for other types of interaction with students."

John F. Rockart and Michael S. Scott Morton
Computers and The Learning Process in Higher Education
McGraw-Hill 1975

"A computer should never take over completely the role of educator. Instead, it makes the job of the educator easier and gives him more time for individual interaction with the students."

Bruce A. Carter
In a recent letter to *Creative Computing*

As you can see "individual attention" is the common watchword. No one ever seems to indicate that the time saved by the teacher might be used for other purposes such as gazing out the window, feeling useless, visiting the local pub for a quick glass of wine, or standing in the local unemployment lines!

But, in reality, is all this skillful reassurance actually necessary? Some people might conclude that it is ridiculous to believe that a technology which accounts for a scant 0.5 percent of overall expenditures could have a detectable, much less frightening, impact on overall employment levels. But, on the other hand, CAI has been under development for only about ten years. Did the automobile seem like much of a threat to the horse-drawn carriage when it had been in existence for a single decade? Most contemporary Americans regarded the new contraption not as a threat to their equestrian way of life but rather as a toy for the idle rich. Only after Henry Ford managed to cut the cost of automobiles down to affordable levels were horse-drawn carriages clearly doomed. Will the same thing happen in the field of Computer Aided Instruction? Will we witness a revolution as soon as costs decline? Nobody can say for sure. As we shall see, CAI faces a number of other difficulties. However, if costs do remain high they will surely constitute a more-or-less permanent barrier to the widespread adoption of Computer Aided Instructional routines.

FUTURE COST PROJECTIONS

Two major expenses are associated with CAI: the cost of the hardware and the cost of developing the courseware. If we are to have economically viable electronic tutors, it will be necessary to reduce both of these two costs substantially. Fortunately, this may not turn out to be prohibitively difficult.

Hardware Costs

Since the earliest beginnings of the digital computer age the cost of data processing hardware has been dropping steadily and most experts expect this trend to continue. The graphs in Figure 60 show what has happened to the costs of the computer's processing circuits and its high-speed memory units. Both graphs employ logarithmic scales so that the contour lines have deceptively gentle slopes. However, if you study the values plotted on the graphs, you will see that the required expenditures are dropping precipitously. As computer expert Paul Armer has noted: "The cost per computer operation (processing and storage) has fallen by a factor of ten every four years."

Of course, the costs of certain computer modules—especially those involving relatively large numbers of moving parts—have not dropped as rapidly as those units which are all-electronic. Thus, we would not expect that the various devices in a large-scale CAI system to drop in price uniformly over the next few years. However, we can reasonably anticipate relatively large price reductions especially if the units are produced in quantity. Proponents of the PLATO system for example, expect quantity production to cut the cost of their terminals by a factor of ten or more if their system is widely adopted. Such a projection does not seem entirely unreasonable in view of the fact that hobby computers, once they became popular, experienced similar price reductions.

Software Costs

In 1973 C.C. Gotlieb and A. Borodin published a book entitled *Social Issues in Computing** in which they surveyed CAI courseware

---

*Gotlieb, C. C. and Borodin, A. *Social Issues in Computing*. Academic Press, New York, New York. 1973.

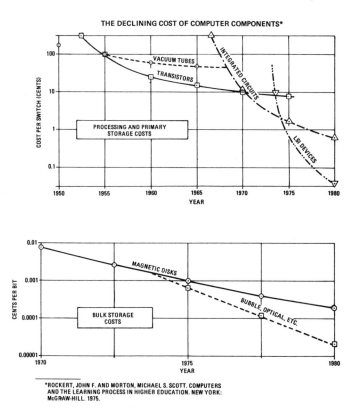

THE DECLINING COST OF COMPUTER COMPONENTS*

*ROCKERT, JOHN F. AND MORTON, MICHAEL S. SCOTT. COMPUTERS AND THE LEARNING PROCESS IN HIGHER EDUCATION. NEW YORK: McGRAW-HILL. 1975.

Figure 60: Throughout the history of computing, hardware costs have experienced a steady decline. The graph at the top of this figure shows the cost of the processing circuits in a digital computer. Similar circuits are used in constructing the computer's high-speed storage arrays. The bottom graph represents the costs of the magnetic disks and more advanced electronic devices which handle the computer's bulk storage requirements. As you can see, the cost of these units has declined almost as rapidly as the solid-state circuits portrayed in the graph at the top of the figure.

preparation costs. Near the end of their treatment they bracketed the prevailing cost values with the following statement: "an estimate of 100 hours is generally taken for the time required to prepare one hour of CAI instructional material. This results in a cost of from $2000 to $10,000 per hour for prepared (courseware) material".*

---

* These courseware preparation times and costs may seem surprisingly high to you. But, in fact, they do not differ appreciably from comparable values associated with the preparation of ordinary textbooks. If we assume it will take you 20 hours to read the material contained in this book, the ratios are: 100 hours of preparation time and $1000 in preparation costs per hour of prepared material.

A few years later John Rockart and Michael Morton arrived at similar conclusions when they studied the courseware costs associated with various CAI research and development projects.* According to their report: "a typical hour of CAI learning materials costs $2420 to create and costs $5280 after extensive field testing and revision."

These quoted courseware costs are high in absolute terms but, if we can manage to spread them over a sufficiently large number of students, they do not constitute a barrier to the development of electronic teaching methods. The graph in Figure 61 shows what happens to the cost of each student contact-hour for a particular course as the number of students varies between 1000 and 5000. As you can see, even if we must spend $10,000 to produce an hour of courseware, the cost per student contact-hour amounts to a modest $2 provided we can get 5000 enrollees. Of course, the number of people who can take any given course is not limited to 5000. The developers of the PLATO system typically assumed an exposure of 100,000 students, or even more, for the various courses they planned to develop.

Thus it seems clear that if CAI is ever to be widely adopted, more widespread sharing of the available courseware modules will be required. But aren't these expensive modules being shared already? To some degree, yes. But not nearly often enough in the opinion of Dr. Harold J. Peters, resident CAI expert at Hewlett-Packard. Dr. Peters views the typical courseware development effort as a monumental tribute to waste and inefficiency. His mood sours as he describes how school districts, in jealously guarding their powers of local control, tend to satisfy their courseware needs mostly by "working in isolation and producing fragmented packages of questionable value at premium prices."** In his opinion "lack of coordination is the principal reason why curriculum costs are so high."

The Big Picture

What then is the bottom line? Barring major changes in our economy, it seems reasonable that hardware costs will decline dramatically but the cost of the basic software producing unit—the programmer—will continue to escalate, paralleling inflation. Today textbooks are widely shared. Tomorrow this capability will surely spread to Computer Aided Instructional routines. If this happens, and if the cost of remote terminals

---

*Rockart, John F. and Morton, Michael S. Scott. *Computers and The Learning Process in Higher Education.* New York, New York: McGraw-Hill, 1975.

**Peters, Harold J. "The Electronic Aristotle." *Computer Decisions.* July 1976. pp. 42-46.

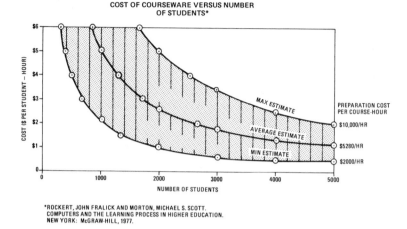

COST OF COURSEWARE VERSUS NUMBER
OF STUDENTS*

*ROCKERT, JOHN FRALICK AND MORTON, MICHAEL S. SCOTT.
COMPUTERS AND THE LEARNING PROCESS IN HIGHER EDUCATION.
NEW YORK: McGRAW-HILL, 1977.

Figure 61: In 1976 Rockart and Morton surveyed the expenditure levels associated with the preparation of the courseware modules used in CAI applications. They found that it costs an average of $2420 to create a typical hour of courseware. By the time the material has been checked out and revised, it ends up costing about $5280 per hour. Gotlieb and Borodin bracketed these values with estimates ranging from $2000 to $10,000 per hour. As the above graph shows, these courseware preparation costs are quite acceptable if we can spend them over a sufficiently large number of users.

begins to drop as more units are produced, CAI should become economically competitive with the more conventional methods of instruction.

Figure 62 shows a distinctly optimistic set of cost projections for the PLATO project. In accordance with these projections, the cost per hour of instruction is expected to decline by a factor of five or more over the next ten years. If these anticipated cost reductions do, indeed, occur the resulting routines would be cheaper than elementary school instruction.* Does this imply widespread acceptance of the CAI concept? Not necessarily. Even if it does become cost-competitive, it still must achieve student acceptance and there will still be serious questions as to the relative effectiveness of CAI when it is compared with other, more conventional, methods of instruction.

STUDENT RESPONSES

How have our students reacted to Computer Aided Instruction? There have been persistent complaints about the mechanical, unyielding

---

*It should be noted that when a CAI system is instituted, the costs of other aspects of the educational process do not necessarily decline. Thus CAI expenditures are best regarded as an *added* cost rather than *substitute* cost.

character of certain routines, some resentment concerning the lack of human contact, some footdragging when their turn comes to work on the terminals. However, hard evidence, from several different sources, indicates that, on balance, the students use it and they like it. For example, Rockart and Morton state flatly that "where computing is of high quality, where it is readily available and where its use by students is encouraged, nearly all students (and faculty) will make some use of it."* This conclusion is amply verified by a survey conducted at Dartmouth University in 1975. The major conclusion: "80 percent of the undergraduates . . . used the computer at some point during the year . . . and 93 percent of the seniors used the computer at some time during their college careers."

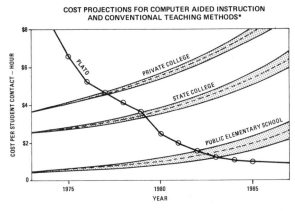

Figure 62: At present the use of the PLATO instructional routines, which were developed at the University of Illinois, are more costly than most competing teaching methods. However, the cost of conventional instruction is increasing while the cost of CAI is declining. If the optimistic projections shown in this figure prove to be accurate, by 1983 the PLATO routines will be cheaper than conventional elementary school instruction.

Indeed, if there is any problem at all with the popularity of CAI it centers around the fact that it tends to be so popular with the students it sometimes causes resentment among the teachers of more conventional courses. Rocco R. Dinapoli, mathematics instructor at Melville High in Seteuket, New York, gives us this rousing account of the reactions of the students in his school:

---

*Rockart, John Fralick and Morton, Michael S. Scott. *Computers and The Learning Process in Higher Education.* New York, New York: McGraw-Hill, 1977.

"They become so engrossed in the course and so 'hooked' on the machine that they'll spend study periods in the school's computer laboratory and either unwittingly show up late for the next class or skip it all together. They stay after school to work with the equipment. Some become so adept that they can even tell the customer engineer what's wrong with a machine."

In this age of affirmative action programs with continuous pressures toward equal opportunity and performance in the classroom some educators are concerned that CAI may help the advantaged child more than it helps the disadvantage. This belief is apparently based on the notion that if students are given a "self paced" course the brighter ones will speed up while the slower ones will tend to lag even more. However, no one seems to have conducted any controlled experiments to verify this speculative conclusion. On the other hand, *National Observer* reporter Patricia Fanning stumbled upon some fairly convincing evidence that disadvantaged youngsters are quite enthusiastic about Computer Aided Instruction:

"Teachers at an inner city high school discovered that their students had carefully jimmied a heavy, steel mesh panel in the door to the computer learning center and were sneaking in after hours to practice. The principal of the school, which is set in the midst of a black neighborhood, says that PLATO-taught math is the hottest thing going and that the pupils now come back after school to work on the computer terminals as long as the building is kept open."*

Thus we see that if a cost-effective version of CAI is developed it will not likely be kept out of our schools because of student resistance. If it sinks it will sink because it is ineffective—or because of widespread teacher opposition.

COURSEWARE EFFECTIVENESS STUDIES

Direct, clear-cut comparisons between the effectiveness of CAI and conventional instructional methods are surprisingly difficult to obtain. This is true, in part, because programmed instructional routines rarely cover exactly the same material covered in the classroom; CAI routines are usually structured to be a *supplement* to regular classroom teaching rather than a *substitute*. However, there have been a few scattered studies

---

*National Observer, May 8, 1976.

in which the two teaching methods have been pitted against one another in a direct head-to-head competition.

One of the earliest comparative studies of this type was conducted in 1967 at Florida State University in connection with a freshman-level physics course. In this controlled experiment 23 students in an autonomous CAI group were matched against two other groups of comparable size. One of them consisted of students who took the course by conventional means; the other consisted of students who attended the regular classroom lectures and were exposed to periodic computer-assisted review sessions.

The elapsed time required for all three groups to complete the course was essentially the same: 11 weeks. However, the actual instructional time for the autonomous CAI group was 23.8 hours compared with 27.8 for the other two groups. This represents a 17 percent saving in exposure time. How did the grades of the various groups compare? Carefully-administered standardized tests showed that the final grades of the autonomous CAI group were statistically superior to the two control groups. How did the participants feel about trusting their schooling to the computer? A series of post-test interviews reflected a generally positive attitude on the part of the students.*

In another experiment conducted in 1969, a Russian language program funded by the United States government was studied for effectiveness. An experimental group taught by computer was matched against a control group taught by conventional methods. According to the resulting research report: "(the) CAI students performed significantly better than the control students on final examinations for two of the three academic quarters." Their grades were only slightly better on the midterm; however, their performance was clearly superior on the final. What made the difference? In the opinion of the researchers who conducted the study, the students' enhanced performance apparently stemmed from the greater concentration required when they were operating the remote terminals:

"To keep pace with the programmed exercises, the student (had to) concentrate more directly on the language and not return to an internal monologue in English. The concentration required at a computer-based terminal precludes the student's attention from

---

*Mosmann, Charles. *Evaluating Instructional Computing.* Irvine, California: University of California at Irvine, 1976.

wandering and achieves a degree of efficiency which would be difficult to match in the best organized classroom."*

The course completion rate of the experimental group was surprisingly high: over 70 percent of the students in the experimental CAI group completed the course compared with about 30 percent in the control group. Moreover, the participants seemed to enjoy dealing with the computer more than they enjoyed dealing with their human teachers. A number of students voluntarily switched from the control group into the CAI group.

Unfortunately, some critics of Computer Aided Instruction do not see the results of these two experiments as being entirely conclusive. They suspect that the improved performance of the CAI groups may have resulted from the Hawthorne Effect. The Hawthorne Effect refers to an often-observed improvement in a subject's performance which can be attributed to his heightened sense of importance as a result of the interest and encouragement of the experimenters. The Hawthorne Effect was first noticed in a series of experiments at the Western Electric Corporation in Chicago in 1927.

The Western Electric researchers set up a carefully-controlled series of experiments in hopes of determining the effects of lighting levels and other working conditions on worker productivity. At first the experimental results were quite puzzling. In the first week the lighting levels in the plant were increased and productivity increased. The second week the lighting levels were decreased and productivity increased. The third week the lights were left alone and productivity increased. Indeed, no matter how the lights were adjusted, productivity always increased. What was causing these strange reactions? After an exhaustive investigation, the experimenters discovered that the lighting levels in the plant were essentially irrelevant. The critical factor affecting the productivity of the workers was the extra attention and support they were receiving from the experimenters themselves!

Ever since these experiments were conducted, doctors who work on experimental procedures have known that they must employ elaborate precautions in order to guard against possible distortions resulting from the Hawthorne Effect. For example, when drugs are being tested, placebos (sugar pills) are commonly given to control groups so that they won't have any way of knowing if they are getting the drug under test.

---

*Rockert, John F. and Morton, Michael S. Scott. *Computers and The Learning Process in Higher Education.* New York, New York: McGraw-Hill. 1975.

The use of "double blind" experiments is also widespread. In a double blind experiment neither the participants nor the experimenter knows which subjects are in the control group until the experiment is completed. The use of similar masking procedures would obviously be advantageous in attempting to guard against the Hawthorne Effect in CAI experiments. Unfortunately, there is no such thing as a CAI placebo and there seems to be no way to trick the control group subjects into believing that they are being taught by computer.

SOME PROFESSIONAL MISGIVINGS

Because of the obvious hazards of the Hawthorne Effect (and other experimental difficulties) many researchers remain unconvinced that CAI is, in any important respect, superior to conventional classroom instruction. For example, Rockert and Morton, after a detailed discussion of the relative merits of the two conflicting methods of teaching, arrive at this distinctively negative conclusion:

"The impact of CAI systems has been hard to measure, and there have been no clear-cut successes of the use of tutorial and drill-and-practice instructional methodologies at the college level. At the time of writing this report, there exists no published results that unambiguously establish a positive impact."[*]

Charles Mossman is somewhat more generous in his assessments but he can hardly be credited with runaway enthusiasm:

"In some environments and under some conditions, computer-based instruction may be more cost-effective than conventional instruction. These environments include particularly those in which increased speed of training is important. In military and industrial schools, for example, the student's time is a factor in the financial equation and computer-based techniques may be financially advantageous."[**]

There are a few exceptions but, in general, the people who sell terminal hardware and those who develop the courseware packages are considerably more enthusiastic about Computer Aided Instruction than are most of the faculty members who are expected to use it. As Dr. Peter

---

[*]Rockert, John Fralick and Scott, Morton S. *Computers and The Learning Process in Higher Education.* New York, New York: McGraw-Hill, 1975.

[**]Mosmann, Charles. *Evaluating Instructional Computing.* Irvine, California: University of California at Irvine, 1976.

A. Wolitzer of the Center for the Study of Higher Education at Pennsylvania State University has observed: "One of the most persistent problems encountered in the development of computer-based education at the college and university level has been the indifference of faculty members to the challenge of using computers for instructional purposes."*

J. A. Wolcos at the Alfred P. Sloan School of Management at MIT put it this way: "Faculty members are *not* optimistic about the introduction of learning technology into the curriculum . . . (they are) fairly certain that, despite the probable availability of technology, the rate of introduction into curriculums will be relatively slow."

What is behind all these negative, pessimistic assessments of the future of CAI? One root cause is fairly obvious: workers everywhere tend to engage in a little foul-tempered foot-dragging whenever they encounter a machine that could conceivably take away their jobs. Teachers are no exception. As John F. Rockert and Michael S. Scott Morton have tersely concluded: "Professors will tend, consciously or unconsciously, not to replace themselves with machines." Of course, as we have seen, it is possible to argue that Computer Aided Instruction will merely free teachers for more significant tasks in the classroom rather than pushing them aside. However, teachers have heard this seductive line of reasoning so often, they have a tendency to develop queasy feelings whenever it is voiced anew. Of course it is obvious that teachers will never be completely obsolete. They will always be needed for such varied tasks as providing motivation, developing confidence, finding meaningful rewards, and encouraging new efforts. On the other hand Computer Aided Instructional routines are so expensive, it is impossible to envision how they could be adopted on a large scale unless there are some compensating savings in labor. Clearly, if money is spent on machines from outside vendors it will not longer be available to pay professional salaries.

Some educators seem to feel that computers have already resulted in appreciable budget shifts away from teachers toward machines. However, a quick examination of a typical college budget quickly dispells this notion. A recent survey showed that the average American college is currently spending about $160,000 on computers, or about 2 percent of its total instructional budget. This figure includes administrative, research, and other non-instructional uses of the campus computers.

But job security considerations aside, there are several, perhaps more compelling reasons, why faculties are resistant to the inroads of computers

* Wolitzer, Peter A. "Faculty Perspectives on Computer-Based Education." *Journal of Computer-Based Instruction*. February 1977. pp. 76-83.

in the classroom. After a lengthy study of faculty reactions to CAI, Dr. Peter A. Wolitzer, a computer specialist at Pennsylvania State University, devised the following itemized rationale as to why it may be many years before we find large numbers of computers in the classroom:*

1. The Research Orientation of Faculty

Every university has a three-pronged mission—teaching, research, and public service—but the three items on this list are far from equal. In the university environment, research productivity is the major criterion for success. Teachers are only human and, like people everywhere, they are "apt to spend most of their time and effort in areas that will be directly rewarded." Thus, the introduction of new technology into the classroom (including CAI) is apt to take a secondary position to research.

2. The Need to Learn a New Discipline

In order to create useful courseware materials and to use CAI effectively, professors must study and absorb the new learning technologies. Unfortunately, expert researchers tend to be people who are not especially interested in things outside their own discipline. To be effective, a researcher must in some sense be a superspecialist. This intensive specialization conflicts directly with any desires he may have to master and use CAI technology.

3. Unionization

A unionized industry is typically one in which innovation is stiffled. Years ago the railway unions required that diesel-powered locomotives carry a fireman who ostensibly handled the job of shoveling "coal" into the boiler. Today about one-third of all faculty members work in a unionized situation. It is widely suspected that these individuals are less prone toward innovation than their colleagues of yesteryear who are not unionized.

4. Inherent Faculty Conservatism

Professors are intensely trained in scientific methods of scholarly analysis. Quite effective in the laboratory, this highly-structured approach to problem solving does not always serve them well in everyday life. For one thing they are often unwilling to take any action unless they can predict the consequences. "Being right is terribly important; being wrong leads to gradual disqualification as a scholar." Such an atmosphere does not tend to encourage risk-taking and bold innovation.

---

*Wolitzer, Peter A. "Faculty Perspectives on Computer-Based Education." *Journal of Computer-Based Instruction*. February 1977.

5. Role Overload

There are so many simultaneous demands on a college teacher's time that the combined expectations far exceed what he is able to do. In such a situation no person willingly gives up significant blocks of time to anything unless it has a high payoff. This role overload "will tend to minimize—if not completely negate—any time or effort spent on learning innovation." In such an atmosphere, CAI (which typically requires 100 hours of programming effort to yield a single hour of instructional time) is one of the earliest casualities.

Thus we see that the single greatest barrier to the widespread adoption to CAI in the classroom may turn out to be the teacher, the one who stands to benefit the least. Is there any way around this difficulty? One thing would surely help: devise a system of royalties to be paid to the authors of successful CAI routines. This would encourage those who may have an interest in Computer Aided Instruction to produce useful courseware modules in much the same way royalties now encourage expert teachers to produce college textbooks. The result will not be instant, worldwide adoption of CAI procedures, but this approach will help release one constraining barrier. If something isn't done we could easily spend the remainder of this century waiting for the computer to make even modest inroads into the way we go about the business of educating the students in our schools. Dr. Robert D. Barr, Professor of Education at Indiana University is not optimistic that anything much will change no matter how glistening and impressive the new technologies may appear to be. As he puts it: "Schools today are basically the same as they were 50 years ago. They have resisted all our good ideas and best efforts. The new era has not yet arrived."

ELECTRONIC TUTORING IN THE HOME

While this lively, but abstract, debate rages in academia, a promising new development may soon make it possible for Computer Aided Instruction to bypass schools and go directly into the home. This new technological miracle is the videodisc in which television images (and other materials) are recorded on plastic platters similar to ordinary phonograph records. These disks, which can store still pictures, television images, stereophonic voice recordings, and computer commands, can be mass-produced for about 40¢ each. Their developers believe millions of people will buy a small electronic device for about $500 permitting them to play videodisc "records" through their television sets.

Of course most disks will be used for entertainment—major league ballgames, a night at the opera, first-run movies, Broadway plays. But it is also easy to envision a system of instruction using a videodisc and a remote control device with three or four extra buttons that would have unusual quality and versatility. For one thing, the videodisc system produces extremely colorful images of remarkable clarity and either the finest-quality stereophonic sound or two separate monophonic sound channels either of which can be played at the flick of a switch under the user's discretion. Demonstration records have been made in which a Broadway play or a movie has two separate sound tracks—one in English, the other in French.

The computer commands necessary to control the sequencing of a CAI lesson can also be stored on the surface of the disk so that the unit itself would have extremely small storage requirements and simple processing electronics. The disk could easily be "programmed" to help you master a specific subject such as the assembly of a Heath kit or the repair of your family automobile. If you were taking such a lesson, you would see detailed "photographs", full color sketches, strips of motion picture film, and typewritten messages on your TV screen and you would hear verbal descriptions in crisp, stereophonic sound. The computer would ask you questions at intervals, either verbally or in printed form. According to your responses, as indicated by punching the buttons on your remote control device, it would sweep to different segments of the disk instantaneously. If you were mastering the material, it would automatically skip over any redundant descriptions. If you were having problems, it might reroute you through certain specific parts of the disk several times. The net result would be an amazingly responsive method of helping you master a wide variety of practical skills.

The cost of the disks will be surprisingly low. It is anticipated that one-hour videodiscs on various specialized subjects can be marketed for perhaps $5.95 each. In other words, a videodisc will be priced lower per hour than a conventional stereo LP album.

The motion pictures on the disk can be stopped and held, played in slow motion, speeded up, or even shown backwards. A one-hour record can hold up to 54,000 still pictures any one of which can be located rapidly by pushing a button. According to the November 25, 1978 *TV Guide:* "A slide show of all the world's great art masterpieces could be recorded on just one side of one disc. If you watched each slide for five seconds, starting Sunday at 8 P.M. without stopping to eat or sleep, it would be 11 o'clock Wednesday night before you saw them all."* Moreover, no matter how often you might decide to view a particular masterpiece, the picture quality would never deteriorate. The videodisc system uses laser scanning

---

*Lachenbruch, David. "What Looks Like a Phonograph Record, Works on a Laser Beam and Shows 'Jaws'?" *TV Guide.* November 28, 1978. pp. 4-8.

techniques; no wear occurs because nothing ever touches the surface of the disk except a hair thin beam of monochromatic light.

If an instructional system based on videodisc technology is eventually implemented, it will make many of the current debates concerning the relative merits of Computer Aided Instruction largely superfluous. Regardless of the attitudes of professional educators, system materials could be shipped directly into the home. And, given the vast scale of operations associated with the home consumer market, it could surely be done at economically feasible rates.

BIBLIOGRAPHY

1. Ahl, David H. "Computer Power to the People." *Creative Computing,* May/June 1977, pp. 40-47.

2. Barstow, Daniel. "Computers and Education: Some Questions of Value." *Creative Computing,* February 1979, pp. 114-119.

3. Bork, Alfred. "Computers and The Future of Learning." *Journal of College Science Teaching,* November 1977, pp. 88-90.

4. Bork, Alfred. "Computer Videodiscs and You." *Computer Decisions,* November 1976, pp. 46-50.

5. Butman, R.C. "Mind and Machine." *Technology Review,* June 1976, p. 71.

6. "Conference on Intelligent Videodiscs." *Creative Computing,* March/April 1978, p. 100.

7. Douglas, John H. "Learning Technology Comes of Age." *Science News,* 11 September 1976, pp. 170-174.

8. "Educator Reaction to 'Via Technology'". *Phi Delta Kappan,* February 1977, pp. 454-457.

9. Fitzpatrick, Michael J. "Utilization of Educationally Oriented Microcomputer Based Laboratories." *Journal of Computer-Based Instruction,* May 1977, pp. 123-126.

10. Franklin, Stephen and Murasco, Joseph. "Interactive Computer-Based Testing." *Journal of College Science Teaching,* September 1977, pp. 15-20.

11. Gotlieb, C. C. and Borodin, A. *Social Issues in Computing.* New York, New York: Academic Press, 1973.

12. Hunter, Beverly; Kastner, Carol S.; Rubin, 'Martin L.; and Seidel, Robert J. *Learning Alternatives in U. S. Education: Where Student and Computer Meet.* Englewood Cliffs, New Jersey: Educational Technology Publications, 1975.

13. "IBM Videodisc?" *Consumer Electronics,* June 1978.

14. Kearsley, Greg P. "Some 'Facts' About CAI: A Quantitative Analysis of the 1976 Index to Computer Based Instruction." *Journal of Computer Based Instruction,* November 1976, pp. 34-41.

15. Kearsky, Greg P. "Some 'Facts' About CAI: Trends 1970-1976." *Journal of Educational Data Processing,* April 1977, pp. 1-11.

16. Lachenbruch, David. "What Looks Like a Phonograph Record, Works on a Laser Beam and Shows 'Jaws'?" *TV Guide,* 28 November 1978, pp. 4-8.

17. Logsdon, Tom. *The Computers in Our Society.* Fullerton, California: Anaheim Publishing Co., 1974.

18. Mayo, John S. "The Role of Microelectronics in Communication." *Scientific American,* September 1977, pp. 192-209.

19. McLaughlin, Laura L. "CAI: Interaction Between Student and Computer." *Creative Computing,* March/April 1978, pp. 44-50.

20. Mossman, Charles. *Evaluating Instructional Computing.* Irvine, California: University of California at Irvine, 1976.

21. Peters, Harold J. "The Electronic Aristotle." *Computer Decisions,* July 1976, pp. 42-46.

22. "Review: Learning Alternatives in U. S. Education: Where Student and Computer Meet." *Journal of Computer-Based Instruction,* February 1976, pp. 80-82.

23. Rockart, John Fralick and Morton, Michael Scott. *Computers and The Learning Process in Higher Education.* New York, New York: McGraw-Hill, 1975.

24. Rothman, Stanley and Mosmann, Charles. *Computers and Society.* Chicago, Illinois: Science Research Associates, 1972.

25. Skavaril, Russell V.; Birky, William C. Jr.; Duhrkopf, Richard E.; and Knight, Jeffrey A. *Journal of Computer-Based Instruction,* August 1976, pp. 13-20.

26. Teague, Robert and Erickson, Clint. *Computers and Society.* Los Angeles, California: West Publishing Co., 1974.

27. "What Looks Like a Phonograph Record, Works on a Laser Beam and Shows 'Jaws'?" *TV Guide,* 25 November 1978, pp. 3-8.

28. Wolitzer, Peter A. "Faculty Perspectives on Computer-Based Education." *Journal of Computer-Based Instruction,* February 1977, pp. 76-83.

EXERCISES

1. Describe a typical Computer Aided Instructional routine. What basic hardware elements are needed to make such a system practical and effective? What other, more advanced, hardware systems can be used to supplement its capabilities?

2. What are some of the more forceful arguments against the long-term practicality of CAI? Do you find these arguments convincing? Explain your answer.

3. Describe PLATO and the TICCIT Computer Aided Instructional systems. What is the primary difference between the two approaches? In your opinion which type of system seems most likely to prevail in future years?

4. Briefly describe the cost trends that have been occurring in CAI over the past two decades. Do you think economics will be the deciding factor in the widespread adoption of CAI procedures? Defend your answer.

5. What is the "Hawthorne Effect"? When was it first noticed? If you were setting up a test of the effectiveness of CAI in comparison with conventional classroom instruction, how would you minimize any distortions of the results due to the Hawthorne Effect?

6. According to the author, home-based Computer Aided Instruction may become a practical reality within the next few years. Do you think this would be a better approach than developing CAI in the schools? Defend your position.

7. Approximately what fraction of our college-level educational expenditures are being spent on the computers in our schools? What fraction goes toward Computer Aided Instruction?

8. List the three major approaches to Computer Aided Instruction and, in your own words, briefly describe each one.

9. What are some of the advantages of CAI over conventional classroom instructions? What are some of the disadvantages?

10. What is the economy-of-scale concept? Why is it important to the ultimate future of the PLATO and the TICCIT Computer Aided Instructional techniques?

STUDENT PROJECTS

1. Many people have misgivings about being taught by computer. Others seem to prefer this method of instruction. Team up with several of your calssmates and design a questionnaire to assess the attitude of your fellow classmates toward CAI. Now conduct an unofficial survey and summarize your findings by constructing a series of graphs and charts.

2. In the long run one of the most exciting new developments in the field of Computer Aided Instruction will likely be the videodisc. Go to the library and read up on this new technology and summarize how it works, how it is now being used, and how it will likely be used in the next few years. Report your findings in a written or an oral report. Include sketches and photographs if this will help clarify what you have learned.

SUGGESTED REFERENCES:

a. "Conference on Intelligent Vidoediscs". *Creative Computing*. December 1978. pp. 100-101.

b. Lachenbruch, David. "What Looks Like a Phonograph Record, Works on a Laser Beam, and Shows 'Jaws'?" *TV Guide*. November 25, 1978. pp. 4-8.

c. Bork, Alfred. "Computers, Video, and You." *Computer Decisions*. November 1976. pp. 46-50.

3. Although CAI seems rather promising, there are, at present, certain problems with its widespread acceptance. Pretend you are an advertising copy writer assigned to produce

an advertisement for the PLATO project to appear in one of the educational trade journals, a journal read primarily by college teachers. Adopt a strong, postive attitude in favor of CAI and attempt to write the copy and lay out the visuals to allay any fears the reader might have about costs, effectiveness, and any possible adverse reactions of his students.

CHAPTER 9

THE ERA OF INTELLIGENT MACHINES?

WHAT IS INTELLIGENCE?

THE COMPUTER AND THE BRAIN

ARTIFICIAL INTELLIGENCE

GAME-PLAYING MACHINES
Tic-Tac-Toe
Checkers and Chess
Machines That Learn

LANGUAGE TRANSLATIONS
Syntax and Semantics
Ambiguity and Context
Language Comprehension Programs
Turing's Test for Machine Intelligence

PROBLEM SOLVING AND PATTERN RECOGNITION

SOME CRITICAL OPINIONS

THE FUTURE

BIBLIOGRAPHY

EXERCISES

STUDENT PROJECTS

For a decade or more America's popular periodicals have carried a series of stories documenting the exploits of technology's cleverest, most intelligent, digital computers. In November of 1970, for example, *Life* magazine featured these rousing paragraphs explaining how a curious, goal-directed robot named "Shaky" spends his time creeping through the empty halls at the Stanford Research Institute like some impulsive mechanical lapdog exploring his own private world:

It looked at first glance like a Good Humor wagon sadly in need of a spring paint job. But instead of a tinkly little bell on top of its box-shaped body there was this big metallic whangdoodle that came rearing up, full of lenses and cables, like a junk-sculpture gargoyle.

"Meet Shaky," said the young scientist who was showing me through the Stanford Research Institute. "The first electronic person."

I looked for a twinkle in the scientist's eye. There wasn't any. Sober as an equation, he sat down at an input terminal and typed out a terse instruction which was fed into Shaky's "brain," a computer set up in a nearby room: PUSH THE BLOCK OFF THE PLATFORM.

"Guides himself by watching the baseboards," the scientist explained as we hurried to keep up. At every open door Shaky stopped, turned his head, inspected the room, turned away and rolled on to the next open door. In the fourth room he saw what he was looking for: a platform one foot high and eight feet long with a large wooden block sitting on it.

"He'll never make it." I found myself thinking. "His wheels are too small." All at once I got gooseflesh. "Shaky," I realized, "is thinking the same thing."

Shaky was also thinking faster. He rotated his head slowly till his eye came to rest on a wide shallow ramp. Whirring briskly, he crossed to the ramp and then pushed it straight across the floor till the high end hit the platform. Rolling back a few feet, he cased the situation again and discovered that only one corner of the ramp was touching the platform. Rolling quickly to the far side of the ramp, he nudged it till the gap closed. Then he swung around, charged up the slope, located the block and gently pushed it off the platform.*

Did Brad Darrach, who provided us with this stimulating reenactment of "Shaky's" impressive exploits, actually witness clearcut evidence of *intelligent* machine behavior? He certainly thought he did. Indeed, in

---

* Darrach, Brad. "Meet Shaky, The First Electronic Person". *Life* Magazine. November 20, 1970.

the remainder of his article he expressed the opinion that Shaky can "see", "understand", "learn", and, in general, has demonstrated "that a machine can think". Moreover, he quoted the predicitons of a distinguished computer scientist who stated that in "three to fifteen years we will have a machine with the general intelligence of an average human being . . . and in a few months (thereafter) it will be at genius level . . ."

A chilling possibility, indeed, but by no means an isolated account of what some highly-respected experts believe to be the future of machine intelligence. In 1968 Marvin Minsky, director of the Artificial Intelligence group at the Massachusetts Institute of Technology, wrote an article for the *Science Journal* in which he gave this optimistic evaluation of the progress that had been made up to that point in making machines intelligent:

> "At first machines had simple claws. Soon they will have fantastically graceful articulations. Computers' eyes once could sense only a hole in a card. Now they recognize shapes on simple backgrounds. Soon they will rival man's analysis of his environment. Computer programs once merely added columns of figures. Now they play games well, understand simple conversations, weigh many factors in decisions. What next?"
>
> "Today, machines solve problems mainly according to the principles we build into them. Before long, we may learn how to set them to work upon the very special problem of improving their capacity to solve problems. Once a certain threshold is passed, this could lead to a spiral of acceleration and it may be hard to perfect a reliable 'governor' to restrain it."*

In other words, computers are already impressively smart—and they're getting smarter at a frightening rate.

Another talented researcher, Herbert Simon is convinced that computers can do anything people can do, only better. Right after he developed a highly acclaimed program called the "General Problem Solver", in 1957, he wrote these words describing what he believed would be the ultimate capabilities of intelligent machines:

> "It is not my aim to surprise or shock you . . . But the simplest way I can summarize is to say that there are now in the world machines that think, . . . learn, and . . . create. Moreover, their

---

*Minsky, Marvin. "Machines Are More Than They Seem". *Science Journal*. October 1968. p. 3.

ability to do these things is going to increase rapidly until—in the visible future—the range of problems they can handle will be coextensive with the range to which the human mind has been applied."*

Are these enthusiastic experts on the right track? Are we, indeed, on the threshold of a new era in which computers will duplicate human thought processes and behave in intelligent ways? In this chapter we shall attempt to find out what has happened in the field of artificial intelligence over the past decade or so and what is likely to happen throughout the next few years.

WHAT IS INTELLIGENCE?

"Intelligence" is not easy to define; but even if we can't formulate a workable definition, most of us are convinced that we can recognize an intelligent person by the way he behaves. For example, you would probably be inclined to agree that my 17-year old cousin in Tennessee is "intelligent" once I have explained to you that he speaks halting French, makes good grades in college calculus, and has learned to beat most of the people in his home town at checkers and chess. What convinces you that he is intelligent? Most of the characteristics he displays are imbedded in the following definition which has been adapted for our purposes from a more abstract version that appeared in the 1976 edition of the *Encyclopedia of Computer Science:*

"An intelligent person is able to understand relationships between facts, discover meanings, and recognize truth. He also adapts himself to novel situations and exhibits the ability to learn; i.e., to improve his level of performance on the basis of his past experiences."**

The key words are "understand", "adapt" and "improve".

Colliers Encyclopedia echoes the same fundamental concepts in a slightly different definition. Here are the characteristics they regard as being indicative of human intelligence:
1. The ability to deal with abstract symbols, concepts, and relationships.
2. Learning, or the ability to profit from experience.

---

*Dreyfus, Hubert L. *What Computers Can't Do.* New York, New York: Harper and Row, 1972.
**Ralston, Anthony and Meek, Chester L. *Encyclopedia of Computer Science.* New York, New York: Petrocelli/Charter, 1976.

3. The ability to adapt to new situations, or problem solving in the broadest sense.

Of course, in practice, we don't usually go through this checklist in deciding if a specific person is intelligent. Instead, we tend to base our judgment on how well he scores on a particular I.Q. test. Accordingly, one sarcastic critic of the I.Q. concept has proposed that we should define intelligence as "Whatever an I.Q. test measures".

We can administer a test to a person, but how can we measure the intelligence of an animal or a machine? Indeed, should they be regarded as intelligent entities? Or is intelligence an exclusively human trait?

In a broad-ranging discussion of animal intelligence *Van Nostrand's Scientific Encyclopedia* proposes this simple definition: "The ability to adapt to changes in environmental conditions through changes in behavior." By this yardstick, it is clear that all animals exhibit at least some degree of intelligence. However, even highly-evolved primates such as chimpanzees seldom rise above the performance level of a three year old child. Thus, if they were adult human beings we would be forced to classify them as idiots.*

On occasion, however, specific animals have exhibited spontaneous behavior patterns that would suggest that they are reasonably intelligent even in comparison with mature adults. In 1925 W. Kohler published a landmark study in which he attempted to estimate the intelligence levels of anthropoid apes and other advanced primates. When fruit was suspended beyond his reach, one enterprising ape fetched a box upon which he could stand upright as a means of gaining access to the tempting morsels. One of his blood relatives, who spotted a tantalizing bunch of bananas suspended outside his cage, managed to snag them—after signs of considerable difficulty and frustration—by inserting one bamboo shaft inside another to make a pole long enough to reach.

Cornell University Professor Carl Sagen in his book, *The Dragons of Eden,* describes far more complex adaptive behavior as displayed by a family of chimps living on Tenerife in the Canary Islands. On one occasion two chimpanzees were observed maltreating a chicken: one would extend some food encouraging the fowl to approach whereupon the other would thrash it with a piece of wire concealed behind his back. The chicken would retreat but soon allow itself to approach again—only to receive another beating. According to Sagen "Here is a fine combination of behavior sometimes thought to be uniquely human: cooperation,

---

*An idiot has an I.Q. rating of 25 or lower, the lowest classification of mental deficiency. In accordance with British traditions, an idiot is one who is unable to guard himself against common dangers.

planning a future course of action, deception, and cruelty."

Chimpanzees have also been taught to use language in reasonably effective ways. Because their jaw and tongue structure is not conducive to the production of spoken words and, because they do not pass through the natural "babbling" stage of human infants, the best approach is to teach them either sign language or a "push-button" language using a computer console. By applying these two imaginative techniques, two psychologists at the University of Nevada, Beatrise and Robert Gardner, have been able to teach certain selected chimps to use and understand more than 100 vocabulary words. The chimps construct complete sentences such as "Please machine give Lana juice". Occasionally, they have been observed to invent new compound nouns in novel situations. After testing watermelon for the first time, a fiesty young chimp named "Lucy" described it as "candy drink" and, after she burned her mouth on her first radish, she described radishes forever after as "cry hurt fruit".*

In these limited experiments the chimps were taught to communicate only with human beings or with machines. But in a more recent test series, conducted at the Yerkes Regional Primate Research Center in Atlanta, a few chimpanzees have been taught to communicate with one another.

In one experiment the researchers alternately selected either of two chimps to be led off into another room where he or she was allowed to watch as an opaque container was filled with any of eleven different kinds of food such as bananas, bean cake, or candy. Led back into the original room, the chimp was encouraged to press the buttons on a computer console in an attempt to communicate to his or her roommate what the container held. If the other chimp understood, and correctly identified the food item by punching out the correct sentence on his own console, the chimps were allowed to share the food. In one series of trials two chimpanzees named Sherman and Austin got the message (and the snack) 60 times out of 62 attempts.

In another series of trials the two chimps were separated by a transparent plastic barrier only one of them being supplied with food. Spontaneously, without prodding by the experimenters, the unfed chimp would punch out a request for a mouth-watering morsel. More often than not, his or her companion would comply. At first, as reported in a 1978 article in *Time* magazine, "Sherman, an older and apparently more quick-witted chimp, seemed to make 'errors'. When asked to share an especially

---

*Sagan, Carl. *The Dragons of Eden* New York, New York: Random House, 1977.

tasty item—say, chocolate—he occasionally ignored the request, seemed to feign ignorance, or proffered something less desirable."*

Upon being exposed to accounts of this type, we find it relatively easy to accept the fact that animals can be regarded as intelligent creatures. But, for some reason we tend to be more resistent if a colleague attempts to attribute the same intellectual powers to an inanimate machine. Are we merely exhibiting what NASA engineer Robert Jastrow has characterized as "carbon chemistry chauvinism"?** Or is there more to it than that? Perhaps we develop those uneasy feelings because we need to reserve some uniquely human characteristic for ourselves? Or is it that machines really can't think and our best instincts are protecting us from a gross misinterpretation?

Perhaps the easiest way out of this dilemma is to avoid the issue altogether and talk not about the "intelligence" of our machines but about their "*artificial* intelligence". Thus, many researchers have adopted a convention first proposed by Marvin Minsky who defined "artificial intelligence" as follows: "the science of making machines do things that would require intelligence if done by men."*** Incidentally, if you find this definition acceptable, you have already inadvertently attributed "artificial intelligence" to an inanimate machine. You see, my cousin in Tennessee is not a person: he is a computer built by IBM. As will be explained elsewhere in this chapter, skillful programmers have already managed to teach him to speak halting French, score well on college calculus exams, and beat most local enthusiasts at checkers and chess.

THE COMPUTER AND THE BRAIN

A few years ago digital computers were often described in glowing terms as "giant brains" by excited journalists looking for a flashy headline. If the computer was, indeed, a giant brain, it seemed to follow naturally that it was an intelligent entity. Proponents of the giant brain theory of computer operation never seemed to pass up an opportunity to point out that the interconnections in the human brain resemble the electronic circuits in a digital computer. Specifically, the brain's dendrites, like the computer's logic gates, are believed to transmit electrical pulses in a binary format. (See Figure 63)

However, it is easy to get too carried away with the superficial similarities between brain function and computer processing. In 1822 an

---

*"Chimp by Chimp". *Time*. August 28, 1978. pg. 61.

**"Toward An Intelligence Beyond Man's". *Time*. February 20, 1978. pg. 59.

***Minsky, Marvin. "Artificial Intelligence". *Scientific American*. September 1966.

Englishman named Charles Babbage sketched up the plans for a general-purpose machine that would have been able to solve any problem solved by a modern high-speed digital computer.* Yet it would have utilized neither electrical pulses nor binary arithmetic.

Moreover, there are functional dissimilarities between the brain and the computer's electronic circuits. For example, the brain, unlike the computer, can still function when parts of it have been destroyed by accident or disease. Another critical difference between the brain's component parts and those of a digital computer is that the brain seems to have at least limited self-repair capabilities. A brain injury may be temporarily incapacitating but, with rehabilitation, the patient is often able to re-establish some of the inoperable neural pathways. By contrast, if we snip a few parts from a computer's primary storage region, it will become permanently useless.

Still, even if the computer doesn't resemble the human brain in every respect, it could eventually turn out to be a thinking machine. After all, a Cheyenne helicopter doesn't look or act much like a bald eagle or a

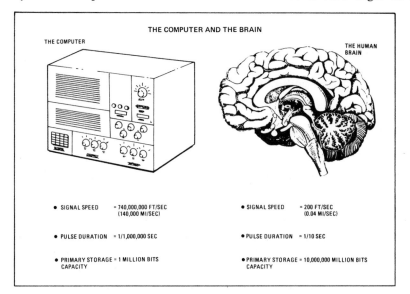

Figure 63: The human brain resembles a digital computer in that if processes discrete electrical pulses in a binary format. However, the signal transmission speeds, the packing densities, and the fundamental operating principles of the two mechanisms are grossly different. Specifically, the human brain is about ten thousand times more densely packed with information but it transmits its binary pulses ten billion times slower.

*Morrison, Philip and Morrison, Emily. *Charles Babbage and His Calculating Engine.* New York, New York: Dover. 1961.

California Condor but, nevertheless, almost everyone would agree that a Cheyenne helicopter is able to fly at least as well as any of nature's free-flying creatures.

ARTIFICIAL INTELLIGENCE

Much of the original work in artificial intelligence has been carried out at Stanford University and the Massachusetts Institute of Technology. In general, the researchers at these two locations attack their problems by using either the *simulation* mode or the *performance* mode. Those who use the *simulation mode* attempt to duplicate, in some sense or other, the way we use our brains in thinking. Those who use the *performance mode* attempt to duplicate some of the end results of our thought processes but no attempt is made to duplicate the way we actually think. In general, the *simulation mode* has not been notably successful; the *performance mode* seems to be far more practical.

Using a different type of classification system, we can divide the efforts devoted to artificial intelligence into four major areas:

1. Game Playing
2. Language Translation
3. Problem Solving
4. Pattern Recognition

In the next few subsections we shall discuss these major areas one by one. We start with game playing machines which have a surprisingly long history.

GAME PLAYING MACHINES

The first successful chess-playing "robot" was built in 1769 by Baron von Kempelen in Presburg, Hungary. His machine, which consisted of a box-like device with magnetic counters, successfully defeated such famous men as Geroge III, Frederick the Great, and Napoleon (who incidentally, made several unsuccessful attempts to cheat!). Edgar Allen Poe maintained that the device was a clever fraud—a charge which he was never able to substantiate. However, he did publish a detailed monograph forcefully arguing that a genuine chess playing machine would never be possible. "Arithmetical . . . calculations are from their very nature, fixed and determinate." he wrote. "Certain data being given, certain results . . . inevitably follow." And he went on to explain why the choices made by men could not possibly be tackled by a deterministic mechanism. In concluding his essay, he surmised that if von Kempelen's "Chess Player" was truly a machine, it would be "the most wonderful of the inventions of mankind."*

Well, Mr. Poe was right about one thing—the device was, indeed, a clever fraud—its cabinet concealed a hidden chess master. But he was wrong about the ultimate game playing capabilities of "fixed and determinate" machines. It is not at all impossible to program a computer to play competitive games. Today's computers play perfect tic-tac-toe, world-class checkers, and legal, but uninspired, chess.

Tic-Tac-Toe

Tic-tac-toe is probably the most common competitive game programmed on a digital computer. This simple game is played on a grid formed by four intersecting lines:

The players alternate, one placing X's in the open slots in the grid, the other placing O's. The object of the game is to get three X's in a row

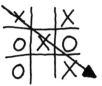

before your opponent gets three O's. In a session between sober experts, every game ends in a draw.

How is the computer programmed to play the game of tic-tac-toe? There are several easy methods. One of the most straightforward ways of visualizing a workable approach is to regard the various possible moves as being diagrammed in "tree" fashion as shown in Figure 64. In this particular instance, the machine moves first and it uses the X symbol. As you can see, the computer has three fundamentally different choices for its first move: it can put the first X in a corner, in the center, or along one of the edges. Depending on the choice the machine makes, its opponent

---

*Logsdon, Tom and Logsdon, Fae. *The Computers in Our Society*. Fullerton, California: Anaheim Publishing Co. 1977.

has either five viable responses or two.* Only the first two steps in the complete game tree are shown in Figure 64, but you can easily visualize what the rest of the diagram would look like. Some of the branches end in victories, some in defeats, and some in draws. At every opportunity the computer chooses a move that could, depending on the opponent's response, lead the game along one of the victorious branches.

For a simple game like tic-tac-toe the entire game tree (or its equivalent) can be stored inside the computer. Thus, the machine can be programmed to play a perfect game. This means that if its opponent makes a mistake at any point, the machine will win, if not, the game will end in a draw.**

---

*Note that because of obvious symmetries, certain "equivalent" moves have been deleted from the tree.
**Some programs are laid out so that the computer will lose an occasional game. This is done simply to make the game more interesting for the human participants.

A PARTIAL GAME TREE FOR TIC-TAC-TOE

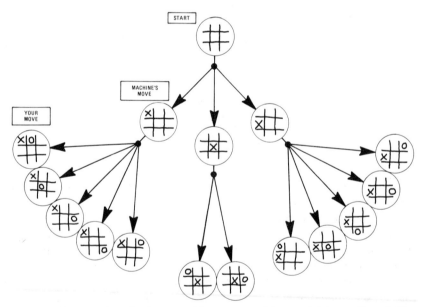

Figure 64: Tic-tac-toe is a simple competitive game used in entertaining restless children. Quite easy to master, it can be programmed on a digital computer in such a way that the machine never loses a single game. One method of developing a winning strategy is to sketch the various moves in tree fashion, each permissible move being represented as one of the branches on the tree. Whenever the human player makes a mistake, the machine response with a series of moves that drives it along a winning branch.

Checkers and Chess

If the construction of the game tree for tic-tac-toe allows us to program a perfect winning strategy on a digital computer, why don't we do the same thing for checkers and chess? It sounds like a good idea and if we could do it, it would definitely work. Unfortunately, checkers and chess are much more complicated than tic-tac-toe. If we attempted to draw their complete trees, we would need a very large sheet of paper! Arthur Samuel, who developed a highly successful checkers program in 1967, has estimated that a complete checkers tree would involve approximately 10^{40} = 10,000,000,000,000,000,000,000,000,000,000,000,000,000 branches. Even if we could program a computer to examine a move every one-thousandth of a second, it would take it 300,000,000,000,000,000, 000,000 years to consider all of the possibilities. Chess is even more complicated. According to Samuel's careful estimates, a complete chess tree would involve approximately 10^{120} = 1,000,000,000,000,000,000, 000,000,000,000,000,000,000, 000,000,000,000,000,000,000,000,000, 000,000,000,000,000,000,000,000,000,000,000,000,000,000,000,000,000 branches.*

In view of their complexity how is it possible to program a computer to play checkers or chess? The trick is to "prune" some of the branches from the tree by using *heuristic* rather than *algorithmic* programming techniques. The distinction between these two different programming methods is relatively easy to make. Most of the programs we hear about use algorithms. An algorithm is a fixed step-by-step procedure which will inevitably lead to the solution of a particular problem—assuming that the computer keeps at it long enough. By contrast, a heuristic program is one which uses clever rules of thumb to help the computer move toward a solution. The solution is not guaranteed but it is likely provided the heuristic rules are properly chosen. Thus, for example, a heuristic checkers program might be programmed in accordance with the following rules of thumb:

1. Always play to cause your opponent to have fewer pieces than yourself.
2. In counting the pieces on each side equate two kings with three men.**

---

*Desmonde, William H. *Computers and Their Uses.* Englewood Cliffs, New Jersey. Prentice-Hall. 1964.

**In checkers kings are more powerful pieces than ordinary men. They are allowed to move in either direction across the board whereas ordinary men are allowed to move only in one direction.

In accordance with these rules, the computer will set up a trade with its opponent if in so doing it will gain an advantage. Note that when heurestic programming procedures are used, the computer, like its human counterpart, cannot foresee the ultimate outcome of the game.

The first clear description of the heurestic methodology ultimately used in developing checkers and chess programs was published in 1950 by Claude E. Shannon, a well-known expert in information theory. Shannon, however, did not develop a computer program to execute his plan.

Checkers, which is vastly simpler than chess, has yielded well to computer analysis. It turns out that there are practical ways to determine the probable value of a particular move on the basis of such quantifiable parameters as control of the center position, advancement, etc. This, plus the fact that there are relatively few possible moves at any given point (because some pieces block one another and captures are forced), makes it possible to explore all plausible possibilities to a depth of as many as 20 moves which proves sufficient for excellent play.

The first operational chess program was coded at Los Alamos in 1956 for a machine called the MANIAC I. In order to keep the computing time within reasonable bounds, the game was played on a six-by-six board with no bishops. Two years later in 1958 Alex Bernstein developed a program for the IBM 704 played on a standard board. It examined seven selected moves from each position looking ahead four moves. The examination of each move took about 2 minutes of computer time. The following heurestic rules were used in selecting the seven moves to be considered:

1. If in check, capture the checking piece, interpose a piece, or move the king away.
2. If exchanges that gain material are possible, make the capturing move to start the exchange.
3. If castling is possible, castle.
4. Develop a knight or bishop.
5. Occupy an open file with a queen or a rook.
6. Move a piece into a pawn chain so that it cannot be attacked by a pawn.
7. Move a pawn.
8. Move a piece.

Upon examination the results of each selected move were compared on the basis of the resulting board position, pieces captured, etc. Thus we see that the program operated somewhat in the manner of a real chess player who studies the board trying to find special opportunities which he can exploit to his advantage. Unfortunately, although there was great optimism for chess playing programs in the 1950's they still play, at best, only a mediocre game. By 1970 several programs had reached the level of grade C tournament play but have not progressed much beyond that level in the intervening years. Moreover, any gains in proficiency that have been attained are due mainly to faster computers and greater programming effort rather than to any conceptual breakthroughs in the art of chess programming.

Thus we see that the best of the modern chess playing machines probably couldn't have beaten the earliest version as developed by Baron von Kempelen in 1769 (assuming that he concealed the finest available player inside its empty cabinet). But why haven't our experts been able to develop grandmaster-level chess programs as has been done with tic-tac-toe and checkers? The fundamental problem is that the tree structure of chess is enormously complicated. By using heuristic programming techniques we can "prune" the tree to some extent but, if we prune it too much, the computer will miss promising lines of play that would be spotted by a human expert.

It might seem that we could increase the skill of the computer by having it analyze more branches on the tree. However, careful studies of the way human grandmasters approach the game have shown that they do not analyze more lines of play than players of lesser ability, nor do they look ahead any further—typically only 6 or 7 moves. Instead, the grandmasters owe their expertise to the fact that they can "zero in" on the most promising areas of the board—in short, they have a highly-developed sense of what is *important* in the game.

Can we program our computers to approach chess in the same way? It's conceivable, but nobody seems to know how to do it. However, there is another possible approach: in theory we could program the computer to "learn" from its past experiences in much the same way a human being learns to master the game. A few years ago this concept created a wave of excitement when Arthur Samuel incorporated learning capabilities in his checkers program. In playing a series of games against qualified opponents it quickly improved its strategy.

In fact, it learned so rapidly that after playing against Samuel a few dozen times, it was able to clobber him in every subsequent game. Given further training, it also beat the champion of Connecticut in one well-publicized game although the world's champion checkers player beat it four games out of four. At first there were high hopes for improving chess programs by using the same "learning" approach. To date, however, none of the attempts have been notably successful.

How do we program a computer to learn from its experiences? A good question. In the next subsection we shall attempt to answer it by developing a "game-playing robot" that "learns" to improve its strategy in the play of a game called Hexapawn. Both the game and the learning robot were designed by Martin Gardner the Games Editor of *Scientific American*.*

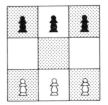

Machines That Learn

Hexapawn is a very simple game. It is played on a three-by-three board similar to the grid used in tic-tac-toe. As is shown in Figure 65 there are three chess pawns on each side and there are only two legal moves: A pawn may advance straight forward one square to an empty square or it may move diagonally one square to capture an enemy. The captured piece is removed from the board. Either player wins the game by advancing any of his pawns to the third row, by capturing all the enemy pieces, or by blocking his opponent so that he is unable to make a move. It is relatively easy to devise a winning strategy in Hexapawn. However, it is much more instructive and more enjoyable to build a "learning machine" which gradually—over a large number of trials—learns to play a perfect game.

The Hexapawn learning robot is sketched in Figure 66. It consists of 24 matchboxes capped with color-coded sketches of all the possible board configurations. In this particular instance, the human player is allowed to make the first move; the robot always goes second. All together there are 24 boxes, 2 corresponding to the second move, 11 corresponding to the fourth move, and 11 corresponding to the sixth move.

Are we ready to begin playing the game? Not quite. Before beginning, we must place color-coded beads in the boxes. Moving from box to box we insert one colored bead to match each colored arrow on the box top. When the human opponent makes his moves, we select the appropriate box and draw a bead from it at random. Its color tells us

*Gardner, Martin. *The Unexpected Hanging and Other Mathematical Diversions*. New York, New York: Simon and Schuster, 1969.

THE GAME OF HEXAPAWN

OPENING POSITIONS

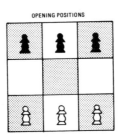

EXAMPLES OF TWO KINDS OF LEGAL MOVES

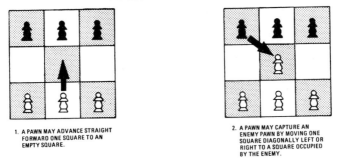

1. A PAWN MAY ADVANCE STRAIGHT
FORWARD ONE SQUARE TO AN
EMPTY SQUARE.

2. A PAWN MAY CAPTURE AN
ENEMY PAWN BY MOVING ONE
SQUARE DIAGONALLY LEFT OR
RIGHT TO A SQUARE OCCUPIED
BY THE ENEMY.

Figure 65: Hexapawn is played on a three-by-three board with three pawns on each side. The players move their pawns alternately under the following groundrules: (1) A pawn may advance straight forward one square to an empty square or (2) diagonally forward one square to capture an enemy occupying the square. The game is won if one of the players moves a pawn to the third row, captures all the enemy's pieces, or traps his opponent so that none of his pieces can be moved.

which move to make. Here is how Martin Gardner describes the play of the game.

"Make your first move. Pick up the matchbox that shows the position on the board. Shake the matchbox, close your eyes, open the drawer, remove one bead. Close the drawer, put down the box, place the bead on top of the box. Open your eyes, note the color of the bead, find the matching arrow and move accordingly. Now it is your turn to move again. Continue this procedure until the game ends. If the robot wins, replace all the beads and play again. If it loses, punish it by confiscating only the bead that represents its *last* move. Replace the other beads and play again. If you should find an empty box (this rarely happens), it means the machine has no move that is not fatal

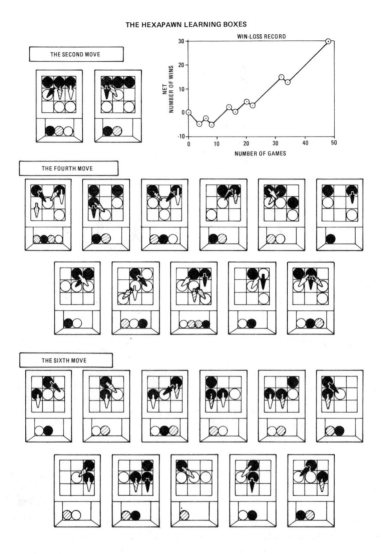

Figure 66: Twenty-four matchboxes, each capped with a sketch of a specific board position and containing up to four types of color-coded beads, constitute a "learning robot" which gradually develops a winning strategy in Hexapawn. At the beginning of the session we insert in each box a single colored bead corresponding to each of its colored arrows. Each time the robot loses a game, one of its color-coded beads is confiscated. As the graph at the top of the figure shows, the robot learns to play a perfect game after a series of 36 trials in which it is defeated eleven times.

and it resigns. In this case confiscate the bead of the preceding move."*

The sketch in the upper right hand corner of Figure 66 shows what happened when the robot was allowed to play 36 games in one particular session. It was defeated 11 times but soon learned to play a perfect game. As is the case in real life, the robot learns faster if it plays against strong opponents.

Martin Gardner's learning robot is conceptually similar to the learning routine in Arthur Samuel's checkers program which has been so widely praised by those in the field of artificial intelligence. Does it seem to learn in any meaningful sense? It definitely improves its performance on the basis of past experiences, but most people who get a chance to watch it operate are somewhat disappointed by its rather primitive learning capabilities. Generally speaking, the learning routines now being programmed on computers are not much more impressive. As Marvin Minsky has observed: "(Some) programs use . . . processes that might be called learning; they remember and use the methods that solved other problems; they adjust some of their internal characteristics for the best performance, they 'associate' symbols that have been correlated in the past. No program today, however, can work any genuinely important change in its own basic structure."**

On the other hand, we are often impressed with what machines do until we learn that they are machines. Peter J. Sandiford, director of operations research for Trans-Canadian Air Lines, demonstrated this point rather clearly when he exposed two young students to the robot in blind trials—without telling them they were playing against a machine. As we shall see, they were much impressed with the results. Sandiford arranged the game so that the two students, a boy and a girl from a local mathematics club, would think they were playing against one another. "Each contestant was alone in a room, and indicated his moves to a referee," explained Sandiford in a letter to Martin Gardner. Unknown to the players, the referees reported to a third room which contained two learning-box robots, their actual opponents. "With much confusion and muffled hilarity, we in the middle tried to operate the computers, keep the games in phase, and keep score." During the session the two students were encouraged to make running comments on their own moves and those of their opponents. Here are some sample remarks:

---

*Gardner, Martin. *"The Unexpected Hanging and Other Mathematical Diversions"*. New York, New York: Simon and Schuster. 1969.
**Minsky, Martin. "Artificial Intelligence." *Scientific American*. September 1966.

"It's the safest thing to do without being captured. It's almost sure to win."

"He took me, but I took him too. If he does what I expect, he'll take my pawn, but in the next move I'll block him."

"Am I stupid?"

"Good move! I think I'm beat."

"I don't think he's really thinking. By now he shouldn't make any more careless mistakes."

"Good game. She's getting wise to my actions now."

"Very surprising move . . . couldn't he see I'd win if he moved forward?"

"My opponent played well. I guess I just got the knack of it first."

After an extended session the two students were brought into the room with the robot they had been playing. They were astonished. They could hardly believe they hadn't been playing against a real person!

Was this then an impressive demonstration of the ability of an inanimate machine to mimic the learning capabilities of intelligent human beings? Perhaps. But those of us who understand how the robot actually works are left with the nagging feeling that it really doesn't do much of anything after all. If we want someone to learn to swim or ride a bicycle we often give them only the skimpiest of instructions. However, at present, we can develop a learning program only if we can explicitly define (usually in numerical terms) what it means to execute a successful strategy.

Contrary to some current science fiction accounts, it should be relatively easy for us to control the learning capabilities of our digital computers. For one thing it has been found that they eventually reach a stage beyond which they exhibit no measureable improvement. For another, we control the color-coded beads. Judy Gomberg of Maplewood, New Jersey, after playing Hexapawn against a matchbox robot of her own construction, found that contrary to expectations, she mastered the game faster than the machine. This enterprising young lady who used jelly beans as counters explained with a grin: "every time it lost I took out a candy and ate it!"

LANGUAGE TRANSLATIONS

Of all the activities in the field of artificial intelligence, the computer translation of natural languages has probably attracted the heaviest funding. In addition, there have been large expenditures for developing mechanical and electronic devices to understand the content of spoken or written messages without translating them into another language.

Syntax and Semantics

Until the 1950's most linguists believed that natural languages could be analyzed in two separate phases: first syntax, then semantics. *Syntax* deals with the formal *structure* of a language whereas *semantics* deals with the *meanings* of the individual words. In keeping with this strategy, many early researchers were convinced that if all the proper word meanings were stored inside a computer, accompanied by the proper rules of grammar, the machine would be able to develop effective translations from one of the languages to another. It seemed like a good idea at the time. So good that various government agencies, mostly the military, ended up spending more than $20 million on language translation procedures of various types. Unfortunately, as Bertram Raphael pointed out in his book *The Thinking Computer,* "these experiments failed miserably, producing translations whose meanings differed from the original in all kinds of strange, unexpected ways."*

After much careful analysis it was learned that the boundary between syntax and semantics is much fuzzier than anyone had previously suspected and that we constantly use subtle real-world clues in extracting meaning from sentences. For example, a syntactic analysis of such utterances as

"I ain't never been here."
"Me Tarzan, You Jane."
"Them's them."

produces only empty and profound confusion. Yet most people have little difficulty interpreting these awkward strings of words—and many others like them—in entirely meaningful ways. On the other hand, an expression like "Colorless green ideas dream furiously" is semantically correct (as well as we can tell) but it conveys no clear or useful meaning.

Ambiguity and Context

The *context* of an utterance also has an important impact on its proper interpretation. As Hubert L. Dreyfus the author of *What Computer's Can't Do* has pointed out, a simple phrase like "stay near me" can mean anything from "press up against me" to "stand one mile away"

---

*Raphael, Bertram. *The Thinking Computer.* San Francisco, California: W. H. Freeman. 1976.

depending upon whether it is addressed to a child in a crowd or a fellow astronaut exploring the moon.*

Similar ambiguities based on context crop up with discouraging regularity in machine translations. For example, if we attempt to translate the seemingly simple English phrase "It is beautiful" into French, the proper translation should turn out to be "C'est beau" if we are referring to a *concrete object* such as the Statue of Liberty, but "Il fait beau" (literally "It does beautiful") if we are referring to an *abstract concept* such as the weather or a theatrical performance.

Because of these, and a host of similar difficulties, computer translations have begun to lose favor in recent years. The early vision of workers in the field was that high-quality translations could be produced by machines supplied with sufficiently detailed syntactic rules, a large dictionary, and sufficient speed to examine the context of ambiguous words for a few words in each direction. Unfortunately, after nearly 20 years of developmental efforts, computers are still not producing high-quality translations. Of course it can be argued that with larger expenditure and more years of hard work, acceptable translations might be forthcoming. Would this happen? According to Joseph Weitzenbaum "Every serious worker now agrees that the answer to this question is simply 'no'."** Today we have machine-aided translations but it would appear that some sort of conceptual breakthrough will be required if we are ever to have complete and meaningful translations made solely by computer.

Language Comprehension Programs

Even though language translation by machine has encountered seemingly intractable difficulties, the use of machines to understand and duplicate human speech patterns is still receiving widespread attention. In these efforts the computer does not attempt to translate languages; instead, it attacks the simpler task of *attempting to extract meaning from a single language.* If computer programs of this type could be perfected, it could open up the use of computers to ordinary citizens who would not have to learn a special programming language in order to communicate with machines in many useful ways. Unfortunately, even this simpler task is plagued with serious difficulties. Consider the following passage which

---

* Dreyfus, Hubert L. *What Computer's Can't Do.* New York, New York: Harper and Row. 1972.

** Weizenbaum, Joseph. *Computer Power and Human Reason.* San Francisco, California: W. H. Freeman, 1976.

has been devised by a group of researchers at the Xerox Corporation to test the reading capabilities of various computer programs:

"Tommy had just been given a new set of blocks. He was opening the box when he saw Jimmy coming in."

In order to pass the Xerox test, a language comprehension program must be able to answer these three questions:

1. Who was opening the box?
2. What was in the box?
3. Who came in?

Although a typical inattentive first grader would have little difficulty answering these apparently simple questions, language comprehension programs find them surprisingly hard to handle. What causes the difficulty? One thing is clear, the questions can't be answered simply by repeating words directly from the passage. This strategy would lead the computer to reply to the first question: "Who was opening the box?" with the nonsense answer: "He was opening the box." Unfortunately, our language is structured in such a way that pronouns like "he" make sense only if they refer to a particular person.

The second question, "What was in the box?" calls for specialized knowledge of the real world. Nothing in the passage tells us what the box contains; however, we effortlessly use our background knowledge of how the world works to decide what the correct answer must be. We know from experience that new items often come in boxes—and we conclude that the blocks must be in the box.

To answer the third question: "Who came in?" we must understand the full implications of the phrase: ". . . he saw Jimmy coming in." But this phrase is ambiguous. It could be interpreted to mean either "He saw Jimmy as he was coming in." or "He saw Jimmy come in." Again we use our real world experiences, in making the proper interpretation—we realize that Tommy is probably not opening a box and walking through a door at the same time.

Thus we see that in order to extract meaning from everyday language, we need to know numerous subtle things about the world in which we live. The difference between "Join me in the pool" and Join me in a cup of coffee" has nothing to do with syntax and everything to do with the difference between a cup and a pool. As Dr. Terry Winograd assistant professor of Electrical Engineering at MIT has explained: "A sentence does not 'convey' meaning the way a truck conveys cargo, complete and packaged. It is more like a blueprint that allows the hearer to reconstruct the meaning from his own knowledge." Language comprehension programs encounter many different difficulties, the most serious of which stems from the fact that a computer has no sense of what it is to be alive and participating in the many experiences that give us a common heritage with those whose communication we seek to comprehend.

Turing's Test for Machine Intelligence

In 1936 a full decade before the first electronic digital computer was placed in operation, a gifted English logician named Alan Turing proposed a clever technique for determining whether or not a particular computing device is actually a thinking machine. In Turing's scheme, a human interrogator would be seated in front of two teleprinter terminals—one linked to an intelligent human subject and the other linked to a digital computer. The interrogator would type a series of questions on any desired subjects. After a suitable delay, man and machine would answer the questions via the teleprinters. In Turing's view if the interrogator couldn't distinguish the man from the machine—on the basis of the typed replies—then the machine would have to be regarded as being capable of intelligent thought processes. Turing himself anticipated that by the year 2000 machines would be built that could pass his ingeniously contrived test.*

It seems clear that a computer can pass the Turing test only if it has genuine knowledge of the real world. A typical exchange might go something like this:

Q. HOW MANY CASUALTIES DID THE U. S. FORCES SUFFER IN WORLD WAR II?
A. Most historians place the figure at 450,000.
Q. WHO WOULD HAVE A PERSONALIZED LICENSE PLATE THAT READ 10S NE1?**
A. Jimmy Connors.
Q. WHAT WAS THE LEAD STORY IN TODAY'S NEW YORK TIMES?
A. I'm not sure I remember, but I think it dealt with the settling of the coal miner's strike in Pennsylvania.

---

*Bernstein, Jeremy. *The Analytical Engine*. New York, New York: Random House, 1963.
**10S NE1 = "tennis anyone?"

It certainly looks impressive but is it actually possible to store enough real-world information in a computer to allow it to answer such a broad range of questions? After all, our brains contain an incredible amount of data.

In order to give you at least a vague feel for the storage capacity of a digital computer, we add a few lines to the graph in Figure 45 of Chapter 6. You will recall that this particular graph dealt with the total information content of the human brain and the estimated information content of our society. The new version is presented in Figure 67. As is indicated by the dark horizontal line near the bottom of the figure, the primary storage region of a typical large-scale digital computer can store approximately a million bits—or only about 1/10,000,000 the information content of the human brain. However, the computer's auxiliary storage devices are considerably more spacious. The Unicorn memory system used by the Illiac 4 is among the largest in existence. It stores a trillion bits of data ($\frac{1}{10}$ the capacity of the human brain) by using a laser beam to burn tiny holes in a thin mylar sheet. Thus, as technology develops over the next few years, it does not seem entirely unreasonable that we might develop a storage system that could handle as much data as is contained in the human brain.*

The problem is that the brain doesn't just store data in a passive way. It is equipped to set up remarkably complicated links between the various data entries being held in storage. It is not clear how we could ever institute all the necessary crosslinks—a job of stupendous proportions! Computer expert Charles Taylor has aptly described the problems that would be encountered by a computer trying to duplicate the thought processes of a handicapper who is planning to make a bet in today's fifth race at Belmont Park. Listen as Taylor explains some of the problems the computer would encounter in trying to determine what is important in the current situation, a task which the human handicapper can handle with ease:

> "The handicapper is concerned to pick a winner. As a human being he has a sense of what is involved in the enterprise of winning, and his being concerned means that he is aware of the horse, jockey, etc., in a way in which dangers are salient. Hence he notices when he reads in the obituary columns that Smith's mother died yesterday (Smith being the jockey, and one he knows is very susceptible), and for once he bets against the form. The machine would pick out

---

*However, the preparation of the necessary data would not be an inexpensive undertaking; the keypunching operations alone would cost in excess of $2 billion.

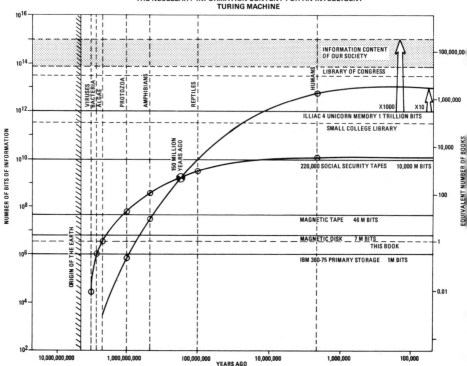

THE NECESSARY INFORMATION CONTENT FOR AN INTELLIGENT TURING MACHINE

Figure 67: No computer can be expected to pass the Turing test for machine intelligence unless it can store a vast amount of data. As this figure shows, the primary storage region of a digital computer typically has only about 1/10,000,000 the storage capacity of the human brain. However, its auxiliary storage units are considerably more spacious. The Unicorn memory system used in connection with the Illiac 4, for example, can store a trillion bits of data or about $\frac{1}{10}$ the brain's information content. Unfortunately, raw information storage is not the only problem associated with the Turing test, the computer must also be programmed to handle an enormous number of crosslinks between the various data entries being held in storage.

Smith's mother's death, as a fact about Smith, along with all the others, such as that Smith's second cousin has been elected dogcatcher in some other city, etc., but will then have to do a check on the probable consequences of these different facts before it decides to take them into account or not in placing the bet."

But, if the computer needs to know the connection between a death in the family and the probable outcome of the race, why don't we just program that in? Unfortunately, it's not quite that simple. As Mr. Taylor goes on to explain:

"We (might) store the information that people often do less than their best just after their near relations die, but we can't be expected to tag a connection with betting on horses. This information can be relevant to an infinite set of contexts."

"The machine might select on the basis of the key concepts it was worrying about, horses, jockeys, jockey Smith, etc., and pick out all facts about these. But this too would give an absurdly wide scatter. Via jockey, man and horse, one would find oneself pulling out all facts about centaurs!"*

Thus we see that the fundamental problem we encounter in attempting to equip a computer with human judgment is not that we find it hard to tell it what is *true*. Instead, our difficulties center around telling it what is *important*.

PROBLEM SOLVING AND PATTERN RECOGNITION

The ability to recognize subtle patterns is closely related to native intelligence. In fact many popular intelligence tests consist mainly of pattern recognition procedures of various sorts. Figure 68 presents an item from a highly-popular pattern recognition test. It is in the form of a *ratio and proportion,* i.e., "A is to B as C is to...?" Can a computer be taught to select the proper answers on a test of this type? You bet it can! Dr. Marvin Minsky at the Massachusetts Institute of Technology has programmed a computer to make exactly the kind of choices indicated. The geometrical analogues he used were obtained from a popular college entrance exam. In general, his program matches the performance of a tenth-grade student—not good enough to get into Harvard or Yale but still surprisingly good.**

The sketches in Figure 69 portray another type of task that can be executed by a digital computer. This particular routine, which was developed by Terry Winograd at MIT, can "understand" (to a limited extent) both verbal language and geometrical manipulations. Among other things, it is programmed to carry on protracted conversations, recognize and use colloquial sentence fragments, correctly interpret

---

*Dreyfus, Hubert L. *What Computer's Can't Do*. New York, New York: Harper and Row, 1972.

**Information*. San Francisco, California: W. H. Freeman, 1966.

PATTERN RECOGNITION TEST

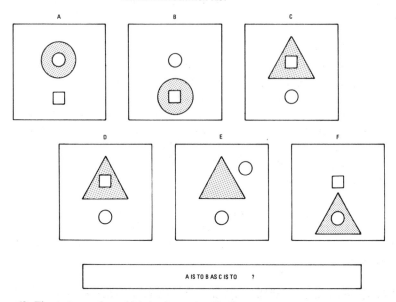

Figure 68: The test question which is shown in this figure was taken from a well-known college entrance exam. Students who score high on this exam tend to do well in college and are said to be highly intelligent. Marvin Minsky at MIT has coded a computer program to recognize the analogues involved in a test of this type. Although the computer does not yet do as well as the average applicant at Harvard or Yale, it does consistently score at or above the tenth grade level.

pronouns, and assume the most meaningful interpretations of almost all ambiguous constructions. The geometrical figures it handles are drawn on a CRT screen and, when it does its manipulations, the pictures move.

It is an impressive program in many respects, but it suffers from several nagging limitations. As Winograd himself points out, the program cannot understand commands that involve compound nouns such as: "Build a three-block stack." Nor can it handle sentence fragments or implied meanings which make up most of our daily conversation. Moreover, it is baffled by commands like "Build a stack without touching any pyramids." The difficulty stems from the fact that it has no way of working on one goal (building a stack) while keeping track of another (avoiding contact with pyramids).

To Winograd these shortcomings, and others like them, indicate that his program—which is one of the most advanced in existence—has a long way to go before it will understand language the way human beings do. As he wryly comments: "At present, it takes a huge computer and sophisti-

DR. WINOGRAD'S GEOMETRICAL PROGRAM

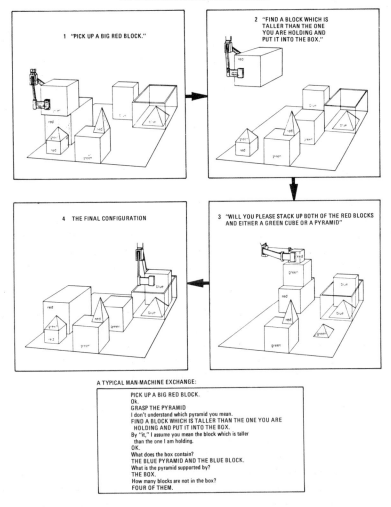

Figure 69: In 1971 Dr. Terry Winograd at MIT developed a program which can "understand" to a limited extent both verbal communication and geometrical relationships. The program operates by sketching solid geometrical shapes on a CRT screen. At the request of the operator, it rearranges the objects and answers questions about their new relationships. One of the most impressive programs of its type yet developed, it, nevertheless, suffers from several easily-identifiable limitations.

cated programming to do a small part of what a young child does naturally."*

---

*Minsky, Marvin L. "Artificial Intelligence." *Scientific American.* September. 1966.

SOME CRITICAL OPINIONS

Most of the wide-ranging evaluations of artificial intelligence tend to be rabidly enthusiastic, especially those published by workers in the field. As MIT electrical engineering professor Hubert Dreyfus has candidly observed: "The value of a program is often inversely proportional to its programmer's promises and publicity." However, several more conservative evaluations have also appeared in print. For example, in 1968 researcher Fred Tonge edited this rather sober assessment:

> "While many interesting programs (and some interesting devices) have been produced, progress in artificial intelligence has not been exciting or spectacular."
> "This is due in part to lack of clear separation between accomplishment and conjecture in many past and current writings. In this field, as in many others, there is a large difference between saying that some accomplishment 'ought to' be possible and doing it. Identifiable, significant *landmarks* of accomplishment are scarce."*

If Dreyfus and Tonge are correct, how have workers in the field been able to create such a favorable impression of progress despite the fact that so little substantial progress has actually been made? In part, this is possible because of a clever choice of problems which create the *illusion* of complexity without being nearly as complex as they seem. To the uninitiated observer, for example, checkers seems nearly as complicated as chess. However, as we have seen, checkers is, in fact, a relatively simple game to which the computer seems admirably suited. When a computer program is pitted against grandmaster in chess, however, it usually is in for a sound trouncing.

Another difficulty most people encounter in attempting to evaluate the progress that has actually been made in the field of artificial intelligence is called "the fallacy of the first step". If a researcher shows that he has made a tangible first step—such as the development of a program that responds to English statements about a set of children's blocks—we often assume that this same program can be modified to understand more subtle and complicated material such as the Watergate transcripts. Inevitably, we tend to interpret any tangible progress toward an ultimate goal as a concrete indication that the goal itself will eventually be reached. However, as Dreyfus points out, if we push this line of

---

*Tonge, Fred M. "A View of Artificial Intelligence". *Proceedings, Association of Computing Machinery*. National Meeting. 1966. pg. 379.

reasoning to its logical conclusion we would have to say that: "the first man to climb a tree could claim tangible progress toward reaching the moon." He goes on to observe that "Rather than climbing blindly, it is better to look where one is going." Accordingly, in his opinion, it is time to study in detail "the specific problems of confronting workers in artificial intelligence and the underlying difficulties that they reveal."

What are some of these difficulties? Dreyfus makes this penetrating observation: "The basic problem facing workers attempting to use computers in the simulation of human intelligent behavior should now be clear: all alternatives must be made explicit." Unfortunately, even when we have a fairly clear idea how we perform a task requiring intelligence, we usually can't quantify all the possible alternatives. In effect, the computer is so literal minded that we can devise no reliable way of helping it master what it needs to know in order to duplicate our simplest feats such as understanding the content of a seemingly ambiguous sentence.

As we have reviewed the exploits of computers that play games, translate languages, solve problems, and recognize patterns we have discovered several other specific difficulties faced by the researchers in the field. For example, when computers are programmed to play competitive games such as bridge or chess they often encounter a game tree that branches exponentially. Heuristic programming techniques and computer learning methods can help prune the tree to some extent but what remains is often a complicated tangle of branches that can't be further simplified even with the most ingenuous programming procedures.

Researchers in the field of language translation are stopped by several more intractable difficulties. These include the complicated interplay between syntax and semantics, intrinsic language ambiguities, and the problem of deducing the proper context of words and sentences without having real-world knowledge. Although it is theoretically possible to store a significant fraction of all the knowledge mankind has accumulated over the centuries, no one has any idea how to set up all the necessary crosslinks between the various data entries.

One of the primary difficulties encountered in problem solving and pattern recognition is that the computer has no effective way of distinguishing between important foreground elements and those that more properly belong in the background. Moreover, we can train a computer to distinguish a particular pattern under distortion and in the presence of noise and static only if we can explicitly state what its primary characterisitcs are supposed to be—something which requires more knowledge and judgment than we normally have. As Dreyfus reasons "The assumption which cannot be avoided is that computers treat observations as data which are represented in memory as a fixed structure, and which are operated on by an essentially fixed program. But humans interpret observations in the total context of the situation."

In short, in any given situation there are an indefinite number of facts that are possibly relevant and an indefinite number that are definitely irrelevant. Unfortunately, since the computer is not a participant in the situation, it must treat *all* facts as possibly relevant at all times. This leaves the workers in the field of Artificial Intelligence with a dilemma; they are faced either with storing and accessing an infinity of facts, or with having to exclude some possibly relevant facts from the computer's range of calculations.

THE FUTURE

The present seems somewhat discouraging but what is the future of artificial intelligence? In recent years an increasing number of researchers have turned their attention to the problem of helping the computer sense the characteristics of the real world. Today's computers are being fitted with artificial eyes, ears, sense organs, feedback control systems, manipulative "hands", etc. As they are perfected, these devices are having important impacts on various industrial activities.

Other researchers are attempting to come to grips with the fundamental differences between man and machine and to apportion the appropriate parts of any complicated task to the proper entity. Donald N. Streeter has provided us with an interesting account of the fundamental differences between people and their computers. In his view:

"Man is inventive and flexible. He perceives, abstracts, and associates quite well, drawing on broad experience to make decisions and check reasonableness. However, he is forgetful of detail, inaccurate, and subject to boredom and fatigue."

On the other hand, in Streeter's view, machines have completely different strengths and weaknesses:

"Computer systems, compared to humans, are fast, accurate, and consistent in recalling and processing information, but are inflexible, requiring detailed programming for all situations to be dealt with."

---

*Garrett, Lewis E. "Primer on Artificial Intelligence." *The Best of Creative Computing, Volume 2*. Morristown, New Jersey: Creative Computing Press 1977.

Because of these contrasting capabilities, many thoughtful individuals have urged that we set up beneficial cooperative relationships in which we would capitalize on the talents and abilities of both man and machine.

For example, a chess player who could focus on a few promising possibilities and then call on the computer to check them out would be a truly formidable opponent. Similarly a human language translator who could easily display the various meanings of obscure words on a CRT scope would be a more efficient translator than one working without electronic aids.

Will we end up using our computers in these and similar ways that will keep for the machine what it does best while preserving for the man what suits his special talents and capabilities? One certainly hopes we will. For if we do, we should be able to build for our children and for their grandchildren a brighter, more efficient world.

BIBLIOGRAPHY

1. Adams, J. Mack and Haden, Douglas H. *Social Effects of Computer Use and Misuse.* New York, New York: John Wiley, 1976.

2. Ahl, David H. "Can Computers Think?" *The Best of Creative Computing, Volume 2,* Morristown, New Jersey: Creative Computing Press, 1977.

3. "Artificial Intelligence: When Will Computers Understand People?" *Psychology Today,* May 1974, pp. 73-79.

4. Baer, Robert M. *The Digital Villain.* Reading, Massachusetts: Addison-Wesley, 1972.

5. Bernstein, Jeremy. *The Analytical Engine.* New York, New York: Random House, 1964.

6. "Can a Computer Really Play Winning Chess?" *Creative Computing,* May/June 1978, pp. 58-59.

7. "Chimp to Chimp." *Time,* 28 August 1978, p. 61.

8. "Computers Learn to Make Their Own Decisions." *Business Week,* 6 April 1974, pp. 30-33.

9. Darrach, Brad. "Meet Shaky, The First Electronic Person." *Life,* 20 November 1970.

10. Dreyfus, Hubert L. *What Computer's Can't Do.* New York, New York: Harper and Row, 1972.

11. Findler, Nicholas V., "Computer Poker." *Scientific American,* July 1978, pp. 144-151.

12. Gardner, Martin. *The Unexpected Hanging and Other Mathematical Diversions.* New York, New York: Simon and Schuster, 1969.

13. Garrett, Lewis E. "Primer on Artificial Intelligence." *The Best of Creative Computing Volume 2*, Morristown, New Jersey: Creative Computing Press, 1977.

14. Gotlieb, G. C., and Borodin, A. *Social Issues in Computing.* New York, New York: Academic Press, 1973.

15. Jastrow, Robert. "Toward an Intelligence Beyond Man's." *Time*, 2 February 1978, p. 59.

16. Logsdon, Tom and Logsdon, Fae. *The Computers in Our Society.* Fullerton, California: Anaheim Publishing Co., 1974.

17. Minsky, Marvin L. "Artificial Intelligence." *Scientific American*, 17 September 1966.

18. Nelson, Ruth. "The First Literate Computers?" *Psychology Today*, 18 March 1978, pp. 73-80.

19. Ralston, Anthony, and Meek, Chester L. *Encyclopedia of Computer Science.* New York, New York: Petrocelli/Charter, 1976.

20. Raphael, Bertran. *The Thinking Computer.* San Francisco: W. H. Freeman, 1976.

21. Sagan, Carl. *The Dragons of Eden.* New York, New York: Random House, 1977.

22. Sanders, Donald H. *Computers in Society.* New York, New York: McGraw-Hill, 1977.

23. Weizenbaum, Joseph. *Computer Power and Human Reason.* New York, New York: W. H. Freeman, 1976.

24. Winston, Patrick Henry. *Artificial Intelligence.* Reading, Massachusetts: Addison-Wesley, 1977.

EXERCISES

1. How would you define intelligence? In accordance with your definition are people intelligent? Plants? Animals? Vending machines? Computers?

2. In what ways does the operation of a digital computer resemble the functioning of the human brain? In what ways does it differ?

3. What are the four major areas in which computers have been used in the field of artificial intelligence? In what areas has it been the most successful? The most unsuccessful?

4. What do the words *syntax* and *semantics* mean? Why is it not possible to analyze them separately in attempting to obtain a useful language translation?

5. What are some of the games that have yielded to computer game-playing routines? What games cause difficulties for the computer? Explain why.

6. What 18th century chess-playing machine could have beaten any modern chess-playing computer? Why don't modern researchers use the same techniques to build a similar device?

7. What are some of the things animals have done to indicate that they are intelligent creatures? What are some similar things machines have done? Judged solely on this basis, which entity do you believe is the most intelligent?

8. Draw a partial game tree for the game of Hexapawn. How does a tree of this type help programmers develop a winning strategy? Why is it impractical to use such an approach for a game like checkers or chess?

9. Apparently a complete understanding of natural language requires genuine real-world knowledge. What are the major difficulties we would encounter if we tried to feed large amounts of real-world information into a computer?

10. Describe Turing's test for machine intelligence. In your opinion is it a valid test? Explain your answer.

STUDENT PROJECTS

1. In this chapter the plans were sketched for building a "learning machine" which gradually learns to master the game of Hexapawn. Team up with several of your classmates and build a similar model. Now run it several dozen times to see if it learns to win. When you have completed your trials, make a sketch showing the final location of the color-coded beads and draw a graph similar to the one in Figure 66 showing the rate at which it learns.

2. Some of the most interesting work in Artificial Intelligence has dealt with game-playing devices. Research these fascinating applications with emphasis on learning machines. Document your results informally.

   a. Baer, Robert M. *The Digital Villian.* Reading, Massachusetts: Addison-Wesley, 1972.

   b. "Can A Computer Really Play Winning Chess?" *Creative Computing,* May/June 1978, pp. 58-59.

   c. Findler, Nicholas V. "Computer Poker". *Scientific American,* July 1978, pp. 144-151.

   d. Gardner, Martin. *The Unexpected Hanging and Other Mathematical Diversions.* New York, New York: Simon and Schuster, 1969.

   e. Raphael, Bertram. *The Thinking Computer.* San Francisco: W. H. Freeman, 1976.

   f. Winston, Patrick Henry. *Artificial Intelligence.* Reading, Massachusetts: Addison-Wesley, 1977.

3. Although the field of Artificial Intelligence has many ardent supporters, there are those who argue that it is not producing noteably fruitful results. Read some of the writings of the critics and assemble a report summarizing the results.

SUGGESTED READING LIST:

   a. Weizenbaum, Joseph. *Computer Power and Human Reason.* New York, New York: W. H. Freeman, 1976.

b. Raphael, Bertran. *The Thinking Computer*. San Francisco, California: W. H. Freeman, 1976.

c. Garrett, Lewis E. "Primer on Artificial Intelligence". *The Best of Creative Computing, Volume 2*. Morristown, New Jersey: Creative Computing Press, 1977.

d. Dreyfus, Hubert L. *What Computer's Can't Do*. New York, New York: Harper and Row, 1972.

CHAPTER 10

COMPUTERS AND AUTOMATION

HUMAN LABOR VERSUS AUTOMATIC MACHINES

INDUSTRIAL ROBOTS
Feedback Control
The Friendly Robots in Your Future

UNEMPLOYMENT LEVELS

HISTORICAL PROGRESS IN WORKER PRODUCTIVITY

MECHANIZATION AND JOB QUALITY TRENDS

ALIENATION AND WORKER DISSATISFACTION

THE FUTURE

BIBLIOGRAPHY

EXERCISES

STUDENT PROJECTS

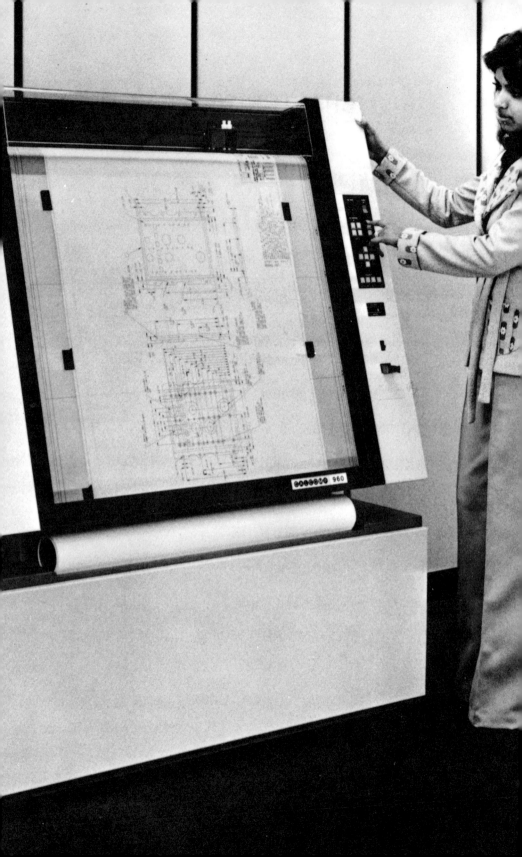

In 1811, as the Industrial Revolution rumbled across the English countryside, profit-minded British industrialists began stuffing their cavernous factories with new weaving looms of superbly-efficient design. Everywhere they were installed, the new looms increased worker productivity with dramatic swiftness. As a result, thousands of skilled craftsmen could be dropped from company payrolls. It was a terrific way to cut expenses but, like many schemes that look good on paper, it had unexpected consequences. Angered and bewildered by the new realities, the unemployed craftsmen soon organized themselves into vengeful clots of destructiveness. They called themselves the Luddites.

To be as generous as possible, the Luddites were modern barbarians. They roamed from factory to factory smashing every valuable machine they could find. Unfortunately, it soon became apparent that mindless temper tantrums were not a practical way to halt technological progress. By 1813, two years after the movement had begun, a mass trial consigned the worst offenders to the gallows and scattered their cohorts to the distant reaches of the empire. The depression of 1815 triggered a brief revival of Luddite fanaticism. But repression and prosperity eliminated fresh recruits and, within a year and a half, the movement had forever vanished into the shadows of history.

Unlike the compact, heavily-populated regions of Northern Europe, our own country has almost always suffered from chronic labor shortages. Slavery, loosely-restricted immigration, neighborly cooperation, and large farm families have helped alleviate this problem to some extent. But old-fashioned yankee ingenuity—the ability to substitute simple technologies for large masses of labor—has been our most consistently effective solution. Unfortunately, as hightly-organized research teams began displacing the basement inventor, a growing distrust of advancing technology became increasingly apparent. By the 1950's fear of unemployment due to the introduction of computers and other fancy gadgets had become a touchy emotional issue. Indeed, judging by their most outlandish tirades, many people living in that era could easily have been mistaken for Luddite reactionaries.

In part, their fretful reactions were engendered by a number of stark evaluations of the probable consequences of widespread automation. The respected futurist, Herman Kahn, for example, made a highly-publicized statement that our country would soon require "less than one half...of one percent of its work force to produce all the goods needed by American consumers." A few months later, in his book *The Human Uses of Human Beings,* computer expert Norbert Wiener painted an even bleaker word picture of the hazards of automation:

"The automatic machine...is the precise economic equivalent of slave labor. Any labor which competes against slave labor must accept the economic conditions of slave labor. It is perfectly clear that this will produce an unemployment situation, in comparison with which...the depression of the thirties will seem a pleasant joke. This depression will ruin many industries...possibly even the industries which have taken advantage of the new potentialities."*

No one knew exactly how accurate these frightening projections would turn out to be, but even the most sober editorialists could see unprecedented hazards in the new wave of automation. For example, an article in *U. S. News and World Report* predicted in appropriately somber tones that "The careers of fully 50 percent of the present work force will be disrupted by the new wave of automation at some time during their productive years."

Politicians also scrambled onto the bandwagon. Congress talked of imposing controls on the pace of automation and in 1962 President John F. Kennedy was not contradicted when he asserted that "the major domestic challenge in the sixties is to maintain full employment at a time when automation is replacing men."

But what was actually about to happen? Were we, in fact, approaching an era in which we would need only a few hundred thousand workers to keep our economy running at full productive capacity? Were we really sinking inevitably into another great depression? Was automation, indeed, our most serious domestic challenge? As is so often the case, things weren't as bad as they seemed. In this chapter we shall attempt to show that the disruption of our labor market caused by the computer was much less dramatic than had been anticipated; that those few problems which did occur were not unique to the age of computers; and that, so far, the net overall effect of automation on employment levels has been essentially insignificant.

HUMAN LABOR VERSUS AUTOMATIC MACHINES

One of the author's colleagues has defined work as: "something you wouldn't do if nobody paid you to do it." It's a surprisingly accurate definition and, in view of its distinctly negative tone, it may seem curious that anybody would object if computers took over all our work thus freeing us to engage in activities we would be willing to tackle without remuneration. However, even if our economic system could survive in a

---

*Logsdon, Tom and Logsdon, Fae. *The Computers in Our Society*. Fullerton, California. Anaheim Publishing Company. 1977.

world without work, this jolting change would entail serious cultural and psychological difficulties. For one thing, those of us who have been reared in keeping with the tenets of the protestant work ethic* tend to view our jobs as inseparable parts of our personalities. Work gives us an opportunity to be a part of something bigger than ourselves. It enhances our feelings of status and importance. It helps shape our social lives. And it gives us constructive ways of filling our time.

Abundant leisure is not as beneficial as commonly supposed. Some retirees are delighted with their well-earned freedom. But others, especially those who retire while they are still healthy and robust, soon find time hangs heavy on their hands. Their wives complain about having them underfoot. Even long-term vacations can create serious problems. As Alvin Toffler noted in his book, *Future Shock,* our death and accident rates go up when we are on vacation.** We often see bumper stickers singing the praises of leisure. But at Kaiser Steel when production line workers were granted 13-week sabatical leaves every five years, one of the primary results was an alarming increase in the consumption of alcoholic beverages. At another plant where the workers were given a choice between extra time off and higher pay, they chose fatter paychecks.

Thus we are beginning to see why men and women everywhere develop queasy feelings of disorientation whenever they try to picture a fully-automated society in which almost nobody holds a steady job. On the other hand, we want our machines to relieve us of some of the burdens of work; but not permanently, not completely, and not irrevocably. If automation threatens to take away all of our jobs forever, we quickly lose enthusiasm for it. But is this likely to happen? Is it happening already? Before we attempt to answer these questions, we need a workable definition of automation. Webster defines it in this way: "Automatically controlled operation of an apparatus, process or system by mechanical or electronic devices that take the place of human organs of observation, effort, and decision."***

It's hard to find a flaw in this formal definition but, unfortunately, it's not particularly useful in helping us to understand the process of

---

*The protestant work ethic, which can be traced back to the writings of the 16th Century Swiss theologian, John Calvin, refers to a philosophical system in which hard work and diligence are highly admired and, in some interpretations, playful spontaneity and idleness are regarded as mildly sinful.

**Toffler, Alvin. *Future Shock.* New York, New York: Bantam Books, 1972.

***Originally, the term "automation" was used only in connection with the computerized mechanization of production processes. In recent years, however, it is also being used in connection with the mechanization of services. Today we talk about automating our airline reservation systems or the automation of the insurance business.

automation. Ted Silvey of the AFL-CIO has provided us with a more complete and useful description of what actually occurs when process is automated. When a man works, he makes use of (1) his skills, (2) his senses and (3) his decision-making capabilities. When we automate the same task, this is what we do:

1. Replace the man's physical strength with highly-engineered mechanization.
2. Replace the man's perceptive senses and personal control with instrumentation and automatic adjustments.
3. Replace the man's simple, repetitive decision-making functions and memory capabilities with the electronic computer.

In analyzing the component parts of the above description, we find that automation provides the equivalent of human dexterity and skill. As we shall see later in this chapter, a computer, properly equipped with sensors (devices that measure the properties of its environment) and effectors (devices that interact with and change that environment) can, indeed, duplicate—and improve upon—many of the physical and mental capabilities of a skilled workman.

INDUSTRIAL ROBOTS

The machines used in automation can take many different forms. An ordinary digital computer can be used in automating many of the tasks in an office building; a time-sharing computer equipped with disk storage devices is sufficient to automate the reservation system for a major airline; several acres of production and control mechanisms might be needed in automating an entire facility such as a brewery or an oil refinery; but, perhaps, the most glamorous machines yet developed for the purpose of automation are *programmed machine tools* and *industrial robots*.

A programmed machine tool is a relatively complicated device equipped with milling machines, drill presses, etc., directed by discrete electrical pulses produced by a magnetic tape, a punched paper tape, or, in some cases, an on-site minicomputer. The enormous cost associated with the development of programmed machine tools has fostered a unique cooperative venture between the Federal Government and twenty large American companies. A special computer language called APT (*Automatically Programmed Tools*) was specifically developed for this application. Work began in 1956 and, at last count, the APT translation routines, which contained over 60,000 machine-language instructions, had required more than 50 man-years of programming effort.

Modern industrial robots are the offspring of a favorable marriage between programmed machine tools and the teleoperator mechanisms developed for the remote handling of radioactive isotopes. Although they are just now becoming widely known to the general public, industrial robots have been available for nearly 20 years. To date they have provided us with more than 10 million hours of robot labor in such diverse applications as spot welding, spray painting, press loading, and component assembly.

At least 350 different types of industrial robots are manufactured by about 150 companies. They range in size from the Japanese Seiko used in manufacturing wrist watches to the 350-pound capacity Unimate 4000. The Unimate machine is sketched in Figure 70. This particular version is rigged to take a casting from a die caster, quench it in a tank, and insert it into a press.

Almost all robots are equipped with at least one manipulator arm. A typical version is able to move its arm vertically or horizontally and to rotate its end effector (hand). Usually the robot is stationary but, in some cases, it is mounted on rails or an overhead conveyor so that it can move to a number of different work stations.

Most robots have hydraulically powered arms and pneumatically-operated end effectors which hold and operate tools, spray guns, welding heads, etc. All have built-in memory systems to command the arm and hand to move in the desired manner. Some are programmed by conventional techniques; others are programmed in a much simpler way by switching in the "program" mode and moving the hand of the robot through the desired motions. Once recorded, the motions will be repeated precisely, time after time, with an accuracy of at least 0.008 inches.*

A typical robot costs around $32,000 but prices range from $3000 to over $250,000. Experience has shown that the Unimate 4000 is functional about 97 percent of the time. Typically, it repays its investment in two or three years.

Feedback Control

Mindless, insensitive behavior is widely associated with robots and other automatic machines. Shields and Yarnell skillfully reproduce this mindlessness whenever they perform their hilarious imitations of windup toys. Mindless machines can also be quite terrifying. There is a particularly chilling sequence in the film "The Stepford Wives" in which a

---

*"Putting It All Together...With Robots". *Iron Age.* 13 December 1976. pp. 47-56.

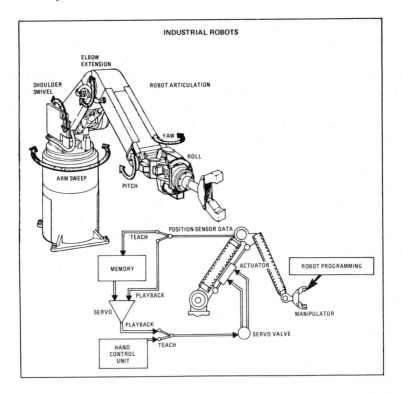

Figure 70: The sequence of operations sketched on the right hand side of this figure shows how an industrial robot "learns" to carry out a simple, repetitive task as the operator moves its arm through the required motions. Once the robot has been "programmed" in this way, it is able to execute the repetitive sequence millions of times with a high degree of precision.

"mechanical" housewife repeatedly executes frightening, machine-like rituals completely oblivious to her surroundings.

Many of the machines in today's factories embody an eerie mindlessness rivaling Hollywood's scariest creations. Consider this lucid description from Bertram Raphael's book, *The Thinking Computer:*

"If a foreign object (or a person) passes through the path of [a robot], the machine will smash into the obstacle without being aware of its existence. If the supply line stops and, say, no more bricks arrive to be moved, the brick-moving arm will continue moving imaginary bricks until some person turns it off. If an object to be picked up is more than a small fraction of an inch away from where it should be, the arm is likely to break it or drop it, without knowing that anything has gone wrong."*

Thus it seems clear that one primary difference between the behavior of a person and that of a typical machine is that the person responds to changes in the local environment. When you attempt to thread a needle, you don't program youself to execute all the precise movements once and for all. Instead, you watch what is happening as you proceed, constantly make subtle corrections to your movements. An engineer would call this process *feedback control.*

What exactly is feedback control? Webster's Third International Dictionary defines it as a process in which we "return to the input...a part of the output of a mechanism, this part of the input constituting information that reports discrepancies between intended and actual operation and leads to a self-correcting action." Even to a professional engineer it's a somewhat incomprehensible definition. Fortunately, Don Fabun in his respected best-seller, *The Dynamics of Change,* gives us a much simpler explanation of how a feedback control system actually works:

"Feedback control can best be described as a subtraction process. Think about picking up a glass of water. You have willed the action, and your arm and hand respond to the will. You determine how close you are to your goal by substracting the motions you already have made toward it. In the end, the result is zero; no more impulses are needed, because you have reached the glass." **

The human body contains dozens of feedback control mechanisms. When you sneeze, cough, or shiver, your body is making feedback control responses to changes in your environment. The same thing is happening when your heart beats faster during a vigorous tennis match.

By using sophisticated feedback control systems driven by special sensors, we can significantly enhance the precision and versatility of our robots. One of the most advanced robots of this type, "Shaky", was constructed several years ago at the Stanford Research Institute in Palo Alto, California. Shaky's picture is shown in Figure 71.

Shaky was an experimental robot, never intended for commercial production. But simpler industrial robots that can sense their surround-

---

*Raphael, Bertram. *The Thinking Computer.* San Francisco, California: W. H. Freeman. 1976.

**Fabun, Don. *The Dynamics of Change.* Englewood Cliffs, New Jersey: Prentice-Hall, 1967.

SHAKEY

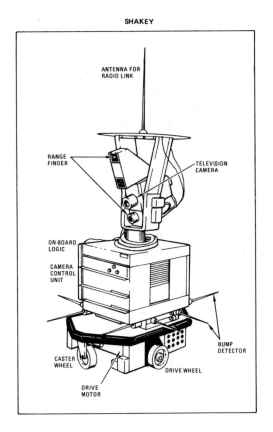

ANTENNA FOR
RADIO LINK

RANGE
FINDER

TELEVISION
CAMERA

ON-BOARD
LOGIC

CAMERA
CONTROL
UNIT

BUMP
DETECTOR

CASTER
WHEEL

DRIVE WHEEL

DRIVE
MOTOR

Figure 71: This is an adaptive robot named "Shaky" who was born at the Stanford Research Institute in Palo Alto, California. Although Shaky was mothballed shortly after this picture was taken, thousands of simpler industrial robots are, at this moment, working in factories and on various production lines in the United States.

ings, and respond to the conditions they encounter, are being marketed. Various models produced by Japanese and American companies utilize television cameras, pressure sensors, and laser-ranging devices. These measurements allow them to perform in a surprisingly versatile manner.

The Friendly Robots in Your Future

Robot technology has come a long way in the past few years—in Japan alone the sale of robots and their replacement parts brings in $300 million per year. But Joseph F. Englberger, President and founder of Unimation, Inc., the world's largest producer of industrial robots is convinced that in the near future it will become an even bigger business. He predicts that someday you will drive your car into robot-run hamburger stands and robot-run service stations. "In such an establishment an arriving customer would feed his or her credit card into the robot. The credit card would contain credit information and also the make and model of the car, directing the robot to the location of the gasoline tank filler spout." Moreover, Englberger believes that in the future you will be served by robot garbage collectors and robot housekeepers. Among other things, they will probably be able to "repair broken appliances and detain unannounced intruders!"*

UNEMPLOYMENT LEVELS

More than two decades have elapsed since Herman Kahn and Norbert Weiner issued their stern verbal warnings that we would soon experience extensive job losses as a result of galloping automation. But, somehow, things haven't turned out to be as bad as they had anticipated. The two historical graphs in Figure 72 will help you see what has actually occurred during this supposedly-devastating 20-year interval. As you can see, the growth in computer sales does not seem to have created large-scale domestic unemployment. In 1955 when Kahn and Weiner made their dire predictions, unemployment was 5.5 percent of our work force. Today, after more than 300,000 computers have been installed, the current unemployment figure stands only a trifle higher, at 6.2 percent. Moreover, the fluctuations in Figure 72 are to some extent fallacious. They reflect not only actual variations in our country's unemployment levels but also gradual changes in the demographic composition of our population as well as abrupt changes in the morale of our labor force.

Unemployment statistics are gathered by surveying a carefully-selected sample population. Each person interviewed is asked if he currently holds a job. If not, he must have looked for a job during the previous month in order to be counted among the unemployed. As you can readily appreciate, this method of gathering the statistics can create sizeable variations in the unemployment rate even if the number of people actually holding jobs does not change. The unemployment rates published by the government in any given month are strongly dependent upon the hope and determination of the average American job hunter.

A recent column written for the *Boston Herald American* by Warren T. Brooks** illustrates how the attitudes of our work force can have large

---

*Robots in Your Future". *Technology Review*. January 1975. pp. 52-53.

**Boston Herald American*, December 29, 1976.

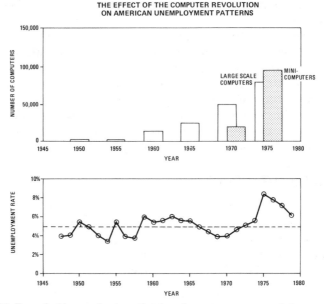

Figure 72: Fear of widespread automation has, for many years, worried our country's most vulnerable workmen. However, as shown by the two graphs in this figure, the introduction of computers and other automatic machines has had little impact on long-term unemployment statistics. Between 1950 and 1978, our country's computer population grew from virtually zero to a little over 300,000 machines. In that same interval, our unemployment rate increased only a trifle, from 5.5 to 6.2 percent of our total work force.

impacts on our "unemployment" rates. According to Brooks, the *unemployment* rate in Massachusetts went from 7.5 percent of the labor force in October 1974 to 11.1 percent in October 1975 to 7.1 percent in October 1976—yet *employment* changed hardly at all. What produced these phantom variations? According to Brooks, the extension of unemployment benefits in January of 1975 "brought 100,000 people out of the woodwork and onto the unemployment rolls—not because they had lost their jobs, but because the state and federal government was offering a good deal."

"About a year ago, the governor and the legislature tightened up the state's unemployment-compensation program—making it impossible for people who quit their jobs voluntarily to collect benefits." The result? "The work force declined by 120,000...while jobs went up about 19,000...unemployment plummeted—not because our economy was booming, but because the benefits were no longer available."*

---

*Quoted in "Behind the Unemployment Numbers" by Milton Friedman, *Newsweek*. February 7, 1977. pg. 63.

Because of the rather confusing nature of conventional unemployment statistics, many statisticians prefer instead to deal with the "employment level" of the working-age population. The employment level is defined as that fraction of our working-age population (ages 16 through 64) that holds a steady job. A plot showing the historical trends in America's employment level is presented in Figure 73. As you can see, it has been hovering near 55 percent-plus or minus a percentage point or two—for more than 20 years.

The working-age unemployment rate is plotted across the top of Figure 73. It varies more than the employment level because, as we have explained, unemployment depends on hope and determination. The middle portion of the graph represents those who are neither employed nor unemployed. Some of the individuals in this category are idle. But also included are college students, housewives, people in hospitals and mental institutions, and some of those who are in the process of making a transition from one job to another.

Thus, we see from the curves in Figures 72 and 73 that early prophesies of mass unemployment due to automation were, at best, somewhat premature. However, it should be noted that these gross statistics give us no useful information about what happens in a particular industry when automated equipment is suddenly introduced. Surely there must be some impact on employment. After all, the owner of a company automates his or her operations in order to save labor, otherwise, he or she would invest his money in some other way to obtain a higher return. Herbert A. Simon in a *Science* magazine article put it this way:

> "When (an) accounting system is mechanized, fewer clerks and bookkeepers are needed, else there would be no economic motivation for mechanizing."*

But then he went on to explain how mechanization and automation could conceivably result in *increased* employment despite improved worker efficiencies:

> "Of course, if part of the motivation for the change is to improve the quality of the system's output, the operation may be expanded, and the net reduction in personnel may be smaller than would be estimated solely from the increase in efficiency. If there is sufficient elasticity of demand for the activity, personnel may actually increase."

*Simon, Herbert A. "What Computers Mean to Man and Society". *Science*. 8 March 1977. pp. 1186-1191.

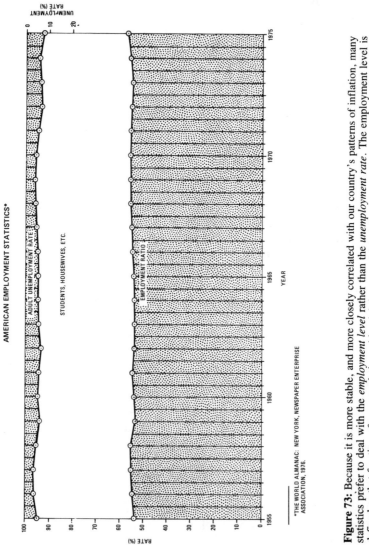

Figure 73: Because it is more stable, and more closely correlated with our country's patterns of inflation, many statistics prefer to deal with the *employment level* rather than the *unemployment rate*. The employment level is defined as that fraction of our population with a job between 16 and 64 years of age. As you can see from this graph, America's employment level has been remarkably constant throughout the past two decades, consistently hovering around 55 percent.

But does this happen in actual practice? Indeed, it does. Several separate studies indicate that work force levels don't change much when computers are introduced.

For example, the U. S. Labor Department recently reviewed twenty companies with a total work force of 2800 that installed computers. This is what had happened to their payrolls after one year: "One-third of the employees had been reassigned to new positions within the companies, one-sixth had retired or quit, and the majority remained at their old jobs. A total of only nine people were laid off!"

In 1965 a similar study was conducted by the Ministry of Labour at a number of offices in Great Britain.* Their summary report indicated that, despite the introduction of more than 600 computers, there was an 8 percent *increase* in the aggregate number of employees. The report went on to predict that there would not be any substantial change in office employment in England over the next five years. This prediction has since been confirmed by follow-up research.

Another study, which was conducted by the International Labour Office, ended with this general conclusion:

"For various reasons the introduction of automation in offices has thus far not brought about any significant dismissal of personnel nor resulted in a decline in the general level of employment for office workers."**

Apparently, it is possible for us to keep our jobs despite the fact that we are becoming more productive primarily because we are also becoming more enthusiastic consumers. The *Encyclopedia of Computer Science* lists three other reasons why employment levels have held up so well in automated industries:

1. Full automation has been attempted only in a very few cases.
2. Computerization usually requires years of planning, especially where services cannot be interrupted during installation.
3. Computers are often not brought in to save labor...but rather to achieve improved accuracy, better resources utilization, or simply to do a job that cannot be done without them.***

---

* "Computers in Offices," Manpower Study Number 4, Ministry of Labour, Great Britain, HM Stationary Office, London, 1965.

** "Labour and Automation". Bulletin 1-7, International Labour Office, Geneva, Switzerland, 1964-1968.

*** Ralston, Anthony and Meek, Chester L. *Encyclopedia of Computer Science*. New York, New York. Petrocelli/Charter. 1976.

Item Number 3 was underscored by the experiences of the airlines when they introduced automated reservation systems. When reporters kept insisting that these expensive automated systems must have reduced his company's payroll costs, one airline official became increasingly exasperated: "In some cases," he said, "automated equipment has made more work for people, not less." And he went on to observe that "cost is really not a critical criterion in cases like the reservation problem where it is necessary to automate to exist. Savings are possible with automation...but the image of the computer replacing people is more myth than reality." *

The data processing industry itself provides another interesting example of *increases* in labor costs resulting from automation. According to A. F. Donovan of Space Technology Laboratories (now TRW Systems):

> "When electronic computers first came into use, there was a lot of discussion on how they would reduce the cost of computation. The cost of a particular computation (was reduced), but computer staffs grew like mad...there is probably thousands of times as much computation, or more, done now than there was before we had computers, because we now attempt computations that we formerly would have considered absolutely impossible."

When automation arrives at a particular plant, the employees inevitably become edgy about the future of their jobs but, apparently, they are protected by a well-known variation of Parkinson's law which states that "the work will always expand to consume all available resources".

HISTORICAL PROGRESS IN WORKER PRODUCTIVITY

Contrary to what we might expect, automation has resulted in no *abrupt or unusual* gains in worker productivity. As Figure 74 shows, recent productivity gains have merely continued the trend we had already established long before computers and other automatic devices began passing into widespread use. Trend lines are included in the figure to help you gauge the rate of progress we have actually experienced in the first four-fifths of this century. As you can see, our productivity gains have consistently averaged about 2.5 percent per year. In large part, these surprisingly consistent gains have been made through mechanization and a better-educated work force.

As a result of these long-term gains in worker productivity, the

---

* "Automating the Airline System". *Aviation Week and Space Technology*. October 22, 1973.

average American employee of today can produce five times more output per hour than his or her counterpart did in 1900. This increased productivity has resulted in both a higher standard of living and increased leisure time. In 1900 the average non-farm worker stayed on the job 56 hours per week but, as Figure 75 shows, by 1960 this work-week had declined by 32 percent to only 38 hours.

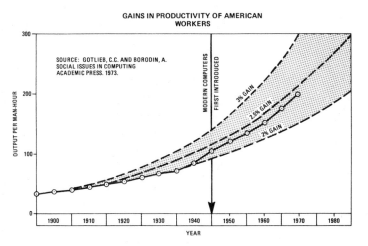

GAINS IN PRODUCTIVITY OF AMERICAN WORKERS

SOURCE: GOTLIEB, C.C. AND BORODIN, A. SOCIAL ISSUES IN COMPUTING ACADEMIC PRESS. 1973.

Figure 74: Contrary to popular belief, automation has resulted in no dramatic or unusual gains in worker productivity. Throughout the first four-fifths of this century, mechanization and automation of various sorts have resulted in consistent productivity gains of about 2.5 percent.

As we shift toward an automated economy, the devices responsible for automation—high-speed digital computers and other complicated machines—require a great deal of servicing and maintenance to remain in operation. Large numbers of programmers and system analysts are also needed. Thus, to some extent the number of *primary* workers is reduced but there is often a compensating increase in the number of *secondary workers*. *Primary workers* are those necessary to the task at hand. If they walk off the job, production stops almost immediately. *Secondary workers* act in supporting roles. In the long run their presence is necessary to the task being performed, but, if they walk off the job, the operations will grind to a halt only after an appreciable delay. Consequently, although little experience has been gained so far, it is believed that automated industries will turn out to be more strike-proof than those industries involving larger numbers of *primary workers*.

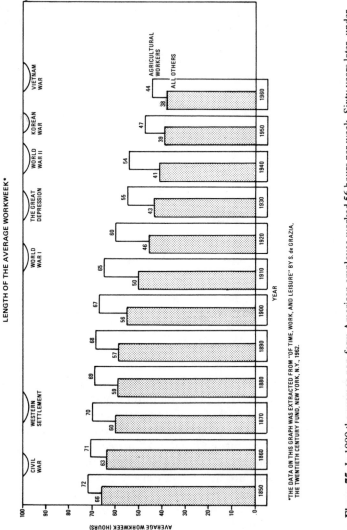

Figure 75: In 1900 the average non-farm American employee worked 56 hours per week. Sixty years later, under the pressures of increased mechanization (and unionization), his or her stay on the job had shrunk each year by an average of one-half of one percent. If these trends continue up to the turn of the century, we will see the average work-week shrink down to a little less than 28 hours.

MECHANIZATION AND JOB QUALITY TRENDS

Many early studies concerning the future of automation seemed to indicate that, when an industry had been fully automated, there would be a general upgrading of employee skills—a frightening possibility for those workers clinging to the bottom of the economic ladder. In practice, however, the actual effect was much more complicated than was predicted. When office workers are replaced by computers there is more work for engineers and programmers, probably at a higher educational level. However, as Figure 76 shows, there is an even greater need for computer operators and data entry specialists, probably at a lower educational level. What then is the net overall effect? Statistics indicate that there is a slight change but it is not as great as we might anticipate. Gotlieb and Borodin summarize the attendant situation with these carefully-measured words:

"After more than a decade of study, the consensus is that skill levels are both increased and decreased, and that the nature of the process has a greater effect than the technological change itself. For example, experience with numerically-controlled machine tools has shown that the requirements for worker skill are often decreased with the advent of automatic control."*

In an article on "Computers and Society" in their *Encyclopedia of Computer Science,* Ralston and Meek echo the same sentiments:
"It is an open question whether on the whole, the introduction of computers tends to produce a net gain or reduction in the skill requirements for jobs...Studies show that in certain operations (e.g., demand deposit accounting), significantly increased skill levels are needed; in others (e.g., plant operation for electric utilities), less skill is needed...In general, the net changes in skill levels (taking both *direct* and *indirect* labor into account) are not large."**

ALIENATION AND WORKER DISSATISFACTION

As we have seen, in 1811 the Luddites were so upset by the introduction of labor-saving devices into British factories they systematically smashed dozens of weaving looms. In our own era the

---

*C. C. Gotlieb and A. Borodin, *Social Issues in Computing,* New York, New York: Academic Press 1973.
**Ralston, Anthony and Meek, Chester L., *Encyclopedia of Computer Science.* New York, New York: Petrocelli/Charter, 1976.

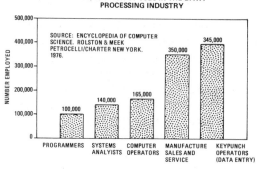

DISTRIBUTION OF JOBS IN THE DATA
PROCESSING INDUSTRY

Figure 76: A few years ago many commentators were convinced that the widespread use of computers would result in a general upgrading of the skills needed to get and hold a good job. However, various studies now indicate that the skills mix of a company is not substantially altered with the introduction of automated equipment. The data processing industry itself, which employs about two million workers, is a good case in point. As can be seen from the above barcharts, the industry needs substantial numbers of highly-educated people but it needs even greater numbers of people with more moderate skills and educational attainments.

sporadic destruction of data processing devices and other expensive equipment has caused some commentators to suggest that we may be entering a new era of worker alienation and dissatisfaction. In particular, Detroit's assembly line workers are said to suffer from such severe morale problems that many Americans prefer to purchase Japanese or European automobiles. But is it acutally true that automation and more widespread mechanization have brought about a new era of worker dissatisfaction?

Several different studies have indicated that workers have never been particularly satisfied with their jobs. Herbert A. Simon reporting in a *Science* magazine article entitled "What Computers Mean for Man and Society" notes that objective data on national trends in job satisfaction have been available for only around 20 years. In that interval approximately 15 national surveys have been conducted. "The polls provide absolutely no evidence for a decrease in job satisfaction over this period," he writes. "If alienation has been increased by automation, the increase somehow does not show up in answers by workers to questions about their attitudes toward their jobs. Notice that the polls do not show that workers are enthusiastic about their jobs, only that they do not seem to like them less today than they did in 1958."*

R. Blauner conducted a separate survey attempting to pinpoint worker dissatisfaction in four different industries.** He found few indications of alienation in printing and chemicals, considerably more in textiles, and most of all in automobile assembly. It is interesting to note that the industry which best typifies modern automation—chemicals—was substantially less alienating than the other three which typify older kinds of mechanization.

But weren't workers much more contented with their simpler lives before the age of mechanization? Many people assume they were, but Alasdair Clayre doesn't agree. In his book *Work and Play* *** Clayre examined attitudes toward work as expressed in preindustrial folk literature and popular ballads. He found "few indications of a Golden Age in which work was generally regarded as pleasurable and satisfying." In general, daily work in those days was "the same burdensome necessity for peasants and craftsmen as it is (today) for factory workers and clerks." Life's satisfactions and pleasures were mainly sought, then as now, in leisure not work.

THE FUTURE

In order to gain useful insights into how the industrialization process is likely to evolve over the next few years, it is best to regard the introduction of automation equipment not as an isolated event but rather as a part of a much longer process of technological innovation which has been going on in human society since its inception. Accordingly, the invention of the wheel, the development of the printing press, and the harnessing of steam are far more significant than the more recent developments in which we have been using computers to streamline the productive process. As Gotlieb and Borodin put it:

---

*Simon, Herbert A. "What Computers Mean to Man and Society". *Science*. 8 March 1977. pp. 1186-1191.

**Blauner, R. *Alienation and Freedom: The Factory Worker and His Industry*. Chicago, Illinois: University of Chicago Press, 1964.

***Clayre, Alasdair. *Work and Play: Ideas and Experience of Work and Leisure*. New York, New York: Harper and Row, 1975.

"In industrialized countries, the present evidence indicates that computing has not had the unsettling effect on employment forecast by many...the effects have been similar to those accompanying other technological innovations."

And yet, despite these soothing reassurances, when we consider the future, we still find it hard to shake the bothersome feeling that automation could eventually create jolting and widespread unemployment. In Gotlieb and Borodin's words:

"The possibility that large segments of the work force will be replaced by machines, that work will be the privilege of the elite, still persists as a nagging, if remote fear."*

This fear is not entirely groundless. True, after decades of rampant mechanization, more Americans are working today than ever before; however, the amount of time they spend on the job is inevitably declining. As is shown by the barcharts in Figure 75 for several decades our average workweek has been shrinking around a half of one percent per year. If we extrapolate this trend to the turn of the century, it would appear that by the year 2001, the average American worker will be on the job only about 1400 hours per year. This corresponds to a 28-hour workweek or roughly 50 percent of what it was at the beginning of this century.

The proponents of high technology often insist that technological advancements result in more jobs, not less. There must be something in what they say because, by and large, the countries with big labor forces and low unemployment rates live and breathe high technology. And yet, when we examine specific industries that have adopted new technological innovations, we find that, in some cases employment has declined, occasionally in dramatic ways.

For example, as you can see from the graph at the top of Figure 77, in the past 50 years tractors and other mechanized farm implements have cut our country's farm population from 30 million to less than 10 million. In that same interval, for much the same reasons, the number of coal-mine workers has declined about 50 percent. In both cases the quantity of materials being produced experienced sharp increases at the same time employment was declining. Between 1930 and the present day wheat production went from 0.9 billion to 2.1 billion bushels and coal production rose from 300 million to 600 million tons.

---

*Gotlieb, C. C. and Borodin, A. *Social Issues in Computing*. New York, New York: Academic Press, 1973.

The 19th century British dramatist Oscar Wilde strongly identified with the profoundly personal feelings of his country's ragtag army of laborers being displaced by advancing mechanization. But he also realized that the increased productivity made possible by new machines was the key to a richer, more meaningful civilization. Excess productive capacity gives us the surplus to create cathedrals, concerts, paintings, great plays. As Wilde himself put it in a famous essay praising the benefits of mechanization:

"Civilization requires slaves...unless there are slaves to do the ugly, horrible, uninteresting work, culture becomes almost impossible. Human slavery is wrong, insecure, and demoralizing. On mechanical slavery—on the slavery of the machine—the future of the world depends."

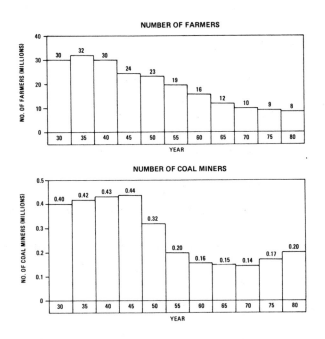

Figure 77: Although there are no documented examples of situations in which automation has created widespread unemployment, the simpler, long-term process of mechanization has had far-reaching impacts on the composition of our country's labor force. Farming and coal mining provide two instructive examples. In 1930 America's farm population consisted of 30 million people; today it numbers less than 10 million. In that same interval, under similar pressures of increased mechanization, the number of coal miners has dropped by 50 percent.

BIBLIOGRAPHY

1. Abraham, R. B., and Yaroshuk, N. "Advanced Robotics." *Mechanical Engineering,* December 1975, pp. 32-36.

2. "America The Inefficient." *Time,* 3 March 1970, pp. 72-80.

3. Aronson, Robert B. "Let the Robots Do It." *Machine Design,* 27 November 1975, pp. 54-59.

4. "The Blue Collar Computer." *Technology Review,* May 1975, p. 63.

5. "Computers That Learn to Make Their Own Decisions." *Business Week,* 6 April 1974, pp. 30D-30H.

6. Darrod, Brad. "Meet Shaky, The First Electronic Person." *Life Magazine,* 1970.

7. Doi, Yasuhiro. "Robots Get Smarter and More Versatile." *IEEE Spectrum,* September 1977, pp. 65-68.

8. Fabun, Don. *The Dynamics of Change.* Englewood Cliffs, New Jersey: Prentice-Hall, 1970.

9. Friedman, Milton. "Behind the Unemployment Figures." *Newsweek,* 7 Feburary 1977, p. 63.

10. " 'Friendly' Computers Will Cut Computer Labor Costs." *The Futurist,* December 1977, p. 396.

11. Gotlieb, C.C., and Borodin, A. *Social Issue in Computing,* New York, New York: Academic Press, 1973.

12. "Mechanical Handling: The Industrial Robot." *Engineering,* May 1977, pp. 399-400.

13. Newman, Joseph. *The Computer: How It's Changing Our Lives.* Washington, D. C.: Books by U. S. News and World Report, 1972.

14. Noll, Michael A. "Man-Machine Tactile Communication." *Creative Computing,* Jan-Feb 1976. pp. 52-57.

15. Parks, J. R. "Intelligent Machines—Commercial Potential." *The Radio and Electronic Engineer,* August/September 1977, pp. 355-367.

16. "Perils of the Productivity Sag." *Time,* 5 February 1979, pp. 126-127.

17. "A Problem List of Issues Concerning Computers and Public Policy." *Communications of the ACM,* 17 (Sept. 1974): 495-502.

18. "Putting It All Together...With Robots." *Iron Age,* 13 December 1976, pp. 47-56.

19. Ralston, Anthony. *Encyclopedia of Computer Science.* New York, New York: Petro-celli/Charter, 1976.

20. Rathel, Bertram. *The Thinking Computer: Mind Inside Matter.* New York, New York: W. H. Freeman, 1976.

21. "Robots Are Getting Smarter." *Modern Plastics,* February 1977, pp. 44-45.

22. "Robots in Your Future." *Technology Review,* January 1975, pp. 52-53.

23. "Robots Lend a Hand in a New Aus-forming Line." *Iron Age,* 7 February 1977, pp. 58-59.

24. "Robot Sights Objects on Table." *Electronics,* 24 November 1977, pp. 46-48.

25. Rorvik, David. *As Man Becomes Machine.* New York, New York: Pocket Books, 1970.

26. Rosen, Steven. *Future Facts.* New York, New York: Simon and Schuster, 1976.

27. Rothman, Stanley and Mossman, Charles. *Computers and Society,* Chicago, Illinois: Science Research Associates, 1972.

28. Shepherd, Mark Jr., "Distributed Computing Power: A Key to Productivity." *Computer,* November 1977, pp. 66-74.

29. Takeyasu, K.; Goto, T., and Inoyama, T. "Precision Insertion Control Robot and Its Application." *Journal of Engineering for Industry,* November 1976, pp. 1313-1318.

30. "The Undersea Robot." *Mini-Micro Systems,* May 1978, pp. 54-55.

31. Weizenbaum, Joseph. *Computer Power and Human Reason,* San Francisco, California: W. H. Freeman, 1976.

32. Will, George F. "Good Grief." *Newsweek,* 27 November 1978, p. 120.

EXERCISES

1. The introductory paragraphs of this chapter contained a series of frightening predictions concerning the effects of automation on future American unemployment levels. Yet, according to the arguments presented elsewhere in the chapter, hardly any unemployment can be traced directly to automation. Explain why you think things turned out better than most people had been anticipating.

2. What is an industrial robot? How is it used today? What new jobs do you think it will be able to handle in the distant future?

3. What is a feedback control system? Give examples of feedback as practiced by Mother Nature and examples as practiced by design engineers.

4. Who were the Luddites? What happened to them? Are there any modern Luddites?

5. It can be argued that an industrialist would never be willing to purchase an expensive computer unless he or she envisions appreciable savings in labor. Yet, so far, those industries that have bought and installed large numbers of computers have experienced harldy any employee reductions. Explain why.

6. What did the author mean by the statement "Contrary to popular opinion the era of automation has produced no abrupt or unusual gains in worker productivity"?

7. What is the difference between a *primary* worker and a *secondary* worker? Which type is likely to increase with increasing automation?

8. What is Yankee ingenuity? Does it still live today? If not, why not? If so, list modern examples.

9. Both Norbert Wiener and Oscar Wilde compared automatic machines with slave labor, but they arrived at completely different conclusions as to the desirability of increased mechanization. Write a paragraph or two contrasting the attitudes of these two intelligent men.

10. We usually think of leisure time as desirable. But some of the difficulties of leisure were highlighted in this chapter. List as many difficulties as you can. (Feel free to enlarge the list with ideas of your own.)

STUDENT PROJECTS

1. Robots are fascinating creatures. Research their use in present-day industrial applications. Summarize what you have learned in a 5 or 6 page report.

SUGGESTED REFERENCES:

a. Abraham, R. G., and Yaroshuk, N. *Mechanical Engineering*. December, 1975. pp. 32-36.

b. Aronson, Robert B. "Let The Robots Do It". *Machine Design*. 27 November 1975. pp. 54-59.

c. Doi, Yasuhiro. "Robots Get Smarter and More Versatile". *IEEE Spectrum*. September, 1977. pp. 65-68.

d. " 'Friendly' Computers will Cut Computer Labor Costs". *The Futurist*. December 1977. pg. 396.

e. "Putting It All Together...With Robots". *Iron Age*. 13 December 1976. pp. 47-56.

f. Parks, J. R. "Intelligent Machines—Commercial Potential". *The Radio and Electronic Engineer*. August/September 1977. pp. 355-367.

2. Automation has come to many production plants and various service industries. But, so far, with minor exceptions, it has not had much of an impact on our educational institutions. Suggest ways in which we might go about automating one or more of the operations that take place on a college campus, e.g., cleanup, patrol, athletic programs, teaching, etc. Make crude sketches showing how your automatic devices would work, compete with explanatory comments.

3. Band together with six or eight of your classmates and set up a debate with the following point of contention: Resolved: technological advancements result in more jobs, not less.

CHAPTER 11

THE SCANNER REVOLUTION

CASH DRAWERS THAT TALK COMPUTER
The Universal Product Code
The Scanners
Operating Procedures

POTENTIAL COST SAVINGS

CUSTOMER CONCERNS
Paying for the Hardware
The Fears of Unemployment
The Price Marking Controversy
New Opportunities for Deception and Fraud

APPROACHING THE STATUS QUO

A METHOD FOR MAKING THE SCANNERS OBSOLETE

BIBLIOGRAPHY

EXERCISES

STUDENT PROJECTS

As you maneuver your wobbly-wheeled shopping cart up and down the aisles at your neighborhood supermarket, the entire production seems to operate like a carefully-oiled machine. But as you approach the checkstand, everything quickly grinds to a mind-numbing halt. Shifting impatiently from foot to foot, each customer is temporarily held captive while the checker laboriously punches in the prices, one individual item at a time. Fortunately, the era of the manually-operated cash register is coming to a close. A few years ago *Time* magazine described a promising alternative in these most eloquent terms:

> "Like pickle barrels and nickel candy, the ring of the grocery store cash register may soon belong to nostalgia. In its place will come the soft whir and occasional beeping of electronic equipment. Seven large supermarket chains in the U. S. are quietly testing an automated pricing and checkout system that can 'read' coded prices on each item, tote up the bill and do nearly everything but pack the groceries in a bag. Advocates of the system, who describe it as the biggest advance in retailing since the tin can, say that it promises big savings in both shopping time for consumers and operating costs for store owners."[*]

How do the new electronic checkout systems operate? They use laser scanning devices to decipher black and white patches factory-imprinted upon bottles, boxes, and cans. The *Time* magazine article goes on to explain:

> "Postage-stamp-sized rectangles printed on boxes or labels by the packager carry both the product's code number and a set of light and heavy lines that allow an optical scanner set in the new fangled checkout counters to identify each item. The scanner feeds the data to a computer programmed with the store's current prices . . . and the machine does the rest."

At the time this article was written, many in the grocery industry expected rapid computerization of America's 33,000 major supermarkets. "Within two or three years, mechanical cash registers will not be available any more," predicted Douglas Steward, Automation Director for a Montreal supermarket, "all manufacturers will convert to electronic equipment."[*] Nor was Mr. Steward alone in his rather enthusiastic

---

[*]"Bringing Home the 33900-10020." *Time*. December 30, 1974. pg. 20.

[*]Howard, Grover A. "Future Shock in the Supermarket". *The Futurist*. June 1975. pp. 143-146.

assessment. Once a few systems had been installed and demonstrated, the trade journals loudly trumpeted both their slick operation and their attractive profit potential.

Have the new electronic marvels worked as smoothly as planned? Not entirely. Things seldom do. In the early days there were a few inevitable snags: Coded stickers came unstuck from milk cartons and frozen foods. Consumers were bewildered by computer-printed sales slips said to be "about as easy to read as alphabet soup." Legislative difficulties and formal regulations hampered the local adoption of the devices and, in several states, labor unions and consumer groups—in a rare coalition—banded together to prevent or delay their installation. However, in the main, electronic checkout has succeeded in doing the things it is supposed to do. It saves time—and money. And, once the equipment is in place, organized customer resistance gradually begins to crumble. In this chapter we shall retrace some of the tortuous steps that led to the beginnings of supermarket computerization and we shall review some of the emotional controversies its proponents encountered along the way.

CASH DRAWERS THAT TALK COMPUTER

Even as early as the 1960's electronic checkout devices had been operated experimentally in a few innovative supermarkets. Unfortunately, the developers of these pioneering systems all had their own ideas as to proper design of the scanning devices and the types of coding systems that should be used. In those days if you carried a box of Post Toasties from one computerized market to another, the scanner at the second location would be completely confused. Standardization was obviously necessary if the scanners were to achieve widespread adoption. Unfortunately, a variety of technical and political problems had to be resolved before it was possible to devise a realistic set of standards. It was tiresome, irritating work; sometimes it seemed as though agreement would never actually be reached. However, on March 30, 1973, after six hard years of more-or-less continuous haggling, the Universal Product Code was finally adopted by a special consortium representing the various, special-interest groups from within America's food-marketing industry.

The Universal Product Code

In essence, the Universal Product Code consists of a series of black and white stripes representing the ten decimal digits; letters and punctuation marks are not included in the code. For grocery store applications the first digit is always a decimal zero (0). The next five denote a particular manufacturer; the last five identify the specific item being sold. Thus, for example, 0-35000-50500 represents a 3-ounce tube of Colgate toothpaste and 0-20000-10023 denotes a 15-ounce can of Green Giant extra-long asparagus spears.

As is shown in Figure 78, each of the ten decimal numbers is represented by seven consecutive binary digits. From the computer's viewpoint, a white band is a binary 0; its black counterpart is a binary 1. The sticker is partitioned into two parts by a "tall center bar" which is always coded as 01010. In order to allow the checker to run the food item across the scanner in either direction, each decimal digit is represented in a different way depending on whether it is to the left or to the right of the tall center bar. The decimal digit 4, for instance, is represented as 0100011 if it is on the left; but 1011100 if it is on the right. Notice that there is a simple relationship between these two binary sequences: the ones and zeros have merely been interchanged.

To the left of the tall center bar the sticker contains the following four items of coded information:

1. A *white space* at least seven binary characters wide.
2. A *left guard band* (101) used in signaling the scanner that it has just encountered a coded symbol.
3. A *number system character* telling the scanner which version of the Universal Product Code is being used (there are five slightly different versions).
4. *35 binary digits* (five decimal digits) specifying the product manufacturer.

The right side of the sticker contains four similar items of information:

1. *35 binary digits* (five decimal digits) specifying the particular product.
2. A *modulo check character* which helps insure that the decoding procedure will be successfully achieved.
3. A *right guard band* (101).
4. A *white space* at least seven binary characters wide.

The modulo check character is similar to the "parity checking bit" which we reviewed in Figure 12 of Chapter 2. It eliminates any erroneous reading that might be caused by wrinkled labels or fingerprint smudges. If this special checking character was not included, the store could, in the words of one worried manager: ". . . be charging out ham for the price of broccoli".

Figure 78: In essence, the Universal Product Code consists of a series of black and white stripes representing the ten decimal digits 0 through 9. Each coded symbol includes two 5-digit decimal numbers, one representing the manufacturer, the other representing the specific product being sold.

Any time the modulo check character fails to match the other numbers extracted from a particular sticker, the scanner automatically signals the clerk that an error has occurred. The modulo check character and the other self-checking characteristics built into the code allow the scanners to operate with remarkable accuracy and precision. In one widely-publicized test seven million items were scanned without encountering a single undetected error.*

The Scanners

The scanning unit used in deciphering the Universal Product Code utilizes a helium-neon laser to illuminate the sticker with four pencil-thin beams of monchromatic light. A schematic sketch of the scanner is presented in Figure 79. As you can see, its laser beam shines through a focusing lens onto a series of partially-silvered mirrors. These mirrors split the light into four distinct beams which are then reflected onto a rotating multifaceted mirror. This causes each beam to sweep across the sticker at a rate of 240 times per second. The reflected light is focused onto a photodetector capable of determining exactly when one of the bands changes from dark to light—or vice versa. This produces a set of square waves which can be converted into a string of binary ones and zeros representing the various products being sold.

Operating Procedures

Although the laser scanner is based on relatively complicated design principles, it is surprisingly easy to operate. The salesclerk merely slides the food item across an open slot in the checkout counter as shown in Figure 80. In many markets the item is placed in a paper bag in the same smooth motion. This eliminates the need for separate bagging operations. The prices are not called out during checkout; instead they are displayed optically for visual verification by both the customer and the checker. In addition, each price is printed on the register tape beside a 12-letter description of the purchase it represents.

The scanner also relieves the checker of several other tedious chores. For example, if Del Monte string beans are priced at three Number 2 cans for 77¢ the checker need not save and group them. If the cans are passed over the scanner interspersed with other items, the computer will "remember" the first two until the third one appears. If and when it does, a single price of 77¢ will be charged and printed on the tape.

The computer also simplifies the checkout procedures in several other ways. Specifically, it takes care of sales taxes, handles cents-off promotions, and reminds the clerk of Sunday sales bans. Moreover, it determines the requisite number of trading stamps, calculates federal food stamp payments, and, in some cases, maintains a bad-check memory.

---

*"Supermarket Scanning and You" a consumer-oriented pamphlet being distributed by the National Cash Register Company in Dayton, Ohio.

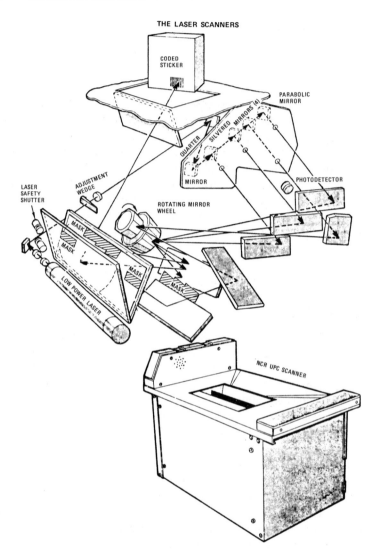

THE LASER SCANNERS

CODED STICKER

PARABOLIC MIRROR

QUARTER SILVERED MIRRORS (4)

MIRROR

PHOTODETECTOR

LASER SAFETY SHUTTER

ADJUSTMENT WEDGE

ROTATING MIRROR WHEEL

MASK

MASK

MASK

MASK

LOW POWER LASER

NCR UPC SCANNER

Figure 79: The laser scanning device used in deciphering the Universal Product Code generates four laser beams which are reflected from a multifaceted mirror rotating at a high rate of speed. These pencil-thin beams are, in turn, reflected from the UPC symbol thus producing a binary pulse train which is routed to a dedicated minicomputer located in the back of the store.

ELECTRONIC CHECKOUT PROCEDURES

Figure 80: The scanning devices used in deciphering the Universal Product Code are surprisingly easy to operate. The checkout clerk merely slides each item across an open slot in the counter thus illuminating its sticker with monochromatic laser light. Shoppers seem to enjoy buying their groceries in markets equipped with the scanners: checkout is considerably faster, the clerks are more relaxed, mistakes are less frequent, and the customer ends up with a clearer, more detailed register receipt.

POTENTIAL COST SAVINGS

The proponents the electronic scanning point out that the system has a number of important advantages over manual methods. In particular, it results in shorter waiting lines, better inventory control, closer monitoring of the effectiveness of media advertising and more comprehensive register records for customers. However, cost reduction is by far, the most important benefit of switching to electronic checkout.

Price-conscious housewives may find it a little hard to believe but, for nearly a decade America's major supermarkets have been earning less than a penny in profit for every dollar's worth of food they sell. In such a tight, competitive industry even small percentage savings are seen as significant gains.

The barcharts in Figure 81 represent some of the more obvious cost reductions that result when electronic scanners are bought and installed. A relatively large market, one which grosses $560,000 per month, was assumed in this particular illustration. As you can see, four types of cost savings are included in the listing:

1. Underrings
2. Pricing and Marking
3. Cashier Labor
4. Shrinkage Control.

Underrings: Underrings occur when the checker rings up less than the proper price for an item—a surprisingly common and costly mistake. It may seem curious that the clerk would be inclined to undercharge customers at the expense of his employer, the supermarket chain. However, several studies have shown that checkers feel more of a kinship with their customers than they do with the market; consequently, they tend, perhaps unconsciously, to charge less than the going rate. Another reason they may tend to undercharge is that the customer is standing at the register available for an argument whereas the store manager is usually not present. In a typical market the savings that result from using scanners to reduce underrings amount to about $900 per month.

Pricing and Marking: Each year approximately 170 billion price labels must be imprinted upon or attached to individual packages and cans According to an industry spokesman testifying before the Subcommittee for Consumers of the U. S. Senate Commerce Committee: "Item price marking is estimated to cost approximately $1 per thousand items marked and . . . *repricing* approximately $3 per thousand items . . . thus, current pricing and repricing practices add between $250 million and $300 million annually to food distribution costs."* If a typical market could eliminate individual price marking as a result of using scanners (i.e., by putting the prices only on the shelves), it could save another $2100 per month.

---

*Thornton, Zane. "The Consumer Comes Face to Face with the Computer." *Dimensions.* September 1976. pp. 3-7.

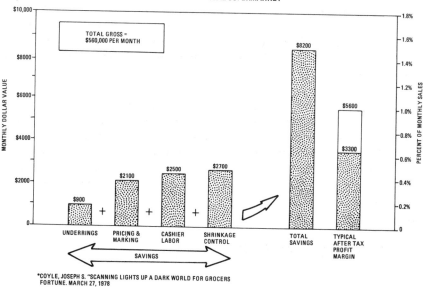

THE TOTAL SAVINGS RESULTING FROM ELECTRONIC
CHECKOUT AT A TYPICAL SUPERMARKET*

*COYLE, JOSEPH S. "SCANNING LIGHTS UP A DARK WORLD FOR GROCERS
FORTUNE. MARCH 27, 1978

Figure 81: When electronic checkout devices are installed in a typical supermarket the total hard savings usually amount to 1.5 to 2 times the store's after-taxes earnings. Most of the savings result from the elimination of underrings, better shrinkage control, cuts in the labor required for pricing and marking, and reductions in salaries for cashier and checkout personnel.

Cashier Labor: Scanning technology will cut cashier labor substantially because the checkout procedures are considerably faster and in many situations boxboys are not required. Some of the earliest studies pointed toward 30 to 40 percent reductions in supermarket staffs. However, more recent evaluations indicate staff reduction of more like 15 percent. Converted into monetary terms, this saving averages about $2500 per month.

Shrinkage Control: At one time supermarkets operated under shrinkage allowance that amounted to a small fraction of one percent of total sales; today in some neighborhoods these allowances range upwards to 2 percent. Most of the losses result from employee theft, shoplifting, bad checks, and improper delivery from vendors and suppliers. Electronic checkout helps the supermarket pinpoint its shrinkages thus giving managers a better chance to work out effective measures of control. Preliminary estimates indicate monthly savings of about $2700 in a typical store.

Total Savings: The total hard savings resulting from automated checkout in our hypothetical market total about $8200 per month or around 1.5 percent of gross revenues. Although this may not seem like a particularly large savings, it is nearly twice the after-taxes earnings at a typical store. If all 33,000 American supermarkets would convert to the scanners, the total nationwide saving would exceed $1 billion per year. Moreover, electronic checkout offers additional soft savings aside from the hard savings listed in Figure 81. A soft saving is a clearly-defined benefit which is difficult to quantify in monetary terms. The soft savings include greater customer satisfaction, closer control of inventories, more accurate monitoring of the effects of advertising campaigns, and easier stocking of stores to suit neighborhood tastes. Even if the store managers end up sharing a portion of these savings with their customers, it is estimated that the laser scanners (which carry price tags of about $80,000 to $120,000 per store) will pay back their costs within two to four years.

CUSTOMER CONCERNS

Customer reactions to electronic scanning have generally been quite favorable; however, some individuals have also expressed certain serious concerns: Who will end up paying for the hardware? Will widespread job losses occur? Will the scanners be used to deceive those who buy their groceries at supermarkets—or ensnare them in outright fraud? These are all reasonable questions, questions which we shall examine in some detail in the subsections to come.

Paying for the Hardware

At this writing 15 of the top 20 American supermarket chains have at least one store with the scanners installed and operating. Giant Foods is the industry leader with nearly one-third of its 114 stores having already converted. However, the Winn-Dixie chain will soon overtake them. Winn-Dixie's executives recently signed a four-year contract with IBM to install scanners in all 500 of its stores.

Those who are marketing the hardware contend that increased profits will pay for the devices in approximately three years thus making the scanners an extremely attractive investment. Because of this unusually favorable payoff interval, it is anticipated that total sales of electronic checkout systems may soon approach a billion dollars per year. So far two major corporations have assumed a dominant position. IBM got a late start but now claims to have captured 57 percent of the market followed by NCR (National Cash Register) with 25 percent.

Although the scanners appear to be an attractive investment, their high cost has, to some degree, slowed their widespread installation. In 1978 only about 200 of the nation's 33,000 major supermarkets were using registers capable of reading the code. Even if installations stay on schedule, the scanners are expected to be in use in only about 20 percent of the available markets by the early 1980's.* A total conversion of every supermarket in the United States would probably cost between $3 and $4 billion dollars, a sum that may not be available to an industry in which profits are often tissue-paper thin.

When the scanners were first introduced, industry experts joyously maintained that they would help counteract rising food prices by increasing worker productivity. Consumer advocates can forsee substantial savings but they are afraid the high initial cost of the hardware will be passed on to grocery shoppers and that any eventual savings will likely end up in the pockets of local merchants or corporate chains.

Dr. Thomas V. Sobczak writing in *Computers and People* sees the scanners as a giant ripoff. He argues that supermarket managers are installing the equipment for only one reason "profits". He goes on to ask consumers a pointed question: "Have you noticed any savings from other supermarket gimmicks?" In his opinion the cost of installing and maintaining the devices will inevitably be passed on to consumers while the owners of supermarkets will keep any savings that may result. "With the Universal Product Code, you pay more and know less" he maintains.**

Professor Ray Boche, Computer Center Director of California Polytechnic State University at San Luis Obispo, California, is quite aware that in some circles the term "profit" is regarded as a dirty word. But he is not shaken by the emotional appeal of Dr. Sobczak's arguments. The fact that businessmen are attempting to achieve higher profits "does not surprise me at all", he writes in reply "as I believe that private industry's motivation for adopting any new technology must be either directly or indirectly their opportunity to profit from its adoption. As a consumer, I support that potential profit improvement. I cannot expect significant reductions in prices while supermarket profits remain at only one percent."*** As for the lack of past savings from supermarket "gimmicks", Dr. Boche offers this informative reply: "I am not prepared to argue the cause and effect relationship relating to 'savings from other

---

*"Supermarket Scanning and You." National Cash Register (NCR). Dayton, Ohio.

**Sobczak, Thomas V."The Universal Product Code: An Introduction to What It Means for Consumers." *Computers and People.* December 1975. pp. 7[+].

***Boche, Ray. "The Universal Product Code—A Defense". *Computers and People.* February 1976. pp. 16[+].

supermarket gimmicks' but to the extent that the supermarket is the sum of those 'gimmicks', the difference in pricing by contrast to the convenient neighborhood 'mom and pop store' seems fairly apparent."

Because some consumers seem to be offended by the idea that substantial savings might be pocketed by others, industry spokesmen have recently toned down some of their more outlandish claims. In many cases they have dropped any references to monetary savings. Instead, they now, more typically, talk about "the potential for reduced prices."

In 1977 Jim Stell, President of Lucky Stores, made a public statement that typified this cagey attitude. On visiting a San Leandro establishment that had just installed $250,000 worth of checkout equipment, he was asked by reporters if the new devices would result in savings for consumers. His answer: "We can't guarantee anything."*

The Fears of Unemployment

When the scanners first began to appear in large numbers, many supermarket clerks were afraid the new technology might cause them to lose their jobs. Kenneth Edwards, President of Retail Clerk's Union, Local 770 testified before the California State Assembly that, with total computerization, his union might experience labor cuts amounting to as much as 30 to 40 percent. Other union leaders forecast a series of strikes and a slowdowns as a result of supermarket computerization.

In practice, labor unrest didn't turn out to be a particularly serious problem. However, the unions did, on occasion, join forces with certain militant consumer groups, sometimes secretly contributing money to help support their activities. Today, however, there is little organized union resistance when the scanners are installed. In part, this is true because the conversion process is usually so gradual that any labor cuts—which now seem far less formidable than was first suspected—are almost always handled by attrition. According to the latest estimates, a conventional 8-lane supermarket with 22 employees will end up, after conversion, with approximately 18 still on the payroll.** Since the industry as a whole has an annual employee turnover rate approaching 20 percent, many stores guarantee in writing that no worker will be laid off as a result of computerization.

---

* Howard, Grover A. "Future Shock in the Supermarket." *The Futurist.* June 1975. pp. 143-146.
**"Electronic Pricing Faces an Uphill Fight." *Business Week.* March 31, 1975. pg. 23.

The Price Marking Controversy

Whenever you get an opportunity to watch a supermarket clerk stamping prices on laundry detergent boxes or fruit cocktail cans, it seems to be an extremely efficient procedure which, indeed, it is. However, taken on a nationwide scale, price marking is such a big job, total costs quickly escalate. Each year our supermarkets dispense more than 700 food items for each person living in the United States—a total of 170 billion bottles, boxes, and cans. The process of stamping the individual prices is currently costing the industry an estimated $300 million per year.

Because of this high cost, grocers would prefer not to pricemark each individual item, instead putting the prices only on the supermarket shelf. Off hand, this may sound like a fairly reasonable cost-saving measure. Unfortunately, when it is proposed to consumers, some of them become livid with rage. Dr. Thomas V. Sobczak, for example, is suspicious that grocers want to remove the prices from packages in order to create customer confusion. In his view, the absence of prices makes it much more difficult for consumers to compare the costs of various brands. "Suppose the house brand was priced higher than the so-called premium brand; without pricemarking how does the consumer know?" He is also convinced that the introduction of electronic scanners will inevitably have a negative impact on the retail food industry on the whole—especially the small, neighborhood groceries. "What will be the effect on price as marginal manufacturers drop out of competition?" he asks pointedly. And then he answers his own question. "Could it be that the wheeler-dealers have an even bigger innovation planned—a sellers market? Supermarket 1984 is watching. Big Brother is small in comparison to what the control of food-stuffs can do."*

But does the scanner revolution actually represent a serious attempt to confuse the housewife and make her more insensitive to individual food prices? Computer expert Ray Boche isn't convinced. "I am certainly not opposed to pricemarking" he writes, "I am, in fact, a strong advocate of unit pricing but I believe that I could become quite satisfied with both pieces of information on the shelf . . . I don't seem to suffer when I select fresh fruits and vegetables from marked bins."

However, he goes on to explain that the procedures for placing prices on the shelf could stand some improvement. For one thing it is not always clear which price applies to which product. Another difficulty occurs when a shopper decides against keeping a particular item and returns it to a

---

*Sobczak, Thomas V. "Universal Product Coding: Who Profits and Who Loses?" *Computers and People.* February 1976. pp. 17-19.

different shelf. Fortunately, Dr. Boche has an easy solution: "It seems to me that an image of the product label could be coupled with marking information to protect us from mis-shelving or sloppy shelf returns by our fellow customers. A glance at the shelf to verify that the item I am selecting matches the indicated price seems to me a small sacrifice for which I will feel amply compensated by the item identification that appears on the lengthy register tape."*

Still, despite all the soothing things that have been said about shelf prices and fancy register tapes, consumers have consistently objected to the removal of package prices. As a result consumer groups have lobbied for government intervention—and their elected representatives have been quite responsive to their voiced concerns. At this writing 14 states have passed laws requiring individual pricing of the items stocked on supermarket shelves.

But why are supermarket customers so upset by unmarked cans? San Francisco consumer advocate Betty Lederer points out that without individual package prices: "There is no way for the customer to check the accuracy of the computer . . . When you are cooking in the kitchen, it helps to be able to see the price on the package and know how much a meal will cost."** Ms. Lederer also contends that the shopper needs to know the prices on the individual items so she can comparison-shop while she is wheeling her cart around the store.

Barbara Beizer of the National Consumers Congress is also sold on the possibilities for cost comparisons provided by individual price labels: "Most shoppers don't examine closely the cash-register tape when they get home, but every time they open the refrigerator door they see the price stamped on top of the grape jelly. It allows for comparison with items bought a month ago, and makes consumers continually aware of food-price trends."***

Alan Haberman the current President of First National Stores, is not entirely unsympathetic with these consumer concerns, but he voices what he believes is a perfectly reasonable reply: "If consumers are really interested in having prices on merchandise, the supermarkets would be glad to supply grease pencils so they can do the marking themselves." As a matter of fact, Steinberg's, a supermarket chain in Montreal, is doing precisely that.

---

*Boche, Ray. "The Universal Product Code—A Defense." *Computers and People.* February 1976. pp. 16[+].

**Howard, Grover A. "Future Shock in the Supermarket." *The Futurist.* June 1975. pp. 143-146.

***"Grocery Checkout by Computer—What It Means to Shoppers". *U.S. News and World Report.* December 30, 1974. pp. 56-57.

Carol Foreman, Executive Director of the Consumer Federation of America is not entirely satisfied with this approach; to put it mildly the practice infuriates her. She maintains that it is "typical of the public-be-damned attitude the industry takes." The idea of handing out grease pencils, in her opinion, "equates on a public relations equivalency scale with 'let em eat cake'".

Ironically, one of the early motivations for the development of the Universal Product Code was the chronic inaccuracy and illegibility of the prices marked on individual bottles and cans. An independent survey conducted by the Federal Trade Commission several years ago indicated that America's supermarkets were plagued with "mismarked, misplaced, unmarked, and illegible . . . prices". Another survey, carried out by the Retail Clerks Union revealed that pricemarking was inaccurate between 30 and 60 percent of the time.

And yet, if individual prices are really what the public wants, individual prices are what the public will get. In the final analysis the American housewife will cast the deciding vote with her pocketbook. However, if the struggle does end up that way Paul Korody, Consumer Affairs Director of the National Association of Food Chains, thinks it would be a shame. "The removal of prices from goods is not necessary to install the system" he observes, "But by insisting that the price remains on the cans, you just lose the benefits".*

If individual pricing does win out in the long run, we will lose another important efficiency gain in shelf restocking. It is called "modularized packaging". This is how *U.S. News and World Report* described the modularized concept in December of 1974:

> "Modularized packaging . . . allows stores to bring cartons from delivery trucks to the grocery shelves, remove the top and side panels and place the entire carton of packaged items on the shelf, each package already stamped with its code."**

No reliable estimates are currently available as to the probable savings associated with modularized packaging, but it would surely be much cheaper and more efficient than the shelf stocking practices now in common use.

---

*Howard, Grover A. "Future Shock in the Supermarket." *The Futurist.* June 1975. pp. 143-146.
**"Grocery Checkout by Computer". *U.S. News and World Report.* December 30, 1974. pp. 56-57.

New Opportunities for Deception and Fraud

Supermarket managers often talk about employing the information gathered by their backroom computers for such benign purposes as inventory control or checking the effectiveness of their advertising campaigns. However, this same information could conceivably be used in more exploitive and sinister ways.

For example, in one well-publicized instance, a supermarket chain tested a substantial price increase for its private-label orange juice at two of its scanner-equipped stores, carefully programming the computer to monitor any fluctuations in daily volume. When no sales losses resulted, they decided to adopt the higher price at the other markets in the chain.* Of course, this experiment in price gouging was entirely legal and moral. In a free-market economy the sellers have every right to raise their prices to whatever their customers are willing to tolerate. However, since the average market includes 15,000 separate items, it would have been impossible without computers to pinpoint the public's precise buying patterns in such fine detail.

Another underhanded way of using the backroom computers to boost profits was recently suggested by James Turner, a Washington, D.C., lawyer who has made a careful study of computerized marketing. Turner envisioned this hypothetical possibility:

"A store could program its computer to raise the price on every hundredth item 1 cent for three hours on a Saturday afternoon, or during the busy evening rush hour. It would be hard for consumers to detect such a misuse of the system...and yet it would significantly increase the store's revenues."**

Industry spokesmen have called such a suggestion "preposterous". Paul A. Korody, Director of Governmental Affairs for the National Association of Food Chains, had this to say in direct response: "If a store was caught doing that, it would . . . be roasted by the publicity. It's just too big a chance to take. People forget that big grocery chains are in just about the most competitive business in the country, and abuses are pretty quickly uncovered."

The invasion of customer privacy is another prominent worry. In

---

*Coyle, Joseph S. "Scanning Lights Up a Dark World for Grocers". *Fortune.* March 27, 1978. pp. 76-80.

**"Grocery Checkout by Computer—What It Means to Shoppers." *U.S. News and World Report.* December 30, 1974. pp. 56-57.

particular, if the systems are used to authorize credit or to determine bad check risks—as industry leaders now plan—the customer's identity could be linked to his or her purchases. It doesn't take a particularly vivid imagination to visualize slightly dishonest store managers programming their computers to pick out those customers who purchase certain specific items such as teething rings or canned dog food. Armed with this information, the managers could sell specialized name lists to encyclopedia salesmen, car dealers, or mail order firms. Records of magazine purchases could also be sold to publishing houses who might then hound supermarket customers to subscribe to certain magazines or join specialized book-of-the-month clubs. Although this practice may seem relatively harmless, it does constitute a clear-cut invasion of privacy, in that, personal information would be used for purposes other than those for which it was originally collected.

APPROACHING THE STATUS QUO

In the opinion of Dr. Thomas Sobczak, the Universal Product Code has been silently imposed on an unwary public and, now that it has taken root, it is spreading like well-watered crabgrass in an Orange County housing tract. "It started at the grocery", he writes "but since drugs and health-related items are sold in supermarkets, the Food and Drug Administration was convinced (lobbied?) to change the National Drug Code and the Health-Related Item Code to the UPC format. Books are sold in supermarkets, as are magazines. The publishers were the next to give in. Look at the UPC on the cover of 'Family Circle' . . . The trend continues with stationary and business supplies. The logic is the same. In time everything must be scanned mechanically."

At this point he gleefully mocks the Uniform Grocery Product Code Council which has been pleading with customers to ignore any short-term difficulties they may be encountering with the scanners and "Give the system a chance."

"Did you ever hear of a system, once started, that could be stopped for less than twice its startup cost? Do you really believe that those people investing $292 million to gain a 35% return on investment after taxes will give up their profit? If you do, then you can believe in the tooth fairy."*

---

*Sobczak, Thomas V. "The Universal Product Code: An Introduction to What It Means for Consumers." *Computers and People.* December 1975. pp. 7[+].

But, today, if you interview the clerks and customers at those stores using the scanners, you will likely find more peace than struggle. When a new technology emerges from the laboratory, strong resistance tends to build up but after a short time it often collapses, almost imperceptibly, as widespread adoption begins to seem inevitable. Often none of the people in the resistance movement actually believe they can halt progress. They are merely exerting pressures in hopes of sharing in the benefits of the new technology. In a wide-ranging article carried by *The Futurist* Dr. Grover A. Howard described this struggle and its eventual outcome with these carefully-chosen words:

"For the last and most important battle, groups tap their political credits obtained in the previous conflicts. Each cause is documented by favorable statistics. In the end, the interplay of these forces usually produces constantly evolving compromises, leading to a more equitable distribution of new benefits. With each succeeding compromise, support for the innovation widens, until, finally, it became part of the status quo."*

Those who have been following the scanner revolution are already beginning to see the hazy outlines of the new status quo. For several years the Retail Clerks Association fought a pitched battle against the scanners. They even surreptitiously contributed money to various consumer groups fighting the adoption of the new technology. However, in 1977 the Retail Clerks suddenly dropped their opposition. Apparently, they realized that computerization wasn't actually creating substantial job losses in their industry.

"The Retail Clerks International Union, which had feared that scanners would be bad for employment, has reconsidered the evidence on that point and retreated to a posture of neutrality" reported Joseph S. Coyle in a *Fortune* magazine article, "Labor's allies in the consumer movement have also quieted down—perhaps because the consumers they presume to speak for have fallen in love with scanners. Grocers who introduce the systems are consistently witnessing abrupt jumps in volume—as high as 25 percent—and the higher sales persist long after the novelty has worn off."**

Of course, not everyone is overjoyed with the effects of electronic checkout. Some shoppers are still dismayed by the speed with which

*Howard, Grover A. "Future Shock in the Supermarket." *The Futurist*. June 1975. pp. 143-146.

**Coyle, Joseph S. "Scanning Lights Up a Dark World for Grocers." *Fortune*. March 27, 1978. pp. 76-80.

prices flash on and off the digital display. Housewife Arlene D'Agosto, who shops at an automated Pathmark store in South Plainfield, New Jersey is not always sure she understands what is going on. "I feel that I have to watch more, than when the girl was ringing it up", she points out with a nervous frown. But another customer of the same store sees the advantages of scanning and thinks the system is "fantastic". One day she clocked her passage through the checkstand. The 25 items she had bought were tallied, paid for, and packed in 99 seconds flat—half the time it had taken with the old manual system.*

A METHOD FOR MAKING THE SCANNERS OBSOLETE

Thus we see that after nearly a decade of technical, political, and social struggle, the scanners are finally becoming acceptable to most supermarket customers. But even as the devices are making solid inroads into the marketplace, a more advanced technology is beginning to take shape half a world away. Someday, this new idea in marketing (See Figure 82) could make the scanners completely obsolete. This is how U.S. News and World Report described the salient features of the new technology in a story datelined Kokubunji, Japan:

"When the O.K. supermarket chain opened its 35th store, . . . almost one third of its 16,000 square feet was reserved for testing a new, computerized selling system developed by the Japanese Government over the past five years at a cost of 1.5 million dollars."

"There are 67 vending machines, some refrigerated, displaying 3,000 items from soup to sausages and edible seaweed. All are linked to a computer."**

The article goes on to explain how a customer at the market inserts a special magnetic card chained to his or her shopping cart into the slots in the machines and punches individual buttons to select the desired items. Each time a purchase is made, the computer records it and unlocks the door so that the shopper can retrieve the selection. When he or she reaches the checkstand, the items are not removed from the paper bags in the shopping cart. Instead, the magnetic card "is inserted into a slot in the cash register (whereupon) the computer instantly provides an itemized sales slip."

---

* "Bringing Home the 33900-10020." *U.S. News and World Report.* December 30, 1974. pg. 20.
**"Now: 'Unmanned' Supermarkets." *U.S. News and World Report.* June 30, 1975. pp. 56-57.

In general, the Japanese enjoy using the system, but there are a few nagging complaints. Specifically, the products can't be touch-tested prior to purchase and the merchandise can't be returned as easily as it can in a conventional market. Moreover, selections are somewhat limited because the markets that have been set up so far are only about one-fifth as large as their full-sized American counterparts.

PUSHBUTTON SUPERMARKETS

Figure 82: This Japanese supermarket uses vending machines to dispense more than 3000 food items ranging from Hershey bars to edible seaweed. The various machines are activated by inserting a stiff plastic card into a slot, then punching one or more buttons to make it dispense the desired item. When the customer leaves the store the plastic card is inserted into a slot in the register which instantly produces an itemized receipt. Tests show that this approach cuts checkout time by a factor of seven and reduces retail food prices 5 to 8 percent.

On the other hand, the vending system provides substantial benefits. For one thing the stores are virtually unmanned. Only two cashiers are needed compared with twenty before the computerized system was installed.* In addition, the vending machines are stocked with only 9 man-hours of labor, mostly provided by part-time workers. Shoplifting, employee pilfering, and cashier mistakes are all but eliminated and checkout is seven times faster. But the most important advantage is the one that will be of the greatest interest to American consumers. Once the system reaches its full operating potential, food prices are 5 to 8 percent lower than those charged at competing markets.

---

*"Click, Click, Click." *Newsweek*. June 30, 1975. pp. 57-58.

BIBLIOGRAPHY

1. Asimov, Isaac. "The Super Market 2077 A.D." *Progressive Grocer,* June 1977, pp. 50-53.

2. "Bringing Home the 33900-10020." *Time,* 30 December 1974, p. 20.

3. Bryngdahl, Olof, and Wai-Hon, Lee. "Laser Beam Scanning Using Computer-Generated Holograms." *Applied Optics,* January 1976, pp. 183-194.

4. "The Coming Battle at the Supermarket Counter." *Fortune,* September 1975, pp. 105-110.

5. "The Consumer Comes Face-to-Face with The Computer." *Dimensions,* October 1976, pp. 10-12.

6. Coyle, Joseph S. "Scanning Lights Up a Dark World for Grocers." *Fortune,* 27 March 1978, pp. 76-80.

7. "'Electronic Money' - What It Is and The Changes It Will Bring." *U. S. News and World Report,* 5 August 1974, pp. 50-52.

8. "Electronic Pricing Faces an Uphill Fight." *Business Week,* 31 March 1975, p. 23.

9. "Future Shock in the Supermarket." *The Futurist,* June 1975, pp. 143-146.

10. "The Great Checkout." *Newsweek,* 27 November 1978, p. 89.

11. "Grocery Checkout by Computer - What It Means to Shoppers." *U.S. News and World Report,* 30 December 1974, pp. 56-57.

12. Harrison, Shelly A. and Swartz, Jerome. "Needed: Better Quality Control for UPC." *Food Engineering,* October 1976, pp. 61-63.

13. Hastings, Susan. "Retail Marking Code." *Creative Computing,* January/February 1978, p. 47.

14. "How Universal is the UPC?" *Infosystems,* July 1974, pp. 22-23.

15. Koch, W. E. *Engineering Applications of Lasers.* New York: Plenum Press, 1975.

16. "NCR 255 Universal Product Code Scanning System." *NCR Corporation,* (Dayton, Ohio), SP-1478-01 0574.

17. "NCR 782 UPC Scanner Site Preparation." *NCR Corporation,* Dayton, Ohio: Pub. No. 2, May 1975.

18. "Packaging for the Space Age Checkout Counter." *Industry Week,* 18 February 1974, pp. 40-41.

19. "Point of Sale: Registering Gains for Retailers." *Infosystems,* July 1974, pp. 20-25.

20. "Retailing: Click, Click, Click." *Newsweek,* 30 June 1975, pp. 57-58.

21. "Scanning Gains More Ground. *Chain Store Age Executive,* February 1977, pp. 21-22.

22. Simon, Herbert A. "What Computers Mean to Man and Society." *Science,* 195 (March 1977): 1186-1191.

23. Sobczak, Thomas V. "Machine-Readable Marking Codes: Who Specifies What Type of Symbology?" *Computers and People,* February 1978, pp. 12-23.

24. Sobczak, Thomas V. "The Universal Product Code: An Introduction to What It Means for Consumers." *Computers and People,* December 1975, pp. 7-20.

25. Sobczak, Thomas V. "The Universal Product Code and the High Cost and Long Task of Conversion to it for Many Manufacturers." *Computers and People,* January 1976, pp. 8-11.

26. Sobczak, Thomas V. "Universal Product Coding: Who Profits and Who Loses?" *Computers and People,* February 1976, pp. 17-19.

27. Sobczak, Thomas V. "The Use of Coding Systems in Manufacturing." *Computers and People,* April 1978, pp. 9-26.

28. "Supermarkets: Brave New Checkout." *Newsweek,* 17 February 1975, pp. 79-80.

29. Triplett, B.L. "UPC Creates Data Revolution." *Data Management,* August 1975, pp. 24-29.

30. "UPC Moving Faster than Expected." *Datamation,* November 1974, pp. 111-112.

31. "UPC Scanning." *NCR Corporation,* (Dayton, Ohio) *SP-1500 0974.*

32. "When Food and Soft Goods Talk Different Codes." *Business Week,* 30 March 1974, pp. 64-66.

EXERCISES

1. What are some of the principal advantages to the consumer of electronic checkout in supermarkets? What are the principal advantages to those who own and operate the store?

2. How many different types of alphanumeric symbols can the Universal Product Code handle? How do the symbols differ when they are on opposite sides of the tall center bar? How does the manufacturer guard against scanner errors to avoid "charging out ham for the price of broccoli?"

3. Here is part of a scanner label taken from a popular supermarket product:

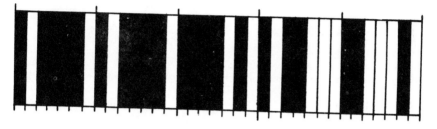

   Decipher its numerical code.

4. What are some of the major hard savings resulting from the use of electronic scanners? What are some of the soft savings?

5. What is the annual cost of price-labeling food items in American supermarkets? Approximately how much money would the scanners save a typical American grocer per year if we continue to require individual price labels? How much would be saved if we abandon individual pricemarking?

6. Describe the new supermarkets being tried experimentally in Japan. From the consumer's viewpoint what are some of their advantages? Their disadvantages?

7. Once retailers have installed electronic checkout systems, what are some of the shady things they could conceivably do with the hardware? Do you believe these are genuine hazards? How might they be prevented?

8. At present, placing prices on supermarket shelves does not seem to satisfy all the needs of the typical housewife. Describe two solutions mentioned in this chapter. Now describe at least one solution of your own.

9. When the scanners were first introduced, labor unions feared that they might cause large-scale job losses among their members. Why has this problem been less severe than they had anticipated? In general, how do labor unions react to the scanners today?

10. Fourteen states have passed laws requiring that supermarkets pricemark individual food items despite the fact that removing the prices would result in substantial cost savings. Do you approve or disapprove of this legislation? Explain your answer.

STUDENT PROJECTS

1. Go to a supermarket in your area with electronic scanners. Interview a few of the customers and a few of the supermarket employees to find out how they feel about the new technology. Summarize your finding in a four or five page report.

2. The price marking controversy was one of the most emotional issues ever to sweep through the American food industry. Go to the library and research the controversies surrounding the introduction of the scanners. Now summarize the key issues involved from the viewpoint of any one of the following:

   a. The supermarket managers.

   b. A typical housewife.

   c. The president of a local union representing supermarket workers.

Make no attempt to be fair but rather plead your case from a typically partisan viewpoint.

SUGGESTED READING LIST

a. "The Coming Battle at the Supermarket Counter." *Fortune*. September 1975. pp. 105-110.

b. Coyle, Joseph S. "Scanning lights Up a Dark World for Grocers." *Fortune*. 27 March 1978. pp. 76-80.

c. "Supermarkets: Brave New Checkout." *Newsweek*. 17 February 1975. pp. 79-80.

d. "When Food and Soft Goods Talk Different Codes." *Business Week*. 30 March 1974. pp. 64-66.

e. Sobczak, Thomas V. "Universal Product Coding: Who Profits and Who Loses?" *Computers and People*. February 1976. pp.17-19.

f. Sobczak, Thomas V. "The Universal Product Code: An Introduction to What It Means for Consumers." *Computers and People*. December 1975. pp. 7-20.

3. Shortly after Winn-Dixie signed a contract with IBM to purchase 500 scanner systems at a cost of something like $50 million, several popular magazines carried stories about the "vending machine" supermarkets in Japan that might soon make the scanners obsolete. Pretend you are the head of the board of directors at Winn-Dixie and compose a letter to a worried stockholder explaining why this large purchase makes sound economic sense.

CHAPTER 12

COMPUTERS AND OUR MONETARY SYSTEM

HISTORICAL PERSPECTIVES
Coins and Paper Money
Checks
Credit Cards
Electronic Funds Transfer Systems

**THE COSTS AND THE BENEFITS
OF ELECTRONIC MONEY**

THE AMERICAN WAY OF DEBT

GOVERNMENTAL RESPONSES TO EFTS
Restrictive Banking Laws
The Federal Reserve
Negative Reactions from The Postal Department

CUSTOMER RESPONSES
Learning to Live Without the Float
Privacy Worries
Special Security Concerns

CONCLUDING REMARKS

BIBLIOGRAPHY

EXERCISES

STUDENT PROJECTS

Gertrude Stein once wrote that "the money is always there, only the pockets change". Today the pockets are changing at an almost incomprehensible rate. Last year the average American family engaged in nearly 5000 business transactions.* Approximately 4000 of them were handled with folding money and metal coins. Another 500 were made with personal checks, at least 100 with plastic credit cards. A few were handled by direct barter—or Electronic Funds Transfer Systems, an exciting new technology in which coded impulses clattering through a telephone line can pluck money from your bank account and redeposit it somewhere else.

HISTORICAL PERSPECTIVES

Partly because of well-known biblical injunctions forewarning us against its moral hazards, we tend to feel guilty whenever we express enthusiasm for money. The love of money may well be "the root of all evil" but the money itself is among mankind's most important inventions. Money promotes complicated social organizations involving efficient teamwork and job specialization. It raises cathedrals, motivates armies, fosters science. It allows us to convert our assets and our labor into a form which can be conveniently exchanged for other, more desirable, things. Before money was in common use, barter helped satisfy pressing human needs but, as the German people learned during the Great Depression when their monetary system suddenly collapsed, barter is capable of handling only the simplest transactions.

Coins and Paper Money

Cattle, corn, shells, and trinkets have all, at times, served as the preferred medium of exchange, but the most practical of the early monetary systems utilized precious metals, especially gold. Gold fever, a highly contagious mental abberation, has played a preeminent role in shaping human history. In an article providing background for a National Geographic telecast, the noted journalist, Adam Smith, produced this rousing account of the way men infected with gold fever have impacted civilization:

"Gold! The very name has romance, yet the metal itself has no more intrinsic use than other simple metals such as copper. Throughout

---

*Thornton, Zane. "The Consumer Comes Face-to-Face With The Computer." *Dimensions.* October 1976. pp. 10-11.

history, men have braved hardships, plundered, died—to bring a metal from one hole in the ground to another. 'Get gold!' Spain's King Ferdinand wrote to his men in South America. 'Humanely if you can, but at all hazards get gold.' In the late middle ages, alchemists sought to turn base metals into gold; they were looking for the philosopher's stone that would do it. 'More men have been knocked off balance by gold than by love,' wrote British Prime Minister Disraeli. In American history gold rushes helped to spur the migrations to California in 1849 and Alaska in 1898."*

Why is gold so highly prized? For one thing its intrinsic physical properties make it ideal for monetary transactions. As the editors of *Colliers Encyclopedia* put it: "(gold) combines the attributes of portability, divisibility, durability, homogenity, recognizability, and stability of value."

Of course its use for commerce also entails certain practical difficulties. For one thing pure gold tends to wear away when handled extensively, for another, large quantities of it are quite heavy. Because of these problems, and others, we have been led to use paper money as a viable substitute.

The wonder of it was that anyone would actually swallow the notion that paper money had any genuine worth. It is a medium of exchange based on nothing more substantial than widespread mutual trust. Of course at first the greenback was an abstract symbol secured by an equivalent amount of gold and silver. Every dollar placed in circulation was backed by a dollar's worth of precious metals. However, over the years the gold backing for paper money has been gradually diluted. Today the United States government owns 275 million ounces of gold worth $53.2 billion but, even by the narrowest definition of our "money supply" (cash plus bank deposits) we now have $356.7 billion in circulation.

Because printing presses are consistently more productive than sluice gates, modern governments can no longer redeem their paper money with an equivalent amount of precious metals. The Canadian dollar bill carries an inscription promising that the Bank of Canada "will pay to the bearer on demand" one dollar. What it does not say is that the Bank of Canada has nothing to pay with, except more dollar bills.

Thus we see that paper money is pumped up mostly with blind faith in the integrity of our government and in the strength of the prevailing economic system. If people should suddenly lose confidence in its future,

---

*"Gold!" Adam Smith, *TV Guide*, January 6, 1979. pp. 33-34.

the value of our paper money could suddenly evaporate. Given a sufficiently devastating sequence of events, confidence could, indeed, disappear. Twelve decades ago Confederate money lost its value when it became apparent to all but die-hard fanatics that Lee's battered armies inevitably faced defeat. Seventy years later it happened again—this time to the German Deutchmark—as the Great Depression descended over the Rhineland like a black curtain of despair.

Checks

Paper money is far more portable and in a sense more indestructible* than the precious metals it supposedly represents. Unfortunately, it can be lost or stolen in transit and a particular transaction can be made only if the parties involved can manage to produce the exact change. Personal checks circumvent these difficulties to some extent. A personal check is essentially a signed legal document instructing your banker to take money from your account and turn it over to someone else.

To a degree a check is protected from theft. Unlike money it cannot be stolen in transit especially if you have not yet filled it out. And, even after you have written in the face value and signed a check, theft is made more difficult because the endorsement procedures required in cashing it are legally equivalent to writing a fresh check. A check is thus considerably more secure than an equivalent amount of cash, so secure we even feel comfortable sending it through the mail. Changemaking problems are also largely eliminated. In making a purchase you can write any appropriate amount on the face of the check.

Although personal checks are reasonably safe and convenient, they can give rise to serious papershuffling difficulties. Money keeps its own records. If someone pays you with a dollar bill there is no need to inquire about this bank account; no need to write anything down. But you dare not accept a check in payment unless you are convinced that the person writing it actually has the money in his account.

But even good checks cause us a few minor bureaucratic nightmares. Between the time you fill it out, and the time it is returned to you by your bank, each check must be handled and sorted several different times. As long as checks were few in number and labor rates low, manual check sorting procedures were adequate to the task. But when checks became

---

*Paper money is, of course, physically less durable than gold or silver but, when a dollar bill begins to show serious signs of wear, an identical replacement can be produced at an extremely low cost.

more popular in the late 1940's it appeared that our banking system might collapse under the extra work.

Fortunately, technology provided a superior approach. Those funny, futuristic numbers running across the bottom of your paycheck were put there by the banking industry to allow computers to decipher and process its coded contents. The characters are printed with a special magnetic ink to promote electronic sensing. Last year the banking industry used automatic deciphering devices (See Figure 83) to sort and process a record 33 billion personal and commercial checks.

Credit Cards

Cash and checks work reasonably well for those who plan their personal finances carefully. But what about those who arrive at the big Persian rug sale only to find themselves stuck with sagging billfolds and embarrassing bank accounts? Credit cards are a modern solution.

A credit card allows us to make credit purchases within a specified price range through an advanced agreement to repay the credit card company principal plus interest at some future date. The forms we sign at the point of purchase are later returned to us; in many cases serving as official receipts to be used in backing up any questionable items on tax returns and expense accounts.

Today there are approximately 280 million plastic credit cards stuffed into the pockets and purses of American citizens. (See Figure 84.) Each year they are used in connection with 7 billion credit transactions. The two most popular: Master Charge and Visa (formerly BankAmericard) are running neck-in-neck with 62.9 million and 62.4 million cards in circulation respectively.*

One third of the people who make credit card purchases escape direct interest charges—by making their payments promptly during the interest-free grace period. The other two-thirds typically pay 18 percent true annual interest until the principal is fully repaid, usually in installments.

No one advertises the utility of cash or checks but the purported advantages of credit cards are heavily touted in all the major advertising media. Here is how *Changing Times* summarizes the pitch used in these highly-intense advertising campaigns:

"You don't have to risk carrying a wad of (bills) or pass up a sale because you're short of cash; you don't have to worry about a

---

*"Credit Card Use Gains Wide Popularity." *Los Angeles Herald Examiner*. September 7, 1978. pp. A-18, A-19.

MAGNETIC CHARACTER RECOGNITION DEVICES

Figure 83: The futuristic characters running across the bottom of this check are printed with magnetic ink to allow automatic sensing devices to decipher their coded contents. If this technique had not been developed in the early 1950's, a substantial fraction of the entire American labor force would now be needed to sort and process the banking system's annual flood of 33 billion personal and commercial checks.

personal check being turned down; you get a handy record of your purchases; you don't have to study a complicated contract every time you want to charge something because a single agreement gives you preapproved credit at hundreds of thousands of stores, restaurants, hotels and other establishments; you get a single bill payable with one check; and in the case of bank cards you can stretch out payments."*

In the 1960's credit cards were promoted as a luxury item with clearcut snob appeal. In those days if you were lucky enough to be

---

*"Compare The Big-Name Credit Cards." *Changing Times.* August 1978. pp. 37-39.

POPULAR CREDIT CARDS*

TYPE OF CARD	COST TO GET CARD	GOOD FOR –	INTEREST ON THE UNPAID BALANCE
DINERS CLUB DINERS CLUB 556/0043-50026 JOHN DOE	$20 per year	Travel, dining and entertainment and in some retail shops in U.S. and abroad	1 per cent per month on payments 30 days past due and on extended-payment travel tickets
MASTER CHARGE master charge THE INTERBANK CARD	free	Retail purchases of all kinds and many professional and other services in U.S. and abroad	1 1/2% per month
VISA (formerly BankAmericard) FIRST TRUST VISA	free	Retail purchases of all kinds and many professional and other services in U.S. and abroad	1 1/2% per month

*SOURCE = "AS THE RACE TO 'SELL' CREDIT CARDS HEATS UP –."
U.S. NEWS AND WORLD REPORT. SEPTEMBER 5, 1977. PP. 62-64.

Figure 84: Today there are 280 million plastic cards in circulation in the United States. Each year they are used in connection with approximately 7 billion business transactions. A status symbol, as well as a practical necessity, the cards are collected by a few enterprising hobbyists. One of them, Walter Cavanagh a 33-year old bachelor pharmacist with an annual income of $27,000, managed to collect, in his own name, 805 cards granting him a line of credit said to exceed $9.3 million.

granted a card, your status was instantly enhanced. Later, as the industry expanded, the cards were routinely issued to anyone with the slightest traces of financial stability. They were even sent through the mail to people who had not requested them—a practice which triggered shrill cries of protest and later became illegal.

Today credit cards—and the instant credit they represent—are viewed not as a luxury but as a modern necessity. As a staff-written article in *Time* magazine put it: "The Affluent Society has become the Credit Society and an insistence on buying only what can be paid for in cash seems as outmoded as a crew cut. Those who cannot get credit are second-class citizens. Those who try to limit their borrowing are sometimes viewed as economic subversives."* Indeed, when one of their staff members confided to a Boston banker that she rarely used her two charge cards she was told that: "You're just not doing your part for the American economy." Of course there's no need for alarm, other credit-happy Americans are more than making up for her unpatriotic frugality.

*"Merchants of Debt". *Time*. February 28, 1977. pp. 36-40.

Last year installment buying commitments reached a record level: $224 billion—about a thousand dollars per capita. The editors at *Time* are definitely a part of the credit card economy but even they had to marvel at the remarkable variety of goods and services that can be purchased on the cuff:

"Houses, cars, furniture barely begin the list. Rents at the Promenade Apartments in Los Angeles, ski-lift tickets in Aspen, Colorado, taxi rides in St. Louis, veterinary services in Jacksonville, and treatment in the emergency rooms of Atlanta's hospitals can all be charged on credit cards. So can admission to a nudist camp in Yugoslavia, birth-control counseling by Planned Parenthood of Pittsburgh and funerals conducted by the Parkside Memorial Chapel in New York City . . . culture, virtue and vice are all available on credit . . . the Cottontail Ranch, a legal brothel between Las Vegas and Reno, posts signs over each of the beds advertising its willingness to take Diners Club, Master Charge or BankAmericards."

Electronic Funds Transfer Systems

After a brief period of adaptation, both checks and credit cards have been embraced enthusiastically by a majority of modern Americans. Last year they were used in making a total of 40 billion business transactions. The necessary operations are highly automated, but the mountain of paper which must be processed is beginning to put a noticeable strain on available facilities. Is there any way we could eliminate some of this costly paperwork? Those who have studied the problem see at least one tempting possibility: the installation of a nationwide Electronic Funds Transfer System.

Electronic Funds Transfer (EFT) utilizes modern computer technology coupled with advanced telecommunications techniques. With such a system you could pay your creditors instantly by switching funds from your account to theirs. No actual movement of bills and coins takes place; the process merely rearranges a set of pulses on a magnetic disk or a magnetic tape. As banking technicians fondly observe: "Money is information." When you barter or make a cash purchase the necessary information is transferred by exchanging physical objects. When you write a check or fill out a credit card form the information is recorded on paper. When you make a purchase using an Electronic Funds Transfer System the information is recorded electronically.

An ideal EFTS network would provide for instantaneous nationwide transactions between any pair of bank accounts. No such broad-ranging system is presently in existence. However, several, less ambitious, versions have already been implemented. For example, large financial institutions have their choice between two nationwide Electronic Funds Transfer Systems which operate on an immense scale. Each day Bank Wire, a private organization, handles $10 billion worth of transactions; Fed Wire, which is managed by the Federal Reserve, handles $60 billion. There are also systems in operation which are more attuned to the needs of the ordinary private citizen. The Bank of America has installed a nationwide network to transmit electronic credit receipts; dozens of banks have installed electronic tellers—often at remote locations; and a number of regional banks and related institutions are experimenting with point-of-sale remote terminals allowing supermarkets and department stores to clear checks and, in some cases, debit existing bank accounts.

One of the most successful systems of this type is operating in Columbus, Ohio under the skillful guidance of John Fisher, a Vice President at City National Bank. So far, 125 IBM 3608 terminals have been installed in 68 different supermarkets in Columbus and the surrounding area. By inserting either a Visa Card or a special bank-supplied charge card into the terminal, the customer obtains a printed note approving a personal check or a credit card transaction. The terminals (See Figure 85) are connected to the Bank of America'a files of bad credit risks. These files are so extensive that check-writing approvals can be given with a high degree of confidence. At this writing the experiment has been going on only nine months but already the participants are beginning to document measurable benefits. For example, the managers at Krogers estimate that the eliminationof manual check verification procedures at on of their markets has saved at least 40 man-hours per week. By their estimates this translates into an annual saving of around $15,000.*

Customers are also impressed with the capabilities of the City National Bank system. It speeds their transit through busy checkout lines and it allows them to obtain private check-cashing approvals thus eliminating any possibility for personal embarrassment. Moreover, the members of two local credit unions can use the same equipment to validate their share drafts while they are in the supermarket. Technically speaking, it would be relatively easy to modify the terminals so that they could accept bank deposits; however, John Fisher and his team are precluded from offering shoppers this service unless they can obtain a special state permit to form a "branch bank" at each location. The estimated cost: $20,000 per terminal is clearly prohibitive.

---

*Rose, Sanford. "Checkless Banking is Bound to Come." *Fortune.* June, 1977. pp. 118-130.

A TYPICAL CHECK QUARANTEE TERMINAL

Figure 85: This check-guarantee terminal is similar to the ones operated by the Columbus, Ohio City National Bank. Check and credit approvals are handled privately so that the customer need not face the embarrassment of being turned down by a human clerk.

Thus, we see that although the system in Columbus is already approaching the break-even point—after only nine months of actual operating experience—it is not by any means a full-service nationwide Electronic Funds Transfer System of the type envisioned by avid proponents. There are, of course, other systems in operation: twenty-three banks in Iowa are interlinked by an EFT network, as are several dozen others in Nebraska. To date, however, no nationwide system has been instituted, much less run at a profit. Even the few regional systems that have been profitably operated are typically quite limited as to the number of accounts they can handle and the customer services they can provide.

THE COSTS AND THE BENEFITS OF ELECTRONIC MONEY

During the 1960's the proponents of Electronic Funds Transfer calmed their nerves with soothing daydreams about the "Cashless Society" of the future in which, presumably, coins and paper money would virtually disappear. In those days the EFT concept was usually justified by appealing to the widely-accepted argument that it would ultimately constitute a cheaper and more efficient monetary system. The American Bankers Association, the Federal Reserve, and several independent research organizations sponsored studies whose results indicated that the existing paper-based payments system would soon become prohibitively expensive. The conversion from paper to electronics was thus viewed as an opportunity to substitute an inflation-hedged, machine-intensive system for one that was labor-intensive and hence relatively unprotected from the ravages of inflation.

However, as things turned out, the paperbased system they were hoping to replace, was not as inflation-prone as had been predicted. According to a recent Chase Manhattan study, the direct backroom cost of processing a check has held steady for nearly a full decade. Consequently, as Sandford Rose pointed out in *Fortune* magazine, "Superficially, it would seem that, at the moment, paper holds a decisive edge over electronics."*

Now that there has been more time to study the economics and the public acceptability of the EFT concept, even its most enthusiastic backers are beginning to scale down their earliest expectations. Today they seldom predict direct economic savings, preferring to argue that EFT has hidden intangible benefits. As a part of this low-profile approach, the "Cashless Society" is now more humbly referred to as the "less-cash/less check society".

What has happened to cause the advocates of electronic money to abandon their most grandiose dreams? For one thing the Federal Deposit Insurance Corporation has found an inverse relationship between the use of electronic money and bank earnings. Those that do *not* install the systems earn more than those that do.** Perhaps more disturbingly, Glendale Federal Savings and Loan achieved only the most disappointing results when its managers made a large-scale trial of the hardware in the Los Angeles basin. In March of 1977 after sinking $400,000 into a check approval network consisting of 137 terminals in 20 Southern California supermarkets, bank officers reluctantly gave up and pulled the plug on the system. The primary reason: although the terminals were used by large numbers of supermarket customers, they did not, as had been expected, provide the bank with any substantial new accounts. Most customers simply cashed their paychecks without making deposits. "The bigger accounts just didn't materialize", confessed David L. Smith, Glendale Federal's senior vice president.

Another difficulty is that electronic money has turned out to be considerably more expensive than the ordinary kind it was intended to replace. Figure 86 presents cost comparisons between our four most

---

*Rose, Sanford. "Checkless Banking Is Bound To Come." *Fortune*. June, 1977. pp. 118-130.
**Benton, John B. "Economics and Use of Electronic Fund Transfer." *Communications*. May, 1978. pp. 35-41.

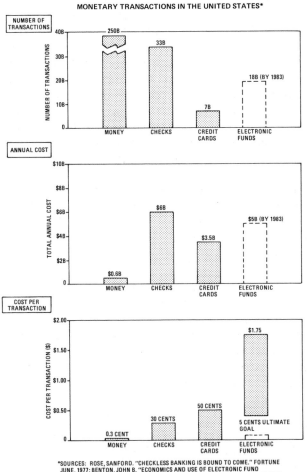

MONETARY TRANSACTIONS IN THE UNITED STATES*

*SOURCES: ROSE, SANFORD. "CHECKLESS BANKING IS BOUND TO COME." FORTUNE JUNE, 1977; BENTON, JOHN B. "ECONOMICS AND USE OF ELECTRONIC FUND TRANSFER." TELECOMMUNICATIONS. MAY, 1978; THORTON, ZANE. "THE CONSUMER COMES FACE TO FACE WITH THE COMPUTER" DIMENSIONS. OCTOBER, 1976; "COMPARE THE BIG NAME CREDIT CARDS" CHANGING TIMES. AUGUST, 1978.

Figure 86: Each year more than 300 billion financial transactions are executed in the United States. Today the cost associated with the average cash transaction is only about one-third of a cent. This compares with costs of 30 and 50 cents respectively for personal check and credit card transactions. Limited experience indicates that present day EFTS transactions are costing somewhere between 40¢ and $1.75. Thus we see that, at present, EFT is not particularly cost-effective. However, its proponents are convinced that it will be considerably cheaper than most competing systems if it is ever utilized on a sufficiently large scale.

popular monetary media. As you can see, transactions using money are by far the most popular—and the least expensive. It is estimated that Americans are currently making 250 billion cash transactions each year at a cost of about $0.6 billion.* Although this may sound like a relatively high cost, it amounts to only about one-third of a cent per cash transaction. By contrast, it costs approximately 30¢ to make the average transaction with a personal check and 50¢ if a credit card is used. Meaningful cost estimates for large-scale Electronic Funds Transfer Systems are not yet available; however, the limited number of experiments that have been conducted to date have resulted in transaction costs ranging from as high as $1.75 to as low as 40¢.

Of course many proponents of electronic money are convinced that, given sufficient volume, they could get the cost of the average transaction down to a much lower level, perhaps as low as 5¢. Other industry experts are not convinced that this is an attainable goal. It costs at least $5000 to install a point of sale remote terminal and upwards to $50,000 to install an automated teller machine with full banking capabilities.

However, even if a cost figure of 5¢ does turn out to be attainable, transactions using electronic money would still be 15 times more costly than transactions using cash. A service that costs only a nickel may not sound like an unreasonable burden but if we made all of our present cash transactions using EFTS hardware our total bill would rise from $0.6 billion to $12.5 billion. It is conceivable that the people in our society might be willing to pick up a tab that large—after all, we are now spending an estimated $6 billion per annum to maintain our check-writing system. However, it seems likely that we would be willing to accept the extra cost only if the proposed electronic system has some compelling and easily perceived advantages.

A full-fledged Electronic Funds Transfer System certainly will perform a wide variety of services—some of them strongly consumer-oriented. This is how *Fortune* magazine described some of its probably capabilities:

"Ultimately, the consumer will be able to perform nearly all essential banking transactions through the use of point of sale remote terminals. He will be able to deposit and withdraw money in whatever form he likes. He will be able to debit his account to make

*This figure breaks down as follows: $45 million per year for the manufacture and replacement money, $90 million for the use of armored cars, and $430 million in payment for the services of various types of protection agencies.

a retail purchase or to pay an outstanding bill, such as a mortgage. He will have the capability of transferring funds from one type of account to another or of getting a cash advance from his bank."*

But what will be the solid advantages associated with these electronic services? The same article goes on to explain:

"It will save the consumer time. It will provide him with 24-hour access to his money. It will give him a greater choice among competing banks and Savings and Loans than he now has, as well as protection from the theft and unauthorized use of checks. Perhaps most important, as EFT matures, people will be able to borrow money on more favorable terms. The cost of consumer credit will either fall absolutely or rise much more slowly than it otherwise would have."

It may not be clear to you why credit might tend to be cheaper in a system that uses electronic money. The reasoning is that paperwork handling and processing costs should be substantially reduced. In an electronic system a line of credit can be prearranged and preprogrammed into the machine. Once this has been done, the procedure for obtaining a loan is surprisingly simple. The customer merely makes a purchase which exceeds his current balance, whereupon the computer checks his allowable line of credit and automatically grants him a loan.**

Loan repayment can also be handled automatically. The computer simply dips into the regular account to pluck out the necessary installments whenever they are due. If such a system should ultimately result in more convenient loan procedures and lower interest rates would this have an important impact on future consumers? You bet it would! At one time Americans regarded the casual use of credit as a serious moral transgression, but in recent years we have become a nation that lives and loves and travels on credit. "Fly now, pay later" is not just an advertising slogan. It could well be regarded as America's new national anthem.

THE AMERICAN WAY OF DEBT

At the present time America's private citizens owe their creditors a total of $224 billion in short-term installment loans. Much of this money

---

*Rose, Sanford. "Checkless Banking is Bound to Come." *Fortune*. June 1977. pp. 118-130.
**It can be counterargued that this bookkeeping simplification would have little actual impact. Today many banks preauthorize "balance plus" accounts yet they usually charge the legal maximum in interest, typically 18 percent.

has been borrowed to purchase solid assets which could be sold to liquidate outstanding debts. However, unsecured loans have also climbed upward at a galloping rate. Today's personal debt level is more than ten times higher than it was only three decades ago. Interest charges alone total approximately $30 billion per year.

A graph showing the rate at which we have increased our installment plan buying is presented in Figure 87. As you can see, the dollar value of our indebtedness has been moving upward but so has our total income. Consequently, for the past decade or so our installment debts taken as a fraction of disposable income has been hovering around 18 or 20 percent. Delinquency rates (payments overdue more than 30 days) have also remained fairly constant. In the years in question they have generally ranged between 1.6 and 3.1 percent.

Thus we see that although installment plan buying may be causing financial difficulties for many families, in general, commitments are being met. On the other hand, divorce and bankruptcy are not uncommon outcomes for those who use their credit in unwise and frivolous ways. In the 1976 fiscal year, 211,348 bankruptcies were filled in the American courts, slightly fewer than the year before but 25 percent more than in 1974.*

In part, this increase may be due to the lack of stigma now being attached to bankruptcy proceedings which have historically been surrounded by shame and guilt. Today bankruptcy is more typically viewed as a reasonable method for obtaining a fresh start. Indeed, it has become so socially acceptable that many creditors are perfectly willing to reopen accounts with those who have just gone through the procedure. One reason: once a family has filed for bankruptcy they are not allowed to do so again for another six years.

GOVERNMENTAL RESPONSES TO EFTS

Even if Electronic Funds Transfer Systems can be shown to be economically feasible and socially desirable, the pace of actual development may be stymied by various political forces. In particular, state banking commissions, the Federal Reserve, and the U.S. Postal Service may push for severe restrictions.

Restrictive Banking Laws

Many states, shaken by widespread bank failures in the 1930's,

---

*"Merchants of Debt." *Time.* February 28, 1977. pp. 36-40.

CONSUMER INSTALLMENT DEBTS*

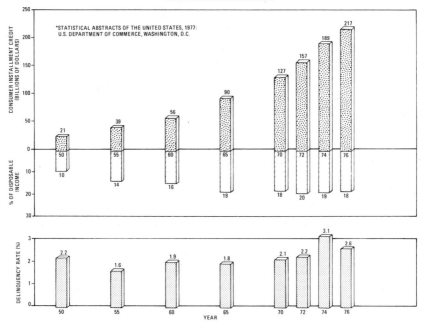

Figure 87: In 1977 America's short-term installment debts totaled $224 billion—more than ten times their peak level of three decades ago. Some observers are alarmed by the increases but, in fact, borrowing rates mirror similar increases in America's family earning power. In recent years short-term installment debts have consistently hovered around 20 percent of disposable income. Default rates have also remained fairly steady. They reached a level of 3.1 percent during the 1974 recession but, otherwise, they have usually stayed below 2.5 percent.

passed laws designed to prevent a limited number of banks from dominating their monetary systems. Some of the most stringent limitations deal with the opening of new "branch banks". Although it may seem obvious that an EFTS terminal is not actually a branch bank, few conservative businessmen are willing to make heavy investments in fancy electronic devices under the tacit threat that their costly efforts might be later declared illegal. Court rulings and administrative decisions have not been particularly helpful. In some cases the terminals are regarded as "branch banks", in others they are judged to be part of the parent facility.

The Federal Reserve

Those who manage our Federal Reserve System are worried about EFTS for a completely unrelated reason. Their responsibilities include the regulation of our money supply which influences, among other things, the interest rates we pay and our average rates of inflation. But how can they manage to regulate that portion of our money supply which consists of a string of pulses on a magnetic disk?

Indirect evidence indicates that they may already have lost some degree of control over the behavior of our monetary system. In 1975 an extra dollar pumped into our "money supply" by the Federal Reserve led to a rise of $5.11 in our country's Gross National Product. By 1977 a new dollar was producing a $5.60 increase. Thus, in accordance with a thesis advanced in an article published in *Fortune* magazine: "If the Federal Reserve had injected too much or too little money into the system in 1975, the economy would obviously have been thrown off the course . . . intended." But if they made the same mistake today "the economy would be pulled further off target than it would have been two years ago."* In other words, our system is becoming increasingly sensitive to any mistakes that might occur at the federal level. If the EFTS concept is widely adopted in future years, the regulatory capabilities of the Federal Reserve may be further weakened. Indeed, if the only available medium of exchange is "electronic money" there may be absolutely nothing left to regulate!

Negative Reactions From the Postal Department

The individuals who manage our postal department are not especially enthusiastic about the widespread adoption of Electronic Funds Transfer Systems. Theirs is a labor-intensive operation plagued with rising costs. Each year America's 31,000 Post Offices handle approximately 90 billion pieces of mail—about 2000 pieces for every American family. But despite growing volume levels, unit costs have been rising at a worrisome rate. In 1960 it cost three cents to mail a first class letter; today the cost for that same service is 15¢. Unfortunately, despite discouragingly regular rate increases, service cuts, and brave attempts at automation, the Postal Department generally operates in the red. Deficits for the past three fiscal years have averaged nearly a billion dollars each.

Because postal rates have been increasing so rapidly, some of the services formerly performed by the Postal Department are being skimmed off by robust competitors. For example, United Parcel has captured much of the package business in major metropolitan areas and small local

---

*Rose, Sanford. "More Bang for the Buck: The Magic of Electronic Banking." *Fortune.* May 1977. pp. 202-226.

outfits are delivering advertising circulars door-to-door. As a result, the Post Office is being left with the most unprofitable parts of its former business (e.g., delivering Christmas presents to distant rural locations). The Postmaster General is afraid he may be forced into further rate increases thus driving away larger numbers of customers. This, of course, would lead to even higher postal rates.

At present, about 65 percent of all first class mail involves financial transactions, e.g., bills, receipts, invoices, etc. These items, which are often dropped off at the Post Office in bulk, are among the most profitable remaining portions of the U. S. mail. If the Post Office should lose this business to a nationwide EFT System, further rate increases would seem inevitable. Consequently, some bureaucrats contend that the Postal Department should circumvent this problem by entering the world of electronic money. However, it seems doubtful that the department, chronically short on cash, running, at best, on wafer-thin profit margins, facing one of the country's most powerful labor unions, could cut through the thicket of objections and justify the capital investments necessary to enter such a risky business enterprise.

CUSTOMER RESPONSES

In most early proposals advocating the use of electronic money, consumers, if they were mentioned at all, were usually portrayed as a group of compliant individuals who would almost certainly be over-joyed with the added convenience of the proposed hardware. In some cases consumers have, indeed, responded favorably, most recently with regard to the partial EFT Systems that have been installed in Columbus, Ohio, and Atlanta, Georgia. However, in many other cases they have largely ignored the new systems or reacted to them with a noticeable degree of hostility. Consequently, modern proposals on EFTS networks tend to speak of the need to "educate the consumer" concerning their obvious benefits and hidden virtues.

One consistent difficulty has been that ordinary people do not see any striking advantages over the payments system now available to them. Even as early as 1974 U.S. News and World Report quoted a banking industry consultant as saying that "consumers are basically happy with the paper-check system we've sold them for the past 50 years."* Some experts

---

*"Automated Finances: Will Consumers Go Along?" U.S. News and World Report. August 5, 1974. pg. 51.

seem bewildered by this quaint obsession with the past. But Bob Kling, one of the department editors of *Computers and Society,* an educational newsletter, explains this conservatism on quite rational grounds:

"Most consumers seem particularly interested in maintaining . . . control over how much they pay to whom and when. Thus, they occasionally will opt for pre-authorized deposits into their accounts (such as payroll) and show remarkable disinterest in pre-authorized debits (such as telephone or utility bills). Generally, consumers seem to have the same kind of economic rationality as do business enterprises: they want to increase the speed with which they receive income, control the speed at which they pay for goods and services, and are unwilling to accept convenience for its own sake without asking what it will cost."*

There are also other rational and irrational reasons for consumer resistance toward full-service EFTS networks. These include the potential loss of interest-free grace periods, possible invasions of financial privacy, and a general fear of the unknown which tends to affect anyone facing an uncertain future.

Learning to Live Without the Float

Checks and credit cards provide their users with a built-in interest-free interval between the time the transaction is consumated and the time the account must actually be settled. This is called a "float." A credit card typically provides a float of one month; a check provides a float of one or two days. If you're brave enough you can race your check to the bank and, at the last minute, deposit money to cover it. Although this may sound like a rather harrowing procedure, millions of people routinely depend on it in order to remain solvent.

Businesses large and small, also depend on the float. Some of them have even set up dummy accounts in Phoenix, Arizona, because the banks in that region provide notoriously slow services. While a check is inching its way through the various processing steps, the business can manage to draw a little extra interest.

An EFT System may be slightly more convenient than a check or a credit card but it does not provide a float. This causes varying degrees of consumer resistance.

---

*Kling, Bob. "EFTS Social and Technical Issues: What are EFTS?' *Computers and Society.* Fall 1976. pp. 3-9.

Privacy Worries

The possibility of having a machine prying into their private affairs also disturbs many potential users of Electronic Funds Transfer Systems. The technicians who install and operate the hardware admit that "a complete financial picture of any bank account holder or credit-card carrier can be assembled in seconds by computer and whisked across the country."* Many people will go to great lengths to keep their finances private. Some even feel compelled to conceal their incomes from the members of their own families. As Sidney A. DaCosta, a vice president at Wilmington Savings and Fund Society in Delaware points out: "A lot of guys still cash their paycheck at the corner bar, take a few bucks off the top and give the rest to their wives. Some men don't want their wives to know how much money they make." It would be hard to maintain this privacy in most proposed EFT Systems. As DaCosta goes on to observe: "Under an electronic system that salary goes right to a family bank account for all to see."**

Of course, there are much larger privacy concerns connected with EFTS networks, particularly in the case of a nationwide system where records of all financial transactions would be concentrated in a single, centrally-located master file. To many the image of Big Brother monitoring all important economic activities is too unthinkable to contemplate. This is what privacy expert Paul Armer said in evaluating this bothersome privacy threat:

> "It would seem prudent to me to slow down the pace at which EFTS (networks) are being implemented. A bit more time might enable us to erect some safeguards."***

The issue of who is responsible for the security of a particular EFTS transaction also gives rise to some formidable difficulties especially in any systems that are spread across large geographical regions. An editorial in

---

*"Electronic Money What It Is and The Changes It Will Bring." *U.S. News and World Report.* August 5, 1974. pp. 50-52.
**"Automated Finances: Will Consumers Go Along?" *U.S. News and World Report.* August 5, 1974. pg. 51.

***Quoted by Semour F. Thompson in "The Invasion of Privacy and Electronic Fund Transfer Systems: Spotlight on the Invaders." *Computers and People.* September 1976. pp. 12-19.

the January 1977 issue of *Datamation* asks this series of unanswered questions: ". . . if an individual who lives in Washington travels to San Francisco and purchases something in a department store, by his action he creates a record but who is responsible for this record? The department store? The local bank serving the department store? The individual's bank in Washington? The owner of the EFT network connecting the banks? All of them, or perhaps, none of them?"* To many observers it seems unlikely that we can provide privacy in a nationwide network unless we can somehow assign clear-cut responsibilities for maintaining that privacy.

Special Security Concerns

The security of an EFT System is also of major concern. After all, if you can withdraw funds from your own account from a remote location what's to prevent a clever criminal from doing the same thing? Actually, the systems operated so far have been relatively secure, but even the most enthusiastic backers of the EFTS concept have to admit that it gives rise to some special security concerns.

The maximum possible theft at an ordinary bank is limited to the amount of cash or negotiable securities actually located on the premises (which is generally only a small fraction of the bank's total holdings). However, in an electronic system, the maximum theft is, in principle, essentially boundless. A clever programmer may have access to all the funds in a particular bank—or in some cases, all the funds in the entire system. Experience has shown that embezzlers who use computers average stealing hundreds of thousands of dollars before they are apprehended. In a nationwide network involving all 13,000 American banks, tens of thousands of programmers and technicians would have access to at least some of the funds in the system. If only one tenth of one percent of these people were overcome by temptation, the losses could be enormous.

CONCLUDING REMARKS

In the early 1970's some of its most avid proponents tended to become huffy and belligerent whenever anybody tried to question them about the probable public acceptability of electronic money. To them point-by-point justification seemed entirely unnecessary. "EFTS is happening because it is a better way. All arguments about the sufficiency of

---

*Heller, Christopher E. "EFT and The Prospects for Individual Privacy." *Datamation*. January 1977. pp. 174-178.

the present paper system are meaningless" sniffed R. H. Long in a special report published by the Bank Administration Institute. "Television did not come about because the radio system was overloaded or breaking down, nor did radio or the telephone develop because the mail was about to collapse. Neither were these systems built because the public was crying for their development. They came about simply because they represented a 'better way' of communication. The same motivation is the driving force behind EFTS developments."*

But now that a few early experiments have been conducted and the public response has not been entirely favorable, many people are having serious second thoughts. The editors of *Business Week,* for example, recently put together this rather sober and pessimistic assessment:

"Suddenly it appears that the great electronic banking revolution that has been 'just around the corner' for a decade may never arrive after all. It has been halted by consumer resistance, soaring costs, legal and legislative snarls—and by a growing belief among bankers that they really do not need and cannot afford a nationwide Electronic Funds Transfer System."

"This is a dramatic turnabout. Until recently, most experts considered EFT both inevitable and highly desirable. In the widely envisioned 'cashless society', dominated by magnetically encoded plastic debit cards, funds would be rocketed across the nation in seconds, eliminating checks and saving both time and the money it takes to process them. With electronic terminals in every retail outlet—and maybe in homes and offices as well—there would be no need for people ever to go near a bank to carry out routine transactions. They would simply use the card for purchases, deposits, withdrawals, payment of bills, and even borrowing money."

"Instead of anything approaching a nationwide EFT system, today, there is a hodgepodge—electronic banking well along in such states as Iowa, hardly off the ground in other states, and in still others totally stymied by custom and law."**

And yet, *Fortune* magazine in reviewing the results of the same inconclusive field trials is considerably more optimistic about the future prospects of the EFTS concept:

---

*"EFTS, Banking and Regulation J: A report by the ACT Division of BAI". R. H. Long, Bank Administration Institute, Park Ridge, Illinois, 1974.
**A Retreat from the Cashless Society." *Business Week.* April 18, 1977. pp. 80-90.

"The nation is a long way from reaching what used to be called the cashless society. There may come a time when the consumer who pays his bills with cash will be looked upon with suspicion and distrust, but that time is still many years away. Within the next ten years, however, the use of electronic money will greatly increase, while the use of checks and eventually cash will begin to level off and decline."

"Money is basically a form of communication, and people are gradually realizing that it makes little sense to communicate with checks when technology is making it much more economical to use electronics. Although there are atavistic attitudes to be overcome, groundless fears to be put to rest, and obsolete ideas to be swept aside, the spread of electronic banking cannot be halted, EFTS simply promises too many benefits for too many people."*

---

*Rose, Sanford. "Checkless Banking is Bound to Come." *Fortune*. June 1977. pp. 118-130.

BIBLIOGRAPHY

1. "The American Banker and Telecommunications." *Telecommunications,* May 1978, p. 42.

2. Arbib, Michael A. *Computers and the Cybernetic Society.* New York, New York: Academic Press, 1977.

3. "As the Race to 'Sell' Credit Cards Heats Up." *U.S. News and World Report,* 5 September 1977, pp. 62-64.

4. "Bank Cards Take Over the Country." *Business Week,* 4 August 1975, pp. 44-46.

5. Benton, John B. "Economics and Use of Electronic Fund Transfer." *Telecommunications,* May 1978, pp. 35-40.

6. "Compare the Big-Name Credit Cards." *Changing Times,* August 1978, pp. 37-39.

7. "Credit Card Use Gains Widespread Popularity." *Los Angeles Herald Examiner,* pp. A-18 - A-19.

8. Diloris, Anthony M. "EFT Today." *Computer Decisions,* March 1976, pp. 20-24.

9. Dorf, Richard C. *Computers and Man.* San Francisco, California: Boyd and Fraser Publishing Company. 1977.

10. "Dough on the Go: Inside an EFT System." *Computer Decisions,* March 1976, pp. 26-30.

11. Dragunas, Deanna J. "EFTS: Living Better Electronically or Is It?" *Creative Computing,* Jan/Feb 1977, pp. 42-44.

12. "Electronic Banking: A Retreat from the Cashless Society." *Business Week,* 18 April 1977, pp. 80-90.

13. "'Electronic Money'What It Is and the Changes It Will Bring." *U. S. News and World Report,* 5 August 1974, pp. 50-52.

14. "A Future That Leaves Currency Behind." *Nation's Business,* January 1978, pp. 53-54.

15. Kling, Rob. "EFTS Social and Technical Issues." *Computers and Society,* Fall 1976, pp. 3-9.

16. Kling, Rob. "Value Conflicts and Social Choice in Electronic Funds Transfer Systems Developments." *University of California at Irvine,* 24 April 1978, ICS Technical Report No. 112.

17. Long, R. H. "EFTS, Banking and Regulation J: A Report by the Act Division of BAI." *Bank Administration Institute,* (Park Ridge, Illinois) 1974.

18. "Merchants of Debt." *Time,* 28 February 1977, pp. 36-40.

19. Much, Marilyn. "Crowding Out This Time Around?" *Industry Week,* 28 June 1976, pp. 43-44.

20. Pease, David L. "EFT Systems are Evolvoing." *Telecommunications,* May 1978, pp. 51-54.

21. "Push Button Banking Is Running into Trouble." *U. S. News and World Report,* 7 July 1975, pp. 76-78.

22. Rose, Sanford. "Checkless Banking is Bound to Come." *Fortune,* June 1977, pp. 118-130.

23. Rose, Sanford. "More Bang for the Buck: The Magic of Electronic Banking." *Fortune,* May 1977, pp. 202-226.

24. Rothman, Stanley, and Mosmann, Charles. *Computers and Society.* Chicago, Illinois: Science Research Associates, 1972.

25. Schwartz, Milton. "Checkout Terminal Takes on Many Supermarket Tasks." *Electronics,* 15 April 1976, pp. 157-161.

26. Smith, Adam. "Gold." *TV Guide,* 6 January 1979, pp. 33-34.

27. "A Sudden Setback for Electronic Banking." *Business Week,* 18 August 1975, pp. 32-33.

28. Thompson, Seymour F. "The Invasion of Privacy and Electronic Fund Transfer Systems: Spotlight on the Invaders." *Computers and People,* September 1978, pp. 12-19.

29. Thornton, Zane. "The Consumer Comes Face to Face With The Computer." *Dimensions,* October 1976, pp. 10-11.

30. Weberman, Ben. "Cash Like a Flash." *Forbes,* 1 April 1977, pp. 42-45.

31. Tobias, Andrew. "Will We Survive Electronic Banking?" *Esquire,* 26 March 1978, pp. 64-65.

EXERCISES

1. Over the past few centuries the civilized people of the world have made use of five different types of monetary media all of which are still in use today. Tabulate some of their relative advantages and disadvantages. Include such criteria as cost, security, convenience, etc., in your tabulations.

2. What do the letters EFT stand for? If we were to institute a nationwide EFT system what would be some of the principal advantages to you and your family? What might be some of the disadvantages?

3. The people who manage our banks, our postal department, and our Federal Reserve have expressed various misgivings about the EFTS concept. List a few of their worries and devise methods to alleviate some of the difficulties they foresee.

4. What is a float? Roughly how much of a float is associated with the five major monetary media now in common use?

5. Many people have worried about the security features associated with a nationwide Electronic Funds Transfer system. Explain why a bank using such a system might have more difficulty maintaining security than a conventional bank.

6. Careful preparation often helps soothe the nerves of those people who must face an unfamiliar situation. If you were the head of a public relations firm how would you go about preparing the public for the introduction of electronic money?

7. Today's banks sort and process 33 billion checks each year—or about 1000 per second. Describe how modern technology is used to help them work their way through this mountain of paperwork.

8. What percent of the American families go bankrupt each year? Why do you think the number is growing?

9. Ordinary people often have vague feelings of resistance toward Electronic Funds Transfer Systems. List some of the causes of these negative feelings.

10. What is the principal difference between a credit card and a debit card? Which type has been most enthusiastically embraced? Explain why.

STUDENT PROJECTS

1. Surveys sometimes help us learn how other people perceive a new societal development. Conduct an informal survey among 4 or 5 of your friends and acquaintances to see how they would likely react to the creation of a nationwide EFTS network. Summarize the various attitudes you encounter. Use graphs and charts if this will help clarify your presentation.

2. According to published figures from the *Statistical Abstracts for the United States,* each year Americans are going deeper and deeper in debt. Draw several graphs showing the changes in our various debt levels. Be sure to include data on the debts of the federal government and private business.

3. Gold fever has had a profound effect on the development of Western civilization. Research the history of gold and the men who went after it and write up the results in a 1000-word report.

CHAPTER 13

THE FUTURE

THE PUBLICATION OF THE LIMITS TO GROWTH
Euphoric Responses
Clinical Evaluations
Sobering Afterthoughts

COMPUTERS AND MILITARY POWER
Maintaining and Enhancing the Strategic Balance of Terror
New Possibilities for Tactical War

THE GEOPOLITICS OF COMPUTERS

CONCLUDING REMARKS

BIBLIOGRAPHY

EXERCISES

STUDENT PROJECTS

HISTORICAL PERSPECTIVES

GLOSSARY

INDEX

Six hundred years ago when the black plague raged across the European continent, there were only about 500 million inhabitants of the planet Earth. Today our population is eight times bigger—and growing. Worldwide increases currently average 1.9 percent per year. Inevitably, in the next decade nearly a billion additional passengers will be welcomed aboard our planetary spaceship. Like their predecessors, these new arrivals must be packed into a thin, life-supporting rim called the biosphere.

Viewed on a human scale, the earth's biosphere seems quite expansive. Even after centuries of relentless population growth, the land masses on our planet still cover nearly 10 acres per person. But if we could see the biosphere from a more distant vantage point, it would appear to be remarkably fragile and tenuous. Imagine a stainless steel ball 12 inches in diameter, polished like a mirror. Hold it up to your face and breathe on it; the film of moisture that now clouds its surface is proportionately thicker than the earth's biosphere.

What is the maximum life-supporting capacity of the biosphere? Today it seems obvious that there is some maximum. But in the middle ages and beyond, any arguments along these lines would have sounded like mere theoretical abstractions. In those days the earth seemed able to swallow up unlimited numbers of human beings—especially after the discovery of the vast, uncharted reaches of the New World. Consequently, most Westerners viewed a growing population as an unmitigated blessing. New births meant more neighbors, stronger armies, larger markets. Measures to control population would have seemed dangerously sacrilegeous. After all, even the Good Book itself instructed man to "be fruitful . . . go forth and multiply."

Yet even in those days a few daring individuals held countervailing opinions. The most carefully-reasoned arguments were advanced by the well-known clergyman/economist, Thomas Malthus, who convinced an influential following that disastrous consequences were awaiting mankind if our population continued to grow. His famous book, *Essay on the Principle of Population,* was based on a simple mathematical model, a model linking future population levels with available food supplies and other finite resources. His thought processes were quite elaborate, but they stemmed from a surprisingly simple proposition. As *Colliers Encyclopedia* explained it: "The population tends to increase geometrically (1, 2, 4, 8, 16) whereas the food supply increases arithmetically (1, 2, 3, 4, 5)." Thomas Malthus was convinced that we have an opportunity to limit our numbers by relatively painless measures: "late marriage, celebacy, birth control". But if these measures are not successfully executed, Mother

Nature imposes more painful controls of her own: "famine, pestilence, and plague."

The arguments advanced by Thomas Malthus are extremely difficult to prove or disprove since they concern prevailing conditions in some distant, vaguely defined future era. However, to many people his fundamental thesis seems to ring true. In particular, the disasters he predicted do occur with frightening regularity—most often in rapidly growing areas of the world. And yet, for all its appealing simplicity, there has always been a paucity of direct evidence to support his basic contention that population inevitably grows faster than available food.

In 1798 when he published the first edition of his famous essay, total world population was 0.9 billion; today it exceeds 4.3 billion and according to recent estimates, is doubling every 35 years.* But despite this rapid growth, (See Figure 88), we are still producing enough food to feed nearly everyone. Distribution bottlenecks often prevail, and vast areas of the world still live at subsistence levels, but, on the whole, this generation is more prosperous and better fed than any of its predecessors. Those born into today's world, especially in industrialized areas, are maturing younger, growing taller, and living longer than ever before.

The conclusion seems inescapable: so far at least, food production has not only increased *geometrically,* it has increased at a faster geometrical rate than population growth.

THE PUBLICATION OF THE LIMITS TO GROWTH

The warnings issued by Thomas Malthus were based on a simple mathematical model that produced vague, pessimistic results. More recently, MIT Professor Jay Forrester, a man who has had a distinguished career in designing and programming computers, arrived at similarly depressing conclusions using a completely different mathematical approach.

The sophisticated computer program he developed was financed by an exclusive international organization of businessmen and scientists called The Club of Rome. It simulated the various high-level interactions between five fundamental quantities: population, pollution, food production, industrialization, consumption of resources. All together Forrester and his colleagues defined more than 100 mathematical relationships linking these five variables, most of them involving autonomous feedback

---

*Ehrlich, Paul R. and Ehrlich, Anne H. *Population, Resources,Environment*. San Francisco, California: W. H. Freeman, 1970.

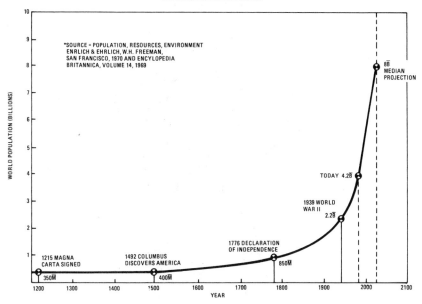

THE POPULATION EXPLOSION*

Figure 88: In 1798 Thomas Malthus published an essay in which he predicted that the population of the earth would eventually outstrip any attempts at adequate food production thus forcing Mother Nature to impose her own painful controls. In the long run his dire predictions could prove accurate, but, so far, in the centuries-long runoff between the stork and the grim reaper, the stork is obviously winning the race.

control. A small segment of the program flowchart is sketched in Figure 89. In a feedback control program of this type, the current inputs touch off numerous chain reactions among the variables so that even the programmers themselves have no clear idea as to the eventual outcome of any particular simulation.

Once the computer had been programmed in accordance with this basic philosophy, dozens of runs were made under varying sets of assumptions. Unfortunately, the results were not entirely encouraging. According to the computer, within less than 100 years mankind will have consumed most of the earth's nonrenewable resources. At that time our civilization will begin to crumble into chaotic disarray.

Is there some way we can mitigate the effects of this bleak scenario for the future? It won't be easy in the humble opinion of Jay Forrester's electronic oracle. Three sample plots from *The Limits to Growth*, the highly-popular summary publication of The Club of Rome, are presented in Figure 90. The first graph, labeled "World Model Standard Run",

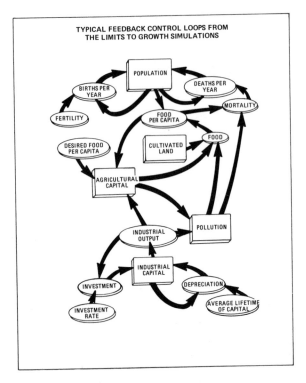

Figure 89: A few of the many feedback control loops forming the backbone of the Limits to Growth simulations are represented schematically in the above sketch. Although the mathematical relationships included in the program were all coded by skilled experts, the overall program is so complicated it is nearly impossible for anyone to predict the ultimate results of any particular simulation.

shows the typical "overshoot and collapse" scenario which occurs in most of *The Limits to Growth* simulations. As you can see, the world's population peaks out in the year 2050 and then slides into an abrupt decline, a decline caused by the virtual depletion of our nonrenewable natural resources. Pollution is also a serious problem, peaking out at several hundred times the level we are now willing to tolerate.

What causes the other disastrous consequences as indicated by the graphs in the "World Model Standard Run?" Here is the explanation provided by the authors of *The Limits to Growth:*

"As resource prices rise and mines are depleted, more and more capitol will be used for obtaining resources, leaving less to be invested for future gorwth. Finally, investment cannot keep up with

THE LIMITS TO GROWTH PROJECTIONS

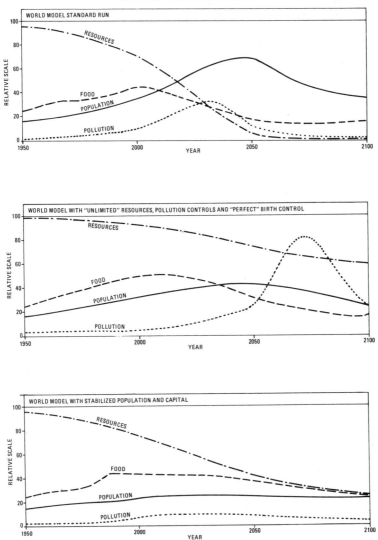

Figure 90: These three computer-generated simulations, which were obtained from the *Limits to Growth,* show that unless mankind responds with uncharacteristic discipline, we inevitably face a disastrous population decline at some time during the next 100 years. In the opinion of the men and women who put together the simulation, there is no way we can avoid this calamity if we continue to overplant our arable land, pollute our environment, and deplete our cheap and abundant mineral resources.

depreciation, and the industrial base collapses, taking with it the service and agricultural systems, which have become dependent on industrial inputs (such as fertilizers, pesticides, hospital laboratories, computers and especially energy for mechanization) . . . Population finally decreases when the death rate is driven upward by lack of food and health services."*

The second graph in Figure 90 shows what would happen if we could somehow acquire three things: (1) essentially unlimited resources, (2) highly effective pollution-abatement procedures, and (3) nearly perfect birth control—that is if each couple could limit themselves to their exact desired number of children. Unfortunately, the results of the new simulation are not much more encouraging: industrial production remains relatively high throughout the interval and pollution reaches its apex considerably later, but the world population level still peaks out in the middle of the 21st century with a subsequent die-off greatly exceeding the great plague. What causes the difficulty under this rather favorable set of assumptions? The authors explain it quite simply: "In this run (population) growth is stopped by a food crisis", a crisis which is clearly portrayed by the shape of the "per capita food consumption" graph in Figure 90.

The third set of curves represents the results of an even more stringent set of controls as proposed by the authors of *The Limits to Growth*. Among other things they believe that we should:

1. freeze total world population at a level only slightly higher than it is today
2. cut resource consumption per unit of industrial output by 75 percent
3. continue to shift our economy away from products toward services
4. reduce pollution per unit of industrial output to one fourth our present-day value
5. divert large amounts of capital away from the industrial sector and use it to enhance agricultural productivity
6. minimize soil erosion and maximize its enrichment and preservation
7. design various items of capitol equipment for a substantially longer lifetime of useful operation.

---

*Meadows, Donella H.; Meadows, Dennis L.; Randers, Jorgen; Behrens, William W., III. *The Limits to Growth*. New York, New York: Universe Books, 1972.

series of projections based on statistics for 1900 and 'proved' that the world economy ought to have collapsed by 1970."*

By now further criticism had become almost pointless, but in 1976, two years after the original study first reached the bookstores, Lincoln Gordon writing in *Resources* magazine put together one final bruising report:

> "The scientific foundations of the study now look even weaker than they did at the time. The study was seriously wrong in its data on resources, wrong in its assumption on the costs of environmental control, faulty in its modeling methodology, defective in its neglect of prices as an allocator of scarce resources, and strikingly oblivious to known technological possibilities, to say nothing of plausible new technologies. There were convincing scholarly refutations in scientific and popular journals (and) in an early analysis by the World Bank staff."**

What was the ultimate outcome of this gushing flood of well-founded criticism? The Club of Rome did not disband its membership. It merely waited four years, then abruptly published a new report. This time the conclusions were masterminded by the Nobel prize-winning economics Professor Jan Tingergen of the Netherlands. Professor Tinbergen, working with 20 other experts who declined to use computers, reviewed the international order and decided that "further global growth is essential". Never mind that this conclusion was completely at odds with the results of the original *Limits to Growth* study!

"The Club of Rome is now prepared to admit that it was wrong back in 1972", concluded a sharply-written editorial review published in the *Los Angeles Herald Examiner*. And what did the authors of the new Club of Rome study indicate we should now do? "Outright transfer payments of vast sums of money (should be made) from the developed nations to countries of the underdeveloped world." It was a course of action that many others had previously advocated, but it sent the *Herald Examiner's* editorialists into a fit of fury: "What ineffable crust these people have! Less than four years ago their first major proposal was the laughingstock of the sophisticated world. Not even they themselves pretend to defend it any longer. Yet here they are again, still peddling their Third World snake

---

*"The Club of Rome Tries Again". *Los Angeles Herald Examiner.* April 25, 1976. pg. A-16.
**Gordon, Lincoln. "Limits to Growth Debate." *Resources.* Summer, 1976.

oil and now claiming the ability to prescribe sound economic policies for all mankind.''

Sobering Afterthoughts

In retrospect it may seem surprising that so many otherwise sophisticated people would have been so quick to accept the validity of the *Limits to Growth* simulations, especially in view of the fact that more conventional projections of the future so often turn out to be hopelessly in error. Consider these revealing examples:

1. A committee organized in 1486 at the command of King Ferdinand and Queen Isabella of Spain reported in 1490 that a voyage such as the one Christopher Columbus contemplated was not possible because "So many centuries after the Creation it was unlikely that anyone could find hitherto unknown lands of any value."

2. After being sent to survey the lands occupied by the Grand Canyon, Lt. Joseph C. Ives, of the Corps of Topographical Engineers said that "The region is, of course, altogether valueless. It can be approached only from the south, and after entering it there is nothing to do but leave. Ours has been the first and will doubtless be the last, party of whites to visit this profitless locality."

3. A committee of the British Parliament in 1878 reported Thomas Edison's ideas of developing an incandescent lamp to be "good enough for our transatlantic friends but unworthy of the attention of practical or scientific men."

4. The astronomer William H. Pickering, said with regard to airflight *after* the invention of the airplane "The popular mind often pictures gigantic flying machines speeding across the Atlantic and carrying innumerable passengers in a way analogous to modern steamships . . . It seems safe to say that such ideas must be wholly visionary . . . even if a machine could get across with one or two passengers the expense would be prohibitive to any but the capitalist who could own his own yacht."

5. In 1922 the Assistant Secretary of the Navy, Franklin D. Roosevelt, stated that "It is highly unlikely that an airplane, or a fleet of them, would ever successfully sink a fleet of Navy vessels under battle conditions."

6. Dr. Vannevar Bush, one of the developers of the modern analog computer said in December of 1945: "There has been a great deal

said about a 3,000 miles high-angle rocket . . . carrying an atom bomb and so directed as to be a precise weapon which would land exactly on a certain target, such as a city. I say, technically, I don't think anyone in the world knows how to do such a thing, and I feel confident that it will not be done for a very long period of time to come . . ."*

It seems clear that a computer-generated projection can never be any better than the quality and timeliness of the inputs nor the validity of the mathematical model being used. And yet many people who might be reluctant to believe a human prophet anxiously embrace the results developed by a digital computer—in some cases even if it appears to contradict their own personal experiences! Pierre Gallois in a recent guest editorial in the French newspaper *Science et Vie* tried to cajole his countrymen into a more realistic view of the limitation of computer simulations. "If we put tomfoolery into a computer, nothing comes out but tomfoolery" he noted, "but this tomfoolery having passed through a very expensive machine is somehow ennobled, and no one dares criticize it." Harvey Lynn, Jr. of the Rand Corporation echoed this same sentiment when he noted that "Few people will argue with the computer, feeling that it combines the qualities of a sorcerer with those of a slightly mad (but competent) scientist."**

Of course those who have had direct experience with the limitations of computers tend to be far more critical than the average layman. For example, Dr. Joseph Weitzenbaum, noted computer expert at MIT, has bluntly pointed out that regardless of how precise and imposing it may seem to be, a computer simulation often tells us absolutely nothing useful about the real world: "A plain typewriter in some sense mirrors the behavior of an autistic child (one types a question and gets no response whatever), but it does not help us understand autism."

Another fundamental difficulty with computer modeling procedures of the type developed by The Club of Rome is that they are simply too big, too complicated, too involved to produce trustworthy results. We are always on shaky ground when we find ourselves using a tool that is so complex we have no clear idea how it actually works. Unfortunately, although we realize that big, complicated computer simulations are not

---

*Bamarra, Nancy T. "Erroneous Predictions and Negative Comments Concerning Exploration, Territorial Expansion, Scientific and Technological Development." Published by The Library of Congress, Washington, D.C., May 29, 1969.

**Logsdon, Tom and Logsdon, Fae. *The Computers in Our Society.* Fullerton, California: Anaheim Publishing Company, 1977.

foolproof, we are often forced into using them in another important area to our lives; future projections of the potentially devastating effects of our military power.

COMPUTERS AND MILITARY POWER

If the ENIAC had been completed on schedule, it would have been used in constructing accurate firing tables for the big World War II artillery guns. As things turned out the war ended shortly before the computer became operational, however, it was used in planning and building some of the earliest atomic bombs. Later, its descendants were put to work on our intercontinental ballistic missiles and our nuclear submarines.

Today, nearly 30 years later, our military establishment is almost completely dependent upon the high speed digital computer. Among other things it is used in simulating the probable results of various wartime scenarios. These simulations have an important impact on the way we shape and spend our military budgets. Since the end of World War II, our government has expended more than $2000 billion in maintaining a powerful and convincing military posture. The necessary expenditure levels and their proper allocation among the various branches of the service are determined by carefully evaluating our own military strength relative to any potential adversaries. Throughout most of this 30-year interval, we have perceived our most likely adversary to be the Soviet Union.

If we should happen to miscalculate and allow ourselves to become weaker than those who oppose us, war is not the only possible detrimental result. As has happened to many different countries in the past, we could also find ourselves being bullied and blackmailed in international interactions. On the other hand, there is no more wasteful way for us to squander our national treasure than to spend it on military weapons we don't need and will never use.

In 1978 America's military expenditures amounted to $116.8 billion and the Carter administration put in a request for $126 billion for fiscal 1979. A graph showing the history of our expenditures (translated into constant 1978 dollars) is presented in Figure 91. In accordance with this particular yardstick, our current spending level is higher than in any previous peacetime era, although it is considerably lower than the peak levels reached during World War II. Unfortunately, even discounting for inflation the dollar buys less military muscle today than it did 30 years ago. The elimination of the draft and the upgrading of the living conditions and other fringe benefits for our soldiers has resulted in much higher costs; consequently, the number of men in uniform has gradually drifted downward. Today a little over 2 million Americans serve in the military. This compares with nearly 4 million in uniform in the Soviet Union and about 3.3 million in the People's Republic of China.

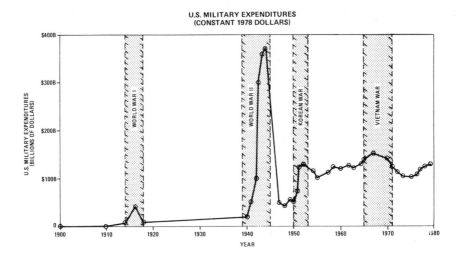

U.S. MILITARY EXPENDITURES (CONSTANT 1978 DOLLARS)

Figure 91: Even if they are expressed in constant, uninflated dollars, our military expenditures have been creeping steadily upward. In large part, these higher costs go toward the purchase of increasingly sophisticated weapons systems which some military critics are afraid may be exposing us to greater dangers rather than giving us a safer world.

Maintaining and Enhancing the Strategic Balance of Terror

For many years America's military planning has been dominated by the concept of "mutual assured deterence", which many people refer to as "the balance of terror". Under this philosophy it is believed that war is best averted if both sides maintain sufficient strategic forces so that they are capable of effective retaliation even after sustaining a nuclear first strike from the other major power.

Today our strategic strike force is based on a three-pronged "triad", an enormously destructive mixture of land-based missiles, missile-carrying submarines and long-range bombers. At present this deterrent force is dependent upon 2090 delivery platforms broken down as follows:

- 1054 land-based missiles
- 656 submarine-based missiles
- 380 long-range bombers.

Theoretically, these weapons' systems could deliver more than 6,500 megatons of nuclear explosives on more than 11,000 enemy targets.* The number of warheads greatly exceeds the number of launch platforms because each platform carries up to 14 warheads each of which can be directed to a separate target.

Most military experts are willing to concede that a sufficiently masterful technological breakthrough might allow the destruction of one part of our country's strategic triad. However, they consider it extremely unlikely that all three portions would suddenly become vulnerable. Unfortunately, a series of gradual technological advances made over the past few years raises the spectre of gradually emerging vulnerability. Recently, *Science* magazine, the highly respected publication of the American Society for the Advancement of Science, stated flatly that "both the Soviet Union and the United States . . . are technically capable of achieving a 90 percent success on the first strike."** Of course this technical capability will not necessarily be translated into a corresponding physical capability. Both sides may hold back because of the enormously high cost of deploying the necessary hardware to achieve an effective first strike. However, the fact that a first strike is technically possible indicates that in the long run the world is not especially safe from nuclear madness. How have we managed to get ourselves into this admittedly frightening fix? In rather undramatic ways in the opinion of the editors at *Science* magazine. In their view it has come about by means of an almost imperceptible process they call "technology creep":

> "Incremental advances in a number of fields—electronics, materials, gravity, geodesy, and others—all contribute to the growing accuracy of the ICBM forces on both sides, and make it virtually inevitable that these missiles (which, when they were first built, were lucky to land within 5 miles of their target) will soon be able to land within a few hundred feet. This capability is sometimes called 'absolute accuracy', since once an ICBM becomes accurate enough, it is virtually certain to destroy its target."***

---

*The nuclear warhead that leveled Hiroshima had a power of less than 0.02 megatons, a megaton being the explosive equivalent of one million tons of TNT.

**"Technology Creep and the Arms Race: A World of Absolute Accuracy." *Science*. September. 1978. pp. 1192-1196.

***"Technology Creep and the Arms Race: A World of Absolute Accuracy." *Science*. September 1978. pp. 1192-1196.

These impressive increases in accuracy have been achieved only through the most painstaking efforts in science and technology. Hundreds of precisely-engineered components are involved. The accelerometers and the gyroscopes used in guiding the rockets toward their targets are among the most demanding. Consider this description from a recent *Scientific American* article:

". . . under certain conditions a dust particle weighing (only) 0.00000005 grams on the test mass of a single accelerometer can cause a 200-meter miss in range and a 70-meter miss in track. A shift of 0.00000005 centimeters in the center of gravity of a spinning (gyro) . . . can cause a range error of 100 meters and a track error of 50 meters. These instruments must remain 'combat ready' for thousands of hours, then be able to tolerate without degradation of their performance the vibrations caused by the burning rocket fuel and still maintain the linearity of their outputs to ten parts per million . . ."*

The Arms Control Agreements we have negotiated with the Soviets have provided for some reductions in certain military items that can be easily counted such as launch silos and nuclear warheads. However, it is not at all clear if an agreement can ever be reached that would halt the destabilizing effects of creeping technology. Part of the problem is that no one even knows how to define creeping technology much less regulate it.

If gradual advances in technology do, in fact, result in "absolute accuracy" is there anything we can do to minimize the possibility of sustaining a first strike? A number of possible strategies have been devised and their probable results simulated using digital computers.

One possible response would entail the construction of a large field of *mobile* ICBM's (Intercontinental Ballistic Missiles). The missiles in this field would be shifted by truck from one empty silo to another at random to confuse any Soviet strategy of attack. Another approach would be to deploy large numbers of ABM's (*A*nti *B*allistic *M*issiles) to defend our land-based silos. There is also the possiblity of launching the missiles on warning of an attack to save them from destruction and to assure that they would be used. Finally, we could do nothing at all in the hope that the

---

*Tsipis, Kosta. "The Accuracy of Strategic Missiles." *Scientific American*. July 1975. pp. 14-23.

weapons we now have would act as an adequate deterrent. Unfortunately, each proposed course of action involves its own worrisome hazards.

The institution of a mobile land force of ICBM's, for example, would give rise to horrendous arms control problems. The Soviets can verify the number of silos we have by using observation satellites but they cannot verify the number of Intercontinental Ballistic Missiles. Thus, they would inevitably suspect that each of our silos contained a live missile—which is not in keeping with the SALT agreements already signed.*

The development of an extensive ABM force to protect our missiles was outlawed by the 1972 ABM treaty. Consequently, we would have to renegotiate the treaty—or break it—in order to use this approach to protect our strategic missile forces.

The "launch on warning" concept also creates certain intractable problems. In particular, many critics are afraid that, since the President would have only 30 minutes to issue the order, he might hesitate too long, thus allowing our missiles to be destroyed. Moreover, in the past few years there have been a number of false sightings by our early warning radars. Among other things they have been confused by herds of migrating caribu and by echos picked up from the rising moon. Would any President be willing to issue an order risking the annihilation of our civilization based on information from such a failure-prone system?

Of course there are those who believe that, given the hazards associated with the first three options, our safest response may be to do nothing at all. It can be argued convincingly that the assured force of retaliation, even if it does seem relatively small by modern military standards, should be enough to deter either side from risking the counterattack that would result from a first strike. How destructive would the resulting retaliation turn out to be? In a recent article scientists Philip Morrison and Paul F. Walker described the destructive potential of an attack on Boston launched from a single submerged nuclear submarine. They then extrapolated the results to cover a more ambitious version involving 5 to 9 nuclear submarines attacking several population centers in the Soviet Union or the United States:

> "Let us imagine a single strike by one missile with 14 reentry vehicles or warheads, on one U. S. city, Boston. If each warhead carries 40 kilotons of nuclear explosives, about three times the power of the Hiroshima bomb, the overlapping circles of 14 warheads (See Figure 92) would kill or seriously injure about 40 percent of the three million

---

*SALT = Strategic Arms Limitation Treaty.

HYPOTHETICAL NUCLEAR STRIKE

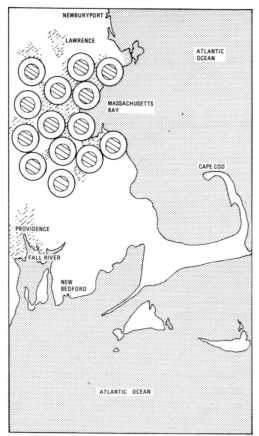

Figure 92: According to recent computer simulations, a nuclear strike on the city of Boston by a single missile equipped with 14 nuclear warheads would kill or seriously injure 1.2 million people. The shaded damage circles are conservatively sized for warheads of 40 kilotons each, or roughly three times the size of the bomb that leveled Hiroshima. Within the dark inner circles the probability of instant death is 50 percent. The lighter donut-shaped regions involve a 20 percent probability of short-term death.

people living in the metropolitan area. Bombs falling in the harbor would send huge waves of radioactive water pouring over the city center. The prevailing wind from the northwest would carry a radioactive fallout plume over all southeastern Massachusetts and much of Cape Cod, causing as many as 100,000 delayed deaths."*

*Morrison, Philip and Walker, Paul F. "A New Strategy for Military Spending." *Scientific American.* October 1978. pp. 48-60.

In using their computers to extrapolate this rather devastating scenario to a larger, but still quite limited, nuclear exchange (See Table 7) the authors conclude that:

"An attack by nine submarines with 1,200 warheads could well kill or gravely injure 70 to 90 million people, counting delayed deaths from radioactive fallout."

Of course, an attack using the same number of warheads against the Soviet Union would be somewhat less destructive since their population is considerably less concentrated; nonetheless, it seems likely to many observers that their probable losses would be large enough to deter them from attempting a preemptive first strike. After all, a loss of, say 50 million lives would be 2.5 times as great as the number they suffered during the entire torturous course of World War II. Moreover, there is no assurance that the retaliation would be limited to 5 to 9 submarines. At the present time, as is shown by the force level comparisons in Table 8, the United States has 70 nuclear submarines in operation; the Soviet Union has 85.

New Possibilities for Tactical War

Thus we see that the computer has profoundly restructured the world's strategic forces; it has also triggered revolutionary changes in tactical war. In World War I, when most defensive battles were fought from protective trenches, the defense had an important advantage. Shelling from the big guns cratered the land separating the two forces so badly it was nearly impossible for the attackers to move forward with their heavy equipment. Consequently the attacking foot soldiers, who were cynically characterized as "cannon fodder", often had a battlefield life expectancy of only a few minutes.

With the advent of World War II, advancing technology and daring new military tactics tipped the balance in favor of the offense. Blitzkrieg tactics* allowed Hitler's mechanized armies to roll across Czechoslovakia, Poland, and France with bonejarring speed.

According to Morrison and Walker there are strong indications that the introduction of modern electronic technologies may be tipping the balance back in favor of the defense. Throughout World War II the key to victory in battle was often raw "firepower". Cheap, plentiful rounds of

---

*Literally translated the word blitzkrieg means "lightning war". It consists of swift, surprise attacks involving precise coordination between ground artillery, close-support aircraft, and highly-disciplined infantry troops.

TABLE 7

HYPOTHETICAL NUCLEAR ATTACKS*

U. S. SUBMARINES ATTACKING RUSSIAN CITIES		
NO. OF SUBMARINES	5	9
NO. OF WARHEADS (40 KILOTONS EACH)	800	1450
NO. OF IMMEDIATE DEATHS	37 million	50 million + delayed radiation deaths

RUSSIAN SUBMARINES ATTACKING U. S. CITIES**		
NO. OF SUBMARINES	5	9
NO. OF WARHEADS (40 KILOTONS EACH)	750	1200
NO. OF IMMEDIATE DEATHS	50 million	60 + 10 to 30 million delayed radiation deaths

*Source = Morrison, Philip and Walker, Paul F. "A New Strategy for Military Spending". *Scientific American*. October 1978. pp. 48-60.
**These projections assume that the Russian submarines would be equipped with missiles of the type now being deployed by the United States. In fact their missiles are, at present, somewhat less sophisticated.

ammunition were used to lay down a metal curtain often even in the absence of visible targets. As a result, it has been estimated that it required the expenditure of approximately 300,000 rounds of small caliber ammunition to kill the average enemy soldier.

Firepower is, of course, still important to a modern mechanized army. However, "smart weapons" provide a reasonable alternative. A smart weapon uses sophisticated electronic sensors coupled with a compact microprocessor to allow an explosive warhead to home in on its

TABLE 8

MILITARY FORCE COMPARISONS*

	UNITED STATES	SOVIET UNION
STRATEGIC MISSILES	1700	2415
NUCLEAR WARHEADS	9500	4000
WARPLANES	5800	8100
TANKS	11,000	50,000
SUBMARINES	70 NUCLEAR 5 DIESEL	85 NUCLEAR 158 DIESEL
MAJOR WARSHIPS	172	240
AIRCRAFT CARRIERS		3
MILITARY SPENDING (% of GNP)	6%	12%

*Source = Wiley, Fay, et. al. "The New Global Balancing Act". *Newsweek*. February 5, 1979. pp. 58-59.

target. Naturally, such a device is much more expensive than conventional ammunition but its kill probability is also considerably higher. Moreover, smart weapons are consistently able to destroy large pieces of equipment such as tanks and airplanes which are themselves becoming increasingly expensive.

Five years ago the U. S. M-60 main battle tank could be purchased for $300,000; today it costs $650,000 and, the cost of the new XM-1 tank, fully equipped, will probably approach $1.5 million. A modern nuclear aircraft carrier costs about $2 billion plus another $3 billion for all the necessary support equipment. And, yet, despite their sky-high prices, these fancy weapons' systems are becoming increasingly vulnerable to the relatively cheap and widely-proliferated "smart weapons".

Smart weapons utilize a variety of methods for locating and destroying selected targets (See Figure 93). Some direct themselves toward the infrared rays emitted by hot surfaces (tank engines, aircraft exhaust gases), some use optical and radar homing devices, others are directed by "pilots" on the ground viewing the battlefield on a special television screen.

The kill rates achieved by some smart weapons are truly amazing. For example, it is estimated that the Tow anti-tank weapon (a wireguided missile which can be launched from a jeep or a helicopter*) has a kill probability of 80 percent up to its maximum range of 2.4 miles. The Maverick air-to-surface anti-tank missile is even more deadly. Recently, it made 208 direct hits in 226 test firings—a kill rate that exceeds 90 percent.**

These tests were, of course, made under idealized conditions. However, when the same devices have been tested in a realistic battlefield environment surprisingly good results have been obtained. Perhaps the most striking example occurred in the 1967 Arab-Israeli war when the Egyptians sank an Israeli destroyer with a Russian-built Styx cruise missile from a range of 20 miles. In this instance, a single $20,000 missile launched from a small patrol boat destroyed a ship worth $150,000,000!

The 1973 conflict between the same adversaries illustrates how much technology had advanced in six short years. Expensive equipment carefully stockpiled throughout the entire interval was converted into useless rubble within a short time after it was positioned on the battlefield. When the war was over General Sa'ad al-Shazli, Chief of Staff on the Egyptian armed forces, arrived at this rather candid appraisal of the wartime situation: "It was now impossible to guarantee the success of any armored attack until the anti-tank weapons of the defense are neutralized."***Offensive blitzkrieg tactics were strangely ineffective.For example, the Israeli 190th Armoured Brigade had attacked the Egyptian

---

*As a wire-guided missile moves toward its target, a thin wire unfurls behind it. The soldier who launched it transmits midcourse corrections along the wire by keeping the target in his sights.
**The Boston Study Group. *The Price of Defense: A New Strategy for Military Spending.* New York, New York: Times Books, 1978.
***Morrison, Philip and Walker, Paul F. "A New Strategy for Military Spending." *Scientific American.* October 1978. pp. 48-60.

SMART WEAPONS ON THE BATTLEFIELD

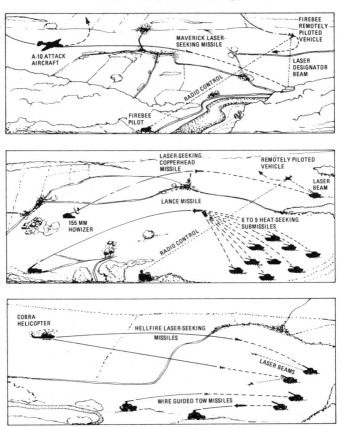

Figure 93: According to a thesis advanced by Philip Morrison and Paul F. Walker in their forthcoming book, *The Price of Defense: A New Strategy for Military Spending,* modern technology seems to be giving the defender a distinct military edge. These sketches show various types of "smart" weapons closing toward their targets by using heat-seeking devices and other electronic sensors. Under certain conditions, a weapon of this type costing perhaps $20,000 has an excellent chance of destroying much more complicated and costly enemy hardware.

Second Army under cover of strong air support in the Sinai. After only a few hours of fighting, the Israeli force had been effectively destroyed. More than 130 Israeli tanks were killed by Russian-made Sagger anti-tank missiles: 25 pound wireguided rockets carried by lightly-armored vehicles.

On the other side of the conflict Major General Claim Herzog of the Israeli army pointed out in his book *The War of Atonement: October, 1973,* that the Israelis made a "serious mistake in assuming that the best anti-tank weapon would be the tank." In fact, tiny, cheap weapons played a decisive role. This is how Herzog described one particularly devastating Sinai battle: "Hundreds of guiding wires of anti-tank missiles lay strewn across the road as if a giant spiderweb had collapsed."[*] Of course the "smart weapons" now on the drawing boards will be even smarter than those available today. Consequently, any aggressor will be forced to take some high level risks in order to reach his military objectives. In attacking he must expose his most expensive and vulnerable pieces of equipment to the destructive capabilities of relatively inexpensive, but quite lethal smart weapons.

Only time will tell if the advantage will remain with the defender. But during the next few years, at least, it would appear that advancing technology has given us a world that is, perhaps, just a little safer for those who would prefer to avoid destructive war.

THE GEOPOLITICS OF COMPUTERS

As we have seen from the previous discussions, technology, especially computer-oriented technology, quickly translates into military might. Small wonder the Soviet Union is constantly trying to gain access to the superb technology of the United States and other non communist powers.

In 1975 it was estimated that there were 175,000 large-and small-scale computers in use in the United States. This compares with approximately 15,000 computers in the Soviet Union including small business machines.[**] These raw numerical values are indicative, but they do not accurately portray the actual qualitative differences between the levels of computer technology in the two countries. For one thing, a much larger percentage of the computers being used in the Soviet Union are obsolete first- and second-generation machines. Are the Soviets likely to close the gap in the immediate future? Computer expert Donald J. Reifer doesn't think they will. After a two-week tour of Soviet data processing installations he summarized his observations in the following way:

> "There is a serious lack of computing power in the Soviet Union that will not be corrected in the near future. Compounding this problem are the lack of reliable peripherals and an absence of sophisticated software for large machines."

---

[*]Herzog, Chaim. *The War of Atonement.* October, 1973: New York, New York: A Sports Illustrated Book, 1975.

[**]Szprowicz, Dohdan O. "Computers from Communist Countries." *Datamation.* September, 1976.

Because of the obvious military implications of data processing technology, the State Department carefully scrutinizes any proposed sales of advanced computer technology to the communist world. Sometimes sales are allowed; more often permission for export is unhesitatingly denied. There are those who believe that these trade barriers are needlessly harsh and restrictive. In particular, William C. Norris, Chief Executive Officer of The Control Data Corporation, contends that we should be more liberal in encouraging freer trade. "The gut issue in high technology trade with the Communists is jobs versus military risk", he maintains forcefully. "in today's atmosphere, however, attention is focused almost entirely on military risk with little or no apparent consideration given to the new jobs that can flow from increased trade . . . yet the nation's number one problem is unemployment. Not only are more jobs needed, but almost as important, more *skilled* jobs."*

In his view it seems obvious that Soviet military leaders will always have first call on everything needed—including any available computers— so that our refusal to trade with them hurts only the civilian sector of their economy; it has little effect on the military. Moreover, the Soviet military, like that of the United States, avoids depending on foreign suppliers. Hence our trade restrictions are actually forcing them to develop their computer technology to a higher level of sophistication than would otherwise be necessary.

"Without doubt, U. S. export controls have forced the acceleration of the development of the Communists' computer industry, thus causing economic and military capability to be created at earlier dates and outside of our control."

What should we do about this problem? Norris unflinchingly offers us this daring proposal:

"The best answer for the United States is cooperation, either through direct exchange of technology, or indirectly through joint projects or jointly-owned companies."

How would we keep them from running off with our advanced technology once such arrangements have been consummated? He comes up with this surprisingly simple solution: "It is practicable—even desirable—to retain some of the . . . component production in the United States."

*Norris, William. "High Technology Trade with the Communists." *Datamation.* January, 1978. pp. 99-131.

Why should we be willing to accept what some see as a profound risk in order to gain at most, a few hundred thousand jobs for our work force? This is how Norris analyzes the probable risks versus the probable gains:

"It is clear that as long as this nation has a healthy economy, it will never fall to Communists, either from within or from abroad. But economic disorder, with widespread unemployment and consequent disillusionment with our economic system, would be an entirely different and threatening setting."

Thus we see that in order to avoid a takeover by the Communists, we should, in the opinion of William C. Norris, increase our mutual trade. What should we trade with them? In his view we should sell them, on a controlled basis, our most sophisticated electronic technology. Most Americans would probably have great difficulty following all the technical arguments involved in this highly emotional debate. But, if they were given a vote in the matter, most of them would, in all likelihood, vote for severely restricted trade.

CONCLUDING REMARKS

At the beginning of this chapter we saw how big, all inclusive, computer simulation of the future can turn out to be grossly in error. But in later sections we discovered that our country has been relying upon the results of somewhat similar simulations for our national survival.

Of course some military leaders realize that the computer does not give us reliable answers, at least not sufficiently reliable for us to base our military decisions on the projections they generate. Vice Admiral Hyman Rickover, the architect of nuclear propulsion in the U. S. Navy, has long been one of the sternest critics of computer-generated simulations. In May of 1966 Rickover pointed out to a congressional subcommittee that "many people are mesmerized into believing . . . a study based on computer calculations must be correct since it (uses) the most modern mathematical techniques."*

Recalling that his nuclear propulsion work employed "the most advanced computers in the world and...a large number of first rank mathematicians" Rickover went on to explain to the committee that:

---

*Wilson, Andrew. *The Bomb and the Computer*. New York, New York: Delta Books, 1968.

"Hardly a day goes by without experience in our test programs and operating plants revealing that the results of many of our computer studies are not correct; had we based our engineering decisions solely on the computer study results, our nuclear plants would not (operate)."

Unfortunately, those who develop war gaming algorithms often operate in a vacuum, without being able to test the accuracy or the validity of their computer-generated results. This can be an extremely risky proposition. As Rickover put it:

". . . all wars and military development should have taught us that . . . a war, small or large, does not follow a prescribed 'scenario' laid out in advance. If we could predict the sequence of events more accurately, we could probably avoid war in the first place. The elder Moltke said 'No plan survives contact with the enemy'."*

BIBLIOGRAPHY

1. Aspin, Les. "The Verification of the Salt II Agreement." *Scientific American,* February 1979, pp. 38-45.

2. Austin, John E. "Computer-Aided Planning and Decision Making in the USSR." *Datamation,* December 1977, pp. 71-74.

3. Boyd, R. "World Dynamics: A Note." *Science,* 11 August 1972, pp. 516-519.

4. Brand, S. "Apocalypse Juggernaut, Goodby?" *CoEvolution Quarterly,* Fall 1975. pp. 4-5.

5. Bremer, John W. "Hardware Technology in the Year 2001." *Computer,* December, 1976, pp. 31-36.

6. Brown, William M., and Martel, Leon. "A Response to Critics of the Next 200 Years." *World Future Society Bulletin,* November-December 1978, pp. 16-20.

7. "Chip Helps Detect Targets Automatically." *Electronics,* 16 March 1978, pp. 41-42.

8. "Club of Rome: Computerizing The World." *Business Week,* 10 April 1971, p. 42.

9. "The Club of Rome Tries Again." *Los Angeles Herald-Examiner,* 25 April 1976, p. A-16.

---

*Congressional Record. Testimony May 11, 1966. " Department of Defense Appropriations for 1967." Subcommittee on Department of Defense, House Committee on Appropriations, 89th Congress, 2nd Session, Part 6.

10. Cole, H. S. D. "Models of Doom: A Critique of The Limits of Growth." *Nation,* 23 March 1974, pp. 376-378.

11. Davis, Ruth M. "Computer Systems in the 1980's." *Dimensions,* February 1976, pp. 10-23.

12. Drell, Sidney D., and Von Hippel, Frank. "Limited Nuclear War." *Scientific American.* November 1976, pp. 14-37.

13. Ehrlich, Paul R., and Ehrlich, Anne H. *Population, Resources, Environment,* San Francisco, California: W. H. Freeman, 1970.

14. Elson, Benjamin M. "Computer's Electronic War Role Growing." *Aviation Week and Space Technology,* 3 March 1975, pp. 43-49.

15. Forrester, J. J. *World Dynamics.* Cambridge, Massachusetts: Wright-Allen Press, 1971.

16. Gillette, R. "The Limits to Growth: Hard Sell for a Computer View of Doomsday." *Science,* 3 March 1972, pp. 1088-1092.

17. Gordon, Lincoln. "Limits to Growth Debate." *Resources,* Summer 1976.

18. Heppenheimer, T. A. *Colonies in Space.* Harrisburg, Pennsylvania: Stackpole Books, 1977.

19. Hobbs, L. C. "A Look at the Future." *Computer,* December 1976, pp. 9-10.

20. Hotz, Robert. "Export Problems Fester." *Aviation Week and Space Technology,* 11 December 1978, p. 9.

21. Hughes, Barry B., and Mesarovic, Mihajio D., "Testing the Hudson Institute Scenarios: Is Their Optimism Justified?" *World Future Society Bulletin,* November-December 1978, pp. 1-15.

22. Kahn, Herman., "Computers and The Future of America." *Computer Decisions,* January 1977, pp. 18-19.

23. Kahn, Herman., "Our Global Growing Pains." *Nation's Business,* July 1973, pp. 32-38.

24. "A 'Lean' Budget." *Newsweek,* 29 January 1979, pp. 59-60.

25. Logsdon, Tom. *Programming in BASIC.* Fullerton, California: The Anaheim Publishing Co., 1977.

26. Meadows, Donella H.; Meadows, Dennis L.; Rangers, Jorgen; and Behrens, William W. III., *The Limits to Growth.* New York, New York: Universe Books, 1972.

27. Morrison, Philip, and Walker, Paul F. "A New Strategy for Military Spending." *Scientific American,* October 1978, pp. 48-60.

28. "New Technology Export Curbs Rejected." *Aviation Week and Space Technology,* 28 August 1978, p. 21.

29. "The Next Big Leap in Electronics." *Business Week,* 24 October 1977, pp. 94B-94L.

30. Norris, William C. "High Technology Trade with the Communists." *Datamation*, January 1978, pp. 99-131.

31. "Processing of Data Key to Missile Defense." *Aviation Week and Space Technology*, 28 August 1978, pp. 12-14.

32. Reifer, Donald J. "Snapshots of Soviet Computing." *Datamation*, February 1978, pp. 133-138.

33. Robinson, Clarence A. "Soviets Boost ICBM Accuracy." *Aviation Week and Space Technology*, 3 April 1978, pp. 14-15.

34. Roth, P. F. "Using Computer Simulation to Solve Problems," *Dimensions*, December 1975, pp. 278-281.

35. Scoville, Herbert Jr., "The SALT Negotiations." *Scientific American*, August 1977, pp. 24-31.

36. "Soviet Threats Spur U. S. Missile Interest." *Aviation Week and Space Technology*, 22 May 1977, p. 16.

37. Stein, Kenneth J. "Realtime Data Aid SAC Mission." *Aviation Week and Space Technology*, 10 May 1976, pp. 47-51.

38. Szuprowicz, Bohdan O. "Computers from Communist Countries." *Datamation*, September 1976.

39. Szuprowica, Bohdan O. "Mini Computer Markets Around the World." *Mini-Micro Systems*, May 1978, pp. 60-63.

40. "Technology Creep and the Arms Race: A World of Absolute Accuracy." *Science*, 29 September 1978, pp. 1192-1196.

41. "Togetherness." *Newsweek*, 21 October 1974, pp. 62-63.

42. Tsipis, Kosta. "The Accuracy of Strategic Missiles." *Scientific American*, July 1975, pp. 14-23.

43. "U. S. Looks for Bigger Warlike Computers." *New Scientist*, 21 April 1977, p. 140.

44. Whitney, W. M. "Processing and Storing Information." *A forecast of Space Technology 1980-2000*, NASA Publication: NASA SP-387, pp. 3-78 to 3-119.

45. Willey, Fay et. al. "The New Global Balancing Act." *Newsweek*, 5 February 1979, pp. 58-59.

46. Wilson, Andrews. *The Computer and The Bomb*. New York, New York: Delta Publishing Co., 1968.

EXERCISES

1. In 1972 a popular bestseller, *The Limits to Growth*, predicted impending disaster for our technological civilization. Briefly describe the major conclusions of the Limits-to-Growth study. Now summarize some of the major objections to the methodology used on obtaining the computed results.

2. What is a simulation? In what fields of human endeavor have simulations been widely used? What are some of the problems associated with accurate computer-based simulations?

3. Morrison and Walker argue forcefully that in the modern tactical warfare the military advantage has shifted toward the defender. What is the basis of their reasoning? Once you have summarized it, give any counter arguments you can manage to muster.

4. What is a smart weapon? Describe how a typical version works. What have been the results when smart weapons have been tested under battlefield conditions?

5. Define the term "absolute accuracy". If the Soviet Union manages to develop absolute accuracy what are some of the ways our government could choose to respond?

6. What is the main argument for restricting trade in high technology items with the Soviet Union? What is the major counter-argument? Which course do you think our government should emphasize? Why?

7. A modern atomic submarine carries 16 nuclear-tipped missiles each equipped with as many as 14 separate nuclear warheads. About how many casualties would such a submarine be able to inflict on the Soviet Union? The United States? How do these casualty figures compare with those suffered by our country during World War II? World War I? The Vietnam war?

8. What is meant by the "balance of terror"? What are some technological developments that could "unbalance" the balance of terror?

9. What is a feedback control loop? How was it used in developing the graphs that appear in *The Limits to Growth?*

10. It has been estimated that the maximum carrying capacity of the earth is about 30 billion people. Starting with the graph in Figure 88, extrapolate to make your own estimate as to when we might expect to reach a population that large.

STUDENT PROJECTS

1. Both Thomas Malthus and Jay Forrester used mathematical modeling procedures to convince themselves that unless world population growth is soon halted, mankind faces impending disaster. Go to the library and research the work of these two men. Now write a short research report comparing and contrasting their methods and the results of their work.

SUGGESTED REFERENCES:

a. Boyd, R. "World Dynamics: A Note". *Science.* 11 August 1972. pp. 516-519.

b. Brand, S. Apocalypse Juggernaut, Goodby?" *Coevolution Quarterly,* Fall 1975, pp. 4-5.

c. Gillette, R. "The Limits to Growth: Hard Sell for a Computer View of Doomsday." *Science.* 3 March 1972. pp. 1088-1092.

d. Gordon, Lincoln. "Limits to Growth Debate". *Resources,* Summer 1976.

e. Meadows, Donella H.; Meadows, Dennis L.; Rangers, Jorgen; and Behrens, William W. III. *The Limits to Growth.* New York, New York: Universe Books, 1972.

2. For the past several years our national security has depended upon a "triad" of nuclear forces to keep the peace by maintaining a strategic "balance of terror". Research the hardware used in sustaining this balance of terror and the new dangers it now faces from advancing technology. Write up your findings in a 5 or 6 page report.

SUGGESTED REFERENCES:

a. Aspin, Les. "The Verification of the Salt II Agreement". *Scientific American,* February 1979. pp. 38-45.

b. Morrison, Philip and Walker, Paul F. "A New Strategy for Military Spending". *Scientific American.* October 1978. pp. 48-60.

c. Scoville, Herbert, Jr. "The SALT Negotiations." *Scientific American.* August 1977. pp. 24-31.

d. "Soviet Threats Spur U. S. Missile Interest". *Aviation Week and Space Technology.* May 22, 1977. p. 16.

e. "Technology Creep and the Arms Race" A World of Absolute Accuracy." *Science.* September 29, 1978. pp. 1192-1196.

f. "Tsipis, Kosta. "The Accuracy of Strategic Missiles." *Scientific American.* July 1975. pp. 14-23.

3. This book has dealt primarily with the controversies surrounding the use of computers in our society. Go back to the table of contents and pick out 8 or 10 controversial issues and state them in question form, e.g., "Are computers taking away our privacy?", "Will computers someday be smarter than people?". Now make up a table consisting of three columns. In column 1 list the controversial questions. In column 2 summarize your answers to the questions when this class first started. In column 3 summarize how you feel about it now. Note any major changes in your attitudes and on a separate sheet explain what caused you to change your mind.

HISTORICAL PERSPECTIVES

10th Century B.C.: The Sand-table abacus was first placed in operation.

9th Century B.C.: The Hindu-Arabic decimal number system was developed into a practical tool.

10th Century A.D.: Pope Sylvester II unsuccessfully attempted to promote the use of the decimal system in Western Europe.

12th Century A.D.: The Chinese perfected the modern-style abacus.

1614: Scottish mathematician John Napier developed logarithms, a special set of numbers to be used in simplifying numerical calculations.

1615: John Napier constructed a pair of bone-white rods embossed with numerical values for use as an aid in performing complicated mathematical calculations.

1620: Edmund Gunter devised the first practical slide rule.

1623. Wilhelm Schickard of Tubingen, Germany designed and constructed the world's first four-function calculator. Largely unpublicized and later destroyed in a fire, the device had no important impacts on later technological developments.

1624: Englishman Henry Briggs published the first comprehensive tables of logarithms.

1642: Blase Pascal, a young French mathematician, constructed the first widely-known mechanical adding machine.

1672: German mathematician Gottfried Wilhelm von Leibnitz developed the first mechanical calculating machine capable of handling automatic multiplications.

1686: Isaac Newton published his landmark work "Principia" unifying virtually all the mathematics and physics developed up to his day.

1725: Frenchman Basile Bouchon used a continuous belt of perforated paper to control some of his early weaving machines.

1769: Baron von Kempelen of Presburg, Hungary, toured Europe to exhibit a chess playing "machine" whose cabinet actually concealed a human chess master.

1798: The English clergyman/economist Thomas Malthus published a widely-quoted essay in which he predicted that, in the absence of conscious controls, the population of the earth would inevitably outstrip all supplies of food and other finite resources.

1801: Joseph Jacquard utilized the first known punched cards to control his complicated weaving looms.

1811: The Luddites, a fanatical group of unemployed laborers, roamed the British countryside smashing weaving looms and other labor-saving machines.

1814: J. M. Hermann designed a special-purpose analog computer, the Planimeter, which is still used today in determining the areas enclosed by continuous curves.

1823: Charles Babbage in England completed work on the *difference engine,* a special-purpose digital computer utilizing a large collection of mechanical gears and cogs.

1833: Charles Babbage started working on the *analytical engine.* Never completed, it would have been the world's first general-purpose digital computer.

1843: The American inventor, Samuel Morse, designed a "read-only memory" whereby binary pulses representing any letter of the alphabet could be transmitted automatically along a telegraph line.

1850: The hairline was affixed to the slide rule at Taverier-Gravet a French manufacturing firm.

1854: George Boole published his first book on symbolic logic later to form the backbone of formal computer design.

1863: The thermionic emission phenomenon, which later formed the basis of the vacuum tube was noticed, but ignored, by the American inventor, Thomas Edison.

1872: William Thomson of England constructed his tide analyzer, one of the earliest special-purpose analog computers.

1889: The American resercher Herman Hollerith conceived the idea of using punched cards to analyze the 1890 census tabulations.

1890: Louis Brandeis and Samuel Warren published a journal article, "The Right of Privacy", in which they contended that people are entitled, under the law, to have privacy.

1905: The thermionic emission phenomenon was used by J. A. Fleming in the construction of the vacuum diode.

1907: John Powers developed the Sperry-Rand card-sorting system, a major competitor to the system developed by Herman Hollerith.

1908: Lee DeForest invented the vacuum triode, a clever electronic amplification device.

1910: The American data processing expert James Powers developed a die-set device capable of punching all of the holes in a 20-column card simultaneously. His patents were later to form the backbone of Remington Rand.

1914: The Spanish researcher Leonardo Torres y Quevedo published detailed plans for the construction of a digital calculating machine using electromechanical design principles.

1919: American researchers W. H. Eccles and F. W. Jordan were the first researchers to describe the flip-flop circuit in one of the popular journals.

1920: Supreme Court Justice Louis Brandeis advanced a passionate argument that the right of privacy was ". . . the most comprehensive of rights and the right most valued by civilized man."

1927: While studying factory productivity, a team of researchers at Western Electric realized that the efficiency of the company's production line workers was temporarily enhanced by the attention they were receiving from plant psychologists. Later called "The Hawthorne Effect" their discovery was to have important impacts on several other branches of scientific research.

1928: Gustav Tauschek of Austria patented an electromagnetic drum storage device.

1928: Leslie John Comrie of Great Britain utilized Hermann Hollerith's electromechanical devices for computing the predicted motion of the moon over a 65-year interval. His work and his lectures helped foster the use of computing machines in conjunction with scientific research.

1931: Vannevar Bush at MIT built the first modern general-purpose analog computer.

1936: Konrad Zuse in Germany designed and constructed the first computing machine to use floating-point binary arithmetic.

1936: English logician Alan Turing proved mathematically that it was possible to build a digital computing machine that could solve virtually any mathematical problem which could be formulated in a clearly-defined manner.

1937: George Stibitz of the United States began to investigate the use of electromechanical relays for computing. Later he built computing machines with build-in self-checking capabilities.

1938: G. A. Philbrick developed the first electronic analog computer in the United States. It was used primarily for military purposes.

1944: Howard H. Aiken developed the Mark I, the world's first general-purpose digital computer. It utilized thousands of electromechanical relays.

1946: J. Presper Eckert and John W. Mauchly at the Moore School of Engineering in Philadelphia constructed the world's first general-purpose *electronic* digital computer.

1946: Computerized Monte Carlo techniques were developed in conjunction with early nuclear weapons research.

1946: After touring the data processing facilities at the Moore School of

Engineering, John von Neumann published a 40-page technical note lucidly explaining his incisive ideas on computer design.

1947: F. C. Williams at Manchaster University in England developed a high-speed data storage method in which millions of charged spots were stored on the face of a cathode ray tube.

1948: John Bardeen, Walter Brattain, and William Shockley invented the first practical solid-state device, the point-contact transistor.

1948: Engineering Research Associates began a technical study monitored by the National Bureau of Standards concerning the most practical methods for developing a magnetic drum computer.

1949: The first mercury delay line computer, the EDSAC, became operational in Cambridge, England.

1950: Claude E. Shannon, the founder of a branch of mathematics called "information theory" outlined a plan for coding a chess-playing routine that would make use of heuristic programming techniques.

1950: Marshal Kincaid, John M. Alden, and Robert B. Hanna described a new concept in computer storage utilizing millions of tiny magnetic cores.

1951: The first LSI devices were marketed by Fairchild Semiconductor and Texas Instruments.

1953: Magnetic drum memories were first marketed commercially.

1953: Core ring memories were perfected by researchers at RCA and MIT.

1954: The first transistorized computer, the TRADIC, was built by researchers at Bell Telephone Laboratories.

1955: The respected futurists Herman Kahn and Norbert Weiner made widely-quoted predictions that automated machinery would soon create widespread unemployment among American workmen.

1956: Work began on the APT programming language to be used in controlling programmed machine tools.

1956: The first successful chess program capable of playing on a 6×6 board was coded on the MANIAC I at Los Alamos.

1956: IBM described its 50-disk magnetic memory system capable of storing 5 million alphanumeric characters.

1957: John Backus working with a special research team at IBM developed the FORTRAN language.

1958: An international conference of computer experts at Zurich, Switzerland, recommended the adoption of ALGOL as a universal computer language.

1959: The BASIC language was developed for use in conjunction with time-sharing applications by Professor John Kemeny at Dartmouth College.

1960: The PLATO Project, a broad-ranging attempt to code and implement Computer-Aided-Instructional routines, was officially instituted.

1961: The first time-sharing system became operational at MIT.

1962: Ivan E. Sutherland at MIT initiated the use of interactive computer graphics using light pen input-output systems.

1964: The IBM 360, which made widespread use of solid-state LSI circuits, was introduced.

1964: Computers with multiprocessing capabilities were first sold.

1965: The American researchers R. C. Platzek and J. S. Kilby first described the concept of the integrated circuit.

1965: The Social Research Council proposed the institution of a Federal Data Center in order to keep stndardized records on the activities of all Americans. The idea quickly became the focus of a raging controversy.

1967: The United States and the Soviet Union signed the ABM treaty restricting the number of anti-ballistic missiles that could be deployed and limiting each country to the protection of a single missile field.

1968: The Digital Equipment Corporation began marketing the first mini-computers.

1969: IBM introduced the first large-scale general-purpose digital computers using solid-state primary storage units.

1970: The Fair Credit Reporting Act became law. Among other things it gave each American the right to know what information was being held on him in credit bureau files and to challenge the accuracy of that information.

1972: The United States and the Soviet Union ratified the ABM treaty limiting each country to the defense of a single geographical region using anti ballistic missiles.

1972: The first Soviet-American disarmament treaty (SALT I) was negotiated. It limited the number of strategic missiles that could be deployed and paved the way for more comprehensive agreements.

1972: The Club of Rome published *The Limits to Growth*, a widely-criticized study which used computer simulation methods to predict the impending collapse of Western Civilization.

1972: Researchers at Micro Instrumation and Telemetry Systems began work on the Altair 8800, the earliest of the hobby-oriented microcomputers.

1972: The Illiac 4 was first operated. When it became fully operational it was expected to be able to execute 200 million operations per second.

1972: Microprocessor chips were first sold in large quantities.

1972: IBM first marketed the 370. A versatile computer which comes in several different models, it utilizes dynamic addressing and metal oxide semiconductor memory chips.

1973: The Universal Product Code was officially adopted by a standing committee selected from among the various special-interest groups in the American grocery industry.

1973: The first floppy disk was introduced by IBM.

1974: Congress passed the Privacy Act of 1974 which delineated strict guidelines on the proper methods for collecting and using personal information stored in computers.

1976: The U. S. Military issued a request for the design of the Phoenix, a supercomputer capable of executing at least 10 billion instructions per second.

1977: IBM announced the first commercially available lock-and-key remote terminals.

1977: IBM released the Data Encryption Standard, a non-military coding system to be used in connection with various unclassified data processing operations.

1977: Bubble memories were first marketed by Texas Instruments.

1977: The first fully-assembled personal computer, the Commodore PET 2001, was introduced commercially.

1977: Ronald Rivest, Adi Shamir, and Len Adleman, three researchers at MIT, made use of some little-known properties of prime numbers in developing an elegant method of implementing trapdoor codes.

1978: Double-density and two-sided floppy disks began to achieve widespread popularity.

1979: The Videodisc, an inexpensive method of storing high-quality television programs complete with stereophonic sound, began to emerge from the research laboratories.

1979: Agreement on the SALT II treaty limiting the offensive military capabilities of the Soviet Union and the United States was finally reached.

GLOSSARY

ABACUS: A simple mechanical device of ancient origins used in performing mathematical calculations by moving a set of beads threaded onto a grid of stiff metal wires.

ACCESS LIMITS: Any body of methods used in restricting the number of people who can read, use, or alter a set of protected data files.

ACCESS TIME: The average amount of time required to retrieve a quantity from its storage location.

ACCUMULATOR: A high-speed, low-capacity storage register that keeps running tabs on the results of a computer's processing operations.

ADDER UNIT: An electronic device inside a digital computer capable of accepting two multidigit binary numbers and summing them.

ALGORITHM: A well-defined mathematical or logical procedure for solving a problem in a finite number of processing operations.

ALPHANUMERIC CHARACTERS: Any letters, numbers, or special symbols (such as punctuation marks) used in data processing operations.

ANALOG COMPUTER: A computer whose processing functions are based on measuring continuous variables rather than counting discrete entities.

ANALYST: A person who defines problems and develops algorithms for their solution.

ANALYTICAL ENGINE: A partially-completed general-purpose digital computer using mechanical design principles conceived by Englishman Charles Babbage in 1832.

AND-GATE: A specific computer circuit with two or more inputs and a single output, which emits a binary one output signal only if all its input signals are binary ones.

ANTI BALLISTIC MISSILE (ABM): Any defensive military rocket used in destroying the enemy's rocket-launched warheads.

ARTIFICIAL INTELLIGENCE: The capability of any device to perform functions that are normally associated with human intelligence, such as reasoning, learning, and self-improvement.

ASYNCHRONOUS COMPUTER: A digital computer that takes a variable amount of time to complete each processing operation, depending on its intrinsic complexity.

AUDIO RESPONSE UNIT (BORROWED VOICE COMPUTER): An information retrieval system in which a computer uses voice snythesizers or previously recorded fragments of human speech to give oral answers to the users questions.

AUTOMATIC: Any device which, under certain conditions, can function without intervention by a human operator.

AUTOMATION: The implementation of a manufacturing process by automatic means using mechanical, electromechanical, or electronic devices.

AUXILIARY STORAGE: A storage device directly accessible to the computer processing circuits used in supplementing its primary storage.

BACKGROUND PROGRAM: A low-priority program which is executed whenever the computers's resources are not required to process higher-priority programs.

BALANCE OF TERROR: A guiding military philosphy in which it is believed that peace is best accomplished if both the United States and the Soviet Union maintain sufficient numbers of nuclear weapons such that either power could devastate the other even after sustaining a first strike.

BASIC (*B*eginner's *A*ll-purpose *S*ymbol *I*nstruction *C*ode): BASIC is a simple procedure-oriented computer language widely used in educational institutions, small business applications, and in hobby computing.

BATCH PROCESSING: A technique in which a number of similar items or transactions to be processed are grouped for sequential processing during a single machine run.

BINARY ARITHMETIC: A positional notation system involving only two digits: zero and one.

BIOSPHERE: A thin shell around the earth which has the proper temperatures, pressures, and other conditions for sustaining life.

BISTABLE DEVICE: A device with exactly two stable states, such as on and off.

BIT (Binary digIT): A single character in a binary number system, i.e., a binary 1 or a binary 0.

BLACK BOX: An electronic or mechanical device which alters its input signals in a predictable way but whose inner workings are often a mystery to the user.

BOOLEAN ALGEBRA: A branch of symbolic logic similar to conventional algebra which deals with logical relationships rather than those linking numerical quantities.

BORROWED-VOICE   COMPUTER   (AUDIO   RESPONSE UNIT): An information retrieval system in which a computer uses voice synthesizers or previously recorded fragments of human speech to give oral answers to the user's questions.

BRANCH POINT: A point in a computer program at which the flow of the computations can be altered automatically, depending on the value of a previously computed quantity.

BREACH: Any successful and repeatable defeat of a computer's security controls which, if carried to consummation, could result in a penetration of the system.

BRUTE-FORCE APPROACH: Any body of mathematical techniques that depends on the raw power of a computer in order to arrive at an inelegant solution to a mathematical or logical problem.

BUBBLE MEMORY: A magnetic, nonvolatile storage medium in which binary digits are represented by tiny counter-polarized domains formed on a thin slab of orthoferrite.

BUFFER: A high-speed, low-capacity storage register used to increase the efficiency of data transfer operations between two storage units of grossly different data transfer rates.

BUG: A mistake or malfunction.

BYTE: A group of adjacent bits operated on as a unit by a digital computer.

CALCULATOR: A mechanical or electronic data processing device which requires frequent intervent by a human operator.

CARD PUNCH: A mechanical device which punches holes into a set of cardboard cards to represent numbers, letters, and special characters.

CARD READER: A device which senses the locations of the holes in a deck of punched cards and translates them into a machine-processible code.

CARD SORTING: The process of separating a stack of punched cards into separate classifications in accordance with the holes punched into the individual cards.

CASHLESS SOCIETY: A computerized system in which financial transactions are handled instantaneously by transferring credits from one bank account to another.

CATHODE-RAY TUBE: A vacuum tube, similar to a television picture tube, in which an electron gun, controlled by electromagnets, directs a narrow beam of electrons onto specific regions of a fluorescent screen or photographic surface.

CENTRAL PROCESSING UNIT (CPU): A special module in a digital computer which houses the primary storage devices and the circuits that control the interpretation and execution of the program instructions.

CHALK-MARK NOTATION: An ancient numeration system consisting of distinct vertical marks, each of which denotes a single concrete object.

CHARACTER: Any symbol, digit, letter, or punctuation mark stored or processed by a digital computer.

CHARACTER READER: An input device which reads alphanumeric characters directly from a printed document.

CHARGED-COUPLED DEVICE: A volatile, semi-random-access storage device in which the binary digits held in storage are continuously circulated around a number of continuous electronic loops each of which is composed of a chain of solid-state switches.

CIRCUIT: A complete electrical pathway designed for the controlled flow of electrons.

CLOCK-PULSE CIRCUIT: A circuit which generates a series of evenly-spaced timing pulses to help orchestrate the operations carried out by a synchronous digital computer.

CODEBOOK: A listing of equivalents between plaintext and code used for encoding and decoding, generally organized into two separate sections to facilitate easy dual-purpose translations.

COMMUNICATION LINK: A physical method of connecting one location to another for the purpose of transmitting and receiving information.

COMPUTER: Any device which accepts coded information and alters it into a more useable form in accordance with a man-made program of instructions.

COMPUTER-AIDED DESIGN: A process involving direct real-time interaction between a designer and a computer, usually by means of a cathode-ray tube and a light pen.

COMPUTER-AIDED INSTRUCTION (CAI): An interactive system linking a student and a computer which uses a natural language such as English to produce long-lasting changes in the cognitive domain (intellectual knowledge) of the student.

COMPUTER WORD: A sequence of bits or characters occupying a single addressable storage location and treated as a unit by the computer.

CONDITIONAL TRANSFER: A transfer of control in a computer program which is dependent upon the outcome of a previous computation.

CONSOLE: A typewriter-like device equipped with buttons, dials, and flashing lights which enables the human operator to communicate with the computer.

CONTROL UNIT: A special module in a digital computer which retrieves and interprets each instruction and insures that the computer's processing functions are executed with maximum practical efficiency.

CONVERSATIONAL LANGUAGE: A computer language in which the user gives direct answers to questions asked by the computer concerning the job being processed.

CORE RINGS: Tiny magnetizable donuts threaded on a grid of electrically conducting wires. Depending upon its direction of magnetization, each core ring stores a binary one or a binary zero.

CORE STORAGE: A form of high-speed primary storage utilizing magnetic core rings.

COURSEWARE: Programmed teaching routines used in conjunction with a Computer-Aided Instructional System.

CREDIT CARD: A small, embossed plastic strip used in making preauthorized credit purchases in accordance with preset limitations.

CRT PLOT (Cathode-Ray Tube Plot): A computer-generated graph or drawing projected onto the screen of a cathode-ray tube.

CRYPTANALYSIS: The steps and operations performed in converting encrypted messages into the corresponding plaintex without initial knowledge of the key employed in the encryption.

CYBERNETICS: A systematic study comparing the control, communication, and information-handling capabilities of higher animals and machines.

CYPHER: A form of cryptography in which the plaintext is made unintelligible to anyone who intercepts it by a transformation of the information itself, based on some key.

DATA: Coded information. Any representations such as characters or analog quantities to which real-world meaning is assigned.

DATA BANK: Any one-line semi-permanent computer storage array retaining large masses of data.

DATA ENCRYPTION STANDARD: A specific modern cypher developed by the National Bureau of Standards in conjunction with IBM for transmitting sensitive, but unclassified, government communications.

DATA PROCESSING: The execution of a systematic sequence of operations on a particular set of data values.

DATA PROCESSING CENTER: A computer center equipped with devices capable of receiving information, processing it in accordance with a man-made program of instructions, and producing the desired results.

DATA SECURITY: The protection of data from accidental or malicious modification, destruction, or disclosure.

DATA WORD: An ordered set of characters, usually of a preset number, which is stored and transferred by the computer's circuits as a fundamental unit of information.

DEBUGGING: The detection, location and removal of mistakes in a computer program.

DECIMAL DIGIT: In decimal notation, one of the characters 0 through 9.

DECIMAL SYSTEM: Our base-10 positional notation system.

DECRYPTION: The process of taking an encrypted message and reconstructing from it the original meaningful message.

DIAGNOSTIC MESSAGES: Computer-generated notes to a programmer which pinpoint improper commands and errors in logic.

DIFFERENCE ENGINE: A specific special-purpose digial computer, based on mechanical design principles, developed by Englishman Charles Babbage in 1822.

DIGITAL COMPUTER: A computer whose processing functions are based on counting discrete entities rather than measuring continuous variables.

DIGITIZE: To convert an *analog* measurement of a physical variable into a number expressed in *digital* form.

DIODE: A vacuum tube equipped with a cathode and an anode which permits a current to flow in one direction but prevents its flow in the opposite direction.

DIRECT ACCESS DEVICE: A computer storage device which provides either random access or semi random access to the data values being held in storage.

DISK PACK: A set of adjacent detachable magnetic disks.

DISK STORAGE DEVICE: A computer storage unit in which binary pulses are stored magnetically on the surfaces of a parallel stack of rotating platters.

DISTRIBUTED PROCESSING: The concept of placing a part of the computer's power and storage at the various locations where the data is generated or where the computed results are needed for effective management.

DOWNTIME: Any interval during which a computer system is inoperative due to a malfunction.

DRUM STORAGE: A method of storing binary-coded information on the curved surface of a rotating magnetizable cylinder.

ECONOMY-OF-SCALE CONCEPT: A principle of economics which states that, all other things being equal, the cost per unit of production is usually lower for large scale operations.

EFFECTORS: Devices that interact with and change their local environment.

ELECTROMECHANICAL RELAY: A magnetically operated mechanical switch.

ELECTRON: A subatomic particle having a specific negative charge orbiting the nucleus of an atom.

ELECTONIC FUNDS TRANSFER SYSTEM (EFTS): A computer system complete with the associated terminals and communication links which can debit or credit individual bank accounts directly, hence providing for paperless financial transactions.

ELECTRONICS: A specific branch of physics concerned primarily with the natural and controlled flow of electrons through various substances.

EMBEZZLEMENT: The theft of valuables by a person who has been entrusted to safeguard them.

ENCRYPTION: The process of altering a message so that it is incomprehensible to anyone except those who have the key to its decryption.

ENIAC: The world's first general-purpose electronic digital computer developed in 1946 at the Moore School of Engineering in Philadelphia, Pennsylvania, by J. Presper Eckert and John W. Mauchley.

ERROR: Any discrepancy between a computed, observed, or measured quantity and the true, specified, or theoretically correct value.

EXPONENTIAL GROWTH: A mathematical rule which approximates the growth rate of an animal population under idealized conditions. The growth rate for each generation is directly proportional to the number of members who reach childbearing ages.

EXTERNAL STORAGE: Any storage medium outside the computer which can store information in a form acceptable to the computer; for example, cards and tapes.

FEDERAL DATA CENTER: A conceptual system in which the personal files now being stored in various government-operated data processing centers would be moved to a single, centralized location where they could be cross-correlated and stored under more secure conditions.

FEEDBACK: The return of a fraction of the output of a process to its input, to provide for self-adjusting control of the process.

FIELD: An adjacent sequence of columns on a punched card devoted to a specific unit of information.

FILE: A collection of related records treated as a unit.

FILE MAINTENANCE: The periodic process of keeping a file up to date by adding, changing, or deleting data.

FILE PROTECTION RING: A plastic ring which can be attached to a reel of magnetic tape. When the ring is removed, the computer cannot erase or reuse the tape.

FLOAT: That interval between the time a transaction is made and the time the actual funds must be transferred to avoid interest charges or other penalties.

FLOPPY DISK: A small, inexpensive magnetic disk unit in which the individual platters are composed of vinyl plastic whose self-lubricating properties permit constant physical contact between the recording heads and the surface of the disk.

FLOWCHART: A sketch consisting of boxes of various specific shapes interconnected by arrows which provides an overview of the structure of a particular computer program.

FORTRAN: (FORmula TRANslation): A symbolic computer programming language used primarily for scientific and engineering applications in which the commands resemble algebraic equations.

FRAUD: A legal term which characterizes the intentional deception of an individual or a business entity for monetary gain.

FREE ELECTRONS: Those electrons occupying the outermost shell about the nucleus of an atom. Free electrons are loosely bound to the atom and hence are easily affected by external forces.

FULL ADDER: A computer circuit capable of adding three binary bits one of which is a "carry" from a previous addition.

GAME: An activity among two or more independent decision makers (people or computers) seeking to achieve known objectives in keeping with an artificially-imposed set of constraints.

GAME TREE: A schematic diagram displaying all the possible lines of play in a competitive game.

GENERAL-PURPOSE DIGITAL COMPUTER: A digital computer capable of solving a wide variety of unrelated numerical or logical problems.

GLITCH: A sudden, often unexplained, electronic surge which causes problems in an electronic device.

HALF ADDER: A computer circuit capable of adding two binary digits.

HARD COPY: A printed copy of machine output in a readable form.

HARDWARE: The physical equipment in a data processing center.

HAWTHORNE EFFECT: A principle of psychology first noticed in 1927 by a team of researchers at Western Electric in which the performance of an experimental subject under study is inadvertently enhanced by the extra attention he receives.

HEURISTIC: A directed, trial-and-error problem-solving method in which solutions are discovered by consistently evaluating the progress made toward the stated goal.

HOBBY COMPUTER: A small, inexpensive computer purchased for recreational and other home-oriented uses.

HOLLERITH CODE: A specific code used to represent alphanumeric data punched into a deck of cardboard cards.

HYBRID COMPUTER: A data processing device using both analog and digital data representation.

IDLE TIME: The time during which a particular computer is available but is not used.

INFORMATION: Data which has meaning to human beings.

INFORMATION RETRIEVAL: The methods used in recovering specific information from computer storage.

INPUT DATA: The user-supplied data to be processed.

INPUT-OUTPUT DEVICE: A computer module used to achieve man-machine communication.

INSTRUCTION: A statement calling for a specific computer operation.

INTEGRATED CIRCUIT: A combination of interconnected circuitry elements, usually highly compact, inseparably imprinted upon a continuous layer of material, called a substrate.

INTELLIGENCE: The ability to think and reason, draw logical inferences, recognize subtle patterns and interrelationships, and to respond appropriately to novel and unforeseen situations.

INTERCONTINENTAL BALLISTIC MISSILE (ICBM): Any offensive military rocket capable of delivering explosive warheads across continental distances.

INTERLEAVING: A multiprogramming technique in which any delays encountered in the processing of a particular program are filled with work on other programs stored within the computer's memory.

INTERNAL STORAGE: The addressable storage inside a digital computer directly accessible to the Central Processing Unit.

INTERNALLY STORED PROGRAM: A program whose commands are stored in the same locations as the data values so that the commands themselves can be altered as computation progresses.

INVERTER: A specific logic gate in which a binary one input produces a binary zero output and vice versa.

ITERATION LOOP: A repetitive computational procedure which starts with a user-supplied first guess of the desired result and uses it to obtain a better approximation, which in turn, is used to obtain a still better approximation. This process is continued until the desired accuracy is obtained.

JACQUARD LOOM: A weaving machine placed in operation by

Frenchman Joseph Jacquard near the beginning of the 19th century. Punched cards controlled the movements of the shuttles in order to produce tapestries of complicated design.

JOB: A collection of specified tasks constituting a unit of work for a computer.

KEYPUNCH MACHINE: A keyboard-actuated device which punches holes in a set of cardboard cards.

LEARNING PROGRAM: Any computer routine which gradually improves its performance by engaging in a large number of competitive trials against qualified opponents.

LIBRARY ROUTINE: A special-purpose program that is permanently stored within the computer for periodic reuse.

LIGHT PEN: A tiny cylindrical device used in sketching graphical computer instructions on the screen of a cathode-ray tube.

LINE PRINTER: A machine that prints a whole line of characters at one time under computer control.

LOCK CODE: A secret password provided by a programmer in a time-sharing system to prevent unauthorized tampering with his program. The computer will refuse any changes to the program unless the user supplies the correct lock code.

LOGIC GATE: An automatically controlled binary circuit which blocks or passes discrete electrical pulses in accordance with specific laws of logic.

LOOP: A sequence of instructions in a program which is executed repetitively until certain specified conditions are satisfied.

LOOPHOLE: An error or omission in software or hardware which allows the system's access controls to be circumvented.

LSI DEVICE: A modern integrated circuit of extreme complexity.

MACHINE LANGUAGE: A computer-coding language which can be understood directly by a particular machine without further translation.

MAGNETIC CARD: A special plastic card on which data can be stored by selectively polarizing portions of its flat, magnetizable surface.

MAGNETIC DISK: A flat circular plate coated with iron oxide on which data can be stored by selectively polarizing portions of the flat surface.

MAGNETIC DRUM: A rotating cylinder coated with ferromagnetic material. Binary digits are stored on its surface in the form of locally-magnetized subregions.

MAGNETIC INK: An ink infused with magnetic granules whose polarity can be detected by magnetic sensors.

MAGNETIC-INK CHARACTER RECOGNITION (MICR): A device which can decode alphanumeric characters printed with a special magnetic ink.

MAGNETIC TAPE: A plastic tape having a magnetic surface for storing data in a code of polarized spots.

MAIN FRAME: A computer system stripped of its peripheral devices.

MANAGEMENT-BY-EXCEPTION PROCEDURE: An automatic routine in which a digital computer makes and executes simple business decisions while highlighting those decisions which fall outside its preprogrammed norms.

MARK-SENSE CARD: A computer-readable card which is marked with an electrically conductive pencil.

MATHEMATICAL MODEL: A body of mathematical and logical relationships representing the important aspects of a particular process or the operation of a device.

MECHANIZATION: The use of machines to replace or simplify work previously accomplished by human workers.

MICROCOMPUTER: A small, self-contained digital computer with a low degree of accuracy and a small price tag.

MICROPROCESSOR: An electronic device consisting of one or more solid-state chips which can perform essentially all of the processing functions for a general-purpose or a special-purpose digital computer.

MICROSECOND: One millionth of a second.

MINI COMPUTER: A small, self-contained general-purpose desktop computer larger, faster and more versatile than a microcomputer.

MNEMONIC CODE: An easy-to-remember computer language code.

MODULE: A packaged functional hardware unit designed for convenient interconnection with other similar components.

MODULO CHECK CHARACTER: A special digital value built into the Universal Product Code used in detecting any erroneous readings made by the electronic scanners.

MONTE CARLO MODEL: A mathematical simulation procedure in which the statistical variability of a particular phenomenon is investigated by making a large number of simulations in which the input values are repeatedly varied in a random fashion.

MULTIPLEXING: The process of transmitting several simultaneous messages over a single communication channel.

MULTIPROGRAMMING: A technique for handling two or more independent programs simultaneously by overlapping or interleaving their execution.

NANOSECOND: One-billionth of a second.

NATURAL LANGUAGE: Any human language such as English, French, Chinese, etc.

NEUTRON: A neutral particle found in the nucleus of an atom.

NONVOLATILE STORAGE: Any storage medium which retains its stored contents in the absence of electrical power.

NUCLEAR WARHEAD: Any explosive projectile deriving its energy from fission or fusion.

NUMERICAL ANALYSIS: The conversion of a complex problem into a series of simple mathematical steps, suitable for processing by a digital computer.

OFFLINE MODULES: Those items of equipment not under the direct control of the computer's Central Processing Unit.

ONE-TIME PAD: A set of privacy transformations or codewords to be used only once and then discarded.

OPERATING SYSTEM: An organized collection of software that controls the overall operations of a digital computer.

OPERATIONS RESEARCH: A special mathematical science devoted to carrying out complicated operations with the maximum practical efficiency.

OPTICAL CHARACTER READER: A light-sensitive device that identifies alphanumeric characters by sensing their shapes.

OPTIMIZATION PROCEDURE: Any well-defined mathematical technique for finding the smallest or the largest value of a bounded mathematical function.

OR-GATE: A computer circuit containing two switches whose output is a binary one if either or both of the inputs are one.

ORTHOFERRITE: A naturally-occurring substance composed of alternate, snakelike regions of opposite magnetic polarity.

OUTPUT: The final result of a sequence of data processing operations.

PACKING DENSITY: The average number of electronic components per unit area or unit volume.

PAPER-TAPE READER: Any device capable of translating the holes in a perforated paper tape into a machine-processable form.

PARALLEL ADDITION: Summing a pair of multidigit binary numbers by the simultaneous operation of a set of adjacent full adders.

PARITY CHECKING: An automatic error-detection procedure which uses extra checking bits that are carried along with the numerical bits being processed.

PATTERN RECOGNITION DEVICE: Any computerized module

which can distinguish among the members of a predetermined set of abstract or realistic symbols.

PERIPHERAL EQUIPMENT: The input-output devices and the auxiliary storage units in a data processing center.

PHYSICAL SECURITY: The use of locks, guards, badges, and similar administrative measures to control access to the equipment in a data processing center.

PICOSECOND: One-thousandth of a nanosecond, i.e., one-trillionth of a second.

PIGGY-BACK ENTRY: Unauthorized access that is gained to a computer system via another user's legitimate connection.

PLAINTEXT: A term used by encryption experts to denote an ordinary message in its original meaningful form.

POINT OF SALE TERMINAL: A device that reads merchandise tags, verifies credit, completes sale calculations, and permits an immediate review of the merchandise items remaining in inventory.

POPULATION EXPLOSION: A term used in popularized publications to describe the recent dramatic increase in the number of human beings inhabiting the earth.

POSITIONAL NOTATION SYSTEM: A numeration system in which a digit's shape determines its valuation and its position within the string of digits determines its place value.

PRECISION GUIDED MUNITIONS (SMART WEAPONS): Destructive projectiles which home in on their targets by using on-board sensors coupled with electronic microprocessing devices.

PRIMARY STORAGE: The main memory unit of a digital computer. The primary storage region usually consists of a high-speed direct-access unit with moderate storage capacity.

PRINTED CIRCUITS: Electronic circuits printed or vacuum deposited on thin insulating sheets.

PRINTER: A computer output device capable of imprinting alphanumeric characters on paper.

PRIVACY: Those parts of a person's life and personality he chooses to shield from public scrutiny..

PROCESSING UNIT: The mechanism used by a computer for altering the input quantities in accordance with the program instructions.

PRODUCTIVITY: A measure of the amount of useful work accomplished per man-hour.

PROGRAM: A man-supplied set of instructions provided to a computer in a machine-readable form.

PROGRAMMER: A professional technician who codes instructions in a language amenable to computer solution.

PROGRAMMING LANGUAGE: Any well-defined language used in preparing instructions for computer execution.

PROTON: A positively charged particle found in the nucleus of an atom.

PULSE: A sharp voltage change.

PUNCHED CARD: A cardboard card used in data processing operations in which tiny holes at hundreds of individual locations denote numerical values and alphabetic codes.

PUNCHED PAPER TAPE: A long strip of paper in which holes are punched to record alphanumeric information for computer processing.

RANDOM ACCESS DEVICE: Any computer storage device in which the time required to retrieve a particular data value is not significantly affected by its physical location.

RANDOM NUMBERS: A patternless sequence of digits generated by a computer for use in Monte Carlo simulations.

RAW DATA: Data which has not yet been processed or reduced.

READ-ONLY MEMORY (ROM): A memory in which the information is stored at the time of manufacture. The information is readily available to the user, but it can be modified only with great difficulty.

READ-WRITE HEAD (RECORDING HEAD): A tiny electro-magnet used to record information on a thin, magnetizable film.

REAL-TIME PROCESSING: Data processing operations in which the computed results are received so quickly they can be used to influence the operation of the process being simulated.

RECORDING HEAD (READ-WRITE HEAD): A tiny electro-magnet used to record information on a thin, magnetizable film.

REGISTER: A high-speed device used by the Central Processing Unit for temporary storage of data values during processing.

RELAY (ELECTROMECHANICAL RELAY): A magnetically operated switch.

RELIABILITY: The quality of freedom from failure. The reliability of a system is usually expressed as the probability that a failure will not occur in a given amount of time or a given amount of useage.

REMOTE TERMINAL: An array of input-output devices connected to a distant computer by means of telephone lines or other communication channels.

ROBOT: A practical or an experimental machine equipped with sensors and feedback control mechanisms which is intended to perform complex tasks usually thought to require human intelligence and dexterity.

ROUTINE: A set of machine instructions for carrying out a specific processing operation.

RUN: A single, complete execution of a computer program.

SCANNER: Any optical device which can recognize a specific set of visual symbols.

SECRET PASSWORD: A carefully-guarded string of alphanumeric characters known only to certain authorized personnel. Those who know the secret password can use it to gain entry into a time-sharing system or to gain access to certain secure data files.

SECURE KERNEL: A well-defined segment of the system software which is carefully protected by specific, often elaborate, access controls.

SECURITY. The methods adopted for making valuable property or private information safe from theft or harm.

SELF-CORRECTING CODE: A numerical coding system in which transmission errors are automatically detected and corrected.

SEMANTICS: A branch of linguistics concerned with the study of the meanings of words and speech forms and their historical evolution.

SEMICONDUCTOR: A substance, such as selenium, which normally insulates against the flow of electricity but which under certain conditions can be made to conduct the flow.

SEMI RANDOM ACCESS: A computer storage medium such as a magnetic disk or drum in which the computer must wade through a small portion of the values being held in storage in order to reach the particular one it needs.

SEQUENTIAL ACCESS DEVICE (SERIAL ACCESS DEVICE): A computer storage unit in which a stored quantity can be retrieved only by passing through a large number of the other similar quantities being held in storage.

SENSOR: A device capable of measuring the properties of the local environment.

SERIAL ACCESS DEVICE (SEQUENTIAL ACCESS DEVICE): A computer storage unit in which a stored quantity can be retrieved only by passing through a large number of the other similar quantities being held in storage.

SERIAL ADDITION: The repeated use of the same full adder to sum a pair of multidigit binary numbers.

SIMULATION: Computer modeling of real-world problems using time-sequential methods which resemble the functioning system itself.

SLIDE RULE: A hand-operated computing device consisting of a ruler with a sliding center section; both of which exhibit logarithmic scales.

SMART WEAPONS (PRECISION GUIDED MUNITIONS): Destructive projectiles which home in on their targets by using on-board sensors coupled with electronic microprocessing devices.

SOFTWARE: All the instructions and documents needed for guiding the operation of a computer.

SOFTWARE ENCRYPTION: The encoding or decoding of computerized data using programming techniques rather than hardware devices such as scramblers.

SOLID-STATE DEVICE: A non-vacuum electronic device fashioned from semi-conducting materials which performs some of the functions of a vacuum tube.

SOURCE LANGUAGE: A language similar to the user's professional or business language which makes it easier for him to communicate with the computer. FORTRAN, BASIC, COBOL, etc., are source languages.

SPECIAL-PURPOSE DIGITAL COMPUTER: A digital computer capable of solving only a few selected types of numerical or logical problems.

STORAGE CAPACITY: The maximum quantity of information that can be retained in a particular storage device.

STORAGE DEVICE: A device that can accept information, hold it, and deliver it on demand at a later time.

STORAGE HIERARCHY: A computer design concept in which the computer's memory is arranged in stairstep fashion with high-speed, low-capacity primary storage units supplemented by lower-speed, higher-capacity auxiliary and external devices.

STORED-PROGRAM COMPUTER: A digital computer that stores instructions in memory and can be programmed to change its own instructions and subsequently execute them in their altered form.

SUBROUTINE: A subprogram, essentially complete in itself, which is used by the main program one or more times in the process of computation.

SUPERVISORY PROGRAM: A machine-language program stored inside a computer that keeps the over-all data-processing system operating at nearly peak efficiency. The supervisory program automatically schedules the various processing and input-output functions and it optimally transfers stored quantities from one internal location to another.

SYMBOLIC LANGUAGE: Any computer programming language in which the commands resemble scientific equations or business arithmetic.

SYNCHRONOUS COMPUTER: A digital computer that requires the same amount of time to complete each processing operation regardless of its intrinsic complexity.

SYNTAX: The structure of the expressions in a language and the rules governing this structure.

SYSTEMS ANALYSIS: The orgnized step-by-step study of detailed procedures for the collection, manipulation, and evaluation of data about an organization for the purpose of determining what must be done and how it can best be accomplished.

SYSTEM SECURITY: An organized body of technological safeguards and managerial procedures which are applied to computer hardware, software and data in order to protect company assets and individual privacy.

TAPE DRIVE: A device that moves a magnetic tape past the read-write heads at the proper speed.

TELEPROCESSING: The use of telephone lines to transmit data and commands between remote locations and a data-processing center or between two computers.

TERMINAL: Any device in a data processing system or communication network through which data can enter or leave.

THROUGHPUT: A measure of a system's efficiency; the rate at which useful work can be accomplished.

TIME-SHARING SYSTEM: A system in which a computer's time is sequentially apportioned among several different input-output terminals. Characteristically, the response time is so short that the computer seems dedicated to each user.

TRANSISTOR: A small, solid-state semiconducting device, composed principally of germanium or silicon, which performs dynamic functions such as amplification or switching.

TRAPDOOR: A breach created intentionally in an electronic data processing system for the purpose of later collecting, altering, or destroying data.

TRAPDOOR CODE: A specific data encryption method whose resistance to decryption is based on the mathematical property that it is remarkably difficult to find the inverse (reversal) of certain relatively simple mathematical operations.

TRIGONOMETRIC FUNCTION: The ratio of the lengths of two of the sides of a right triangle.

TROJAN HORSE: A computer program that is apparently or actually useful and contains a trapdoor.

TRUTH TABLE: A systematic tabulation associated with a binary circuit listing all possible combinations of input values and indicating, for each combination, the resulting outputs.

TURN-AROUND TIME: The interval between the submittal of a computer job and the time it is returned in finished form to the user.

UNCONDITIONAL TRANSFER: A transfer of control in a computer program which is not dependent on the outcome of a previous computation.

UNIT-RECORD SYSTEM: An accounting system in which each separate business transaction is recorded on a single card.

UNIVERSAL IDENTIFIER: A standard multidigit number assigned to a particular individual to be used in establishing his or her identity.

UNIVERSAL PRODUCT CODE: A specific binary code used in grocery stores and other retail establishments whereby the ten decimal digits are represented by patterns of black and white strips that can be decoded by a computer equipped with optical scanners.

USER: Anyone who utilizes the services of a data processing center.

VENDING MACHINE SYNDROME: A systematic shift in moral judgements experienced by those individuals who feel that cheating a machine or a large organization is not the same as cheating an individual.

VERIFICATION MACHINE: A device, similar in appearance and operation to a keypunch machine which is used to check the accuracy of a previously punched deck.

VIDEODISC: A plastic platter resembling a phonograph record which uses low-intensity laser beams to store visual materials to be displayed on a television screen.

VOICEPRINT: The numerical or graphical description of the time varying frequency and amplitude of the human voice when articulating a selected sequence of sounds.

VOLATILE: A storage system in which the information vanishes if the power is turned off or temporarily interrupted.

WORD: A group of characters which have one addressable location and are treated as a single unit by the computer.

ZERO: A special symbol with no intrinsic numerical value used for spacing in positional-notation systems.

ZONE BITS: Binary bits stored within a digital computer which are used in conjunction with the numerical bits to represent alphabetic characters and special symbols.

ZONE PUNCH: A punch in a Hollerith card in the 11, 12, or 0 row. The zone punches are used in conjunction with the numeric punches in the coding of alphabetic or special characters.

INDEX

Abacus, 365, 371
ABM, 349–350, 371
ABM treaty, 369
Absolute accuracy, 348
Access
  controls, 175
  limits, 173, 371
  time, 95, 97, 371
Accumulator, 45, 371
Adder unit, 45, 371
Adleman, Leonard, 180, 370
Affirmative action, 207
Aiken, Howard H., 35, 367
Alden, John M., 368
ALGOL, 368
Algorithm, 231, 371
Allen, Brandt, 164
Alphanumeric characters, 35, 59, 61, 69, 89,
  93, 95, 371
Altair 8800, 19–20, 369
Ambiguity and context, 239
American way of debt, 321
Analog computer, 3–4, 366–367, 371
Analyst, 371
Analytical engine, 371
And-gate, 371
Animal intelligence, 224
Animals use of language, 225
Analytical engine, 366
Anti ballistic missiles, 349–350, 369, 371
A point of sale remote terminal, 320
Apple II, 17, 19
Arab-Israeli Wars, 355
Arbib, Michael A., 117
Armer, Paul, 140, 147, 202, 327
Arms control agreements, 349
Arnhem bridge, 131
Arrest records, 145–146
Artificial intelligence, 226, 228, 238, 248–
  250, 371
Asynchronous computer, 371
Atom bomb, 345
Audio response unit, 371–372
Auditing, 164
Automated reservation systems, 270
Automatic, 372
Automatically programmed tools, 260
Automation, 257–260, 266, 269–271, 273–
  274, 277, 372
Auxiliary storage, 79–80, 86–89, 97, 372

Babbage, Charles, 227, 366
Background program, 372
Backus, John, 37, 368
Balance of terror, 347, 372
Bankruptcy, 138, 322
Bank wire, 316
Bardeen, John, 368
Barr, Robert D., 213
Barter, 309
BASIC, 37–38, 40, 42, 368, 372
BASIC desk, 15
Batch processing, 64, 372
Battle for the Arnhem Bridge, 130
Beizer, Barbara, 296
Benson, Bernard S., 134
Bernstein, Alex, 232
Bernstein, Jeremy, 30, 36
Binary
  arithmetic, 28–29, 367, 372
  code, 57, 285
  coded decimals, 32–34
  notation, 31–32
  numeration, 4, 29
  pulses, 61
  pulse train, 29–30, 35
Biorhythm charts, 181
Biosphere, 335, 372
Bistable denice, 372
Bistable switches, 4, 29–30
BIT, 372
Bitzer, Donald, 197
Black box, 372
Black plague, 335
Blitzkrieg, 352
Boche, Ray, 293, 295
Boddy, Jack, 65
Boehm, Barry W., 103
Boole, George, 366
Boolean algebra, 372
Barodin, A., 202
Borrowed voice computer, 72–73, 371–372
Bouchon, Basile, 365
Boyd, Robert, 342
Brain, 127, 226–227, 243
Branch banks, 316, 323
Branch points, 115, 189, 372
Brandeis, Louis, 136, 366–367
Brattain, Walter, 368
Breach, 373
Brennan, Edward J., Jr., 142

Briggs, Henry, 365
Brooks, Frederick P., Jr., 103, 108, 111, 113
Brooks, Warren T., 265
Brute Force
  approach, 373
  procedures, 177
Bubble
  detector, 90–91
  eraser, 90–91
  generator, 90–91
  memory, 73, 88–91, 97, 370, 373
Buffer, 88–92, 373
Bug, 373
Bugs Bunny, 30
Bush, Vannevar, 344, 367
Byte, 373

CAI
  costs, 199, 202
  routines, 196
  student response, 205–207
  systems, 198
  terminals, 195
Calculator, 373
Calvin, John, 259
Cancer studies, 130
Carbon chemistry chauvinism, 226
Card
  punch, 373
  punch machine, 60
  reader, 61, 373
  sorting, 366, 373
  sorting machines, 60
Carter, Bruce A., 201
Cash register, 283
Cash transactions, 320
Cashier labor, 290–291
Cashless society, 317–318, 329, 373
Cathode-ray
  tube, 373
  tube plot, 375
  tube plotters, 69–70
Census tabulations, 57
Central processing unit, 43–44, 46, 79, 373
Chain printer, 67–68
Chalk-mark notation, 373
Character, 373
Character reader, 374
Charged couple device, 91, 97, 374
Check-guaranteed terminal, 317
Checkers, 231–233
Checks, 326
Chess, 231
  playing machine, 365
  program, 233, 368
Chief programmer, 116
Chief programmer teams, 115–116

Circuit, 374
Clarke, Arthur, 55, 70
Clayre, Alasdair, 275
Club of Rome, 336–337, 341, 343, 345, 369
Clock pulse circuit, 44, 374
Coal mine workers, 276–277
Codebook, 374
Code reviews, 117
Coding errors, 113
Columbus, Christopher, 344
Communication link, 374
Computer
  based, 164
  clubs, 20
  con artists, 161–162
  costs, 79, 90
  crime, 181
  criminals, 159
  definition, 3
  errors, 33
  fraud, 159, 167, 173
  murder, 182
  program, 38
  programmers, 166
  related crimes, 167–168
  sales, 15
  speed, 9–12, 35
  translations, 240
  word, 374
Computer-aided
  design, 65, 67, 374
  instruction, 189–190, 192, 194–195, 197,
    200, 202, 204–205, 207, 209–211, 213,
    215, 369, 374
Computerized
  checkers, 232
  chess, 232–233
  data files, 146
Comrie, Leslie John, 367
Conditional transfer, 374
Console, 374
Constitutional rights, 136
Control, 42, 44–45
Control unit, 374
Conversational language, 374
Cook, Lawrence H., Jr., 115
Core
  rings, 82–83, 89, 368, 375
  storage, 80–81, 375
Cost of computation, 6–7, 9, 11–12
Cost per bit, 95
Costs of crime, 167
Courseware, 196–197, 204, 375
  costs, 202–205
  effectiveness, 207
Credit
  cards, 149, 312–315, 320, 326–327, 375
  investigations, 131
  verifications, 182

Crichton, Michael, 159
Crime losses, 166
Criminal data files, 145
CRT plot, 375
Cryptanalysis, 375
Crypotgraphic keys, 178, 181
Cybernetics, 375
Cypher, 375
Cyphertext, 176

Da Costa, Sidney A., 327
D'Agasto, Arlene, 301
Daily surveillance sheet, 150–151
Darrach, Brad, 221
Data, 375
  bank, 375
  encryption, 176, 178
  encryption standard, 176–180, 370, 375
  processing, 375
  processing center, 11, 13, 375
  processing industry, 103
  security, 160, 175, 375
  word, 375
Debit cards, 329
Debugging, 375
Decimal
  digit, 375
  notation, 29–31
  system, 375
Decryption, 176, 178, 180, 376
De Forest, Lee, 366
Dendrites, 226
Diagnostic messages, 376
Die set principle, 60
Difference engine, 366, 376
Diffie, Whitfield, 177
Digital computer, 3–4, 376
Digitize, 376
Dinapoli, Rocco R., 206
Diode, 376
Direct access device, 376
Disk
  pack, 89, 376
  storage device, 376
Distributed processing, 376
Donovan, A. F., 270
"Double blind" experiments, 210
Downtime, 376
Dreyfus, Hubert L., 239, 248
Drill and practice method, 192
Drum storage, 376
Dynamic addressing, 370

Eccles, W. H., 367
Eckert, J. Presper, 367

Economy-of-scale concept, 197, 376
EDSAC, 368
Edison, Thomas, 344, 366
Education costs, 199
Educational revolution, 189
Edwards, Kenneth, 294
Effectors, 260–261, 376
Electromagnet, 62
Electromechanical relay, 376, 384
Electron, 376
Electronic
  checkout, 283–284, 291, 300
  embezzlement, 162
  funds transfer, 316
  funds transfer system, 176, 309, 315, 317,
    320, 322, 324, 327, 329, 377
  money, 317–321, 324–325, 328
  scanners, 290, 295
  tutor, 189
  tutoring, 190–191, 213
Electronics, 377
Embezzlement, 163–164, 181, 377
Employment level, 267–268
Encrypting, 180
Encryption, 176, 178, 180, 377
Englberger, Joseph F., 264
ENIAC, 6, 28–29, 35–36, 79, 82, 346, 377
Error, 377
Evolution, 127
Experimental experiences, 194
Exponential growth, 377
External storage, 79–80, 92–93, 97, 377

Fabun, Dan, 263
Fair credit reporting act of 1970, 136–138,
  369
Fallacy of the first step, 248
Fanning, Patricia, 207
Farm population, 276–277
Fed wire, 316
Federal data banks, 132
Federal data center, 134, 369, 377
Feedback control, 263, 336, 338, 377
Ferdinand, King, 310, 344
Field, 377
File, 377
  maintenance, 377
  protection ring, 169, 170, 377
First strike, 347–348, 351
Fisher, John, 316
Fleming, J. A., 366
Flip-flop circuit, 367
Float, 377
Floppy disk, 93–95, 97, 370, 378
Flowchart, 39–42, 378
Flowcharting symbols, 39
Food additives, 130

Ford Foundation, 129
Foreman, Carol, 297
Forrester, Jay, 336–337
FORTRAN, 37, 106–109, 368, 378
Fraud, 378
Free electrons, 378
Full adder, 378
Function-oriented design philosophy, 28–29, 40
Functions of a digital computer, 42–43

Galbraith, Kenneth, 165
Gallois, Pierre, 345
Game, 378
    playing, 228
    playing machines, 228
    tree, 229–233, 249, 378
Garbage in-garbage out, 342
Gardner, Beatrise, 225
Gardner, Martin, 234–237
Gardner, Robert, 225
General problem solver, 222
General purpose computer, 5
General purpose digital computer, 378
Genes, 127
Geopolitics of computers, 357
Germanium, 84
Giant brains, 226
Gibson, Joseph L., 141
Glitch, 378
Gold, 309–310
Goldstein, Robert, 143
Goldstine, Herman, 28
Gomberg, Judy, 238
Gordon, Lincoln, 343
Gotlieb, C.C., 202
Government dossiers, 132
Green revolution, 128–131
Greenlee, Blake, 180
Griswold versus Connecticut, 134
Guard band, 285
Gunter, Edmund, 365

Haberman, Alan, 296
Hal, 70, 72–73
Half adder, 378
Hanna, Robert B., 368
Hard copy, 378
Hard sectored disks, 94–95
Hardware, 103–104, 194, 197, 378
Hardware costs, 104, 202–204, 292
Hawthorne effect, 209–210, 367, 378
Health-related item code, 299
Hellman, Martin, 177
Heppenheimer, Tom, 342

Hermann, J. M., 366
Herzog, Major General Claim, 356
Heuristic, 378
Heuristic program, 231–232
Hexapawn, 234–238
High speed printers, 67
High technology, 276
Hobby computers, 16–17, 20, 369, 379
Hollerith, Hermann, 57, 60, 366
Hollerith cards, 57, 59, 92, 379
Howard, Grover A., 300
Hybrid computer, 379

ICBM's, 348–350, 379
Idle time, 379
Individualized instruction, 189, 191, 200–201
Industrial revolution, 96, 257
Industrial robots, 260–261, 264
Information, 243, 379
    machine, 3
    retrevial, 379
    storage, 127
    theory, 368
ILLIAC4, 243–244, 370
Input data, 379
Input-output, 42
    device, 379
    media, 56
Installment buying, 315, 322, 323
Instruction, 379
Integrated circuit, 369, 379
Intelligence, 223, 379
    experts, 130
    tests, 245
Intelligent machines, 221–222
Interactive computer graphics, 67
Intercontinental ballistic missile, 379, 347–350
Interleaving, 379
Internal storage, 379
Internally stored programs, 28–29, 35–36, 379
Inventory control, 298
Inverter, 379
I.Q. tests, 224, 245
Isabella, Queen, 344
Iteration loop, 379
Ives, Joseph C., 344

Jacquard, Joseph, 57–58, 365
Jacquard loom, 379
Jastrow, Robert, 226
Job, 380
    loss fears, 294, 300
    quality, 273

Johnson administration, 134
Jordan, F. W., 367

Kahn, Herman, 257, 265, 368
Karger, Paul, 171
Karman, Theodore von, 27
Kearsley, Greg P., 198
Kemeny, John, 38, 369
Kempelen, Baron von, 228, 233, 365
Kennedy, John F., 258
Keypunch machine, 60, 380
Kilby, J. S., 369
Kincaid, Marshal, 368
Kling, Bob, 326
Kolata, Gina Bari, 179
Konheim, Alan, 179
Korean war, 126
Korody, Paul, 297–298

Language comprehension programs, 240, 242
Language translation, 228, 238–239
Large scale integrated circuits, 6
Laser, 287–288
    scanner, 214, 287–289, 292
"Launch on warning" concept, 350
Leachim, 196
Learning
    programs 233, 380
    machine 234–237
    robot, 234, 236–237
Lederer, Betty, 296
Less-cash/less-check society, 318
Library routine, 380
Light pen, 65–66, 194, 369, 380
Limits to growth, 336–344, 369
Line printers, 68, 380
Linowes, David F., 150
Lipner, Steven, 171
Lock and key terminal, 175–176, 370
Lock code, 380
Logarithms, 365
Logic gate, 380
Loop, 38, 380
Loophole, 380
LSI
    circuit, 6–9, 369
    device, 368, 380
Luddites, 257, 273, 365
Lynn, Harvey, Jr., 345

Machine
    intelligence, 242
    language, 45, 380

Machines that learn, 233–234, 236–237
Magnetic
    bubble, 88, 90–91
    card, 380
    core rings, 80, 86–87
    cores, 368
    disk, 88–89, 97, 380
    drum, 86, 88–89, 97, 368, 380
    ink, 380
    ink character recognition, 381
    MICR, 381
    tape, 61–64, 93, 95, 97, 146–147
Main frame, 381
Major loop, 90
Malthus, Thomas, 335–337, 365
Management-by-exception procedure, 381
Manipulator arms, 261
Manual data files, 143
Mark I, 5, 35, 367
Mark-sense card, 381
Mathematical Model, 381
Mauchly, John W., 367
Maverick missile, 355
McWilliams, Erik, 199
Mechanical
    plotters, 69, 71
    printers, 67
    slavery, 277
Mechanization, 260, 271, 273–274, 276–277, 381
Medical records, 130
Medium of exchange, 309–310
Mercury delay line, 368
Microcomputer, 16–17, 19–21, 369, 381
Microminiturization, 5
Microprocessor, 353, 370, 381
Microsecond, 381
Military expenditures, 346–347
Military manpower, 347
Mills, Harlan D., 103
Minicomputer, 11, 14–15, 21, 198, 260, 369, 381
Minor loops, 90–91
Minsky, Marvin, 222, 226, 237, 245–246
Mnemonic code, 381
Modular construction, 46
Modularized packaging, 297
Module, 381
Modulo check character, 285–286, 381
Monetary systems, 309
Monetary transactions, 319
Money, 309, 330
Monte Carlo
    model, 381
    techniques, 367
Morgan, Edward P., 341
Morris, Robert, 179
Morrison, Elting E., 96
Morrison, Philip, 350, 353, 356

Morse, Samuel, 366
Morton, Michael, 201, 204, 211
Mosmann, Charles, 201, 210
Multics system, 170–171
Multiplexing, 381
Multiprocessing, 369
Multiprogramming, 64, 381

Nanosecond, 382
Napier, John, 365
National Crime Information Center, 135,
    147–148
National Drug Code, 299
National health insurance program, 150
National Security Agency, 179
Natural language, 382
Nazi death camps, 145
Neutron, 382
Newton, Isaac, 365
Nonrenewable resources, 342
Nonvolatile storage, 382
Nordheim, Lothar, 28
Norris, William C., 358–359
Noyce, Robert N., 17
Nuclear submarine, 350, 353
Nuclear warhead, 382
Number system character, 285
Numeric punches, 57
Numerical bits, 33–34
Numerical analysis, 382

Oettinger, A. G., 191
Offline modules, 382
One-time pad, 382
Operating systems, 172, 382
Operation code, 45
Operations research, 382
Optical character reader, 382
Optical scanner, 283
Optimization procedure, 382
Or-gate, 382
Orthoferrite, 90–91, 382
Output, 382

Packing density, 85–86, 90, 382
Paper money, 309–311
Paper-tape reader, 382
Paper trail, 164
Papert, Seymour, 191
Parallel addition, 382
Parallel processing, 33
Parity checking, 33–35, 285, 382

Parker, Donn, 163–164
Parkinson's law, 270
Pascal, Blase, 365
Pattern recognition, 228, 245, 382
Peccei, Aurelio, 341
Performance mode, 228
Peripheral equipment, 383
Perils of complexity, 172
Personal checks, 311, 313, 320
Pet 2001, 17, 19, 370
Peters, Harold J., 199, 204
Philbrick, G. A., 367
Phoenix, 370
Photo-cell reader, 61
Photelectric sensors, 61
Physical security, 383
Pickering, Williams H., 344
Picosecond, 383
Piggy-back entry, 383
Placebos, 209–210
Plaintext, 176, 383
Planimeter, 366
Plato, 197, 199, 202, 204–207, 369
Platzek, R. C., 369
Poe, Edgar Allen, 228
Point-of-sale remote terminals, 316
Point of sale terminal, 383
Population explosion, 38, 335–337
Positional notation, 31
Positional notation systems, 29
Positional system, 383
Powers, James, 366
Precision guided munitions, 383, 385
Preore, Andrew Del, 179
Price Marking, 290, 295
Primary storage, 79–80, 86, 97, 243–244, 383
Primary workers, 271
Prime numbers, 180, 370
"Principia," 365
Printed circuits, 383
Printer, 383
Printwheel, 67–68
Privacy
    abuses, 135
    Act of 1974, 137–138, 140–142, 370
    and the law, 136
    costs, 142–144
    intrusion, 125
    invasion, 298–299
    needs, 125, 131
    regulations, 140
    rights, 136, 149
    worries, 327–328
Problem solving, 228, 245
Processing, 42, 44–45
Processing unit, 383
Product ciphers, 176
Productivity, 383

Program, 383
  coding, 105
  librarian, 116
  maintenance, 107
  specifications, 105
Programmer, 383
Programmed machine tools, 260, 368
Programmer efficiency, 115
Programming languages, 37, 41, 384
Protecting your right of privacy, 139
Protestant work ethic, 259
Proton, 384
Pulse, 384
Pulse trains, 44
Punched cards, 55–59, 92, 97, 366, 384
Punched paper tapes, 58, 384
"Push-button" language, 225

Quevedo, Leonardo Torresy, 366

Random access, 89, 92, 97, 384
Random numbers, 384
Raphael, Bertram, 239, 262
Raw data, 384
Read-only memory (ROM), 384
Read-write head, 62, 89, 384
Real time processing, 14, 384
Recording head, 384
Red Dye Number 2, 130
Register, 384
Reifer, Donald J., 357
Reiner, Kip, 16
Relay, 384
Reliability, 384
Remote teleprocessing, 11
Remote terminal, 13, 64, 176, 384
Richardson, Elliot, 341
Rickover, Vice Admiral Hyman, 359
Rifkin, Mark, 163, 167, 169
Right of Privacy, The, 136, 366
Rivest, Ronald L., 180, 370
Roberts, Edward, 19
Robot, 196, 221, 228, 234, 260–261, 263–264, 384
Rockefeller Foundation, 129
Rockart, John, 201, 204, 210–211
Roosevelt, Franklin D., 344
Rose, Sandford, 318
Routine, 384
Run, 385

Sagan, Carl, 125, 224
SAGE program, 107
Sagger anti-tank missiles, 356

SALT agreements, 350
SALT treaty, 369–370
Samuel, Arthur, 233
Sanders, Donald H., 201
Sandiford, Peter J., 237
Scanner revolution, 300
Scanners, 287, 385
Schickard, Wilhelm, 365
Schneider, Jerry, 159, 161–162, 168, 175
Schwartz, Jules I., 107, 117
Scott, Morton S., 210
Second Industrial Revolution, The, 96
Secondary workers, 271
Secret password, 168–171, 385
Secure kernel, 172–173, 385
Secure machines, 170
Security, 385
Seiko, 261
Self-correcting code, 385
Semantics, 239, 385
Semiconductor, 385
Semi-random access, 88, 97, 385
Sense wire, 82
Sensors, 260, 385
Sequential access, 93
Sequential access device, 385
Serial access device, 385
Serial addition, 385
Shaky, 221, 263–264
Shamir, Adi, 180, 370
Shannon, Claude E., 232, 368
al-Shazli, General Sa'ad, 355
Shields and Yarnell, 261
Shockley, William, 368
Shrinkage control, 290–291
Space shuttle, 65–67
Silicon, 84
Silvey Ted, 260
Simon, Herbert, 222, 267, 274
Simulation, 338–340, 351–352, 369, 385
  mode, 228
  and games, 192, 194
Skinner, B. F., 191
Skinner box, 191
Slide rule, 385
Smart weapons, 353–356, 383, 385
Smith, Adam, 309
Smith, David L., 318
Snoopy calendars, 181
Sobczak, Thomas V., 293, 295, 299
Social Security numbers, 135
Soft sectored disks, 94
Software, 103–104, 111, 113, 386

  costs, 104, 107, 182, 202–204
  development, 104–105
  encryption, 386
  engineering, 105
  maintenance, 104

Solid state
  devices, 6, 9, 82, 84–86, 95, 97, 203, 386
  memory, 82–83
  switches, 44, 84–85
Solzhenitsyn, Alexander, 150
Source language, 386
Soviet data processing, 357
Space Odyssey 2001, 70
Space war, 182
Special-purpose digital computer, 386
Special-purpose computer, 5
Speech recognition, 73
Star Trek, 20
Stein, Gertrude, 309
Stell, Jim, 294
Stepford Wives, The, 261
Stetten, Kenneth, 197
Steward, Douglas, 283
Stibitz, George, 367
Storage, 42, 46, 79
  capacity, 95, 386
  device, 386
  media, 95
  hierarchy, 79, 95, 386
Stored program computer, 386
Strategic Arms Limitation Treaty, 350
Stratified access, 170
Streeter, Donald N., 250
Structured
  programming, 114
  walkthroughs, 116–117
Subroutine, 386
Substitution cipher, 176
Supermarket
  computerization, 284
  vending machines, 301–302
Supervisory program, 386
Suppes, Patrick, 189
Sutherland, Ivan E., 369
Symbolic
  language, 386
  logic, 366
  programming languages, 37
Synchronous computer, 44, 386
Syntax, 239, 387
System security, 387
Systems analysis, 387

Tactical war, 352
Tall center bar, 285
Tape drive, 387
Tape transport speeds, 62
Tauschek, Gustav, 367
Taylor, Charles, 243
Taylor, Edwin, 193
Technology, 342, 357
Technology creep, 348–349
Teleoperators, 261

Teleprocessing, 387
Teller, Edward, 27
Terminal, 387
Test cases, 106
Thermionic emission phenomenon, 366
Thinking machine, 227, 242
Thomson, William, 366
Threshold principle of magnetization, 81
Throughput, 387
TICCIT, 197
Tic-Tac-Toe, 229–231, 233
Tiger Teams at Zarf, 171
Time sharing, 11, 13–15, 37, 64, 134, 145
  176, 182, 260, 369
Time sharing systems, 387
Tingergen, Jan, 343
Toffler, Alvin, 259
Tonge, Fred, 248
Top-down design, 115
Tow anti-tank weapon, 355
TRADIC, 368
Transaction costs, 320
Transistor, 6–7, 82, 84, 368, 387
Transposition cipher, 176
Trapdoor, 171, 387
  code, 180, 370, 387
  functions, 180
Trignometric functions, 387
Trojan horse, 387
Truth table, 387
TRW Credit Data, 140, 142, 182
Turing, Alan, 5, 242, 367
Turing's test, 242, 244
Turn around time, 387
Turner, James, 298
Tutorial method, 192

Unconditional transfer, 388
Underrings, 290
Unemployment, 258, 265–268, 277, 294,
  300, 368
Unicorn memory system, 243–244
Unimate 4000, 261
Unit record
  concept, 59
  system, 388
Universal identifier, 135, 388
Universal product code, 284–289, 293, 297,
  299, 370, 388
User, 388
User identification methods, 173, 175

Vacuum sensors, 62
Vacuum triode, 366
Vacuum tubes, 6–7, 79, 83

Vandalism, 82
Van Tassel, Dennie, 150
Vending machine syndrome, 161, 388
Verification machine, 388
Videodisc, 213–214, 370, 388
Voiceprint, 388
Voice recognition systems, 174
Voice synthesizer, 73
Volatile, 388
Volatile storage, 90, 92, 97
Volatile storage media, 86
von Leibnitz, Gottfried Wilhelm, 365
von Neumann, John, 27, 29, 35–36, 41, 43, 46, 368
von Neumann's corners, 27
Newman, Joseph, 190
Vyssatsky, V. S., 109

Walker, Paul F., 350, 353, 356
Warren, Samuel, 136, 366
Weiner, Norbert, 257, 265, 368
Weizenbaum, Joseph, 145, 193, 240, 345
White collar crime, 159, 165

Wilde, Oscar, 277
Williams, F. C., 368
Winograd, Terry, 241, 245, 247
Wire brush reader, 61
Wireguided missiles, 355
Wolcas, J. A., 211
Walitzer, Peter A., 211–212
Word, 388
Work, 258–259
Worker dissatisfaction, 273–274
Worker productivity, 270–271
Work week, 272, 276

Yourdon, Edward, 116

Zarf, 171
Zero, 388
Zone bits, 32–34, 388
Zone punch, 57, 388
Zuse, Konrad, 367

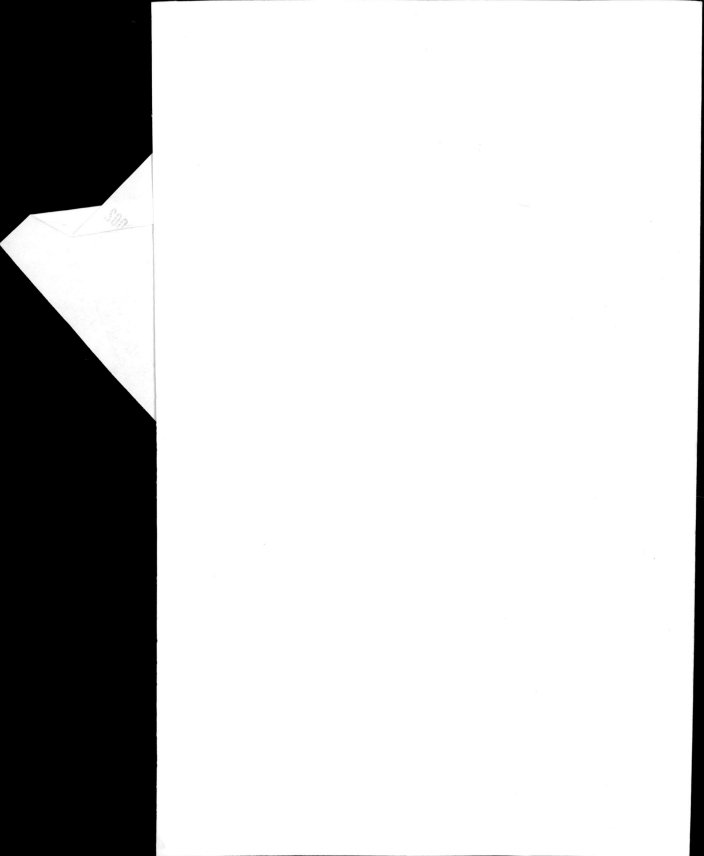

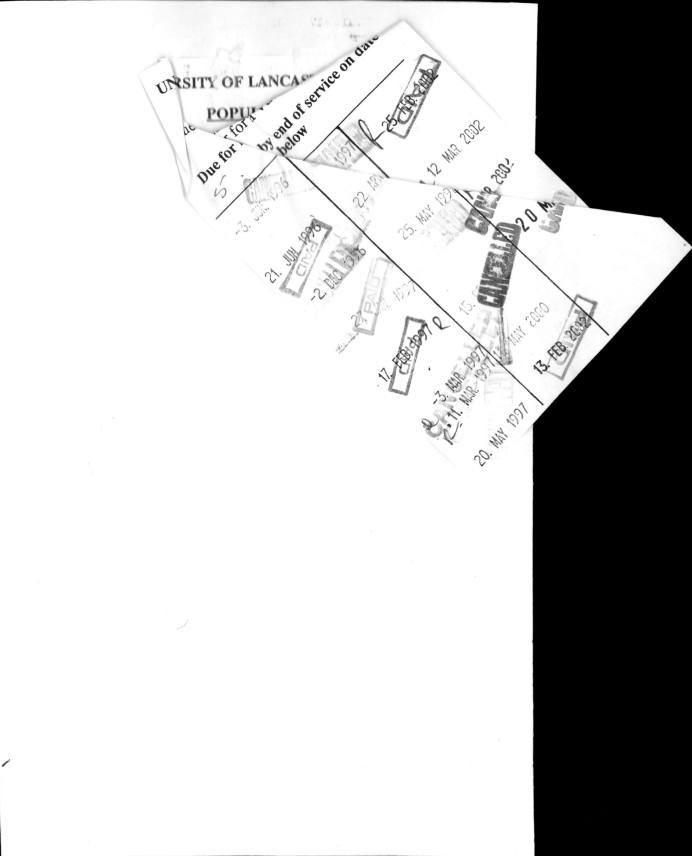